The
Psychoanalytic
Study
of the Child

VOLUME TWENTY-NINE

The Psychoanalytic Study of the Child

VOLUME TWENTY-NINE

New Haven
Yale University Press
1974

Designed by Sally Sullivan
and set in Baskerville type.
Printed in the United States of America by
The Colonial Press Inc., Clinton, Massachusetts.

Contents

ASPECTS OF NORMAL AND PATHOLOGICAL DEVELOPMENT

CLINICAL CONTRIBUTIONS

APPLICATIONS OF PSYCHOANALYSIS

Contents

IN MEMORIAM

The Editors regretfully announce the deaths of Dr. Edward Glover and Dr. Lawrence S. Kubie. These two distinguished psychoanalysts were original members of our Editorial Board.

The Contributions of Berta Bornstein to Psychoanalysis

Introduction
RUTH S. EISSLER, M.D.

THE PAPERS INCLUDED IN THIS SECTION HONOR THE MEMORY OF Berta Bornstein, who died on September 5, 1971. They were presented at the Memorial Meeting for Berta Bornstein, held at the New York Psychoanalytic Society and Institute on October 16, 1973, a meeting that was organized by Ted E. Becker, M.D., Peter Blos, Ph.D., Sylvia Brody, Ph.D., Charles I. Feigelson, M.D., Gerard Fountain, M.D., Robert J. Kabcenell, M.D., Maurice S. Nadelman, and myself.

Although each contribution was presented and written by an individual analyst, the papers were from the beginning planned to be parts of a whole. In the preparation of their contributions, the authors not only relied on Berta Bornstein's publications but also had access to her unpublished lectures on the Technique of Child Analysis, now in the Archives of the New York Psychoanalytic Institute. We are indebted to the Institute for allowing the contributors to use those lectures as the basis for their presentations.

From the wealth of Berta Bornstein's work on child analysis each contributor selected one or several aspects for discussion and illustration by case histories. Thus, taken together, these papers reflect the scope of Berta Bornstein's interests and contributions to psychoanalysis. It is our hope that the depth of her work and her particular way of approaching the child will become as alive in the published presentation as they did in the oral one at the Memorial Meeting.

The question how Berta Bornstein acquired the deep knowledge and theoretical and clinical understanding of pathology and normalcy of childhood and of the child can best be answered with the words: *"Et in Arcadia Ego."*

On Latency

TED E. BECKER, M.D.

THE PERIOD OF LATENCY WAS ONE OF BERTA BORNSTEIN'S CENTRAL interests and she made the most important contributions to our understanding of latency since Freud first described it in *Three Essays on the Theory of Sexuality* (1905). I shall review some of her ideas.

The child enters the latency period with the partial resolution of the oedipus complex and the establishment of the superego. Throughout the latency period he is engaged in a struggle to ward off incestuous wishes and the temptation to masturbate. While this overall task remains, Berta Bornstein discerned two major divisions: early latency, roughly from $5\frac{1}{2}$ years to 8 years, and the second period of latency, roughly from 8 to 10 years.

We can marvel at the complicated changes that are set in motion in the two to three years of the first phase of latency and be amazed that such changes occur in such a short time. Incestuous attachments are partially replaced by identifications with the incestuous objects. The ego is modified by this identification and adopts the task of observing the demands of the drives and the outside world—the superego is formed. The child takes over the regulation of conflicting demands by inner threat rather than outside threat—guilt appears. The ego develops its set of defenses against the drives and external hurts. Character development and sublimations are on their way toward consolidation.

In the first period of latency the self-regulating mechanisms are new and undependable. The superego is at times inordinately strict

Faculty, New York Psychoanalytic Institute.

3

and at times ineffectual. Berta Bornstein describes *temporary regressions to pregenital impulses* as a regular line of defense used by the early latency child in dealing with incestuous wishes. It is against this pregenital regression to voyeurism, thumb-sucking, and anality that reaction formations occur, and these leave their impact on character formation. The heightened ambivalence which regularly accompanies this pregenital regression makes itself known in the child's struggle between obedience and rebellion.

The excessive strictness of his superego exposes the child to a new kind of suffering, his guilt. The early latency child finds guilt feelings particularly painful and intolerable. To avoid this new and painful affect, the child adopts two defensive measures: he identifies with the aggressor and he projects the guilt.

An adolescent described this identification with the aggressor (a term introduced by Anna Freud) to sidestep a feeling of guilt as follows: when he was 6 years old, his father criticized and bullied him continuously. He told me that when he was criticized, he did not feel guilty about it; but he was ashamed to say that he became as big a bully to his little brother as his father had been to him.

We are all familiar with the ease with which an early latency child can commit some minor infraction and immediately project the blame; for example, having accidentally spilled something, he instantly pronounces, "You made me do it." It is still very difficult for him to tolerate any self-reproach.

In the second period of latency the defenses against the drives are more dependable. Masturbation, when it occurs, is immediately forgotten. The strength of the instinctual forces may be diminished physiologically. The child has become more masterful in dealing with the world about him and his own inner needs. Reaction formations and sublimations are solidified. The superego is less strict. As the child devaluates his parents and views them more realistically, their inner representation in the superego may also be less threatening to the child's ego. The 8- to 10-year-old may be content with himself and his world. The ego is in one of its relatively strongest positions. For all these reasons, Berta Bornstein felt that the second period of latency is often a less favorable time for analysis than the first.

In contrast, she emphasized that the first period of latency is one of the best times for analysis. In early latency the defenses are not yet consolidated, reaction formations and character formation have not become crystallized. The child suffers. The psychic structure is more modifiable.

The latency child differs from younger children who often present to us their impulses and drives in rather transparent form. The developmental task of latency is to ward off drives and their numerous regressive expressions. As a result, the latency child presents to us defense rather than impulse. Berta Bornstein utilized this difference by placing the emphasis on defense analysis, a signal technical contribution which superseded, in most cases, Anna Freud's introductory phase.[1] Taking as a starting point the latency child's need to defend himself as the normal developmental pattern, she talked with him first about his ways of safeguarding himself against sadness, hurt, guilt, and anxiety, rather than about his impulses and wishes. By talking with him about his protective devices against his painful affects, we pave the way to talking with him about the danger in which he sees himself.

One of my patients, an 8-year-old boy, had his Christmas presents given away as a punishment. He tried to deal with the loss by playing out a sequence in which as a great scientist he was constructing a machine to recover lost objects from hundreds of miles away. Empathizing with his hurt feelings, we can explain that by means of this regressive fantasy of omnipotence he protects and defends himself against hurt and loss.

Although in some of her case reports Berta Bornstein clearly described how she analyzed latency children in the initial phase of their treatment, she herself never drew attention to the fact that she had introduced a modification of the technique of child analysis; namely, *the analysis of defense against affects before analysis of defense against drives.* It remained for others to underscore this important modification.

Berta Bornstein's contributions extend our understanding beyond the area of child analysis. Her description of the developmental processes in latency is especially important for the understanding of

---

[1] This is illustrated in her report on the first 6 months of analysis of an obsessional child (1953b).

a group of adult patients who, because of traumas suffered in early latency, have been unable to deal with the developmental task of early latency.

Although my own clinical experience is confined to several young males, I believe that the same basic problems are found in female cases as well. Like the early latency child, they have reached the phallic phase. They have been unable to deal with their incestuous wishes and remain embroiled in a constant struggle with masturbation which is centered about incestuous fantasies (heterosexual and homosexual). These patients present serious potency disturbances in heterosexual relationships. To these young men, all women in real life or in fantasy are transparently incestuous objects, either on a conscious or an unconscious level. Their superego development is incomplete and defective. They cannot tolerate the pain of the conscious affect of guilt and therefore avoid it by using the early latency child's maneuvers of projection of guilt and identification with the aggressor.

Although in these cases, as in normal development, the first defense against incestuous wishes and masturbation is a regression to pregenital stages, this regression is not followed by the usual reaction formations and sublimations.

Because of their extensive use of projection which interferes with the function of reality testing (their fantasies often have an almost delusional quality) and because severe narcissistic problems are very much in the foreground, the initial impression may be that of a paranoid state or a borderline condition. Only after a long analysis, which requires a great deal of patience on the part of both analyst and patient, and a painstakingly thorough transference analysis, it becomes clear that one is dealing with a pathology based on trauma and fixation in early latency.

One of the determinants of the inability to resolve the incestuous attachment is gross parental seductiveness which has continued into latency, making it impossible for the child to relinquish his incestuous fantasies. The many disturbances can be understood as an unresolved struggle with these incestuous wishes—a struggle that is carried out very much like that of an early latency child who because of his inability to resolve it has not moved into the second phase of latency.

Another determinant is frequently the male child's inability to identify with his father or other male figures because of narcissistic injuries inflicted by the father or father figures. Severe problems in the evaluation of the self and defective superego development result.

Castration anxiety is intense. But, as mentioned above, *conscious* guilt is not experienced and does not appear until late in the analysis. When guilt does appear, it is so painful that it brings severe recriminations against the analyst for being responsible for this dreadful feeling. These patients deal with the painful feeling of guilt in the manner described by Berta Bornstein as typical for the early latency child.

If we therefore keep in mind the usual phase-specific conflicts and defenses of this developmental stage—pregenital regression followed by reaction formation, projection of guilt, and identification with the aggressor—we are sensitized to their reappearance in the analysis of adult patients. In order to illustrate these points I have selected material from the analysis of one such case.

This 20-year-old man sought analysis because of "difficulty in experiencing my feelings"; fears of women so extreme that he had anxiety attacks, even if he only anticipated speaking to a woman whom he did not know; potency disturbances consisting of an inability to have an erection or, if he did, severe premature ejaculation with no sensation; a work inhibition making it difficult for him to learn in school and take examinations. He had dropped out of college and returned to live with his parents.

He was the younger of two brothers. The unspoken rule in the family was to indulge the sons' wishes, no matter what. The father had had a neglectful stepmother, and his sons were to have a gratifying mother. The mother had been the ugly duckling in a large family of sisters and had become the clown and seductress. Until my patient was 8 years old, the parents allowed him to get into their bed and lie between them. Both parents were nude, and the boy could manipulate and suck on his mother's breasts while the nude father lay behind him apparently showing no disapproval. Thus, the mother forced him into an oral regression when he was already in the phallic phase. Analysis revealed that he felt teased and furious. At the same time his mother frightened him by her joking remarks that "incest and masturbation are the two worst crimes." She also must have had some conflict about the breast play because when it occurred in the father's absence, she commented, "Don't let anyone see you do this—not the mailman or the milkman." This seductiveness in the phallic phase overstimulated his phallic desires which were expressly forbidden. The apparent permissiveness was for pregenital oral gratification.

The father on the other hand indulged in his pregenital anal impulses with his sons. Throughout the latency years, the father, the two brothers, and a number of male cousins had a "tushie club." They wrote a regular magazine filled with anal jokes and stories. They all showered together, mutually rubbing their buttocks.

The father had his own struggles with oral indulgences. When the family ate at a restaurant, the father often found the food unsatisfactory and sent it back; then, long after they had finished their meal, he would go on sitting at the table while the waiters tried to get him out. There were angry confrontations over his rights to stay. In fact, outside of the family the father was a rather pugnacious, violent-tempered man, especially when he felt that his rights were being infringed upon. My patient always expected that this violence would be turned against him, an expectation that increased his castration anxiety and forced him into pregenital regression.

My patient recalled no conscious excitement in the repeated erotic physical contacts with his parents. When he first described them to me, he showed no shame or any indication that there might be something questionable about it. The pregenital regression was acceptable as a shield against his phallic incestuous fantasies. The general blunting of his emotional responsiveness (an initial complaint) dated from early latency. That he experienced no orgastic sensation or excitement in lovemaking where phallic wishes could not be avoided is understandable.

Berta Bornstein described pregenital regressions as a regularly attempted solution to the incestuous conflict in early latency. In the case of this man, the transparently incestuous pregenital fantasies from latency continued into prepuberty, adolescence, and young adulthood. He developed no stable reaction formations against incestuous fantasies and impulses toward fusion, cannibalism, and anal-sadistic love relationships. The result was a pathological character formation.

Other traumatic events had interfered with his ability to identify with his father and to form an effective superego. The father and the 4-year-older brother, who was then in puberty, both boasted of their physical strength and bravery and put a premium on not showing the slightest fear or anxiety. The family spent the summer vacations at an isolated cabin by a lake in the woods. Father and brother strutted about nude, flexing their muscles before an admiring mother. My patient, then in early latency, retreated in humiliation. He increasingly became concerned about his penis being smaller than that of any other male and absolutely refused to swim in the nude.

Once the father and the two sons were rowing near a pier where waves were breaking. My patient, lying in the bottom of the boat, was terrified and in tears. His older brother laughed at him and teased him about his cowardice. The father may have teased him or simply may not have supported him. In any event, he merely had his own feelings of inadequacy confirmed. He imagined his father thinking, "You are not my kind of fellow." He felt that he could never be a man like his brother and father, that he would never be able to live without his strong father's care, never make an independent life of his own. And he continued to admire them, maintaining an idealized, sadomasochistic, homosexual relationship toward father and brother.

Behind this hero worship there was an intense seething rage at having been humiliated by them. In the transference this was illustrated by his first dream. After an initial period of professing his love and admiration for me, he dreamed that I was chasing him with my erect penis over which was draped a black cloth. He would have felt better if it had covered my coffin. The rage at his humiliation and the death wishes against his father and brother were reexperienced in the transference. Although he had not been capable of achieving a masculine identification, he had introjected the prohibition against phallic incestuous wishes, both heterosexual and homosexual.

Early in the analysis the patient once asked me, "Where is the nearest library?" My very gentle attempt to analyze rather than answer this question was a trauma for him. For years thereafter he was incapable of asking me another question or expressing transference feelings or thoughts because he feared I would humiliate him. Years later I learned that he felt I had spurned his furtive attempt to identify with me. He felt I had said, "Don't ask me that, you are not my kind of fellow." He was so vulnerable to narcissistic injury that it took five years of analysis before he could expose his sensitivity to slights, openly express his transference feelings, understand his rage, begin a process of identification with me, show signs of a more advanced superego development, and experience conscious guilt.

Much of the analytic work in these years was concerned with the severe failures in his reality testing, as the following examples illustrate.

In comparison with his brother and father he felt he was castrated, weak, defective, his mother's daughter. Their teasing enabled him to project his devaluation of his body, penis, and self. Regressively, he could then experience feelings of grandiosity which at times reached frightening proportions. The first day on a job which was entirely new to him, he challenged the knowledge and authority of the experienced director of the institution. This same intolerance of his feelings of weakness had made him unable to learn from teachers and was responsible for his dropping out of college.

Once he cuttingly criticized a male teacher to the latter's girlfriend, erroneously believing, at that moment, that she was his confidante. This was done without shame, guilt, or even fear that she would carry the tale to her boyfriend, the teacher. Then he imagined that the teacher made some disguised allusion to his comment in class and felt very unfairly treated, elaborating his feelings in an almost paranoid way. When guilt is not experienced, it frequently leads to a failure in reality testing.

One final group of illustrations demonstrate the similarity between this patient's and the early latency child's way of warding off guilt through projection and identification with the aggressor.

When he was walking on the street with a girl, he feared that any passing man would attack him. When he had intercourse with a woman, he feared that a man would break in and beat him up. The daily experience of such fears had for several years a delusional quality. At these times he blamed the woman: she behaved or dressed too seductively and would attract the other man and place the patient in danger. This was an attempt to cover up guilt about his own incestuous fantasies, heterosexual and homosexual. The guilt was projected onto the woman for her sexuality.

If girls wore miniskirts in the street, they should be raped and abused, he felt. Yet he was filled with blind rage with each report of a rape in the city and insisted that the rapist should be castrated and killed. In this his superego was like that of the early latency child: inordinately strict at one moment, and archaically ineffectual at the next moment.

One would assume that this man had had early preoedipal disturbances and fixation points, but in his history no great disturbance in his early development was evident.

Early latency is a time of profound reorganization of the psychic structure. While pregenital regressions normally occur in early latency, traumatic events during this phase intensify these and also provoke partial ego regressions which give rise to narcissistic problems in the evaluation of the self, severe disturbances in superego functioning, extensive failures of reality testing, and paranoid fantasies. If the defensive structure which Berta Bornstein described as typical of early latency appears in the transference of an adult, and the adult initially appears to be suffering from borderline pathology, we should look for *severe trauma* in early latency.

Contributions to Child Analysis

SYLVIA BRODY, PH.D.

THERE HAVE BEEN TWO MAJOR PHASES IN THE EVOLUTION OF TECH-nique in child analysis, the first beginning in about 1920, the second after the war, in about 1945. The work of Berta Bornstein spanned both phases. To give a general picture of her contributions, I must first sketch in a little of the history of child analysis; I should like to say at the outset that my references to Berta Bornstein's develop-ment of technical methods during the same years when Anna Freud was doing so, and later on as well, have no concern with priority. A simultaneity of discovery is not unusual in the history of science.

Play as a therapeutic medium for the analysis of children was introduced in 1920 by Hermine Hug-Hellmuth, and perhaps because play traditionally has promoted learning, Hug-Hellmuth regarded child analysis to be an educational treatment, which needed to be carried out in the child's home. The theoretical status of child analysis was clarified in 1926 by Anna Freud's first series of lectures, in which she described the main technical tasks: the development of the child's insight into his illness, the uses of play, the limitations of transference, and the work with parents. These themes were taken up by others for almost 20 years thereafter, in Europe and in this country.[1] Publications of the time dealt with

Director, Child Development Research Project, City University of New York; Adjunct Professor, Department of Psychology, Graduate School, City University of New York.

[1] Harnik (1926/27), Oberndorf (1930), Fries (1933), Sheehan-Dare (1934), Hoffer (1935), Lippman (1935), Rank (1942), Payne (1943), M. Kris (1944).

ways of handling the child's immaturity, of overcoming resistances and defenses, of making unconscious material conscious, and of relieving anxiety. An assumption of an inherent connection between education and child analysis lingered, however, and was reflected in the title of the journal of the time (*Zeitschrift für psychoanalytische Pädagogik*), which appeared in Vienna from 1926 to 1937.

The next change of focus, to the structural point of view and to understanding of the unconscious ego, was again codified for child analysis by Anna Freud, in *The Ego and the Mechanisms of Defense*, in 1936. With regard to the technique of child analysis, nothing new appeared until the European analysts came to this country.

Berta Bornstein had begun her training in 1925, in Berlin, where she was a student along with Otto Fenichel, Edith Jacobson, Annie Reich, and others, and came to have a leading position in their "Kinderseminar" (seminars of the younger generation of analysts who wanted to avoid being awed by their seniors). When from time to time Anna Freud came with her father to stay at Simmel's sanitarium in Tegel, Berta Bornstein met with her to discuss technical problems of child analysis; and in 1929 Berta Bornstein went to Vienna, where again she took a leading position in child analysis. She had hoped to return to Berlin.[2] Her giftedness as an analyst and her independent development of classic methods were recognized by Anna Freud long before Berta Bornstein immigrated to New York in 1938. Those of her publications which appeared between 1930 and 1936 already showed exceptional insight into the key to the treatment of the child: the child's need to be understood according to the level of his ego development. She was not alone in this, but her clinical descriptions were particularly explicit.

One of her first classic papers, which appeared in 1931, reported the case of a phobia in a 2½-year-old girl with very limited speech development.[3] For many weeks the child provided only two verbalizations: "Ow," and from a dream, "Grandpa naughty." Berta Bornstein succeeded in helping the child to overcome the phobia and in showing the complexity of mental life in the very

[2] I am indebted to Dr. Edith Jacobson for supplying some of this information.
[3] A complete list of Berta Bornstein's writings appears on pp. 39–40.

young child. In that same early paper she discussed the functions of repetitive play, early signs of the oedipus complex, premature genitalization of sexuality, and the need for partial gratification of instinctual wishes to occur before sublimation can develop. In addition, she raised the question of the early onset of defense. In 1936 she published a case report focused entirely upon the analysis of one defense, denial in fantasy.

Berta Bornstein's first major discussion of the handling of the child's defenses and defensive maneuvers appeared in 1945, in the modestly entitled, "Clinical Notes." By a few short examples, she showed the skill with which interpretive comments or questions, as she called them, could be timed and expressed in such a way that the child could become aware of his defensive attitudes and behavior, and still be spared any narcissistic injury. Her talent for transmuting painful statements into those that stirred a child to reflection became well known.

In 1949 came the case of Frankie, in which she explicated with extraordinary clarity the approach to defense analysis through prior understanding of the child's "central emotion," i.e., she explained how interpretation of affect should precede interpretation of defense. There was nothing new in saying that analysis begins at the surface; but Berta Bornstein described the method of doing so, of first working toward ego change in the patient, in order then to deal effectively with demands of the instinctual drives. So, while the manifest content of Frankie's play for many weeks expressed fantasies of heroism and omnipotence, eventually she interpreted only the feelings of sadness and loneliness, which he had suffered several years earlier and which had been too painful to keep undisguised in consciousness. By helping him to experience the original affect, over and over again, she provided the "emotional ground" for subsequent interpretation of unconscious material. The Frankie paper also demonstrated the economy of language and the "light touch" which Berta Bornstein taught her students always to value. It remains the fullest and most complex history of any child analysis in the classic Freudian literature.

In the "Fragment of an Analysis of an Obsessional Child" (1953b), Berta Bornstein gave other examples of defenses woven into the context of a neurosis, with discussion of how their rigidity or extensiveness may alienate a child from reality or weaken his capacity for reality testing. Here she described how the slow transformation of the child's death fear to a death feeling represented a shift from destructive wishes to libidinal desires that were more accessible to ego interpretation.

Berta Bornstein's lectures, her supervisory work, her papers, and her personal communications displayed an uncommon facility to see the world through the senses of the child. With a skillfulness that may be comparable to that of August Aichhorn, she could discern which of the child's affects were consciously acceptable to him, and could articulate them in a way that showed her full concern for his here-and-now experience and for his disregard of past or future experiences. This facility was in keeping with a fine diagnostic skill, and not only for forms of neurosis. An observation of a child's merest glance, gesture, vocal intonation, or facial expression, in the context of a routine activity, at home or in school, revealed to her his emotional state and his capacity for introspection. I remember sitting with her in a restaurant, seeing her watch a boy at a nearby table for a few minutes, and then mentioning the little signs by which she surmised that he might be psychotic. Two other analysts with her, who had not previously noticed anything unusual in the child's behavior, were shortly thereafter able to confirm her impression. She was also able quickly to assess low intelligence, possibly in line with an interest dating from her first three papers, two about pseudostupidity (1930b, 1930c), and one on the relationship between sexual development and the development of the intellect (1930a).

With the exception of Anna Freud's lectures of 1926, a few papers by others, mainly about transference, and the work of Kleinian analysts, Berta Bornstein's work stands alone in its exposition and exemplification of technical methods of child analysis. A reading of any one of her papers illustrates her zeal to find the most precise formulations she could. Glibness or superficiality were anathema to her, in any aspect of her work, to the point where those whom she supervised sometimes were irritated by her pursuit of clinical or theoretical detail. What, then, has she left us to enlarge our knowledge about the psychoanalytic treatment of the child?

By describing how, from the very beginning of treatment, she communicated to the child the ways in which he guarded himself against feeling conflict, she demonstrated the way to help him regard his symptoms as ego alien. By her ingenious use of defense interpretation for creating a treatment alliance, as Anna Freud (1966) has put it, she rendered a nonanalytic introductory period unnecessary.

She showed that the defenses set up against specific affects are the same as those set up against the specific impulses from which the affects had derived; and that both affects and defenses are to be approached with utmost tact, and interpreted with the same delicacy with which one should approach and interpret instinctual wishes. She showed that analysis of defense involves analysis of the superego; yet was concerned not to encroach upon the child's developing system of values. She aimed only to make him as conflict-free as possible, in his own environment.

She tried to teach us that the unconscious content of a child's play can be interpreted effectively only after his typical patterns of defense have been made known to him—lest he be made excessively anxious and turn away from an activity that could lead to a sublimation; lest he be encouraged to deny feelings or wishes, or to take refuge in stereotyped or intellectualized explanations, especially of symbolic material; lest he use play for the purpose of resistance; and lest child and analyst together neglect to pay attention to the multiple determination of conflict. While these points are well known, it is important to emphasize that they spell out some of the principal risks of Kleinian methods with children. Berta Bornstein explained, as no one else has done, the reasons why the theory and technique of Melanie Klein were a disservice to child analysis.

She provided a theoretical explanation for the child's inability to verbalize in the adult manner, i.e., she explained that the child perceives free association as a threat to his still unstable secondary processes and age-adequate defenses; and that play is the child's natural form of expression because it is closer than words to instinctual wishes, and more fitting to his normal narcissism. This again clarified why Klein's direct interpretations of the fantasies expressed in play constituted intrusions upon the child's ego which were liable to increase or damage his narcissism.

She described, implicitly, how the young child can be enabled to join the analyst in his or her task: he can become an observer of as well as a participant in play, and leave the third task of interpretation to the analyst. The role of observer might be unconventional: sometimes, she said, the analyst should consider the child highly cooperative if he merely listens without putting his fingers into his ears.

She made plain to us the child's difficulty in tolerating painful affect, especially when it has been called forth by an adult; and she comprehended as well the analyst's difficulty in maintaining objectivity and remaining unseduced by the child, i.e., in holding the analyst's own affects and defenses in check. The latter problems were discussed with fine sensitivity in the paper on "Emotional Barriers in the Treatment of Children" (1948). Her ability to combine subtlety with kindness in sparing the child's self-esteem may be glimpsed in a small interpretive remark to a child. She told me that one day a little boy had asked her what she would do if he stole something from her desk; she replied, "I would think to myself, 'I wonder what has happened to make an honest person act as if he were a thief.' " She paid full respect to the child's ideals, treated his bad conscience as a nuisance to *him*, and made clear *her* alliance with him.

Berta Bornstein demonstrated that behind every symptom neurosis there is a character neurosis. The child, she said, does not usually suffer from his character difficulties, but one must keep in mind the danger of characterological defenses becoming petrified during the phase of latency. According to this insight, she enabled the treatment of a child to become less of a symptom analysis and more of a character analysis.

She pointed out that the child's love life can be as intense as an adult's, although the child does not yet have the experiences of climax and discharge.

Finally, she brought child analysis well beyond the realm of an educational technique. She had worked for years with educators and understood the relationships between faulty education and distorted ego functions, but her interest was in psychoanalytic theory and method rather than in the application of psychoanalysis to education, or even to the more recent forms of special education.

Although Berta Bornstein illuminated the nature of the ego in childhood, especially in the latency phase, as far as I know she made no references in her teaching or writing to "ego psychology" as an entity. She was disappointed in the current emphasis upon it, believing that "ego psychology" would lead away from psychoanalysis as a metapsychological theory of neurosis. The purpose of her study of the ego was to find ways to grapple with the id and its derivatives and with the superego more confidently; so to undo unconscious conflict that might interfere with normal development. But the study of normative behavior, she thought, belonged to a different discipline. She sustained a single-minded dedication to the unique knowledge to be gained from psychoanalysis as an independent discipline.

Much of Berta Bornstein's teaching about techniques with children is applicable to adults, because analysis of the adult who is neurotic addresses itself to the regressed or arrested elements in his personality. While she found ways to adapt technique to the child patient, she did not treat the child as an immature adult. She did not advocate the use of parameters in child analysis. Her methods were based upon an acute knowledge of the strengths and weaknesses of the maturing psychic structures of the child, and of the qualitative differences between child and adult, to be seen chiefly in the child's more ego-syntonic narcissism, and his potentials for sublimation. In spite of these qualities of the child patient, analysis was always for Berta Bornstein the analysis of transference reactions, of resistance, of defense, and of conflict.

BIBLIOGRAPHY

FREUD, A. (1926), *The Psycho-Analytical Treatment of Children.* New York: International Universities Press, 1946.

——— (1936), *The Ego and the Mechanisms of Defense.* New York: International Universities Press, rev. ed., 1966.

——— (1966), A Short History of Child Analysis. *This Annual,* 21:7–14.

FRIES, M. E. (1933), Play Technique in the Analysis of Young Children. *Psychoanal. Rev.,* 24:233–245, 1937.

Harnik, J. (1926/27), Die therapeutische Kinderanalyse. *Z. psychoanal. Päd.*, 1:28–30.

Hoffer, W. (1935), Einleitung einer Kinderanalyse. *Z. psychoanal. Päd.*, 9:271–292.

Hug-Hellmuth, H. (1920), On the Technique of Child Analysis. *Int. J. Psycho-Anal.*, 2:287–305, 1921.

Kris, M. (1944), Child Analysis. In: *Psychoanalysis Today*, ed. S. Lorand. New York: International Universities Press, pp. 50–63.

Lippman, H. S. (1935), Technical Difficulties Encountered in Child Analysis. *Amer. J. Orthopsychiat.*, 5:27–31.

Oberndorf, C. P. (1930), Technical Procedure in the Analytic Treatment of Children. *Int. J. Psycho-Anal.*, 11:79–82.

Payne, S. (1943), The Principles and Methods of the Training of Child Analysts. *Int. J. Psycho-Anal.*, 24:61–63.

Rank, B. (1942), Where Child Analysis Stands Today. *Amer. Imago*, 3:41–60.

Sheehan-Dare, H. (1934), On Making Contact with the Child Patient. *Int. J. Psycho-Anal.*, 15:435–439.

Play in Child Analysis

CHARLES I. FEIGELSON, M.D.

IN HER WRITINGS AND TEACHING, BERTA BORNSTEIN REPEATEDLY emphasized the need to understand the core conceptions underlying clinical work. Children in analysis communicate by means of their dreams and daydreams, their stories and dramatizations, and their play. I have chosen to focus on Berta Bornstein's thoughts about play in child analysis, its clinical use and the theory which illuminates it.

In adult analysis we ask our patients to free-associate. Through this process our patients reveal themselves. While play is the substance of child analysis, it is not "free association," nor is it the child's "free association." It is the natural medium for the child. Berta Bornstein believed that children do not employ free association because it threatens their ego organization. For the child, free association represents a temptation to regress to the primary process. She wrote (1951): "It is only with great difficulty that the child learns that contradictions exclude each other and that contradictory thoughts must be kept apart in conversation. . . . Any newly acquired accomplishment can easily be undone by regressive processes and the child senses that this would occur were he to attempt to express whatever comes into his mind." She believed that free association is possible only after children have developed the capacity for introspection, and that this "hardly ever occurs before prepuberty when the superego approaches a state of consolidation" (p. 279).

"In contrast to his feelings about free association, the child is not

The author is a member of the New York Psychoanalytic Institute and Society.

ashamed of his wish for play. Play is an age-adequate expression accepted by the world around him." * ¹

Berta Bornstein believed that play therapy (that is, therapy where the child plays and no interpretation is given) as distinguished from child analysis is useful in two situations: in preparing a child for a future experience which threatens to have a traumatic effect; and in helping a child master through abreaction a past experience which has been traumatic.

The use of play in child analysis is different from that in play therapy. In presenting her own guidelines for the understanding of the meanings of repetitive play in analysis, she wrote "I, personally, feel that the material with which we deal (human beings and their environment) is so variable that we may never attain more than an approximation, expressed in the form of limited basic rules." * Her rules for the understanding of play were:

1. Every element in the play has a meaning which is overdetermined.

2. Every *repetitive* play contains an unconscious conflict related to the child's symptom.

3. Repetitive play frequently contains a symbolic expression either of masturbatory activity or of the fantasy connected with it.

4. The content of repetitive play often reflects a particular traumatic experience.

5. Repetitive play which contains more impulsive characteristics seems to indicate that a past reality experience (not just a fantasy) prior to the development of verbalization is being expressed.

Berta Bornstein taught that play is important to the analyst, *not* as a vehicle of interpretation, but as a fruitful and natural source of knowledge about the child. We do not usually interpret play, and we never interpret it symbolically. (This, she believed, interferes with sublimation.)

The following clinical material taken from Berta Bornstein's work—both published (1945, p. 153ff.) and unpublished—illustrates her way of using play in the analytic situation as a vehicle for understanding, which paves the way for interpretation.

---

¹ Quotations followed by an asterisk are from an unpublished lecture in the course on child analysis at the New York Psychoanalytic Institute.

An enuretic boy aged 8½ introduced by means of his dramatic play his oedipal problems, his sexual excitement, and his oedipal fears at the very beginning of his analysis.

For several weeks he assumed the roles of captain, general, or director of a theater. Usually, the general was killed in action, the captain drowned while saving a ship, and the director was prevented from receiving the applause of the audience by the theater burning down just at the moment when he appeared on the stage. The boy played out most of these incidents as though they occurred on a stage or movie screen, assigning to the analyst the role of silent spectator.

In accordance with her understanding that in repetitive play the child reveals his conflict, Berta Bornstein surmised (without interpreting) the boy's unconscious wish to be a grown-up man and his humiliation whenever he wetted himself. (Although she surmised much more, for the purpose of this discussion I leave the rest aside.) In spite of his intention to get rid of the symptom, he was seldom able to tell directly about his nightly accidents. Only the catastrophe that regularly took place in his dramatizations served for the analyst as an indication of his accidents at night. This was not interpreted.

In a later session he invited the analyst to take part in his play. He said, "Let's play that you are a friend of mine, my girl friend, and I am on leave and I am 21 years old. Let's pretend you give me some whiskey and we smoke cigarettes. But while we are pretending, let's make a real fire." He immediately started to do so. This time, he did *not* stage the usual catastrophe in his play, but it showed up in an unforeseen way, namely, in a slip. In the course of the game he broke an ashtray. He was terrified and inconsolable to a degree quite out of proportion to the incident.

He pleaded with Berta Bornstein not to let anyone know about this incident. After the breaking of the ashtray he asked to continue the session in the adjoining room. They moved into the other room and while he was lying on the floor studying the titles of her books, Berta Bornstein sympathetically remarked that "these little accidents in reality are harder to take than all those catastrophes which the captains, generals, and theater directors had to suffer in your shows." He was surprised and wanted to know how she knew this.

She told him that leaving the locale of the accident had told her the story; that he had felt compelled to leave the scene of the accident because he did not want to be reminded of the broken ashtray. She added that she assumed that he dealt with the accidents at night in the same way. He did not want to be reminded of them either. He admitted that he desperately tried to forget his wet bed. He added that when he was in the office, he hardly could imagine that it was he who wet the bed last night.

Then came his defense: "See, how strong I am, I can lift one of the heaviest boards of your bookcase, even when I'm lying on the floor." Here Berta Bornstein interpreted, saying, "Sure you are strong and just for that reason it must be hard for you to be reminded of your infantile behavior at night." She added, "I know, however, that forgetting is not going to help either with bed-wetting or with any broken ashtray."

His depressed mood grew and suddenly he said, "I'm afraid I'll never grow up. Some grownups are grown up when they are born. Or at least they are strong as soon as they are born. Or at least they have the intelligence of grownups. And some people have to be told what to do until they die." He then withdrew the statement about people who are born as adults, saying, "After all, that can't be. No one can be born grown up." Suddenly he burst out in anger, "And I do not believe in anything anymore. I do not believe in Columbus, I do not believe in Washington, and I do not even believe in Abraham Lincoln."

In this verbalization he expressed the same content which Berta Bornstein had deduced from his dramatic play: the wish to be a famous grown-up man and his fear and doubt that he would never be able to reach that aim. The inevitable catastrophe in his play was overdetermined. It expressed not only his aggression against a successful father figure, but simultaneously his need for self-punishment. The aggression showed up in his open rebellion against the great ones, and the need for self-punishment was manifest in his complaints that *he* never would be able to behave like a grown-up man.

Berta Bornstein presented a detailed account of the analysis of this little boy. I have selected only some material to illustrate her use of play in child psychoanalysis—not primarily for interpretation but for understanding. Interpretation is effective when it utilizes the feelings of the child that he recognizes to be *real*. Those are discovered in the "real" experiences in his life and in the analytic situation.

To illustrate how understanding of a repetitive play led to the recovery of an important early childhood experience, I shall present briefly the case of an 8-year-old boy, who began analysis with me at 5½. In the initial history, the parents reported that at 3 he had walked into their bedroom when they were having a vicious fight. Subsequently, he referred to this as the time "Daddy rushed Mommy." When he began his analysis, he easily remembered this.

During his second year in analysis he developed a consuming interest in hockey, and spent session after session playing hockey with me. While many things varied about the play, one aspect remained constant: he always was the goalie. I would shoot the puck and he displayed his prowess in not allowing it to hurt him or go into the goal. Among the many aspects discussed were his wish to beat me and to protect himself from injury. If an occasional puck got through, he felt shame and humiliation. The play continued for weeks, months, so that I sometimes wondered whether I had missed an important clue.

Then, following a session when he had missed blocking a few pucks, he reported a dream. In the dream he was a goalie, playing in Madison Square Garden; thousands of people watched as a puck was hit right toward his face. He committed the cardinal shame of the goalie—he ducked, the puck went into the net, and he felt humiliated. He felt so humiliated in the telling of the dream, he would not allow discussion of it. But, as if it were manna from heaven, and as if it were totally disconnected from the play and the dream, he talked about the time "Daddy rushed Mommy." He said that he had opened the door to the fight at the same moment that his father threw a pillow at his mother. The pillow flew past his mother and hit the little spectator in the face, knocking him to the floor, leaving him ashamed and frightened.

It would be simplistic to say that this alone accounted for his fear of humiliation. The example is not intended to suggest this, but to illustrate the importance of allowing repetitive play to continue and to emphasize that it does have specific meaning. As Berta Borstein wrote, "The content of repetitive play often reflects a particular traumatic experience." *

On Countertransference

ROBERT J. KABCENELL, M.D.

AS A TEACHER, BERTA BORNSTEIN EMPHASIZED IMPORTANT PROBLEMS neglected in much of the literature on child analysis. Those analysts who were fortunate enough to have heard her lectures at the Institute in New York or Philadelphia will need no introduction to these concepts.

In 1948, Berta Bornstein published a paper entitled, "Emotional Barriers in the Understanding and Treatment of Children," in which she focused on the analyst's attitude toward the child. She mentioned fear of the child. She noted that children frighten analysts by their unpredictability, their highly charged emotions, their narcissism, and their closeness to the unconscious. She continued:

> . . . although it has rarely been admitted, children throughout the ages have been considered a threat by their parents and by society in general. It is as if each older generation must prevent the rebellion of children against its cultural standards which are jeopardized by each succeeding generation. Behind this truisim, the analyst recognizes the archaic pattern of the threat of the oedipal crime, the result of which can be found in unnecessary brutalities in training and discipline, for the alleged purpose of changing children into human beings. The opposite—extreme tolerance—constitutes a part of the same problem; it tends to placate the aggressiveness of the younger generation. . . . we are not astonished to find traces of these archaic tendencies in the analyst's relationship to children. . . .

The difference in our attitudes toward a juvenile and an adult

The author is a member of the New York Psychoanalytic Society and Institute.

neurosis . . . reveals a diluted derivative of the archaic superiority-inferiority attitude toward the child. It . . . is likewise traceable in our unrealistic therapeutic expectations in regard to child analysis [p. 693f.].

From this attitude came the expectation of having the genesis of the neurosis laid on a platter before us. Then we not only could cure the juvenile neurosis, but we could forestall later pathological developments.

In another vein, Berta Bornstein added:

Our relationship to the child is based on the assumption of his continuous development and change. It is difficult for adults to experience a child's disturbed behavior without measuring it by the assumed pattern of adult behavior. It is as if the adult were compelled to visualize the child's present projected on the screen of his future. In contrast to this, there is the tendency to consider the adults' disturbed behavior in terms of his past [p. 695].

We tend to deny our helplessness, especially to unenthusiastic parents, and pretend that we can know the future course of the child's illness.

Discussing the technical complications of child analysis, Berta Bornstein stated:

As the result of the child's impulsiveness, of his frequent attempts to seduce and provoke, the analyst may easily be tempted into abandoning observation and interpretation. . . . All these factors may facilitate the analyst's acting out his own unconscious motivations when giving advice to parents and child. . . . A serious complication in terms of the analyst's mental hygiene is the danger of regression, which no one in continuous contact with children can escape. . . . The defenses the analyst unconsciously brings into play against this pressure may block his intuition. He is especially prone to such defense reactions in two instances: when the child's sexual demands toward the analyst appear in a concealed form; and when children change their neurotic symptoms to aggressive and provocative behavior [p. 696].

In such circumstances, the analyst may withdraw, and this brings about more provocation and then more withdrawal. One must remember that the continual acting out of the child is different in its effect on the analyst than the occasional acting out of the neurotic adult. This continual harassment of the analyst threatens his analytic attitude. I have chosen to describe briefly two cases which illustrate some of these points. Berta Bornstein supervised one and discussed the other one at length.

The first patient was a 10-year-old boy, Teddy, who had been referred to analysis because of his parents' concern about his masculinity, his inability to make friends, and his constant bickering with his mother (the father traveled at least half of the year). He had a brother who was younger by several years, and both children had been raised by a series of housemaids who rarely stayed longer than a year. The father was an infantile character, and the mother, herself not very grown up, was so exhausted by catering to her husband when he was home that she took every opportunity to get away from the house at other times.

Teddy was a slight and insipid child, who was ingratiatingly saccharine at first meeting. This in itself brought a feeling of slight unpleasantness. He regaled me with tales of the elegance in which he lived and the adventures in which he had taken part. He claimed to have helped in the capture of a hijacker. Teddy lied knowingly and unknowingly. He used denial as well as lying to prevent the eruption of painful emotions. Early in the analysis, at the beginning of each session Teddy would say that all was well. In spite of his courtly manners, he was soon seen to be rather insolent. Not one adult except his father seemed to be immune from his insults. He ridiculed his mother mercilessly for her self-interest and stupidity. He fired the maid, which unfortunately gave the girl an excuse to leave the burdensome job. I waited my turn. Teddy then told how he had gotten rid of his last therapist, who had been "mean" to him. For a time, the analysis made little progress.

Berta Bornstein spoke early about the deprivation of this boy. No one had time for him except his analyst. Teddy's interest in the analysis lay not in the desire for understanding or relief of suffering. During one hour each weekday an adult gave exclusive, undivided attention to him. Teddy was clever enough to know that he had to produce a semblance of emotional problems or he would be reminded that there was work to be done. While the mother spoke of the boy's noxious behavior, he lavished affection on the analyst.

There was a constant temptation to succumb to the vilification of the parents, a common failing in child therapists.

Each defense was duly interpreted, with no result. However, Teddy began complaining about family, friends, teachers, and schoolmates. For a while, it seemed that he understood some of what was "expected of him." Yet, quite to the contrary, he was mimicking me. He viewed me as complaining about him in my interpretations and confrontations, and the boy then did the same about others. In noticing the emotional poverty of Teddy's life, one was tempted to ignore the vengeful, aggressive strivings that arose in disguised form whenever he was frustrated to the slightest extent. It was striking that the real rage was not expressed by his occasional temper tantrums, which had a theatrical quality, but by the disruption of the analysis. The climate of the analysis alternated between the quiet enjoyment of the undivided attention and the unrelenting provocation. He felt frustrated by every demand for honesty and examination of his mental contents.

The difficulty in the situation was the poignancy of the deprived child who stimulated rescue wishes in me, even though the child was so unappealing. Desperately I wanted to like the child. The feeling of Teddy's deprivation seemed pale, and I often looked in vain for some real charm and goodness of character, at times leaning over backward to do so. This is a frequent pitfall for the child analyst. Berta Bornstein noted how often child therapists describe their patients in cute, adoring terms, leaning backward in this way. The "naughty" child constantly threatens the analyst's competence as well as his ability to order the analytic situation. The analyst might have said with honesty, "Don't you see that I really want to help you, even though no one else does?" Berta Bornstein was alert to this corruption of the analytic position that is so common in treating children.

Teddy had developed traits that would bring him neither friends nor social adaptation. In his habitual behavior it was possible to see the oedipal struggle with the part-time father. However, Teddy also became a caricature of his mother. She was the "Jewish princess bitch," as he was later able to say. His method of relating to all people was to be critical, snide, and grandiose. The other children at school shunned him. In fact, he could be friends only with the outcasts. Teddy himself did not see these problems. When he was finally able to tell how he was ill-treated in school, he denied being provocative. His solution to this particular problem was to change schools or have his father get after the boys who tormented him. Such circumstances arise frequently and are common in the treatment of adult patients as well as children. But in treating a child, there is a temptation to be instructive. The *instructing* position has the disadvantage of elevating the analyst above the field of conflict so as to insulate him from the incessant ridicule and provocation. As Berta Bornstein wrote, this would then lead to an increase in aggression or a withdrawal of the child. Neither one would be a happy solution.

Berta Bornstein paid constant attention to the progress of patients and the progress of the analyst. She was especially aware of the state of the analyst's countertransference. I use this term in the narrow sense of the reactivation of early emotional states and relationships under the impact of the transference.

It was implicit in Berta Bornstein's comments that the principal mode of understanding the analysand comes from perceptions that arise from a resonance between the preconscious awareness of experience and fantasy of the analyst and the congruent counterparts in the patient. Then the ideas of themes and interpretations present themselves to the analyst's consciousness. Yet, this very receptivity to external and internal perceptions also makes the analyst vulnerable to many internal conflict-laden distortions. The vehicle for the analytic understanding also is the vehicle for countertransference reactions which may obscure the analysis.

In the treatment of adults the analyst in this vulnerable position relies on the relative "quiet" of the analytic situation for his comfort and protection. But the child analyst, who often does analysis in a cacophony of activity, cannot do this. The analyst of adults counts on transient regressions and progressions that oscillate within the patient's ego in the therapeutic situation. But the regressive pull of the child patient is ubiquitous, as Berta Bornstein stated. In the child patient the analyst does not have the therapeutically oriented "healthy" ego to join him in antiregressive moves. The child rarely demands that the analyst act "grown up"—certainly not in the early stages of the analysis—unless he is reminded constantly that it is appropriate to do so.

It is easy, dangerously so, for an analyst engaged in play or other activities with the child to ignore the inherent regression. In this regressed state, the perceptions that arise are then "surreptitious," if one can use the word, and the interpretations are made by the voice of the regressed state.

The second patient, Sam, also was a boy of 10. Sam was a mercurial, adventuresome, hyperactive, rebellious young man. He was also very charming. He was always in trouble in school and at home. After many hectic and quiet weeks in analysis, he suddenly came into the office as on a whirlwind. He would slam the office door, start running, throw his body in the air making a complete roll and land on the couch, stomach down and face up. I was astonished and shocked. My first response (there were many others, as this happened many times) was horror that Sam might land on the floor, break the couch, or crash into the wall (he did the latter several times apparently without hurting himself). Later I caught myself admiring this feat. This boy had a remarkable agility and bodily coordination, and I was enchanted by it. The sequence of my responses also contained an element of relief when the boy was not hurt and got through the turn in air. The pleasure in observing it was increased by the tension and relief that all was well. I interpreted Sam's behavior as a communication and followed it by pointing out the defense against speech, but some of my feelings must have crept into the interpretation because the patient beamed, saying, "You didn't think I could do it." Obviously I didn't, but neither did the patient. He was proving he could do something that was difficult and that he was afraid of. His counterphobic attitude was demonstrated many times. He also conveyed that he wanted to be strong, but when he was attempting to be strong his family (as the analyst) let him do dangerous things.

I, too, had been a gawky boy, afraid of many physical challenges. My defense had not been counterphobic. I could not help for a short time admiring the feat of this other boy, who appeared so unfrightened. The connivance with this counterphobic acting out was brief but finally instructive. The patient was terrified of bodily damage, of which his parents were unaware. The parents felt helpless to interfere with this "whirlwind," who begged to be restrained and protected. With this understanding, these fears and wishes could be interpreted. In the end, it was, as Berta Bornstein had said, a difficult but wonderful task.

Berta Bornstein
1899-1971

PETER BLOS, PH.D.

BERTA BORNSTEIN DIED ON SEPTEMBER 5, 1971. SHE WAS VACATIONING in her beloved summer home on the Island of Vinalhaven in Maine. Death approached her while she was walking with a friend along the beachfront of her house on a Sunday morning. A cerebral accident made her suddenly feel exhausted and weak. A doctor from nearby was summoned. He rushed to her and found Bertl lying on the beach paralyzed, yet still talking. She was taken on a stretcher to the doctor's house where she lost consciousness. Twelve hours later she died in the hospital of Rockland. It was the kind of death Bertl had wished for: reaching the end of her life while still actively engaged in her profession, and reaching it before the physical infirmities of recent years would overtake her. Was she expecting the end or did she wish it to come? Be this as it may, we are touched by her inexplicable foresight and devotion to her calling when we contemplate the fact that she had referred her patients to other analysts before she left for her summer vacation. She had, indeed, worked until the end. She died one week before her 72nd birthday.

We all remember her well; even if we did not know her personally, we knew her from her reputation: she had become a legend during her lifetime. The beginnings and the developments of child analysis are so closely linked with her name that they are, indeed, one and the same. In summing up a historical view of child

Read at the New York Psychoanalytic Society and Institute, January 25, 1972.

analysis at the Vienna meeting of 1971, Anna Freud referred to Berta Bornstein as one of the decisive contributors to child analytic technique. There she said: "The introductory phase of child analysis was dropped when Berta Bornstein developed the analysis of defenses." As author, teacher, training analyst, and supervisor, Berta Bornstein has left an indelible mark on two generations of child analysts. My son was supervised by her and so was his father.

Berta Bornstein's analytic work with children reaches back into the 20s when she became part of the Berlin psychoanalytic circle. She had worked as *Fürsorgerin* (combining some duties of social and welfare worker) when she became a close friend of the Fenichels. She entered analysis with the help of Otto Fenichel and, in addition, she became an active participant in the seminar which Fenichel conducted in his home. Steffi, her sister, 5 years older, followed the same career; indeed the Bornstein sisters were an inseparable pair. Unfortunately, I could not trace her life beyond her analytic beginning. She never talked to her friends about her past, her family and background. All we know is the fact that her family came from Poland (Krakau) and settled in Berlin when Bertl was a child. The two sisters were quite poor when they embarked on their new careers as child analysts.

In the late 20s Bertl went to Vienna and became an outstanding contributor to the practice and theory of child analysis. She published a series of papers, and her work as a teacher and supervisor made her one of the leading figures in the field of child analysis. She possessed a unique talent for dealing with very young children, as we remember from the case of a phobia in a $2\frac{1}{2}$-year-old child, Lisa. The treatment report of Lisa (1931) represents a record of a young child's analysis, still unsurpassed in its clarity of detail and technical ingenuity. To the series of Berta Bornstein's classical case histories belong those of "Frankie," a phobic child (1949), and of "Sherry," an obsessional girl (1953).

To read Berta Bornstein's case histories remains a delight, because they convey so vividly her personal style of working with children. In her assessment of cases, especially where they touched on organicity, as well as in her work with parents, she showed her rare acumen for sifting the essential from the transient. An unusual and highly personal gift enabled her to throw light into the dark recesses of the child's mind for others to see.

Her work on latency probably represents her most lasting contribution. She proposed a division of latency into two periods which she defined structurally and illustrated clinically. During the first period (5½ to 8) we observe heightened ambivalence and the beginning of character changes, based on reaction formations as the typical defense against pregenital impulses. "Early animal phobias are replaced by a new wave of separation anxiety and open castration fear is substituted by fear of death." During the second period of latency (8 to 10) we observe a more determined opposition to masturbation, which we recognize in the child's desire that "defenses should not be upset by any interference." The consolidation of ego defenses turns the child's mind toward the mastery of the outside world; he finds more gratification in reality and he is less aware of his suffering. The consequences of these formulations for the refinement of child analytic technique are obvious. Berta Bornstein's research in latency became formulated and published during the 40s and early 50s after she was well established in this country. She came to America in 1938 and rapidly assumed a leading role in the field of child psychoanalysis. She became a Special Member of the New York Psychoanalytic Society, a Faculty Member of the New York Psychoanalytic Institute, a training and supervising analyst, an Honorary Member of the American Psychoanalytic Association, and a Member-at-Large of the International Psycho-Analytical Association.

An anecdote about Bertl seems worth telling. It came to me from an old friend and colleague of hers and it takes us back to her Vienna years. During the seminars at the Institute for Psychoanalytic Education in Vienna, Bertl, more than once, fell asleep during the case presentations. However, when the discussion started, she was wide awake and it was she who made the most penetrating analytic comment about the case. I let this legend stand as an enigma of the unusual person whose memory we honor.

The Writings of
Berta Bornstein

(1930a), Beziehungen zwischen Sexual- und Intellektentwicklung [Relations between Sexual Development and the Development of the Intellect]. *Z. psychoanal. Päd.*, 4:446–454.

(1930b), Ein Fall von geheilter Dummheit: Referat über eine psychoanalytische Krankengeschichte [A Case of Cured Stupidity: Report on a Psychoanalytic Case History]. *Z. psychoanal. Päd.*, 4:455–461.

(1930c), Zur Psychogenese der Pseudodebilität [Psychogenesis of Pseudodebility]. *Int. Z. Psychoanal.*, 16:378–399.

(1931), Phobie eines 2½ jährigen Kindes.*Int. Z. Psychoanal.*, 18:344–367. Phobia in a 2½-Year-Old Child. *Psychoanal. Quart.*, 4:93–119, 1935.

(1934), Enuresis und Kleptomanie als passagères Symptom [Enuresis and Kleptomania As Transitory Symptoms]. *Z. psychoanal. Päd.*, 8:229–237.

(1936), Ein Beispiel für die Leugnung durch die Phantasie [An Example of Denial in Fantasy]. *Z. psychoanal. Päd.*, 10:269–275.

(1945), Clinical Notes on Child Analysis. *This Annual*, 1:151–166.

(1946), Hysterical Twilight States in an Eight-Year-Old Child. *This Annual*, 2:229–240.

(1948), Emotional Barriers in the Understanding and Treatment of Young Children. *Amer. J. Orthopsychiat.*, 18:691–697.

(1949), The Analysis of a Phobic Child: Some Problems of Theory and Technique in Child Analysis. *This Annual*, 3/4:181–226.

(1951), On Latency. *This Annual*, 6:279–285. (Abstract) *Annual Survey of Psychoanalysis*, 2:85–86.

Compiled by Phyllis Rubinton, Librarian, New York Psychoanalytic Institute.

(1953a), Masturbation in the Latency Period. *This Annual*, 8:65–78. (Abstract) *Annual Survey of Psychoanalysis*, 4:113, 272–275.

(1953b), Fragment of an Analysis of an Obsessional Child: The First Six Months of Analysis. *This Annual*, 8:313–332. (Abstract) *Annual Survey of Psychoanalysis*, 4:288–291.

PANEL DISCUSSIONS

(1951), Child Analysis. *Bull. Amer. Psychoanal. Assn.*, 7:344–348.

(1953), On Problems of Identification. *J. Amer. Psychoanal. Assn.*, 1:538–549.

CONTRIBUTIONS TO PSYCHOANALYTIC THEORY

The Genealogy of the Ego Ideal

PETER BLOS, PH.D.

THE ADOLESCENT PERIOD LENDS ITSELF PARTICULARLY WELL TO THE study of psychic structures in relation to origin, content, and function. While psychic structures, at this advanced stage of development, are essentially formed and integrated, it remains a characteristic of adolescence—or of the biphasic development of sexuality in the human species—that a process of psychic restructuring is evoked by pubertal maturation. The course of the ensuing emotional instability is marked by more or less disintegrative processes of a regressive nature, but simultaneously we can also observe a vigorous and integrative forward movement in personality formation. Integration and consolidation proceed in a seesaw fashion with violent or mild, extended or brief alternations of regressive and progressive movements. The relative openness and fluidity of the personality during this period of psychic restructuring grant the psychoanalytic observer of personality development the opportunity to gain important insights into structure formation and transformation which no other period in human life offers in any comparable manner. The dramatic reverberations of this process in the life of the adolescent have never failed, throughout history, to be noticed and recorded.

In the course of my psychoanalytic studies I have used this natural laboratory setting of psychic restructuring in adolescence for the investigation of those structures that are most decisively affected by the adolescent process. The present study extends this research to the ego ideal. Popular observation and academic psychology have always emphasized the proclivity of youth for high

Faculty, New York Psychoanalytic Institute and The Columbia University Psychoanalytic Clinic for Training and Research.

ideals, for idealizations and ideologies. This tendency, usually in conflict with traditional values, taboos, and customs, has given cause either to sanctify or to malign the younger generation. The vagueness of psychological theory in relation to ideal formation in adolescence, in conjunction with the demonstrative, often desperate search for ideals in contemporary youth, makes the study of the ego ideal within the adolescent process a timely issue. My own findings will be viewed in the light of the ego-ideal conceptualizations which have been advanced over the years and have become an integral part of psychoanalytic theory.

THE CLINICAL STARTING POINT

Whatever my contributions to psychoanalytic theory have been, they all have one thing in common, namely, they issued from clinical observations. The same holds true for the study of the ego ideal. Therefore, I begin by recounting the course of my observations which started during the analysis of adolescent boys, especially of those in their late adolescence.

Several male patients in their late adolescence shared one prominent symptom complex. They had high ambitions, yet they were unable to pursue them; they were aimless and dejected, given to extreme mood swings, to sporadic but short-lived spurts of enterprising action and an unfailing return to monotonous dreams of glory: nothing ever congealed into purposeful pursuit, novel experimentation, or the visionary excitement of a realistic goal. These are typical adolescent characteristics; they acquired the specificity of a symptom complex only by the fact that they remained static, repetitive, and beyond volitional control; thus, they affected perniciously the common challenge to youth, such as job performance, academic achievement, and the pursuit of gratifying object relations with boys, girls, and adults alike. The irrefutable evidence of failure rendered the present dismal and the future ominous. Flight into rebellion or restitution in fantasy led into the quicksand of helplessness. Negativism, if present, never lasted long; yet, any effort to transcend it could not be sustained. Occupational goals or short-term objectives were easily lost in indecision and doubt; they were often and abruptly abandoned, despite a seemingly strong motivation that brought them into existence. These and related phenomena have been widely described in the literature, especially in reference to male adolescence. Among the various dynamic and genetic explanations, the male adolescent's rivalry with the oedipal father stands out as the standard model. Defenses against castration anxiety seem to have barricaded the road to progressive development. There can be no question that this theme reverberates through the adolescent struggle of the male. There is always an abundance of direct expressions or associations, ideas, and affects leading in this direction. However, interpretations along these lines, emphasizing this conflict, did not resolve, in my experience, the symptomatology of such pervasive inhibitions and developmental arrests as described above.

It occurred to me that the complementary complex of the male's rivalry with the father, namely, his love of him and his wish to be the recipient of his affection, presented an obstacle to the formation of realistic goals and their active pursuit. In fact, passive aims rose to the surface repeatedly and without fail, even though these aims clashed with conscious ambitions and were subject to severe self-criticism. They obviously received their pertinacity from the secondary gain they secured. The sexualization of ego and of superego functions during adolescence is well known; it applies equally to those ego-ideal formations which preceded adolescence. To illustrate, I shall cite a male student whose vocational ambitions were the same as those which his father had set for his son. Failure had to prevent success because of a four-pronged conflict: as a success he was either offering himself as a love object to the father (castration wish), or he was annihilating him by usurping his position (parricide); on the other hand, as a failure he was renouncing his ambitions and thereby induced the father to treat him like a contemptible woman; yet, in failure he also established his autonomy, even if a negative one, by repulsing the father's seductiveness, by not becoming his best-loved, his ideal son. The complexity of this constellation is due to the fact that both the positive and the negative oedipus complex come into play again at the terminal phase of adolescence. The final resolution of both is of course decisively influenced by the fixation points in early object relations and the implicit bisexual orientation of childhood.

Observations of this kind have convinced me that the ego ideal remained an immature, self-idealizing, wish-fulfilling agency, resisting any transformation into a mature, namely, abstracted, goal-intentional, and action-motivating force, as long as the young man's negative oedipus complex cannot be drawn sufficiently into the analytic work. I am certain that analysts know from experience how impenetrable this aspect of the defensive organization remains in the analysis of the male adolescent. Only after the analysis of the fixation on the negative oedipus complex has been accomplished, can the formation of an age-adequate, workable ego ideal take its normal course. This led me to say that the ego ideal, as it emerges at the termination of adolescence, is the heir to the negative oedipus complex (Blos, 1965, 1972a). By inference, I assume that adolescent psychic restructuring which progresses unaided by therapeutic help follows a similar course.

Before pursuing the theoretical implications of what has been said so far, I must say a word about adolescent idealization in general. These comments apply to boy and girl in equal measure, even though their idealizations are different in content and quality. A good reason exists for making a distinction between the idealization of the self and the ego ideal as such. Even though idealizations have their roots in infantile narcissism, we cannot ignore the fact that the advent of sexual maturation draws these early narcissistic formations into the instinctual turmoil of adolescence. Here we encounter them, either in the area of object relations or in a regressive enhancement of narcissism as seen in self idealizations. These formations are unstable and subject to rapid fluctuations; they are the primitive regulators of self-esteem. Self idealization can provide, at least temporarily, a gratification on the order of infantile need gratification. The ego ideal, in contrast, provides only approximations to fulfillment; it involves delay and a state of anticipation; it is a ceaseless journey without arrival; it is a lifelong striving for perfection. Superego demands can be fulfilled with a subsequent sense of well-being. Ego-ideal strivings can never be fulfilled; in fact, it is the sustained striving for perfection that furnishes a sense of well-being.[1]

The ego ideal has its deepest roots in primary narcissism. Yet, every stage of subsequent development enlarges its scope in terms of content and function. Both ego ideal and superego begin to develop early in life, long before they assume the structure of a psychic agency. They originate in response to the external world and remain, therefore, prone to reexternalization. Here, I want to emphasize the fact that the ego ideal is subject to qualitative changes during the course of development. This is to say, the ego ideal can easily become enmeshed with new drive modalities, as well as with new ego competencies, as both emerge at different developmental stages. By virtue of this fact, we can expect the ego ideal to become drawn into the turmoil of the libidinal and aggressive drives of adolescence. The adolescent reinstinctualization of those psychic structures that derived from the internalization of object relations encompasses the ego ideal as well. Its narcissistic core attaches itself to the narcissistic object libido that finds a renewed outlet within the resurgence of the negative oedipus complex. Its resolution brings the mature ego ideal into existence as the desexualized, i.e., the transmuted, survivor of the negative oedipus complex. Even though the early steps, as well as the final ones, of ego-ideal development are different in male and female, the adolescent structuralization of the ego ideal determines, for both sexes, the end phase of the adolescent process; or, in other words, it marks the termination of psychological childhood.

It is an accepted tenet in psychoanalytic theory that the oedipus complex is reactivated during adolescence. In conjunction with regression in the service of development, the reactivation leads to the loosening of infantile object ties and initiates the second individuation process of adolescence. Ego dominance as well as the

[1] Hartmann and Loewenstein (1962) have discussed the "change of function" (p. 64) in the evolution of the ego ideal. The pertinent comment reads as follows: "the 'striving after perfection' of the ego ideal becomes dynamically a partly independent direction-giving function, which is relatively independent of the objects, and relatively independent also of the instinctual precursors. The aims of the ego ideal are then to a considerable extent no longer identical with the primitive wishes which played a role in its formation" (p. 64).

characterological stabilization of defenses can be observed along the progression of adolescent psychic restructuring. The similarities of this stage with that of the transition from the phallic-oedipal to the latency stage are striking and have attracted the attention of analytic observers.

It has been my impression that the first decline of the oedipus complex at the stage of sexual immaturity forces the positive component of the complex into repression and identificatory transformations (superego), and that this is accomplished by more absolute and stringent measures than appears to be the case with reference to the negative component of the complex. We have always taken for granted that the triadic oedipal conflict is decisively influenced by the precursory object relations of the dyadic period, carrying forward fixations which pertain to specific drive propensities, patterns of object relations, and preferential affinities to one or the other of the component instincts. The little boy's passive love for the father and his identification with the mother seem to find a bypass, often apparent as characterological trait or split-off fantasy, during the resolution of the oedipus complex and the solidification of the superego. The feminine component of the little boy's instinctual life becomes restrained, restricted, or rejected, far more forcefully by narcissistic injunctions, manifest in shame and contempt, than by superego interdictions. His mastery of aggression always skirts close to the dilemma of mastery by passive surrender to moral principles, namely, the father, or by externalizing the conflict through acting out.

It is a well-known fact that the boy's relationship to his father is never better, i.e., less conflicted or more positive, than it is at the dawn of pubescence. The boy enlists the father's assistance in his defense against the regression to the preoedipal—the phallic, castrating—mother. It can be observed how this phase affects the resuscitation of the oedipus complex, regardless of earlier fixations, and how this phase complicates, in some fashion, its adolescent resolution. It is my contention that adolescence not only is faced with the revival of the oedipal conflict as it was resolved or abandoned at its first decline, but that the definitive resolution of the complex is the inherent task of adolescence. This task involves the total renunciation of infantile object ties to both parental figures, i.e., to both as sexual objects. An adjunctive resolution pertains in many cases to an incestuous tie to brother or sister.

For the child, the bisexual position is less conflictual, allowing a host of compromises, than is the case for the adolescent who has attained sexual maturity. The resolution of the negative oedipus complex as an object involvement of a sexual nature confronts the adolescent boy with a relatively novel conflict and task. Displacement to a nonincestuous object can never be a satisfactory solution because this would only extend the complete oedipal constellation, beyond its timing, into bisexual object relations of adulthood. The only road open for the boy lies in the deinstinctualization of the narcissistic, i.e., homosexual, object tie, leading to the formation of the ego ideal in its final form. In the process, all ego-ideal trends that have accrued over time, from primary narcissism to symbiotic omnipotence and later from narcissistic identifications to the stage of homosexual object love, become integrated in the permanent ego ideal that coalesces during the terminal stage of adolescence. From here on, the ego ideal remains an unalterable psychic structure which extends its influence on thought and behavior over a much larger sector of the personality than was the case before adolescence. This shift has to be viewed as a collateral to those changes that the adolescent superego undergoes at the same time. Phenomenologically, these changes are represented by the proverbial adolescent rebellion. Metapsychologically, these changes indicate that ego and ego ideal are taking over some of the superego functions, thereby affecting its scope of influence as well as its dynamic and economic role in mental life (Blos, 1962).

I shall now return briefly to self idealization and ego ideal in adolescence, because the conceptualization of the adolescent ego-ideal formation permits a more precise differentiation between the two. The acquisition of ideals is not identical with an ego-ideal structuralization. One can no less speak of ego ideals than of superegos in the plural. Yet, one frequently encounters the term "ego ideals" in the literature. Both superego and ego ideal denote a cohesive structure or, more correctly, the ego ideal represents an "aspect of the superego system" (Hartmann and Loewenstein, 1962, p. 44). Self idealization is a typical aspect of adolescence; it displays, quite unmistakably, its narcissistic origin and function as the regulator of self-esteem. Concurrently, we discern a more or less malignant impairment of reality testing, objectivation, and object relations. At the point where narcissistic aims of self idealization are externalized, they are easily confused with the manifestation of the ego ideal. Indeed, the adolescent's uncompromising ideals, expressed in word or action, are often mistaken as evidence of a powerful ego ideal. My clinical impressions of some of the angry or activist late adolescents, most of them college students, who seek the creation of a perfect society, have convinced me that the belief in a perfect world is rooted in an archaic belief in parental perfection. The "idealized parent imago" (Kohut, 1971), when externalized, lends a fanatical vision to the striving for such a perfect world, while the narcissistic rage, a response to parental disillusionment, finds a belated expression in the irrationality of violence. An imperfect world must either yield to correction or it must be destroyed. This kind of all-or-nothing principle has been demonstrated in the 1960s with particular virulence on the campus of the American colleges.[2] The Alma Mater, "the fostering mother," became the target of infantile wrath and recrimination as demonstrated in verbal, symbolic as well as in concrete anal defilement. Her refusal to provide need gratification to her foster children was taken literally, in total disregard of the fact that she was fostering (nursing) the mind and therefore was not able to provide instantaneous need gratification. Of course, these comments apply only to a particular segment of campus activists and fringe rebels. The so-called faults of the parent appear to them magnified to the size of unforgivable insults of debasement or evil. In some youthful revolutionaries[3] we find the sense of political or historical logic either distorted by "absolutes" or rendered nonexistent by the overriding belief in perfection. Far from being delusional, this kind of behavior and

[2] A generalization of this thesis on a worldwide scale can only be misleading, because too many heterogeneous factors entered the scene of student uprisings in other countries.

[3] We find their prototypical ancestors in the nihilist students depicted in Arcady and Bazarov in Turgenev's novel *Fathers and Sons* (1862). Arcady eventually settles down in marriage and ancestral life, while Bazarov, in a triumph of self idealization over a thwarted romance, commits suicide.

thinking reflects the externalization of the lost parental perfection; furthermore, it demonstrates how extraordinarily painful the effort is to transcend the loss of the idealized self or object.

Psychoanalytic theory has always emphasized the close connection between the ego ideal and the narcissistic losses of infancy. In accordance with its origin, which also influences its function, the ego ideal is basically averse to object-libidinal involvement; its roots lie in primary narcissism. It perpetuates, so to say, an eternal approximation to the narcissistic perfection of infancy. If we follow the course which the ego ideal takes from infancy to adulthood, we can trace a continuous adaptation of its basic function to the increasingly complex system by which the self measures itself, as it progresses along the developmental lines. Thus, the ego ideal gets further and further removed from those primitive efforts which aim at total narcissistic restitution. In fact, the ego ideal functions as a psychic institution, at least in its mature form, only as long as its goal remains beyond its grasp. Whatever man accomplishes, imperfection remains an everlasting constituent of his endeavors; yet this fact has never held man back from renewing his efforts. While the superego is an agency of prohibition, the ego ideal is an agency of aspiration. "Whereas the ego submits to the superego out of fear of punishment, it submits to the ego ideal out of love" (Nunberg, 1932, p. 146). Many decades later we read again: "Our ideals are our internal leaders; we love them and are longing to reach them. . . . We are driven by our ambitions, [but] we do not love them" (Kohut, 1966, p. 251).

During the formative process of the adult ego ideal in adolescence, preoedipal and pregenital patterns are reinstated and the strength of fixation points becomes glaringly apparent. The same is true of the component instincts, which once more play a role during the upheaval of the instinctual life at puberty, when the advance to genitality draws a more and more distinct demarcation line between forepleasure and genital arousal. In my work with the male adolescent, I was often struck by how intensely his self idealization is cultivated by him as an aim in itself, without being followed up by an act toward realization or achievement. The comparison of this attitude to a fixation on forepleasure is convincing, especially when we observe repeatedly the decline of this mode of functioning with the ascendancy of genitality. This thought, already contained *in nuce* in the clinical starting point, can now be restated: the ego ideal emerges from its infantile state only when, at late adolescence, the narcissistic object attachment to which the infantile ego ideal has become joined has lost its homosexual cathexis. This task is accomplished by the adolescent resolution of the negative oedipus complex.

THE DEVELOPMENT OF THE MALE AND FEMALE EGO IDEAL

Even though we consider the ego ideal to be part of the superego system, they do not evolve from the same conflictual matrix, nor are they overlapping entities at the time of their emergence. Quite to the contrary, their origins are heterogeneous, their starting points are not synchronous, their contents are not identical, and their functions are disparate. What they have in common is their motivational influence on behavior, and their regulatory function of the sense of well-being. We can "distinguish between the superego, as the later and more reality-syntonic structure, and the ego ideal as the earlier more narcissistic one" (A. Reich, 1954, p. 209). However, the chronology of definitive structure formation is reversed: the superego is established earlier at the decline of the phallic-oedipal phase, while the ego ideal reaches its definitive structure only during the terminal stage of adolescence.

It has often been noted that the narcissistic nature of the ego ideal draws, at an early age, the body image into its realm. It is therefore no surprise that the course of ego-ideal formation is not identical for boy and girl. However, for both sexes, the function of the early ego ideal can be recognized in its aim, which is to repair or wipe out a narcissistic hurt caused by comparison with or slight by others. The narcissistic recourse to a state of an illusory self-perfection induces a sense of well-being, which is, however, acquired at the price of a certain reality distortion. With progressing ego development, such isolated distortions extend an insidious influence on the adaptive resourcefulness of the child.

THE DEVELOPMENTAL LINE OF THE EGO IDEAL IN THE GIRL

In the psychoanalytic literature I have come across only one systematic developmental description of the female ego ideal in a paper by Jacobson (1954). It is her impression that "the little girl develops a nucleus of the true ego ideal even earlier than the little boy and in connection with the early onset of her castration conflict." She responds to the discovery of being castrated with a "denial of her supposed deficiency." This conflictual stage leads, over time, to the recognition of her sexual anatomy and, in consequence, to an attempt to recover the lost phallus. During this phase her disillusionment in her mother is marked by accusatory, hostile rejection of the mother and depreciatory feelings about herself (body image). This preoedipal conflict finds a resolution in the recovery of the phallus via her turning to the father and "quite commonly, . . . a premature relinquishment of genital activities, with a withdrawal and shift of narcissistic libido from the genital to the whole body" (p. 118).

My experience confirms this shift, which can be recognized at a later stage in the tomboy when the body-phallus equation is so spectacularly displayed; the same trend can be followed in the older girl, when the body-phallus becomes the exhibitionistic, controlling, and excitatory agent of male sexual arousal. A persistent preoccupation with the body-phallus tends to transport the adolescent girl into the quasi-delusional state in which she perceives all males to lust for her. This, in fact, is often quite correct because the phallic-narcissistic "tease" in her provocative aloofness tends to arouse aggressive and self-assertive sexual behavior in the male.

Jacobson further states:

> My case material left no doubt that these serious conflicts and, in particular, the dangers arising from the little girl's self-deflation and from the devaluation and threatening loss of her mother are mastered by establishment of a maternal ego ideal, though a very premature and immature one: the idea of an unaggressive, clean, neat, and physically attractive little girl who is determined to renounce sexual activities. Frequently we can, indeed, observe that the female ego ideal absorbs and replaces for ever the "illusory penis" fantasy [p. 118f.].

When the little girl turns to the oedipal father, the recovery of the phallus remains an intrinsic aspect of her sexual wishes. In the pursuit of these wishes we can see a reinstatement of oral incorporative modalities which were the phase-adequate mechanism during the premature formation of her ego ideal. I might add here that these "archaic fantasies of oral and genital incorporation" of the paternal phallus constitute a normal (often pathologically fixated) aspect of the late-adolescent girl's strivings for perfection, be this sexually, intellectually, socially, morally, or otherwise. My observations of this stage confirm Jacobson's statement that the girl's tendency to regress to the primitive state of her early ego-ideal formation complicates, delays, or aborts the establishment of an independent ego, as well as an ego ideal of a depersonified, deconcretized, and abstracted nature. In consequence, the girl conserves a lasting tendency to the "reattachment of her ego ideal to an outside person" (p. 119). In other words, the female ego ideal tends to remain enmeshed, or is prone to become reenmeshed, in the vicissitudes of object relations.

Within this context, we have to consider the fact that bisexuality in the female remains, throughout life, less polarized or conflictual than is true for the male; bisexuality is therefore never subjected to a definitive resolution or to a repression as rigid and irreversible as is, normally, the case in the male. We look in vain, during early male puberty, for an unrestrained and ego-syntonic stage, equal to the girl's tomboy stage. Only from the analysis of the young male adolescent have we evidence of his deeply repressed feminine wishes and identifications (Blos, 1962, 1965). These findings only confirm the fact that both issues of the oedipus complex—the first, phallic; the second, the adolescent—follow a different course in boy and girl. At the critical juncture of late adolescence, when the girl's stabilization of her femininity is to be attained, the regressive incorporation of the paternal phallus as the narcissistic regulator of her sense of completeness and perfection has to be overcome by an enduring identification with the mother. The desexualized and deconcretized ego ideal favors the transformation of infantile penis envy into a striving for perfection as a woman, removed from envy, competition, and rapaciousness (sexual "trophy hunting"). This achievement restores a sense of well-being with the attendant assurance that a course of self realization is indeed possible. The inexhaustible reservoir of a propelling force toward this goal constitutes the female ego ideal and defines its narcissistic function.

Remnants of a "reattachment of the ego ideal to an outside person," to a love object, remains, to some degree, the *sine qua non* of the female ego ideal.

Every analyst who has had adolescent girls in analysis has observed the delicate and painful state of transition from the personalized, dependent, and concretized to the autonomous, impersonal, and abstracted ego ideal. In the course toward this end, the girl often attempts to fit her primitive ego ideal into a love relationship. Her pleasure gain here lies more or less exclusively in the exercise of her power and the narcissistic restoration of the phallus; this is achieved either in the vicarious possession during sexual intercourse, or via genital (oral) incorporation. These stages on the road toward femininity often appear juxtaposed with eating disturbances, such as compulsive eating or dietary asceticism, and leave no doubt about the oral mechanisms involved. It is a well-known fact that adolescent eating disturbances are prevalent among girls, but a negligible occurrence among boys.

THE DEVELOPMENTAL LINE OF THE EGO IDEAL IN THE BOY

The first forward step in male ego-ideal development leads from primary narcissism to delusional omnipotence shared with the mother and, beyond that, to narcissistic identifications with idealized objects. These identifications become progressively tempered by the reality principle, which takes a forward leap at the time it is called upon to aid in the resolution of the oedipus complex. The consolidation of the superego keeps flights into omnipotence and aggrandizement in check. The recourse to the state of infantile omnipotence becomes decisively relegated to the world of fantasy. In fact, the creative aspect of fantasy and its expressive modalities (such as play or verbal imagination) reflect, on a metaphorical plane, the potency and power of the procreative, preoedipal mother who has always, to some degree, aroused the envy of the male child. This fact may, in contrast to what has been said about the girl's ego ideal, explain the observation that adolescent boys so frequently pine for creativity, originality, and fame. Girls, indeed, have similar aspirations, but these remain more forcefully attached to the yearnings for a fulfilling relationship. Nevertheless, it remains a fact that large portions of creative efforts and achievements are identified with men; this distribution among the sexes can only partially be attributed to cultural influences. Reverberations of male awe and envy of female procreation can still be detected in the male adolescent's urge to create, be this a gadget, a fortune, a molecule, a poem, a song, or a house. Such wishes fall far short of any characteristic we attribute to the ego ideal, yet they furnish the repertoire for repetitive daydreams and usually remain shackled to these nether regions by strong inhibitions. To illustrate, I shall relate an incident from the analysis of a late adolescent male patient. He reported one day that he had heard himself say aloud, as talking to himself: "Now, Chris, don't be a woman." At the time, he was languishing in daydreams, blissfully hoping that all would turn out for the best. He was startled by his own words, which revealed both his wish and its refutation—and, more pointedly, his neurotic conflict.

If the infantile need for oneness with the archaic mother remains overly strong, the oedipus complex falls under the shadow of this fixation. A regressive component in the resolution of the boy's oedipus complex can be discerned in the narcissistic identification with the archaic, omnipotent, phallic mother. To some extent, this compromise seems to be a rather normal aspect of the male oedipus complex that reaches its final resolution, rather belatedly, during its adolescent resuscitation. Whenever the preoedipal fixation on the phallic mother weakens the rivalrous, phallic assertion of the boy, the oedipus complex is destined to remain incomplete. This abnormal condition certainly becomes evident during adolescence, if it did not already do so during the latency period. The time for the outbreak of the neurosis lies, usually, in the period of late adolescence (Blos, 1972b), because the physiology of puberty tends to render a feeble masculine component more ascendant during this stage, when "the increase in genital libido produces a welcome decrease in pregenitality" (A. Freud, 1958, p. 266). Yet, one characteristic survival of the regressive component, embedded in the oedipus complex, is to be found quite universally in the young adolescent boy's castration anxiety in relation to the phallic mother, or to women in general (Blos, 1962, 1965). This powerful apprehensiveness causes the boy to idealize the father and seek his protective and reassuring peership. Sharing the idealized paternal power and superiority becomes a transient source of narcissistic grandeur that will last until the sexual impulse threatens the arousal of homosexual object libido. At this point, we can observe how the ego ideal again becomes fatefully enmeshed with object-libidinal strivings due to the relatively incomplete resolution of the oedipus complex. Only the analysis of the preoedipal and pregenital fixations and their ominous integration into the oedipal organization opens the path to mature ego-ideal structuralization. This is to say, or repeat, that the resolution of the negative oedipus complex plays a decisive role in the forward development toward adult personality formation.

The structuralization of the mature ego ideal reduces excessive self and object idealizations to the level of more realistic self and object appraisals. The capacity of objectivation serves as a check against any inopportune aggrandizement of the self. From here on, the ego ideal derives its momentum from the unending flow of neutralized homosexual libido. Thus, it sustains the inexorable "striving for perfection," which is the source of narcissistic sustenance, removed from and remote to the vicissitudes of object relations. The male ego ideal enshrines, so to say, its history from primary narcissism to the merger with maternal omnipotence and, beyond, to the oedipal love for the father. This last stage is transcended in the ego-ideal structure. Only in terms of this last and decisive step which integrates the various epochs of the ego-ideal history in its mature structuralization can we speak of the male ego ideal as the heir of the negative oedipus complex (Blos, 1965). The confirmation of these conceptualizations will be served best by a consideration of ego-ideal pathology.

EGO-IDEAL PATHOLOGY

It remains a surprising fact that the normal and often pervasive state of adolescent narcissism has not elicited more extensive investigations of its content, form, and transformation. It is precisely in this psychic territory of fortuitous visibility wherein my observations are made. I intend to use the period that extends from the rise to the decline of adolescent narcissism for the study of the ego ideal.

This period demonstrates its primitive as well as its more mature forms and, beyond that, the steps in the process of its transformation. The failure in the formation of a mature ego ideal exemplifies, as it were, the conditions of adolescent ego-ideal pathology, highlighting the transitional as well as the final steps that are obligatory for the structuralization of an adult ego ideal.

The customary approach to the problem of adolescent narcissism relates this phenomenon to two major dynamic constellations. One pertains to object libido as it is deflected on the self. The narcissistic state of adolescence is, thus, regarded as a concomitant of the second individuation process (Blos, 1967), namely, of the emotional disengagement from the internalized love and hate objects of early childhood. It is a well-known fact that these early and earliest object or part-object relations are endowed with extraordinary resources that satisfy—generally speaking—the narcissistic needs of the immature and dependent organism. Self-esteem and security regulations of this primitive kind are easily reinstituted at periods of a developmental crisis, such as adolescence. The adolescent trends toward idealization of persons, ideas, goals, and endeavors, in conjunction with rebellious self-assertion, have combined to give adolescent idealizations per se an exalted, indeed, a revered position. Should one view the trend toward idealization as a reliable indicator of progressive development, then its potential deterrent to maturation is ignored. It remains no easy task to discern in these idealizing manifestations the correct extent of an adaptive, a regressive, and a defensive component.

The second dynamic constellation effecting an increase in narcissism pertains to the regressive aspect of adolescence. We then observe the revival of the primitive ego ideal as a phase-specific, but transient, self-esteem regulator. This regressive aspect has received special attention, whenever its glaring pathology, especially in adolescent psychosis, dominates the clinical picture. It has received less attention as a concomitant of the regressive movement in the normal development of the ego ideal during the adolescent period. I intend to emphasize, in this process, the temporary enmeshment of the ego ideal in the resolution of the oedipus complex, especially of its negative component, during late adolescence.

The problem of adolescent ego-ideal structuralization has received, over a long period of time, minor attention by authors who have written on this period; only recently has this neglect been corrected. I shall omit, at this point, reference to the many contributions to the concept of the ego ideal, because this will be attended to in the section that follows. Since my focus is, at this moment, ego-ideal pathology, I must first pay tribute to the one outstanding clinician and psychoanalyst who has contributed so profoundly to this subject, Annie Reich (1953, 1954, 1960). Her theoretical formulations are invariably embedded in clinical work and I shall draw freely on these findings in order to lay my own, derived from adolescent analysis, beside them for comparative study. Many features of ego-ideal pathology, as described by Annie Reich in her adult patients, can readily be observed either as transient adolescent symptoms or, in their malignant form, as a pivotal component in adolescent psychosis. Between these extremes lies a spectrum of intermediary clinical phenomena which have attracted my attention.

Archaic elements in the superego system, which includes the ego ideal, often lie in dormant enclaves of a pathogenetic valence whose existence becomes apparent only at adolescence. Even though the personality, in many respects, had advanced in structure formation throughout the various phases of development, the narcissistic, more or less ego-syntonic, frequently concrete fantasies of infantile omnipotence and grandeur have never been sufficiently restrained by the reality principle; consequently, they failed to harmonize with the older child's perceptions, cognition, and memory; to put it briefly, they have obstructed ego development to a catastrophic extent. In that case, the pathogenetic enclaves, mentioned above, continue to serve as the only available and workable regulators of self-esteem via imaginary wish fulfillment during the adolescent disillusionment in self and object. These archaic elements stay outside the realm of object love and remain in the realm of primary narcissism. This portentous condition often remains unnoticed during childhood. "Frequently, narcissistic ego ideals become conspicuous only in puberty" (A. Reich, 1954, p. 215). While this fact generally is amply demonstrated in adolescence, the clinical picture frequently leaves a margin of uncertainty as to the pathognomic or transiently regressive nature of these narcissistic states (Blos, 1962). In order to differentiate between them or "to come to an understanding of narcissistic nonpsychotic states necessitates the concept of the ego ideal" (A. Reich, 1954, p. 216). The undoing of the separation between self and idealized object always entails some disintegration of reality testing. The child's wish to be like the powerful parent, a desire normally mastered by identificatory processes, is, under these conditions, replaced by the magic and megalomanic conviction to be the same, namely, to be his own ideal object (A. Reich, 1953) or, as it is often incorrectly called, his own ego ideal. What is meant, rather, is the merger of self and idealized object, the primitive state of completeness and well-being.

It is implicit in the nature of adolescence that the primitive state of self idealization, including the vast spectrum of magic, omnipotence, and grandiosity, becomes challenged as never before. The oedipal realization of physical immaturity could, at that age level, still find a modicum of perfection, even if only a borrowed one, in simply being the recipient of parental expectations. Expressions of parental overestimation, derived from their own narcissistic needs, are easily taken by the child as promises or predictions that never fail to be called into question during adolescence. It is true that postoedipal superego criticism and the attending sense of guilt counterbalance the primitive powers of self idealization and prevent them from ever dislodging objectivation; however, they never are extinguished. The normal state of a partially integrated and still externally regulated ego ideal of childhood undergoes a radical and lasting change during adolescence. A throwback, in the face of adolescent challenges, to the infantile ego ideal is a rather common occurrence before the more mature appraisal of object and self becomes irreversible. The second individuation process and the consolidation process of adolescence render existing self and object representations less rigid, but more stable and realistic. If the attendant disappointments, compromises, and losses cannot be tolerated, the adolescent process is doomed to miscarry. "The exclusive production of fantasies that aim at one's own aggrandizement reveals a serious disturbance of the narcissistic balance, particularly when these fantasies persist after puberty" (A. Reich, 1960, p. 296). It is no exaggeration, in this context, to say that adolescence is comparable to a continental divide that determines, once and for all, the direction into which the ego ideal will flow from here on: either it will revert to its familiar source of origin, or it will seek a new course, untested and unknown.

Before the rock bottom of ego-ideal pathology is reached in adolescent analysis, a certain amount of preparatory work in all sectors of the personality must be accomplished first. I shall mention only a recurrent theme that bears witness to the complex sources of ego-ideal pathology. What appears as the pathogenetic background is a massive, i.e., cumulative trauma within the narcissistic realm during the preoedipal periods. This extends its pernicious influence on the oedipal conflict, rendering it incomplete, i.e., leaving it interlocked with fixations that lie in the dyadic period. When the oedipus complex in its incomplete state is revived in adolescence, a resolution is attempted in a regressive search for a lost narcissistic completeness through the maternal object of the dyadic period. These early fixations often represent an insurmountable obstacle to progressive development in adolescence and are acted out in an often insatiable need for object possession. This primitive object hunger seeks fulfillment on the level of physical, i.e., sexual, maturity. Sexual relations of this nature are devoid of mutual empathy and the perfection of sexual performance is conspicuously pushed into the forefront.[4]

In cases of this kind, the positive oedipus complex takes on a prominent position early in the analysis, screening off the deeper layers of the narcissistic fixations which have been integrated in the defensive organization. The pathological concomitant of this condition is apparent in defective reality testing and in self-aggrandizement; however, if reality testing is fairly intact, we notice that the narcissistic fantasies are relegated to a split-off segment of the self and object representations, a segment that then displays a florid infantile, sexualized life of its own. These pathological enclaves

[4] This particular pattern of sexual behavior at late adolescence can, at this epoch, be traced to the stereotyping influence of the so-called sexual revolution of youth. Helene Deutsch (1967), an observer of the American college girl, has described this syndrome as one of sexual "infantilism." The reflection of this condition is always discernible in an immature state of the ego ideal.

within the personality are stubbornly preserved by the patient. Any analytic effort to reach them is felt as an aggressive and hostile intrusion or as a narcissistic deprivation. Yet, by this very fact, the analyst is drawn more and more into the realm of the patient's narcissistic needs, both as a provider and as a withholder of gratification. When the patient, finally, experiences these quasi-delusional deprivations as originating and exclusively operating in his own mind, then a decisive step toward a clearer delineation between inside and outside is effected. This step toward introspection and objectivation enhances the analytic work and often carries the adolescent into a period of experimentation, ranging over the whole gamut of human activities. Whatever they might be, they usually lead back to a renewed search for narcissistic perfection in an effort to transcend a pervasive sense of worthlessness, incompleteness, and helplessness.

Sexual relationships of the type described above usually end disastrously; again, the blame for this failure is put on the analyst who brought it about by refusing to extend his omnipotence; now, when everything is lost, he is expected to make amends and undo the loss in a magic way. Through shifting mother and father transferences, the incomplete oedipus complex moves, gradually, forward onto its normal triadic constellation. Its negative component evokes, on the level of sexual maturity, the conflicts of bisexuality and draws the narcissistic "striving for perfection" more and more into the analytic work. Fantasies, wishes, and desires of a homosexual kind become apparent in the analytic material; this fact serves as an indicator that the patient moves toward a resolution of the libidinal attachment to the parent of the same sex. The sex-inappropriate self representation, inherent in this struggle, is an omnipresent occurrence in the analysis of late adolescents and renders the analytic work, for some time, particularly difficult.

The use of clinical material for the demonstration of the aforementioned propositions is encumbered by two conditions. The first encumbrance relates to the fact that ego-ideal pathology as described in the adult can also be observed in late adolescence as a transient phenomenon of seeming likeness. The process of adolescent ego-ideal formation is accompanied by disturbed and disturbing mental states of varied severity. Concomitant regressive, narcissistic, self- and object-idealizing features are apt, at moments, to weaken reality testing to a point where the perception of the self, the body self, and the outer world acquire a quasi-delusional quality. When an arrest on this stage stubbornly precludes progressive development, then many an adolescent seeks psychiatric or analytic treatment. To entertain fantasies about fame, greatness, perfect love is a most common and normal feature of adolescence. It is only the pervasiveness and sameness of these fantasies and their affinity to primitive narcissistic states that render them pathological. To arrive at a differentiation between these narcissistic aspects, normal or pathological, is often no easy task for the clinician.

The second encumbrance to the clinical validation of my propositions lies in the fact that integrative and synthesizing processes remain elusive and proceed in silence. The consequences of new formations—whatever they might be—surface only belatedly in observable manifestations, well after the critical point of their structuralization has passed. This is a common enough observation during analysis. Whatever triggers a new thrust of integrative processes is the consequence of antecedent analytic work and surfaces in quite disparate regions of the mind, often not at all in accordance with the analyst's expectations. This is particularly true for adolescent analysis, which, at one point or other, always leads back to the anxiety of separateness, loss, and death, followed by narcissistic restitution. The ego ideal, anchored in narcissistic self-containment, becomes, so to speak, the triumphant counterforce to the finity of life. In its adaptive aspect, it counteracts regression, shapes adult commitments, and gives them continuity and constancy.

The extent to which the demands or expectations of society, in conjunction with adolescent psychic reorganization, are growth-promoting seems contingent on the concurrent formation of the mature ego ideal. Of course, commitments undergo change in time, but, in order to change, they must first have existed. The critical time of life in which they attain mature form and content is late adolescence. But if the adolescent fails in this task and becomes an analytic patient, then one discovers that there always is a more or less extensive ego-ideal pathology present. Assessing a patient's abnormality in functioning from the side of the ego ideal alone restricts the psychological view by the exclusion of other considerations. To single out the ego ideal for intensive study of this kind is particularly suggestive in relation to late adolescence, because we deal here not only with a normative structure formation, but with one that also represents a critical factor within the structure of a given neurosis. Tracing the development of one psychic agency in relative exclusiveness is not an uncommon methodological approach in psychoanalytic research. The ancients have dignified this approach with the phrase: *ex pede Herculem.*

TRACING THE VICISSITUDES OF THE FEMALE EGO IDEAL
THROUGH THE ANALYSIS OF A LATE ADOLESCENT GIRL

The patient was a girl of 18 who had to abandon a successful college career when she suddenly became the victim of severe anxiety attacks. An affectionate, crushlike, but unfulfilling and unanswered devotion to a female peer precipitated the sudden breakdown.

Early in the analysis it became evident that, for this girl, the ideal self and the ego ideal were still undifferentiated; even more primitive was the pervasive conviction that everything needed for the maintenance of a stable self had an outside source, indeed an idealized source in a withholding object. Through ingratiating and supplicating play-acting, helped along by considerable physical and mental giftedness, she experienced herself as sharing the powers and excellences which others possessed. Object attachment was always founded on the oral modality of greed and incorporation. To be in perfect harmony with herself, she had to incorporate the object and thereby destroy it. Guilt and panic drove her to undo the loss and rescue the source of her narcissistic sustenance by offering herself, again through play-acting, to the needs, real or imagined, of the idealized object. The infantile state of feeling perfect only when unconditionally loved, remained unaltered, far beyond the symbiotic stage; in fact, this stage could regressively be evoked by any disappointment and played out, first in action and then in fantasy, for long periods of her analysis. The bearer of the excellences she admired was loved; associated fantasies of sucking on a breast or a penis revealed the primitive nature of such attachments. Excellences that could arouse her "voracious appetite" might lie in the realm of sexual, physical, academic, ideological, artistic, and intellectual perfection. Material possessions played a rather subordinate role.

This patient's object hunger aimed at oral appropriation or vicarious enjoyment, through merger, of the envied riches which others unquestionably possessed. Her pervasive sense of incompleteness was seemingly dominated by penis envy. In a primitive cognitive style, she attributed to all things that mattered to her, positively or negatively, a male or a female designation. The attainment of perfection was, accordingly, reserved for the boy; once, when she expressed an intelligent thought in public, she experienced a quasi-delusional conviction of possessing a penis. If we speak of an ego ideal in this connection, it would indeed be an infantile one, because the delusional concreteness of the idealized body image reflects a distortion of the self representation that is alien to the mature ego ideal.

The analysis of penis envy was responded to by a consolidation of a vocational direction and of intellectual proficiency, indeed, excellence. Yet, the modality of penis envy lingered on in the exhibitionistic need for intellectual superiority and the sadistic urge to annihilate, i.e., castrate, her male peers. Aggressive self idealization blocked the way to the emergence of a deinstinctualization of the ego ideal. The familiar *dramatis personae* of this emotional configuration were present as usual: the withholding mother, who preferred the younger brother; the seduction trauma inflicted, at a tender age, by a beloved, feared, and aggrandized father; the regressive search for the good and lost nurturing mother; the restitutive resolution through becoming a boy, albeit a tomboy. These matters are too well known to require amplification.

What attracted my attention was the fact that penis envy was, partially, a secondary and defensive formation. In other words, phallic intrusiveness and physical completeness not only were an aim in themselves, but represented, above and beyond, an effort to resist regression to primitive merger with the mother or, later in life, with any object she desired. In this sense, the stage of development as described, aimed clearly, in my patient, not only at a maintenance of her separateness (individuation), but also at a protection of her femininity and at a constant, even if failing, struggle of disengagement from the archaic mother imago. With the receding dominance of penis envy, object idealization shifted to women, with an emphasis on oral gratification and depressive or rage reactions to disillusionment or frustration. Then a sense of hopelessness descended on her; and ego-ideal fragments, which had slowly taken shape within the self as distinct from the object, were swept away in an abysmal sense of worthlessness. Then the withholding object could be saved from destruction only by blaming the self as unworthy to be given to; the sense of guilt moved from dyadic object destruction and its rescue to triadic jealousy, competition and, ambivalence.

A decisive forward step in object relations and, consequently, in identificatory stability was facilitated, when the transference neurosis could deal with the splitting of the object into good and bad, present and absent, giving and withholding. The whole-object representation began to emerge as reliable and constant, without requiring idealization for its survival. The reflection of this more mature object representation became apparent in a more tolerant attitude toward the self. The need to obliterate her self-interests, in order to keep others liking or loving her, gradually gave way to an assertion of her true self, of her unadulterated preferences, opinions, likes, and dislikes. True, such ego-ideal fragments retained, for a long time, a close affinity to object relations, but the threshold of their surrender reached a level which gave the maintenance of self-esteem a larger margin of autonomy. At this stage, fantasy became relegated to the world of play; the reservoir of her rich imagination opened up, invigorating her giftedness and intelligence; in turn, both became more productive as well as gratifying. The same could be said about her relationships and her love life. To conclude: the derivatives of the rock-bottom yearning for the merger with the idealized primary object, the mother, could be traced, through their transformations, and recognized in the autonomous striving for perfection, within a constant, self-determined, even if shared, endeavor toward self-realization. At this stage, the flow of narcissistic libido, derived from the exercise of the ego ideal, became the automatized regulator of self-esteem. Now, she could dispense with the use of idealization, of either self or object, and thus protect her hard-won sense of reality.

TRACING THE VICISSITUDES OF THE MALE EGO IDEAL THROUGH THE ANALYSIS OF A LATE ADOLESCENT BOY

The patient was an 18-year-old college student. Unable to study he was faced with dismissal from college. He was intelligent, seemingly purposeful, personable, well built, and in good health. He had a definite life goal clearly in mind; yet the actions taken in its pursuit were tentative, self-defeating, and erratic.

It became evident early in the analysis that the patient's self representation was extremely labile, i.e., shifting from grandiosity to self-deprecation. His efforts to make himself likable to men of importance, including the analyst, were easily reversed whenever a critical point in his subservience was reached and took the form of negativism, subversion, and procrastination. Emotional withdrawal was noticeable whenever he tried to extricate himself from his passive surrender to idealized objects; then he sought refuge in narcissistic self idealization. The grandiose self of childhood became regressively revived and temporarily served as the regulator of self-esteem. During such episodes, his sense of time as well as his judgment of others and self were disturbed. Words—on the use of which analysis relies—become, under these circumstances, masks, shields, and weapons.

It is most common during adolescence, when sexual identity formation moves into its definitive stage, that the polarity implicit in bisexuality contaminates the cognitive and perceptual spheres. What we observe is the tendency, often obsessive in nature, to assign to any opposites the connotation of male or female. These bisexual conflicts of the patient presented themselves for analysis via their derivatives in the intellectual and behavioral fields. Successful academic study carried, unconsciously, a masculine designation, while going through the motions of studying represented the feminine counterpart. Fright and irritation drew the patient into all kinds of diversions. The fixation on the negative oedipus complex forced the patient repeatedly into failures and, consequently, into a panic of castration wish and fear. His desire to be loved by the

father perpetuated preoedipal yearnings and disappointments in
the mother; these had laid down the lasting foundation for the fear
of women and the belief in their malevolent intent. Early sexual
explorations of his little sister, especially of her incomprehensible
genital (a study that was interrupted by the latency period) left the
little boy with a confused, vague, somewhat dizzying image of the
"vagina." His earliest explanation of the fact that the girl had no
penis was: "She ate it." It had become invisible. The patient
expected from his research to acquire the power of controlling the
castrated, ominous female, or, more accurately, to gain her imputed
power and thus become the master of his impulses, desires,
gratifications, and fears. Here was to be found the link to his partial
identification with the female. When this early research with its
maladaptive resolution was renewed in late adolescence, it took
precedence over any other intellectual or academic curiosity. The
incompleteness of the oedipus complex became apparent, as did the
adolescent reinstinctualization of those internal directives by which
we identify the superego and the ego ideal.

The oscillations from masculine to feminine positions as well as
the shiftlessness from self to object idealizations continued their
stubborn repetitiveness under many disguises. In fact, their circular-
ity gave the impression that they were feeding on each other. The
assault on narcissistic self idealization by reality disappointments
evoked, in turn, the need for object idealization; through this shift,
narcissistic gratification was restored by sharing the object's perfection and being loved by it. To illustrate: when the patient missed
some analytic sessions he entertained the fantasy that his absence
would give his analyst the time to work on a book; thus, the analyst
would more speedily become a famous man and, in turn, a richer
source of narcissistic gratification for the patient, who had been,
after all, a silent promoter of the achievement.

When the patient eventually overcame his sexual inhibitions, he
reformulated, with a sense of conviction, his vocational goal.
However, this progress again came to an impasse through the
rather persistent instinctualization of the ego ideal. The analytic
work revealed a paradoxical finding. As already mentioned, the
preoedipal object tie to the mother was wrought with disappointment, aggression, and fear; these affects, in their full infantile force,

sought alleviation by turning preoedipal object libido onto the father and identifying with the submissive, degraded mother. The father not only had become the recipient of the oedipal idealization, but, in addition, he remained the object of the preoedipal idealizations of the omnipotent mother. Whatever was bad and evil was split off from the idealized object representation and assigned to the female, especially her genital. The ego ideal, at this stage, reflected, in comparable fashion, divided avenues toward perfect self-realization, namely, those of masculine and feminine strivings.

The analysis of the transference neurosis led to the reconstruction and reexperience of infantile ambivalence, which, on the adolescent level, was repeated in homosexual and heterosexual fantasies. Among these, a dream was particularly important because it laid bare the patient's wish for and revulsion of his father's acceptance of him as a girl. It was not until the fixation on the negative oedipus complex was analyzed that the patient's conscious guiding principles, his ambitions and goals, acquired a constancy that remained unaffected by emotional or circumstantial exigencies. The need for instantaneous self idealization in the face of tension was replaced by a rather evenly sustained striving toward a goal that would be, at no point in time, attained; yet, at each point in time, appropinquated. The desexualization of the infantile ego ideal at late adolescence made this shift in ego-ideal functioning possible. In the train of this change, one could observe the emergence of a characterological consolidation which tended, in effect, to integrate and automatize the influence of the mature ego ideal on personality functioning. The attainment of sexual identity appears in this process a prerequisite for the formation of the mature ego ideal.

It is of interest to note that only after the resolution of the negative oedipus complex was accomplished, did the condition arise for the patient to find his way back to the emotional entanglements with the mother of early childhood. To the astonishment of the analyst and, later, to the patient, these had played a most insignificant role in the treatment up to this time. Finally, they appeared in full force, via replications and their attempted corrections, in a love relationship. This attachment was the first one that was not sexually exploitative of the female, but was affectionate and caring, despite the imperfections of the partner. These were realized with chagrin, but they did not render the woman degraded or unlovable. The mature ego ideal afforded the young man constancy of self realization and, in the attendant exercise of the striving for perfection, he had found the reasonable independence from the idealized object and the idealized self. The clear distinction between reality and fantasy had gently closed the door on the world of childhood.

COMMENTS ON THE HISTORY OF THE EGO-IDEAL CONCEPT

I shall not attempt to give a comprehensive historical account of the ego-ideal concept. This has been done by several authors (Sandler et al., 1963; Hammerman, 1965; Hunt, 1967; Bressler, 1969; Steingart, 1969).

There is no doubt that the literature on the superego is voluminous, in contrast to ego-ideal investigations. Yet, cursory references to the ego ideal are ubiquitous, even though the specific meaning of the term can often be inferred only from the context in which it appears. The imprecision of the term plagues us to this day. The distinction between superego and ego ideal has been discussed again and again, and so has the place of the ego ideal in the mental organization. Is the ego ideal a substructure of the ego or the superego? Or is it a separate agency of the mind? Does it acquire an affiliation with both in the course of development and, specifically, during adolescent psychic restructuring? Does its original function change with the maturation of the ego and the adolescent reorganization of the superego? In which way, if at all, is the ego ideal influenced, even determined, by the vicissitudes of object relations? Is shame, rather than guilt, the characteristic response to ego-ideal failures? Furthermore, from which source does the ego ideal draw the energy for its maintenance? Should this source lie in the need to preserve the life line to primary narcissism? Then the question arises how ego-ideal content is altered with the progressive development of the ego. What are the connections of the ego ideal, if any, that become established, over time, with the three structures of the mind? And, finally, what accounts for the faulty development that leads to ego-ideal pathology?

Many of the questions have been dealt with in the literature, often only marginally and suggestively, while some have been singled out for detailed discussion. In this attempt to scrutinize anew the problem of the ego ideal I have chosen to view it from the vantage point of the developmental, but normative, crisis of adolescence. In doing so, I take advantage of the disintegration and reorganization of psychic structure during this period. In the literature of the ego-ideal concept, there are many references which have had a suggestive influence on my own observations and conclusions. Therefore, I shall now return to the historical, even if selective, account of the subject under discussion.

It is a well-known fact that Freud's (1914) original use of the term "ego ideal" blended in its definition with that of the superego, as we define it today. Both terms were, for some time, used synonymously until Freud replaced the term "ego ideal" by the term "superego" in 1923. The original ambiguity of the concept in Freud's writings seemed to have been due to the irreconcilable sources and functions of this single psychic agency. The heterogeneity of origin is to be found in primary narcissism and identificatory processes. In the essay "On Narcissism" (1914) Freud defined the term ego ideal in a way which tries to reconcile its narcissistic origin with the vicissitudes of object libido. The distinction between superego and ego ideal rests progressively on their mode of operation, namely, on the prohibiting and punitive nature of the superego and the nature of wish fulfillment that pertains to the ego ideal (Lampl-de Groot, 1962). This distinction was clearly achieved in *The Ego and the Id* (1923). Following this clarification, the term ego ideal, as a technical term, disappears almost completely from Freud's writings (Strachey, 1961).

I return to Freud's intermediary use of the term ego ideal in which narcissism and object libido are fused (1914), because this amalgamation corresponds to my own observations in adolescent analysis. Of course, Freud did not have the adolescent process in mind, but reflected on his clinical observations in adults and, I venture to say, male patients, when he brought the two concepts together which later became distinct and separate aspects of the same system, the superego. In the adult patient we often encounter great difficulties in tracing the respective influence of one or the other to the period of origin. This is, of course, not surprising because the deviate emotional development that underlies any psychological abnormality implies *ipso facto* that the adolescent process has been left incomplete in one way or another. The importance which I attribute to adolescent psychic restructuring in the final formation of the ego ideal would point to fixations that, strictly speaking, precede those of the superego.

The narcissistic nature of the concept "ego ideal" was implicit in Freud's definition from the very beginning when he used the term; it was but a small step to tie it together with the narcissistic mode of object choice: "what possesses the excellence which the ego lacks for making it an ideal, is loved" (Freud, 1914, p. 101). This primitive mode of object choice reappears in adolescence and generally enmeshes ideal formation with object-libidinal aims. Viewing ego-ideal formation along developmental sequences, I have observed this enmeshment with regularity in adolescent analysis; it renewed my interest in Freud's early clinical findings, regardless of the incomplete state which his theory building had attained at the time. The pertinent lines I have in mind read as follows: "In this way large amounts of libido of an essentially homosexual kind are drawn into the formation of the narcissistic ego ideal and find outlet and satisfaction in maintaining it" (p. 96). It becomes evident from the succeeding paragraph that Freud drew his observation from the paranoid patient who revolts against the "censoring agency" in the effort to "liberate himself from all these influences" and securing his independence by his "withdrawal of homosexual libido" from the parental domination. This is precisely what one frequently observes in male adolescent analysis; I dare assume that this process is a transient and normal state of adolescent development or, more precisely, of the adolescent resolution of the negative oedipus complex.

It should be mentioned at this point that Freud conceived of the ego-ideal content as "imposed from without" (1914, p. 100). In so doing, he went beyond the individualistic meaning of the term and related the ego ideal to a social function, namely, to a dynamic role in group psychology (1921). Due to the fact that group formation "binds homosexual libido," this aspect of social behavior acquires an important function in libido economy: it elevates self-esteem by shared values and aspirations and thus lowers the sense of guilt and social anxiety. A convincing *demonstratio ad oculos* of this phenomenon and the dynamics outlined above can be witnessed in the spontaneous and intense peer group formation of adolescents. These are more prominent among boys than girls; the need for this kind of group formation fades away with the advance to adulthood or, as my analytic observations have convinced me, with the formation of the adult ego ideal. Disapproval by the peer group or its value system possesses a most powerful influence on the individual member and induces him to sacrifice, usually transiently, well-established ego and superego norms.

The distinction between superego and ego ideal became less of a theoretical issue for Freud after he had traced the origin of the superego back to the earliest object cathexes and their transformation into identifications, i.e., introjections (1923). Their conflictual involvement in the triadic constellation of the oedipus complex is resolved by superego structuralization with ego-ideal components closely built into it. As a consequence of this inclusive conceptualization, the ego-ideal concept had become dispensable to Freud's theory building. He did not refer to it again until 1933 when we find a return to the 1914 formulation (Strachey, 1961), for an "important function" attributed to the superego is to act as "the vehicle [*Träger*] of the ego ideal by which the ego measures itself, which it emulates, and whose demand for ever greater perfection it strives to fulfil" (Freud, 1933, p. 64f.). In an editorial footnote, Strachey points out that at this stage of theory building Freud included the upholding of ideals as part of the moral enforcements that constitute the superego.

It is of interest to note that the ego ideal as conceptualized in 1914 represented "the substitute for the lost narcissism of his childhood in which he was his own ideal" (p. 94). In contrast, in 1933 Freud emphasizes that the "ego ideal is the precipitate of the old picture of the parents, the expression of admiration for the perfection which the child then attributed to them" (p. 65). The later formulation presupposes a more advanced ego development than the first one, which refers to the primitive state of primary narcissism. Both views have a bearing on the ego ideal as developmentally conceived.

There are good reasons to assume that the postoedipal consolidation of the superego exerts an influence on the ego ideal as well. Hartmann and Loewenstein (1962) have put this issue succinctly by saying: "To us it seems reasonable to view the specific character of the ego ideal which is part of the superego in close relation to those other developments which originate in the oedipal conflicts and to distinguish the resulting 'ego ideal' from earlier idealizations. We meet here again an issue which is ubiquitous in psychoanalysis . . . the distinction of genetic continuity and functional characterization" (p. 59f.). It is, essentially, this kind of approach that prompted me to view adult ego-ideal formation in the context of adolescence, in which the second and final step in the resolution of the oedipus complex is taken.

Returning to the historical theme, it can be observed that 1923 marked the time when the ego ideal had found its secure place, as the narcissistic component of the superego, within the tripartite structure of the mind. The disappearance of the term from Freud's writings with only a cursory reference to it in 1933, and no mention of it at all in the *Outline* (1940), set a trend that is quite noticeable in the psychoanalytic literature. The distinction between the concepts of the ego ideal and the ideal ego, of the ideal self and of self and object idealizations, often became blurred in their usage, but the term "ego ideal" continued to connote a specialized function of the superego. The relative hiatus in ego-ideal research lasted until the 1950s. Approximately during that decade we notice the upsurge of a renewed interest in the concept of the ego ideal, its place in mental organization, its origin and development, and its specific role in psychopathology. Dating from around this time, an ever-increasing number of papers dealing with the ego-ideal concept in normal and abnormal development attested to the need for an intensive reassessment of the psychic agency called ego ideal. The widening interest can be attributed, at least partially, to the shift, over time, from symptom neuroses to conditions of ego pathology and a prominence of disturbances that are rooted in the narcissistic sector of the personality. No doubt, infant studies, child analytic research, and longitudinal studies in child development aided the clarification of the ego ideal. At any rate, from the extensive research accrued a more useful conceptual tool for diagnostic, therapeutic (technical), and prognostic thinking. The continuity of the concept, from its inception to this day, is reflected in the universal agreement that the ego ideal's roots lie in the stage of primary narcissism.

The clinical papers by Annie Reich (1953, 1954, 1960) stand in the forefront of the renewed interest in the ego ideal; she lucidly described ego-ideal pathology within the context of narcissistic disturbances. Her clinical studies led her to the conclusion that the ego-ideal concept is indispensable for the delineation and understanding of the cases she reported. Her major contributions to the ego-ideal concept have been referred to in the preceding section on pathology and need not be repeated here.

Instead of reviewing the individual contributions to the ego-ideal concept, I shall discuss the literature along five lines of thought. These can briefly be stated as follows: (1) the location of the ego ideal within the psychic structures; (2) the developmental point of view as applied to the ego ideal; (3) the reinstinctualization of the ego ideal at adolescence; (4) the differences and similarities between the infantile and the mature ego ideal; (5) the sociocultural determinants of ego-ideal content.

The question of location within the psychic structures has been tossed about for some time without ever having reached a clear consensus of opinion. Is the ego ideal a substructure of the ego or of the superego? This question of "location" was poignantly brought to our attention by Piers (1953) who discerned discrete affects, elicited by either superego or ego-ideal failures. He refers to the affect of guilt as characteristic for the tension between superego and ego and that of shame as typically derived from violations of the ego ideal. Intrinsic distinctions between the two agencies are further elaborated by Lampl-de Groot (1962) who states that the superego sets boundaries ("prohibiting agency") while the ego ideal sets goals ("agency of wish fulfillment"). Piers draws a distinction between the two agencies by describing their characteristic nature but leaves aside the question of location. One gains the impression that he views the two agencies as separate structures. Bing et al. (1959) have argued that the "ego ideal is 'anatomically' a part of the ego." Viewing the superego and ego ideal along genetic, functional, and structural lines, a separation of the two seems a logical conclusion. Lampl-de Groot (1962), on the basis of genetic and adaptive considerations, concludes that the ego ideal is "an established substructure (or province) within the ego" and can be looked at as "an ego function," but, even in its most highly developed form, it "remains essentially an agency of wish fulfillment" (p. 98). Jacobson (1964), expressing her basic agreement with these opinions, states that it would be "more correct to consider the ego ideal an ego formation rather than a part of the superego system" (p. 186). Even though this quote conveys a definite opinion, it should be mentioned that in her further discussion of the subject Jacobson acknowledges the fact that, with progressive ego development, the ego ideal "gradually bridges the two systems and may ultimately be claimed by both" (p. 187). The aforementioned opinions stand, more or less clearly, in opposition to the formulation advanced by Hartmann and Loewenstein (1962) who consider the ego ideal an aspect of the superego system. This controversy of long standing brings me to the second question.

The fact that so many authors have argued the issue of "location" without ever reaching a consensus is very likely an indication of the intrinsic ambiguity of the term. The concept of the ego ideal has suffered all along from conceptual imprecision, inasmuch as on the one hand it was used to suggest a psychic agency, namely, a component of psychic structure, and, on the other, was defined by content, as apparent in expressions like "this and that are his ego ideals." The intrinsic ambiguity seems to stem from the fact that the ego ideal's affinity to, or separateness from, the systems ego and superego is a mere reflection of various stages in ego-ideal development, namely, along an ongoing process of structure formation. For this very reason, Steingart (1969) has argued that the ego ideal be viewed in terms of "psychic apparatus development" and within the conceptual framework of self and object representations. He thus carries forward the ideas of Hartmann and Loewenstein (1962) who took a developmental approach to the concept of the ego ideal; they pointed out that the preoedipal ego ideal reflects drive-gratifying wishes of aggrandizement, in contrast to the phallic-oedipal period, when idealization encompasses increasingly new issues. Esman (1971) follows the same path of viewing the ego ideal in its changing function, relative to developmental tasks, such as, for example, the support it lends to the sublimatory efforts characteristic of the latency period.

The developmental approach to the ego-ideal concept would imply, then, that the ego ideal takes over functions that for some time had been closely joined to the superego, or the ego ideal receives accretions of content derived from the ego in terms of inculcated or self-chosen values and goals; choices such as these can, of course, be made only on the basis of experience, judgment, or generally on the basis of relative ego maturity. The ego ideal, then, becomes an aspect or a reflection of the individual's identity. In other words, the ego ideal ceases, progressively, to be the agency of wish fulfillment through either fantasy or identification. In the course of development, not only ego-ideal content, but also its functions undergo changes. One crucial stage in the evolution of the ego ideal can best be studied in adolescence when, normally, a reinstinctualization of the ego ideal as well as of the superego occurs. Before we investigate this aspect of the ego ideal, it seems imperative that we consider first the broader question of developmental progression and the theoretical consequences of such an approach.

The distinction between a primitive and a mature ego ideal is widely accepted. The relation between adolescence and ideal formation has generally been recognized since the times of Aristotle, but the genetic antecedents of this adolescent characteristic had still to be explored in their complexity. We distinguish heterogeneous and discrete aspects in the adolescent-specific proclivity to idealization. These trends range from self idealization and its externalization to the integrated and subjectively self-evident nature of thought and action. The automatization of the mature ego ideal weaves its function into the context and function of character. Of course, the decisive role of the ego ideal in the maintenance of the narcissistic balance, experienced as self-esteem, has too often been stressed to need any elaboration at this point.

It has been said that "the ego ideal can be considered a rescue operation for narcissism" (Hartmann and Loewenstein, 1962, p. 61). This statement, undoubtedly, expresses an opinion of general agreement, but leaves a broader question open, namely, the one of changing content and the specific means—even if the aim remains the same—by which the "rescue operation" is kept in a never-ending state of alertness. The above quote might be paraphrased by saying that the gain of narcissistic supplies is as essential to personality functioning as object-directed libidinal and aggressive gratifications. When the latter give rise to the well-known conflicts at adolescence, "object-libidinal strivings are regressively replaced by identifications of the . . . early infantile kind" (A. Reich, 1954, p. 215). It is often only in puberty, as Annie Reich remarks, that the fixation on the infantile ego ideal becomes revealed. Heightened castration anxiety leads to the regressive cathexis of compensatory narcissism, or, I would add, to a retreat from the adolescent resuscitation of the oedipus complex. Under these conditions, neither a mature ego ideal can be formed nor mature object relations can be attained.

The fact that the ego ideal acquires structuralization during adolescence renders it qualitatively different from its antecedent developmental stages. This has been clearly stated by Jacobson (1964, p. 187): "In fact, the final stages [adolescence] in the development of the ego ideal demonstrate beautifully the hierarchical reorganization and final integration of different—earlier and later—value concepts, arising from both systems [ego and superego], into a new coherent structure and functional unit," namely, the ego ideal. Adolescent psychic restructuring in relation to ego-ideal formation has been affirmed by other authors as well. Murray (1964) searches out the pathways that lead to the mature ego ideal; he attributes to the early narcissistic state of the ego ideal the attitude of "entitlement" (pregenital) and postulates a sublimation of narcissism and of the affects attached to libidinal objects that are part of the ego-ideal organization. It is of interest to note Murray's clinical observation which he summarizes by saying "that the narcissistic libido, centered in the ego ideal, returns to the ego to recathect unconscious latent homosexual elements when the ideal is lost or dimmed" (p. 487). While Murray extends Freud's formulation of 1914, he also emphasizes, if I follow him correctly, the object-libidinal affects which predestine the ego ideal to become enmeshed in the adolescent conflict of having to forego pregenital entitlements "in favor of the more ideal-oriented relationships with mature libidinal fulfillments, individual and social aims and relations" (p. 500). Murray considers the ego ideal a psychic agency with close ties to the systems ego and superego. The distinctness of the mature ego ideal is defined and preserved by its intersystemic ties, similar to that of a planet whose orderly motion is regulated by the gravitational interaction with other celestial bodies.

A case report which lays bare the determinants—talent and gift being one of them—as well as the dynamics of the ego ideal in the life of a creative scientist was presented by Giovacchini (1965). The analysis of this patient revealed the child's narcissistic dependency on the overpowering preoedipal mother and the young boy's effort to extricate himself from this stifling, yet exhilarating relationship through the re-creation of an idealized father image, embodied in "the canons of science." However, the repressed, object-libidinal components operating within the patient's extraordinary scientific achievements, which represented his ego ideal, not only disrupted his creativity by periods of depression, but, in addition, rendered his object relations to men and women ambivalent and ungratifying. My propositions regarding the formation of the male ego ideal find a convincing clinical demonstration in Giovacchini's case, even though his formulations are not identical with those I have proposed.

A cumulative consensus can be noted in the literature, asserting that a change in content and quality of the ego ideal and of the superego occurs during adolescence, reviving, in its wake, the infantile states of the ego ideal and of the superego as well (Hammerman, 1965). Ritvo (1971) comes to a similar conclusion by saying: "The ego ideal as a structuralized institution of the mind is a development of adolescence" (p. 255). Kohut (1971), in a more general comment, follows a complementary line of thought: "an important firming and buttressing of the psychic apparatus, especially in the area of the establishment of reliable ideals, takes place during latency and puberty, with a *decisive final step in late adolescence*" (p. 43; my italics). Comparing the primitive and the mature forms of ego ideal and superego, Novey (1955) concludes that the mature ego ideal is acquired later than the oedipal superego. This opinion is widely confirmed; it implies a certain inflexibility of the superego, which is only relatively weakened during the adolescent period by the ascendancy of the ego ideal, as well as by the expansion of the ego. These matters pertain rather to the topic of personality consolidation and character formation in late adolescence (Blos, 1962, 1968); even though they are more than marginal to the subject, I shall not here pursue them further, but stay within the narrow limits I have set myself for this exposition.

The condition *sine qua non* for a successful resolution of the adolescent crisis is "predicated," according to Aarons (1970), "upon the preservation of the ego ideal, inculcated but not yet integrated during childhood" (p. 309). Furthermore, he states that the ego ideal is intrinsically correlated with the attainment of object constancy, which I would place between 18 months and 3 years. This opinion dates the formation of the infantile ego ideal later than is usually accepted. I conceive of the condition for mature ego-ideal formation in the attainment of postambivalent object relations, rather than in terms of object constancy as stated by Aarons (1970): "Adolescence is a test of object constancy and of the integration of the ego ideal. The two are interrelated" (p. 327). His view that the advance from adolescence to adulthood is intrinsically predicated upon ego-ideal development, from primitive to mature, as well as his opinion that the ego ideal at adolescence becomes enmeshed with regressively revived libidinal-aggressive infantile object relations is in agreement with my own observations. Along this line of thought, Alexander's (1970) paper should be mentioned, because it touches on a characteristic of adolescence, namely, the striving toward independence; he assigns to the ego ideal a major role in sustaining this trend. "If the ego ideal contains in a strongly cathected way the ideal of independence, then the ego will expend the drive energies in such a manner as to achieve the skills and masteries which make independence possible, that is, through learning" (p. 55). Of course, what is implied here is the content of the ego ideal rather than the ego ideal as a structural element or psychic agency. Mature emotional independence, so it seems to me, is the by-product of the successful advancement toward genitality or, in other words, not until infantile object dependencies have been transcended, can the mature ego ideal unfold. Both Murray (1964) and Hunt (1967) assign to libidinal fixations and conflicts a decisive influence in determining the vicissitudes of the ego ideal. Murray's statement, based on Freud's 1914 essay, reads as follows: "If the relationship between the ego ideal and its appropriate potential for fulfillment fails, the libido returns to a strong intensification of the homosexual impulses, which in turn create great guilt and great upsurges of social anxiety" (p. 502). Grete Bibring (1964) emphasizes the fact that "genetically it [the ego ideal] derives its strength mainly from positive libidinal strivings in contrast to the superego, in which aggressive forces prevail" (p. 517). This view is supported by the clinical finding that the ego ideal holds its reins in an unambivalent fashion.

Pursuing the interrelation between the ego ideal and the instinctual life, I turn to a paper by Hunt (1967). His case discussion, based on the formulations by Blos (1962) and Annie Reich (1954), among others, affirms the intrinsic relatedness between ego-ideal pathology and insufficiently attenuated homosexual trends. "The ego ideal as discussed here in regard to homosexuality, involves the persistence of a magical, omnipotent form with aspirations of creating an ideal state through forming primary identifications with objects" (p. 242). Whenever homosexuality, latent or manifest, has become the major regulator of the narcissistic equilibrium, the ego ideal remains arrested on an infantile level. The same holds true for the perpetual recidivistic criminal (Murray, 1964) and for the impostor (Deutsch, 1964), who are examples of what Murray (1964) called the "fragmented ego ideal." Ritvo (1971) confirms these findings when he speaks of the reinstinctualization of the ego ideal by predominantly homosexual libido as a normative aspect of the adolescent process.

As a last point of this historical review I shall point to the progressive refinement and sharper delineation of the ego-ideal concept as it emerges alongside the elaborations of the concept of the self. Upon closer scrutiny, we often come to recognize that what appears to constitute an ego ideal is but a self-aggrandizement, an imitation, as it were, of a wishful self-image (Jacobson, 1964). What has been described as a false ego ideal might also be referred to as a primitive, infantile, or archaic one.

In discussing the ontogenesis of the ego ideal, Freud (1914) never failed to point to the fact that the content of the ego ideal is "imposed from without" (p. 100). It includes not only a personal propensity, but also the ideal of such social formations as family, class, nation, and many more. This is to say that prevailing value systems as well as social organizations and institutions always stand ready, in every society, to channel individual narcissistic trends toward goals of a "common ideal." Whatever the ensuing irrationalities and distortions, which are due to persistent narcissistic self and object idealizations, their form and content are always derived from the social system in which the individual lives.

An exploration of some of these sociocultural factors was undertaken by Tartakoff (1966) who traces the interpenetration of ego-ideal content and social institutions in the American culture. Tartakoff concludes that "narcissism may undergo a special fate in our social structure" (p. 226) or, more pointedly, "A sociocultural setting which emphasizes the goal of success may perpetuate narcissistic and omnipotent fantasies" (p. 245). This infantile component of the ego ideal, if not relegated to playful fantasy and corrective self-irony, can permeate the analytic situation, turning it into another chance, where "hard work" will bring about an excellence that was once promised and still waits for fulfillment with that pertinacity so characteristic of infantile narcissistic "entitlements." In following ego-ideal content over time, Tartakoff concludes that narcissistic fantasies do not change, while content (values, goals, norms, institutional means) is subject to epochal shifts. To this I would add that the sociocultural imprint can also be detected in its negative form, e.g., in the adolescent who "opts out."

This brings me to extensions of the ego-ideal concept which, in my opinion, run counter to a developmental conceptualization of the term. Kaplan and Whitman (1965) proposed the concept of the "negative ego ideal." It is defined as "the introjected negative standards of the parents and of the culture" (p. 183). It is suggested that the "devalued parent" forms the core of the negative ego ideal. With this formulation we are forced to abandon the idealizing quality and the genetic history of the ego ideal as it is presently understood. The negative ego ideal is ego-alien, and so is its denigrating content. These conditions, it seems to me, reflect a persistent sadomasochistic tie to the preoedipal parent that is transposed onto the level of values. In accordance with my proposition, this fact alone disqualifies it from the realm of the mature ego ideal and relegates it to an infantile, perverted ideal self. Schafer (1967) also speaks of negative ideals, e.g., "to be a superior con man or a brute" (p. 165), but he does not identify them with the mental structure "ego ideal." The concept of the negative ego ideal can probably best be accommodated, in a similar fashion, within the concept of the self.

In viewing the developmental levels of the ego ideal, we come to recognize a correspondency between function and content of the ego ideal on the one hand, and the age-specific level of ego development and of physical maturation, on the other. The study of the transitions along this path of ego-ideal formation, its deviancy and arrest, has attracted ever widening attention. The concept of the ideal self, in contradistinction to the ego ideal, has been elaborated by Sandler et al. (1963); they point to the difficulties, theoretical and clinical, which are attached to the differentiation between the two, in the indexing of child analytic material at the Hampstead Clinic. This finding only emphasizes the affinity or identity of ideal self and ego ideal, as antecedent to their gradual differentiation that advances within the context of developmental progression.

In the field of applied psychoanalysis, the ego-ideal concept has been used in relation to literary figures for an explication of their characteristic features. Among them are Rostand's *Cyrano de Bergerac,* and Oscar Wilde's *Dorian Gray* (Murray, 1964). But the one personality, studied in depth and portrayed in terms of the ego-ideal consolidation of late adolescence, is Prince Hal. This Shakespearean character displays the enigmatic contradictions of youth—debauchery and high idealism—in flamboyant fashion. All along his bewildering actions, Prince Hal never loses touch with his inner struggle. The consolidation of the ego ideal lies at the center of this struggle, in which he first fails, but finally succeeds by reconciling the idealized father imago he loves with the imperfect, if not downright evil, father person he hates. Had his father, the king, not murdered his own cousin, Richard II, whom Hal had followed to Ireland as a boy, whom he had idealized, and whose favor he had won?

The son-father conflict of Prince Hal has attracted the attention of several psychoanalysts. Ernst Kris (1948) interpreted Prince Hal's conduct within the oedipus complex and the ambivalence conflict that vacillates between obedience, flight, and parricide. The defensive and adaptive role of ideal formation, in the effort to transcend the infantile conflict, is clearly stated. The Lichtenbergs (1969) shifted the focus to that "aspect of adolescent development by which a particular adolescent achieves the formation of his ideals" (p. 874). Again, Prince Hal was made the subject of a study by Aarons (1970) who viewed the son-father conflict in relation to the vicissitudes of the ego ideal. The two components central to this theme are those of object love (the negative oedipus complex) and object idealization, as I had described them earlier in their intrinsic connection to adolescent ego-ideal formation (Blos, 1962, 1965). Prince Hal, indeed, represents a dramatic character of extraordinary plausibility, when viewed by Aarons within the ego-ideal concept. The author illuminates Prince Hal's flight from royal dignity at the court to the carousal at the tavern by pointing out, that through the peer relationship the "tie of dependence is broken" and a "recathexis of the ego ideal for which the father stood" is made possible. Aarons calls this the "renewal" of the ego ideal and defines it "as the rescue and reaffirmation of the ego ideal—a sublimation of the love for the father" (p. 332f.). In surveying the psychoanalytic studies of Prince Hal, from 1948 to 1970, we notice a gradual shift of focus from oedipal strivings to that of idealization and disillusionment, namely, to the problem of adolescent ego-ideal formation. Falstaff, a split-off father imago, with the peer world, his drinking companions, reconstitute a proxy family which—by a grand detour—assists the troubled youth in the formation of the mature ego ideal and the assumption of his princely identity. These tumultuous events illustrate the renewed object enmeshment or the reinstinctualization of the idealized object, from which the mature ego ideal emerges.

I have omitted in this historical commentary any reference to my own work, because the present exposition as a whole rests upon my previous research and, obviously, contains whatever I have found relevant to the presentation at hand.

Epilogue

In using the word "genealogy" in the title of this essay, I had a double reference in mind. One that traces the ancestral sources from which the mature ego ideal emerges during late adolescence, and the other that traces through the psychoanalytic literature the antecedents of the concept as it stands today. These two explorations, ontogenetic and historical, leave no doubt as to the complexity of both the psychic structure formation and the concept as such. In fact, their complexity defies summary or condensation. However, I can state what I endeavored to accomplish, namely, to present a developmental view of the ego ideal as it can be reconstructed in its primitive form and as it can be observed *in statu nascendi* in its mature structuralization during the psychic reorganization of adolescence. Clinical observations of contemporary late adolescents give ample evidence of the fact that ego-ideal pathology represents, in the majority of cases, a considerable sector of any disturbance at this age. Erroneously, derivatives of ego-ideal pathology are, in many instances, subsumed under ego and superego deviations. If the concept "ego ideal" can be defined with sufficient specificity to be useful as a theoretical indicator and instrument, then a refinement and deepening of adolescent analysis and psychotherapy might well follow; to delineate the concept toward this end has been the purpose of this investigation.

The study of the ego ideal has impressed upon me ideas of a speculative nature; somehow, no writer on the ego-ideal concept can escape this invitation. The ego ideal spans an orbit that extends from primary narcissism to the "categorical imperative," from the most primitive form of psychic life to the highest level of man's achievements. Whatever these achievements might be, they emerge from the paradox of never attaining the sought-after fulfillment or satiation, on the one hand, and of their never ceasing pursuit, on the other. This search extends into the limitless future that blends into eternity. Thus, the fright of the finity of time, of death itself, is rendered nonexistent, as it once had been in the state of primary narcissism.

In its mature form, the ego ideal weakens the punitive power of the superego by taking over some of its function; equally, ego aspects become engaged in its service. The realm of the ego ideal, borrowing Nietzsche's words, lies beyond good and evil. Piers (1953) speaks of the ego ideal as a "magic belief in one's invulnerability or immortality to make for physical courage and to help counteract realistic fears of injury and death" (p. 26). Potentially, the ego ideal transcends castration anxiety, thus propelling man toward the incredible feats of creativity, heroism, sacrifice, and selflessness. One dies for one's ego ideal rather than let it die. "Here I stand, I cannot do otherwise" were Luther's words at the Diet of Worms, when he was urged, under great peril to himself, to recant his belief. The ego ideal is the most uncompromising influence on the conduct of the mature individual: its position always remains unequivocal.

BIBLIOGRAPHY

AARONS, Z. A. (1970), Normality and Abnormality in Adolescence. *This Annual,* 25:309–339.

ALEXANDER, J. (1970), On Dependence and Independence. *Bull. Philadelphia Assn. Psychoanal.,* 20:49–57.

BIBRING, G. L. (1964), Some Considerations Regarding the Ego Ideal in the Psychoanalytic Process. *J. Amer. Psychoanal. Assn.,* 12:517–521.

BING, J. F., McLAUGHLIN, F., & MARBURG, R. (1959), The Metapsychology of Narcissism. *This Annual,* 14:9–28.

BLOS, P. (1962), *On Adolescence.* New York: Free Press of Glencoe.

———— (1965), The Initial Stage of Male Adolescence. *This Annual,* 20:145–164.

———— (1967), The Second Individuation Process of Adolescence. *This Annual,* 22:162–186.

———— (1968), Character Formation in Adolescence. *This Annual,* 23:245–263.

———— (1972a), The Function of the Ego Ideal in Adolescence. *This Annual,* 27:93–97.

———— (1972b), The Epigenesis of the Adult Neurosis. *This Annual,* 27:106–135.

BRESSLER, B. (1969), The Ego Ideal. *Israel Ann. Psychiat.,* 7:158–174.

DEUTSCH, H. (1964), Some Clinical Considerations of the Ego Ideal. *J. Amer. Psychoanal. Assn.,* 12:512–516.

———— (1967), *Selected Problems of Adolescence.* New York: International Universities Press.

ESMAN, A. H. (1971), Consolidation of the Ego Ideal in Contemporary Adolescence. *Psychosoc. Proc.*, 2:47–54.

FREUD, A. (1958), Adolescence. *This Annual*, 13:255–278.

FREUD, S. (1914), On Narcissism. *Standard Edition*, 14:73–102. London: Hogarth Press, 1957.

———— (1916–17), Introductory Lectures on Psycho-Analysis. *Standard Edition*, 15 & 16. London: Hogarth Press, 1963.

———— (1921), Group Psychology and the Analysis of the Ego. *Standard Edition*, 18:69–143. London: Hogarth Press, 1955.

———— (1923), The Ego and the Id. *Standard Edition*, 19:12–66. London: Hogarth Press, 1961.

———— (1933), New Introductory Lectures on Psycho-Analysis. *Standard Edition*, 22:5–182. London: Hogarth Press, 1964.

———— (1940), An Outline of Psycho-Analysis. *Standard Edition*, 23:144–207. London: Hogarth Press, 1964.

GIOVACCHINI, P. L. (1965), Some Aspects of the Development of the Ego Ideal of a Creative Scientist. *Psychoanal. Quart.*, 34:79–101.

HAMMERMAN, S. (1965), Conceptions of Superego Development. *J. Amer. Psychoanal. Assn.*, 13:320–355.

HARTMANN, H. & LOEWENSTEIN, R. M. (1962), Notes on the Superego. *This Annual*, 17:42–81.

HUNT, R. (1967), The Ego Ideal and Male Homosexuality. *Bull. Philadelphia Assn. Psychoanal.*, 17:217–244.

JACOBSON, E. (1954), The Self and the Object World. *This Annual*, 9:75–127.

———— (1964), *The Self and the Object World.* New York: International Universities Press.

KAPLAN, S. M. & WHITMAN, R. M. (1965), The Negative Ego-Ideal. *Int. J. Psycho-Anal.*, 46:183–187.

KOHUT, H. (1966), Forms and Transformations of Narcissism. *J. Amer. Psychoanal. Assn.*, 14:243–272.

———— (1971), *The Analysis of the Self.* New York: International Universities Press.

KRIS, E. (1948), Prince Hal's Conflict. *Psychoanalytic Explorations in Art.* New York: International Universities Press, 1952, pp. 273–288.

LAMPL-DE Groot, J. (1962), Ego Ideal and Superego. *This Annual*, 17:94–106.

LICHTENBERG, J. D. & LICHTENBERG, C. (1969), Prince Hal's Conflict. *J. Amer. Psychoanal. Assn.*, 17:873–887.

MURRAY, J. M. (1964), Narcissism and the Ego Ideal. *J. Amer. Psychoanal. Assn.*, 12:477–511.

NOVEY, S. (1955), The Role of the Superego and Ego-Ideal in Character Formation. *Int. J. Psycho-Anal.*, 36:254–259.

NUNBERG, H. (1932), *Principles of Psychoanalysis.* New York: International Universities Press, 1955.

PIERS, G. & SINGER, M. B. (1953), *Shame and Guilt.* New York: Norton, 1971.

REICH, A. (1953), Narcissistic Object Choice in Women. *Psychoanalytic Contributions.* New York: International Universities Press, 1973, pp. 179–208.

—— (1954), Early Identifications As Archaic Elements in the Superego. *Ibid.,* pp. 209–235.

—— (1960), Pathologic Forms of Self-Esteem Regulations. *Ibid.,* 288–311.

RITVO, S. (1971), Late Adolescence. *This Annual,* 26:241–263.

SANDLER, J., HOLDER, A., & MEERS, D. (1963), The Ego Ideal and the Ideal Self. *This Annual,* 18:139–158.

SCHAFER, R. (1967), Ideals, the Ego Ideal, and the Ideal Self. In: *Motives and Thought,* ed. R. R. Holt [*Psychological Issues,* 18/19:131–174]. New York: International Universities Press.

STEINGART, I. (1969), On Self, Character, and the Development of a Psychic Apparatus. *This Annual,* 24:271–303.

STRACHEY, J. (1961), Editor's Introduction to S. Freud: The Ego and the Id (1923). *Standard Edition,* 19:3–11. London: Hogarth Press.

TARTAKOFF, H. H. (1966), The Normal Personality in Our Culture and the Nobel Prize Complex. In: *Psychoanalysis—A General Psychology,* ed. R. M. Loewenstein, L. M. Newman, M. Schur, & A. J. Solnit. New York: International Universities Press, pp. 222–252.

TURGENEV, I. (1862), *Fathers and Sons.* New York: Farrar, Straus & Giroux.

Symbiosis and Individuation

The Psychological Birth
of the Human Infant

MARGARET S. MAHLER,
M.D., SC.D (MED.) h.c.

I WOULD LIKE TO START ON A SOMEWHAT PERSONAL NOTE, TO IN-
dicate how, amidst my reconstructive studies in the psychoanalytic
situation, this observational, normative work, one of whose yields is
the present paper, came about.

During my own formative years when I was still a trainee at the
Psychoanalytic Institute in Vienna, my experiences as head of a
well-baby clinic in the late 1920s brought the (albeit preconscious)
impression again and again to my mind that the human infant's
biological, actual birth experience did not coincide with his "psychological birth." The sensorium of the newborn and very young infant did
not seem to be "tuned in" to the outside world; he appeared to be in
a twilight state of existence.

Then, in the 1930s, when I had a number of neurotic child and
adult psychoanalytic patients, there happened to be among them
two latency-age patients whom I found myself unable to treat with

This paper was read as the Fifteenth Sophia Mirviss Memorial Lecture to the
San Francisco Psychoanalytic Institute and Mount Zion Hospital and Medical
Center on November 5th, 1973. It draws on material that is also presented in a
forthcoming book (Mahler, Pine, and Bergmann, 1974).

Dr. Mahler is Director of Research at the Masters Children's Center, Clinical
Professor of Psychiatry, Albert Einstein College of Medicine; Senior Consultant,
Child and Adolescent Services, Roosevelt Hospital.

the traditional psychoanalytic method. One of them, a highly intelligent 8-year-old boy, was referred by the parents and the school because he did not seem to comprehend the necessary requirements of the reality situation in the classroom, nor was he able to listen to and act upon the reality requirements of family life.

He needed his mother's almost continual attendance. She had to—and sometimes did—guess his primary process thoughts and wishes; otherwise, the patient—with or without an initial temper tantrum—retreated into a bizarre dreamworld of his own. The contents of this dreamworld were discernible in those instances in which he acted out his delusional fantasies; for example, he donned his father's derby hat and walking stick, fully believing that appropriating these paraphernalia of his father actually made him the father, and in addition made him the absolute ruler of the universe.

The analyst was permitted, I soon discovered, to play one of two roles only: either I had to act as an inanimate extension of the patient's ego, a quasi-tool of the delusionary aggrandized self of the patient, or else I had to be completely passive—quasi-deanimated, another (albeit somewhat more significant) piece of furniture in the room.

The animate and individuated existence of the human objects—father, brother, analyst, classmates, and even mother—was blotted out as far as possible. If these deanimation and dedifferentiation mechanisms (Mahler, 1960) did not work, every so often the patient fell into a panic-stricken rage attack, and then slumped into the twilight state of the psychotic.

In spite of the immense difference between these two groups of human beings—the very young infant and the psychotic child—one basic similarity between the two groups made a great impression on me: neither seemed to have been *psychologically* born, that is to say, "tuned in" to the world of reality. What the youngest babies have *not yet* achieved, the psychotics have *failed to* achieve—psychological birth: that is to say, becoming a separate, individual entity, acquiring an, albeit primitive, first level of self identity.

This common feature of a perceptual twilight state of the two groups of human beings slowly percolated in my mind, with the result that I asked myself two questions: (1) How do the vast majority of infants manage to achieve the obligatory second: the psychic birth experience? How do they emerge from what is obviously a twilight state of symbiotic oneness with the mother—an innate given—that gradually allows them to become intrapsychically separated from her, and to perceive the world on their own? (2) What are the genetic and structural concomitants that prevent the psychotic individual from achieving this second birth experience, this hatching from the symbiotic "common boundary with the mothering one?"

After another decade of experience with psychotic children I embarked in the late 1950s on a systematic study of "The Natural History of Symbiotic Child Psychosis," [1] which used a tripartite design.

We attempted to establish what Augusta Alpert would have called a "corrective symbiotic relationship" between mother and child, with the therapist acting as a bridge between them. We became more and more convinced that the "basic fault" in the psychotic was his inability to perceive the self and the mother as separate entities, and thus to use the mother as a "beacon of orientation in the world of reality," as his "external ego." This is in contrast to normal children or to children whose disturbances belong to other categories of pathology.

Soon after initiating the psychosis project (and almost parallel with it), we started a pilot study, in which we endeavored to find out how *differentiation* and *self-boundary formation* do develop in most human beings! (Practically no specific data were available about this at that time.) This pilot study was a bifocal observational study of randomly selected mother-infant pairs, who were compared with each other and compared with themselves over time. The pilot study of the average mother-infant pairs was undertaken with the hypothesis that "there exists a normal and universal intrapsychic separation-individuation process in the average child, which is preceded by a normal symbiotic phase."

It is my conviction that, in the *normal individual,* the sociobiological utilization of the mother, of the "outer half of the self" (Spitz,

[1] This study was conducted at the Masters Children's Center with Dr. M. Furer. It was funded by Grant No. 3363 of the NIMH, 1959–1963, Bethesda, Maryland.

1965), and later on, the emotional availability of the love object—the postsymbiotic partner—are the necessary conditions for an *intrapsychic* separation-individuation process. This is, in fact, synonymous with the *second,* the psychological birth experience: a rather slow and very gradual *hatching out process,* as it were.

As the result of my clinical work in the psychoanalytic situation, and my observational studies of the first years of life, I am now able to state with a fair degree of accuracy what many of my colleagues have found in their mainly reconstructive work: namely, that milder than outrightly psychotic clinical pictures are derived from disturbances in the orderly progression of the subphases of the separation-individuation process. Hence, I shall briefly review that orderly developmental process.

I

The biological unpreparedness of the human infant to maintain his life separately is the source of that species-specific, prolonged, absolute dependence on the mother (Parens and Saul, 1971), which has been designated by Benedek (1949) and myself as "the mother-infant symbiosis." I believe that it is from this symbiotic state of the mother-infant dual unity that those experiential precursors of individual beginnings are derived which, together with inborn constitutional factors, determine every human individual's unique somatic and psychological makeup.

The symbiotic patterning, such as the molding or stiffening of the body when it is held, as well as the specific and characteristic nursing situations and countless other variables within the symbiotic dyad, give us some clues as to what is going on in the infant; but translation of the observable phenomena of early pre-ego states—in our terms, the autistic and early symbiotic periods—into psychological terms is exceedingly difficult. Extrapolations drawn from preverbal behavioral data are even more precarious than the use of hypotheses deduced from observational data of later periods of life. To understand *preverbal* phenomena, as Augusta Bonnard (1958) succinctly stated, "We are . . . compelled to seek out their connotations, either through their pathological or normal continuance in somewhat older individuals than an infant, or else through their regressive manifestations" (p. 583).

As I have described in many of my publications, we have learned a great deal about the symbiotic nature of human existence by intensively studying the preverbal phenomena of symbiosis in their pathological and regressive manifestations.

In our normative study, however, we have tried not only to validate our hypothesis of the *symbiotic origin of human existence,* but to follow development into that period of early life that I named the separation-individuation phase. We studied randomly selected infant-mother pairs, and observed their interaction *beyond* the normal symbiotic phase.

As soon as signs of differentiation appear, the data are considerably easier to read—and constructions appear to be more reliable. This is because the infant's behavior has been polarized and rendered more meaningful through the presence and availability or lack of availability of the mother. The mother's presence and her interaction with the child furnish a circular yet bipolar frame of reference: baby and mother, transacting with each other in a more readable way.

This has enabled us to study the psychological birth of the human infant, the main dynamics of which are: the major shifts of libidinal and aggressive cathexis in the bodily self; and the changing nature and level of the approach and distancing behaviors between infant and mother during the course of the developmental process, from biological birth till the open-ended phase of libidinal object constancy.

In the weeks preceding the evolution to symbiosis, the newborn's and very young infant's sleeplike states far outweigh the states of arousal. They are reminiscent of that primal state of libido distribution that prevailed in intrauterine life, which resembles the model of a closed monadic system, self-sufficient in its hallucinatory wish fulfillment.

Ribble (1943) has pointed out that it is by way of mothering that the young infant is gradually brought out of an inborn tendency toward vegetative-splanchnic regression and into increased sensory awareness of and contact with the environment. In terms of energy or libidinal cathexis, this means that a progressive displacement of drive energy has to take place from the inside of the body (particularly from the abdominal organs) toward its periphery. *The shift from predominantly proprioenteroceptive toward sensory perceptive cathexis of the periphery*—the rind of the body ego (as Freud called it)—*is a major step in development.*

The well-known peripheral pain insensitivity as well as the panic-creating hypersensitivity to enteroceptive ("gut") sensations, which are equated with bad introjects in psychosis, bear witness to the fact that this important and massive cathectic shift has failed to occur.

I believe that this major cathectic shift marks the progression from the normal autistic to the normal symbiotic phase.

The main task of the autistic phase is that with predominantly physiological mechanisms, the homeostatic equilibrium of the organism be maintained, under the changed postpartum conditions.

Through the inborn and autonomous perceptive faculty of the primitive ego (Hartmann, 1939), deposits of memory traces of the two primordial qualities of stimuli of "good"—that is, pleasurable—and "bad"—that is, painful—occur. We may further hypothesize that these are cathected with primordial undifferentiated drive energy.

John Benjamin (1961) found that an interesting physiological maturational crisis occurs at around 3 to 4 weeks. This is borne out in electroencephalographic studies, and by the observation that there is a marked increase in overall sensitivity to external stimuli. "Without intervention of a mother figure for help in tension reduction," Benjamin says, "the infant tends to become overwhelmed by stimuli, with increased crying and other motor manifestations of undifferentiated negative affect" (p. 27).

I believe that this crisis—from our developmental point of view—marks the cracking of the "autistic" shell, the beginning dissolution of the negative, that is to say, uncathected, stimulus barrier. It marks the beginning of its replacement—through the aforementioned cathectic shift—by a positively cathected *protective* and *selective* stimulus barrier which creates a common "shield," as it were, a quasi-semipermeable membrane enveloping both parts of the mother-infant dyad.

The symbiotic phase is marked by the infant's increased attention to and perceptual-affective investment in stimuli that *we* (the adult observers) recognize as coming from the world outside, but which (we postulate) the infant does not recognize as having a clearly outside origin. Here begins the establishment of "memory islands" (Mahler and Gosliner, 1955), but not as yet a differentiation between inner and outer, self and other. The principal psychological achievement of the symbiotic phase is that the specific bond between infant and mother is created, as is indicated by the specific smiling response (Spitz and Wolf, 1946).

The period of 5 to 7 months is the peak of manual, tactile, and near-visual exploration of the mother's mouth, nose, face as well as the "feel" of the mother's skin. With these behaviors, the infant seems to begin to distinguish between contact-perceptual experiences and those originating in his own body and to single out experiences of the hitherto completely coenaesthetic global sensory experiences of mother's and his own bodies. Furthermore, these are the weeks during which the infant discovers with fascination inanimate objects worn by the mother—a brooch, eyeglasses, or a pendant. He begins looking around within the symbiotic dual unity by straining away from the mother's body as if to have a better look at her, and also to look beyond the symbiotic orbit—for example, in the pursuit of toys. There may be engagement in peek-a-boo games, in which the infant still plays a passive role (Kleeman, 1967). These explorative patterns later develop into the cognitive function of checking the unfamiliar against the already familiar.

It is during the first, the differentiation subphase (4–5 to 10 months of age), that all normal infants achieve their initial tentative steps of breaking away, in a bodily sense, from their hitherto completely passive lap babyhood—the stage of dual unity with the mother. One can observe individually different inclinations and patterns as well as the general characteristics of the *stage of differentiation itself.* All infants like to venture and stay just a bit of a distance away from the enveloping arms of the mother; and, as soon as they are motorically able to, they like to slide down from the mother's lap. But they tend to remain or crawl back, as near as possible, to play at the mother's feet.

The baby now begins "comparative scanning," "checking back to mother." He becomes interested in and seems to compare "mother" with "other," the familiar with the unfamiliar, feature by feature, it would seem. He appears to familiarize himself more thoroughly, as it were, with what *is* mother; what feels, tastes, smells, looks like, and has the "clang" of mother. *Pari passu,* as he learns the "mother *qua* mother," he also finds out what belongs and what does not belong to mother's body (such as a brooch, the eyeglasses). He starts to discriminate between mother and whatever it is—he or she or *it*—that looks, feels, moves differently from or similarly to mother.

In children for whom the symbiotic phase has been optimal and "confident expectation" has prevailed, curiosity and wonderment—discernible through the "checking back" pattern—are the predominant elements of the inspection of strangers. By contrast, among children whose basic trust has been less than optimal, an abrupt change to acute stranger anxiety may make its appearance; or there may be a prolonged period of mild stranger reaction, which transiently interferes with pleasurable inspective behavior. This phenomenon and the factors underlying its variations constitute, we believe, an important aspect of and a clue to our evaluation of the libidinal object, of socialization, and of the first step toward emotional object constancy. This inverse relation between basic confidence and stranger anxiety deserves to be emphasized and further verified (Mahler and McDevitt, 1968).

In cases in which the mother showed ambivalence or parasitism, intrusiveness, or "smothering," differentiation in the child was disturbed to various degrees and in different forms. The seeking of distance from the symbiotic partner appeared in some of our babies surprisingly early—at the *peak* of the symbiotic phase. During the differentiation subphase, this distance-seeking seemed to be accompanied by greater awareness of mother as a special person (full establishment of the libidinal object [Spitz, 1965]), even though in very rare cases this awareness may already have been suffused at that stage with negative aggressive affect. This we were able to deduce from primitive, but sometimes quite unmistakable avoidance behaviors.

The differentiation subphase overlaps with the practicing period, which is the second subphase of the separation-individuation process. In the course of processing our data, we found it useful to think of the practicing period in two parts: the *early* practicing phase—overlapping differentiation, and ushered in by the infant's earliest ability to move away from the mother, by crawling, paddling, climbing, and righting himself—yet still holding on; and the practicing period proper, phenomenologically characterized by free, upright locomotion. At least three interrelated, yet discriminable developments contribute to and, in circular fashion, interact with the child's first steps into awareness of separateness and into individuation. They are: the rapid *body differentiation* from the mother; the establishment of a *specific bond with her;* and the *growth and functioning of the autonomous ego apparatuses in close proximity to the mother.*

It seems that the new autonomous achievements, plus the new pattern of relationship to mother, together pave the way for the infant to spill over his interest in the mother onto inanimate objects, at first those provided by her, such as a blanket, a diaper, a toy that she offers, or the bottle with which she parts from him at night. The infant explores these objects near-visually with his eyes, and "tests" their taste, texture, and smell with his contact-perceptual organs, particularly the mouth and hands (Hoffer, 1949). One or the other of these objects may become a transitional object (Winnicott, 1953). Moreover, whatever the sequence in which the infant's functions develop during the differentiation subphase, the characteristic of this early stage of practicing is that, while there is interest and absorption in these activities, interest in the mother definitely seems to take precedence.

Through the maturation of his locomotor apparatus, the child begins to venture farther away from the mother's feet. He is often so absorbed in his own activities that for long periods of time he appears to be oblivious to the mother's presence—yet he returns periodically to the mother, seeming to need her physical proximity.

The optimal distance in the *early practicing subphase* would seem to be one that allows the moving, exploring quadruped infant freedom and opportunity to exercise his autonomous functions at some physical distance from mother. At the same time, however, mother continues to be needed as the "home base," for what Furer named "emotional refueling."

It is worth noting, however, that despite the children's apparent obliviousness to their mothers during the early practicing period, most of them seemed to go through a brief period of increased separation anxiety. The fact that they were able to move away independently, yet remain connected with their mother—not physically, but by way of their seeing and hearing her—made the successful use of these distance modalities extraordinarily important. The children did not like to lose sight of mother; they might stare sadly at her empty chair, or at the door through which she had left.

We had not expected and were surprised by the finding that the advent of the capacity of free upright locomotion seems to take place in a direction not *toward* but *away from* mother, or even in the absence of mother. This is, we feel, an indicator that the normal infant is endowed with an innate given that prompts him at a certain point of his autonomous maturation to separate from mother—to further his own individuation. Walking makes possible for the toddler an enormous increase in reality discovery and the testing of his world through his own control, as a quasi-magic master. It coincides with the upsurge of goal-directed active aggressiveness.

The mother's renunciation of possession of the body of the infant boy or girl, at this point of the toddler's development, is a *sine qua non* requirement for normal separation-individuation. Most mothers recognize—empathically or even verbally—that this quasi-altruistic surrender of the infant's body to himself is a deplorable but necessary step in promoting the infant's autonomous growth. This, I feel, is also the first prerequisite for the development of the child's self-esteem. The practicing toddler's self love and love of the object world, both his narcissism and his potential object love, are at their acme.

The child is exhilarated by his own capacities—he wants to share and show. He is continually delighted with the discoveries he makes in the expanding world; he acts as though he were enamored of the world and with his own grandeur and omnipotence.

The obligatory exhilaration of the practicing period seems to hinge upon the ascendancy of the infant's upright free locomotor capacity. In those children in whom locomotion is delayed, this obligatory exhilaration is also delayed, seems to be of shorter duration, and is much less in evidence. Besides being the function by which the child can physically distance himself from mother or approach her at will, locomotor capacity provides him with a variety of other experiences. His body is more exposed, but his plane of vision and the relation of his upright body in space enable him to see the world from a different—and relatively grown-up—angle. We know from Piaget that sensorimotor intelligence at this point is supplemented by a beginning representational intelligence; thus, symbolic thinking and upright free locomotion herald attainment of the first level of self identity, of being a separate individual entity.

Even though some children were further advanced in their perceptual, cognitive, and other autonomous functions of the ego; more advanced in their reality-testing function—that is to say, in their autonomous individuation—locomotion was the behavioral sign which indicated most visibly to the observer the end of the "hatching process," that is to say, *psychological birth*.

II

Success in goal-directed activity seemed in inverse relation to the manifestations of hostile aggression, which was also involved in this, the second great shift of cathexis in the growing-up process.

Not only is the child in love with himself (narcissism); substitute familiar adults in the familiar setup of our nursery were easily accepted and even engaged. This was in contrast to what occurred during the next subphase, the subphase of rapprochement.

During the entire practicing subphase, the child has evoked the delighted and automatic admiration of the adult world, specifically of his average "ordinary devoted mother" (Winnicott, 1960). Her admiration, when it is forthcoming, augments the practicing toddler's sound narcissism, his love of himself. Every new achievement, every new feat of the fledgling elicits admiration, at first unsolicited, later more or less exhibitionistically provoked by him from the entire adult object world around him. This kind of admiration, which does not even need to be expressed in words or gestures, may be one of the feeding lines that on the one hand promotes progression of the ego's autonomous functioning, and on the other furnishes a great accretion to the practicing toddler's feeling of grandeur—often exalted self-esteem.

In a circular fashion, the mirroring admiration also seems to augment the budding ego's readiness for mirroring the love object. Along with the rapid growth of cognition, it gradually leads to internalization processes of the *now fully born* (structured) *ego*. Eventually, these result in true ego identifications, in Jacobson's sense (1954).

Now, however, the price of this precious progress in development of autonomy has to be paid! As the 16–18-month-old's cognitive development progresses, he becomes more and more aware of his loss of the "ideal sense of self"—of well-being—when he notices his mother's absence from the room. At such times, we observed what we came to call *low-keyedness*: the toddler's gestural and performance motility slowed down, his interest in his surroundings diminished, and he appeared to be preoccupied with an inwardly concentrated attention. It was as if he wished to "image" another state of self—the state that he had felt at the time when the symbiotically experienced partner had been "one" with him.

As the toddler's awareness of separateness grows—an awareness stimulated by his maturationally acquired ability physically to move away from his mother and by his *cognitive growth*—he seems to experience an increased need and wish for his mother to *share* with him his every new acquisition of skill and experience. These are the reasons for which I called this subphase of separation-individuation the period of *rapprochement*.

At the very height of mastery, toward the end of the practicing period, it begins to dawn on the junior toddler that the world is *not* his oyster; that he must cope with it more or less "on his own," very often as a relatively helpless, small, and *separate* individual, unable to command relief or assistance merely by feeling the need for them or even by giving voice to that need. The quality and measure of the *wooing* behavior of the toddler toward his mother during this subphase provide important clues to the assessment of the normality of the individuation process.

The junior toddler gradually realizes that his love objects are separate individuals with their own individual interests. He must gradually and painfully give up his delusion of his own grandeur and participation in the still delusionally believed-in omnipotence of mother and father. Dramatic fights may ensue with mother, and temper tantrums might be the order of the day. (Many years ago, I recognized the significance of temper tantrums as a behavioral indication by which outward directed aggression is turned back onto the "self." Therefore, this mechanism may be looked upon as a precursor of internalization of aggression, and also as a precursor of superego formation.)

Be that as it may, as far as our observational research indicated, this phase of development is a *crossroads* that my co-workers and I termed the *rapprochement crisis*.

From around 18 months on, we observed that our toddlers were quite eager to exercise their rapidly growing autonomy. Increasingly, they chose not to be reminded of the times when they could not manage on their own. On the other hand, the desire to be separate, grand, and omnipotent often conflicted with the desire to have mother magically fulfill all one's wishes—without the need to recognize that help was *actually coming from the outside*. Thus, in a majority of cases, the prevalent mood swung to that of general dissatisfaction and insatiability, and there developed a proneness to rapid swings of mood and to temper tantrums. The period of rapprochement was thus characterized by a sometimes rapid alternation of the desire to reject mother, on the one hand, and to cling to her with coercive, determined tenacity in words and acts on the other hand, a behavioral sequence that the word *ambitendency* describes most accurately. But often at that age there already was a *simultaneous* desire in both directions—i.e., the characteristic *ambivalence* of the 18–22-month-olds.

In the rapprochement period which follows the earlier described psychological birth, the source of the child's greatest pleasure shifts from independent locomotion and exploration of the expanding inanimate world to *social interaction*. Peek-a-boo games as well as games of imitation become favorite pastimes. Recognition of mother as a separate person in the large world goes parallel with awareness of other children's separate existence, their being different from the own self. This was evidenced by the fact that children now showed a greater desire to *have* or to *do* what another child had or did—that is, a desire for mirroring, imitating, and coveting what the other child had. For example, the desire to acquire a "second belly button" (a penis) was sometimes quite openly expressed by girls. Along with this important development, there appeared the "no" along with definitely goal-directed anger, aggressiveness, if the desired aim could not be obtained. We are not, of course, losing sight of the fact that these developments take place in the midst of the anal phase, with its characteristics of anal acquisitiveness, jealousy, envy, and negativism, but also with a much earlier detection than we had previously believed of the anatomical sexual difference.

Depending upon her own adjustment, the mother may react either by continued emotional availability and playful participation in the toddler's world, or by a gamut of less desirable attitudes. If the mother is "quietly available" with a ready supply of object libido, if she shares the toddling adventurer's exploits, playfully reciprocates and thus helps his attempts at imitation, externalization, and internalization—then the relationship between mother and toddler is able to progress to the point at which verbal communication takes over, even though vivid gestural behavior (that is, affectomotility) still predominates. By the end of the second or the beginning of the third year, the predictable emotional participation of the mother seems to facilitate the rich unfolding that is taking place in the toddler's thought processes, reality testing, and coping behavior. In most favorable cases, the toddler is, at this point, on the way to emotional object constancy in our and (I believe) in Hoffer's sense.

III

I should like to conclude my paper with some general statements, which may go beyond the topic that the title of my paper implied.

It is a generally accepted hypothesis among psychoanalysts that unless the child successfully traverses the symbiotic phase, and that first subphase of separation-individuation termed *differentiation,* psychosis will ensue (Mahler and Furer, 1968).

Milder than psychotic disturbances, I believe, occur in children who, though they have passed through a separation-individuation process, have shown ominous deviations from the orderly progression of the subphases. If there is too much overlapping, or other serious disturbances in the differentiation and practicing subphases, and if the rapprochement crises were extreme and did not give way to any degree of object constancy, which is the open-ended fourth subphase of the separation-individuation process, fixation points are created. What may thus ensue is: narcissistic character formation and/or borderline pathology (with splitting mechanisms of the self and of the object world).

More and more, psychoanalysts have become aware of the fact that the pathologies of many of their adult (and, of course, also child) patients derive from the earliest years of life. Either deliberately or without full knowledge of their significance, analysts have been trying to reconstruct not only the preoedipal but also the preverbal genetic roots of their patients' greater or lesser failure to separate intrapsychically.

In my Freud Anniversary Lecture, I gave a vignette of one of my adult patient's borderline features of his analytic material, as I was able to reconstruct it from his dreams and fantasies, from his symbolic or symptomatic behavior, and especially from his body feelings, which he was able to put into words. It had become quite clear that his pathology derived from partial failures of the separation-individuation process (Mahler, 1971).

Many more case histories and vignettes are contained in the works of psychoanalysts who have been the authors of recent books and articles. The most widely read and most influential in this direction are the works of Kernberg (1967, 1970) and Kohut (1971). It has become quite fashionable to compare, juxtapose, or polarize *The Analysis of the Self* with Kernberg's equally important work on the borderline patient, and it is also fashionable now to hint, as a sort of side issue, at certain observational and experimental data of Spitz, Mahler and her co-workers, as well as those of Judith Kestenberg, John Benjamin, T. Gouin Décarie (1963), and many others. It would seem as if those developmental data had *something* to do with psychoanalytic propositions and constructs; but they are referred to as if they were *purely observational*—or *sociobiological* at best. They are not integrated, either as germinal or fundamental, with the lately quite obviously widening scope of psychoanalytic theory and practice. Only a few of my psychoanalytic colleagues have become fully aware that, for this widening scope of psychoanalytic theory, those hypotheses that have been derived from psychoanalytic observational data of the preverbal phase have made meaningful, and indeed indispensable contributions to their own reconstructive work, and offer the promise of further progress in psychoanalytic metapsychology and practice.

Even though most analysts, especially and particularly analysts of adults, may daily encounter material that has the flavor and the patterning of the preverbal, earliest primary-process–dominated phases in the lives of their patients, they shy away from attempts at correlation, let alone from integration of their reconstructive work with those developmental data that Spitz, myself and my co-workers, and others have found. These data, we have postulated, pertain to that period of life which is, especially lately, brought up in the literature as the "unrememberable" and the "unforgettable," (Frank, 1969; Anthony, 1971; Lampl-de Groot, 1973).

Freud himself clearly implied that we will remain handicapped in our efforts at reconstruction unless we learn more and more how to decipher the prehistoric phase of human development. I believe, like Ernst Kris and others, that unless we try to integrate consensually validated preverbal data with the constructs of psychoanalytic theory—which derives from reconstructive material learned in the psychoanalytic situation—we shall remain handicapped in making progress. (It should not be overlooked that even *our* developmental hypotheses are to an extent reconstructive—our constructions and reconstructions, inductive and deductive methods—are intertwined all along in both the analytic and the observational situations.)

In a recent discussion of "The Current Status of the Infantile Neurosis,"[2] I took the standpoint that psychoanalytic metapsychology and our technique would gain greatly if, side by side with the drive theory and our newer structural theory—both of which will remain the foundations of psychoanalysis—we would let ourselves be guided by the steadily growing psychoanalytic developmental theories. These theories have already put at our disposal many consensually validated data of infant observation, which have proved to be of value in reconstructing the data gained in the psychoanalytic situation with regard not only to the oedipal and the

[2] See also Ritvo and Loewald in this volume (pp. 159–188).

preoedipal stages, but also to much that is capable of validation from the preverbal stage.

We are still underestimating the pathogenicity, but also the character-building, the personality-integrative role of preverbal levels of development; and we are underestimating in particular the importance of ego and superego precursors—and especially their capacity for creating hard-to-decipher proclivities to intrapsychic conflicts!

BIBLIOGRAPHY

ANTHONY, E. J. (1971), A Study of "Screen Sensations." *This Annual*, 16:211–245.
BENEDEK, T. (1949), The Psychosomatic Implications of the Primary Unit: Mother-Child. *Amer. J. Orthopsychiat.*, 19:642–654.
BENJAMIN, J. D. (1961), The Innate and the Experiential in Child Development. In: *Lectures on Experimental Psychiatry*, ed. H. Brosin. Pittsburgh: University of Pittsburgh Press, pp. 19–42.
BONNARD, A. (1958), Pre-Body-Ego Types of (Pathological) Mental Functioning. *J. Amer. Psychoanal. Assn.*, 6:581–611.
DÉCARIE, T. GOUIN (1963), *Intelligence and Affectivity in Early Childhood*. New York: International Universities Press.
FRANK, A. (1969), The Unrememberable and the Unforgettable. *This Annual*, 24:48–77.
HARTMANN, H. (1939), *Ego Psychology and the Problem of Adaptation*. New York: International Universities Press, 1958.
HOFFER, W. (1949), Mouth, Hand and Ego-Integration. *This Annual*, 3/4:49–56.
JACOBSON, E. (1954), The Self and the Object World. *This Annual*, 9:75–127.
KERNBERG, O. F. (1967), Borderline Personality Organization. *J. Amer. Psychoanal. Assn.*, 15:641–685.
——— (1970), Factors in the Psychoanalytic Treatment of Narcissistic Personalities. *J. Amer. Psychoanal. Assn.*, 18:51–85.
KLEEMAN, J. A. (1967), The Peek-a-Boo Game. *This Annual*, 22:239–273.
KOHUT, H. (1971), *The Analysis of the Self*. New York: International Universities Press.
LAMPL-DE GROOT, J. (1973), Vicissitudes of Narcissism and Problems of Civilization. Freud Anniversary Lecture, New York.
MAHLER, M. S. (1960), Symposium on Psychotic Object Relationships. *Int. J. Psycho-Anal.*, 41:548–553.
——— (1963), Thoughts about Development and Individuation. *This Annual*, 15:307–324.
——— (1971), A Study of the Separation-Individuation Process. *This Annual*, 26:403–424.

MAHLER, M. S. & GOSLINER, B. J. (1955), On Symbiotic Child Psychosis. *This Annual*, 10:195–212.

———— & FURER, M. (1968), *On Human Symbiosis and the Vicissitudes of Individuation, Volume I*. New York: International Universities Press.

———— & McDEVITT, J. B. (1968), Observations on Adaptation and Defense *in Statu Nascendi*. *Psychoanal. Quart.*, 37:1–21.

———— PINE, F., & BERGMANN, A. (1974), *On Human Symbiosis and the Vicissitudes of Individuation, Volume II*. New York: Basic Books (in press).

PARENS, H. & SAUL, L. J. (1971), *Dependence in Man*. New York: International Universities Press.

RIBBLE, M. A. (1943), *The Rights of Infants*. New York: Columbia University Press.

SPITZ, R. A. (1965), *The First Year of Life*. New York: International Universities Press.

———— & WOLF, K. M. (1946), The Smiling Response. *Genet. Psychol. Monogr.*, 34:57–125.

WINNICOTT, D. W. (1953), Transitional Objects and Transitional Phenomena. *Int. J. Psycho-Anal.*, 34:89–97.

———— (1960), The Theory of the Parent-Infant Relationship. *Int. J. Psycho-Anal.*, 41:585–595.

Levels of Object Representation in Anaclitic and Introjective Depression

SIDNEY J. BLATT, PH.D.

THIS PAPER EXPLORES THE HYPOTHESIS THAT DEPRESSION IS, IN part, a function of impairments in the development of object representation. Based on developmental considerations, two types of depression in adults, an anaclitic and an introjective depression, can be differentiated. Anaclitic depression is characterized by feelings of helplessness, weakness, and depletion. There are intense fears of abandonment and desperate struggles to maintain direct physical contact with the need-gratifying object. Introjective depression, in contrast, is characterized by feelings of worthlessness, guilt, and a sense of having failed to live up to expectations and standards. There are intense fears of a loss of approval, recognition, and love from the object. In each of these types of depression, there are impairments in object representation and there are struggles to maintain contact with objects.

Professor of Psychology, Departments of Psychiatry and Psychology, Yale University; Member, Western New England Psychoanalytic Society. Portions of this paper were presented to research conferences in the Departments of Psychology at Yale University (November 1972) and at Hebrew University (May 1973). This paper was revised and extended during my stay as a visitor at the Hampstead Child-Therapy Clinic, London (January–July 1973). I am grateful to Drs. Alex Holder and Vann Spruiell and Mrs. Doris Wills, to my colleagues Drs. Marion Glick, Stephen Fleck, Patrick O'Neill, and Jean Schimek for their comments, suggestions, and assistance.

These hypotheses are an extension of earlier research (Blatt, 1971; Blatt and Ritzler, 1974; Blatt and Wild, 1974) in which severity of psychosis was differentiated by the degree of impairment in the representation of boundaries between self and nonself and between inside and outside. Severity of psychosis was found to be related to degree of impairment in these earliest stages of object representation. Once basic boundary differentiations have been established between self and nonself and inside and outside, then the developmental task is to establish object and self representations, which become increasingly articulated, diverse, integrated, symbolic, and constant (Jacobson, 1964; Mahler, 1968; Schafer, 1968). It is these later stages of object representation which are relevant to an understanding of depression.

In the first part of this paper I shall review the clinical, theoretical, and research literature on depression in adults and indicate how this literature offers support for the differentiation of two primary types of depression. In the second part of the paper I shall present case material which illustrates an anaclitic and an introjective depression and indicates how specific types of impairments in object representation are particularly relevant in each type of depression. In the third section of the paper I shall review the development of object representations in psychoanalysis and in developmental cognitive psychology and propose a formulation of evolving stages of object representation. Impairments in stages of object representation support the differentiation of two types of depression and clarify why real, apparent, or fantasied loss of an object is often a major precipitant of depression.

DEPRESSION

Depression is defined in this paper as an affect state which can vary in intensity from relatively mild to profound and from a subtle experience to a severely disabling clinical disorder. Depression can be a relatively appropriate response to an accurate appraisal of reality or it can be based on severe reality distortions. Given the ubiquitous nature of depression, it is surprising that it has been such a neglected area of investigation. There has been much more research on anxiety as a dysphoric affect than on depression

(Grinker et al., 1961). The dearth of research on depression may be typical of the studies of affects in general, for, as noted by Rapaport (1953), Jacobson (1953), Benjamin (1961), and Smith (1970), psychoanalysis has thus far failed to develop a consistent and adequate theory of affects. The research on depression as a clinical disorder has also been sparse (Grinker et al., 1961). It may well be that the ubiquitous nature of depression makes it difficult to investigate as a clinical disorder. A differentiation of types of depression, however, may serve to further our understanding of the complex phenomena of depression. There have been some attempts to differentiate types of depression such as psychotic-neurotic, but this distinction is often based on intensity rather than type of disturbance. Another differentiation has been the separation of reactive (exogenous) from endogenous depression, but this distinction is often determined more by the clinician's ability to find an external precipitating event than by an evaluation of personality organization.

Depression has been described as a clinical disorder and as a normal and, in fact, necessary affect state (Freud, 1914; Bibring, 1953; Zetzel, 1960). The term depression has been used to describe reactions to extreme experiences of deprivation in infancy (Spitz and Wolf, 1946; Provence and Lipton, 1962), and as a relatively high-level, developmental stage (Winnicott, 1954; Segal, 1964). It has been described as a character style (Blatt, 1966) in which there is unusual susceptibility to dysphoric feelings, a vulnerability to feelings of loss and disappointment, intense needs for contact and support, and a proclivity to assume blame and responsibility and to feel guilty. Depression has been discussed in terms of infantile feelings of abandonment and helplessness, and also in terms of superego formation and the relatively advanced and complex phenomenon of guilt. Rubenfine (1968), for example, considered depression to be primarily concerned with restoring past pleasure, and to originate in a fixation to a state of narcissistic union with the mother. He saw guilt only as a consequence of the aggression felt toward the frustrating object. In contrast, Beres (1966) states that "an essential determinant of true depression, whether as a transient manifestation or as part of depressive illness, is a sense of guilt which carries with it the assumption of a structured superego and an internalized conflict" (p. 484). Mendelson (1960) pointed to the need to develop a broad conceptualization of depression which can integrate various observations and theories and differentiate between the wide range of phenomena we call depression—the normal and necessary affect state and the various types of prolonged, recurring, and debilitating processes of clinical depression.

The issue of maintaining contact with the need-gratifying object is of paramount importance in depression (Rado, 1928; Fenichel, 1945; Cohen et al., 1954; Segal, 1964; Rochlin, 1965; Beck, 1967). The processes of internalization, described by Freud in 1917, are, in part, an attempt to preserve contact with the object and to retain its love and approval (Nacht and Racamier, 1960). Freud discussed the process of replacing object cathexis by identification, of setting up the lost object within the ego, in several papers (1917, 1921, 1923). Stressing the importance of this process to character formation, Freud stated that the "character of the ego is a precipitate of abandoned object-cathexis and that it contains the history of those object-choices" (1923, p. 29). However, object cathexis and identification can also be maintained simultaneously, and in "such cases the alteration in character has been able to survive the object-relation and in a certain sense to conserve it" (1923, p. 30). But in melancholia there is a strong fixation to the loved object and the object cathexis has little power or resistance (1917, p. 249).

Abraham (1911) initially described depression as similar to obsessive neurosis with an emphasis on anality and intensely ambivalent object ties. Later (1916, 1924) Abraham noted the frequent underlying oral fixations in many depressions, and he maintained that depressed patients often regressed to earlier and more primitive oral fixations. In comparing depression and obsessive-compulsive neurosis, Abraham emphasized that ambivalence was much greater in depression, and that the depressed patient was unable to retain a relationship with the object. Abraham (1924) considered obsessive neurosis to be at a later anal stage. The dividing line between the earlier anal stage of depression and the later stage of obsession is "where object love begins" (p. 432). It is "at this point that the tendency to preserve the object begins to predominate. On the later [anal] level the conserving tendencies of retaining and controlling the object predominates, whereas on the earlier level those hostile to their object—those of destroying and losing it—come to the fore. The obsessional neurotic . . . is able to maintain contact with his object" (p. 432).[1] Klein (1934), likewise, considered the basic fear in depression to be the loss of internal objects and the predisposition to depression as based on the failure to establish firmly "the good internal object." According to Anna Freud (1952), with maturation the libidinal cathexis to absent objects can be maintained for progressively longer times, but mourning, the "gradual process of detaching libido from an internal image . . . cannot be expected to occur before object constancy (phase 3) has been established" (1965, p. 67). Loss of the object can be experienced and fully accepted only when adequate levels of representation have been established in the internalization achieved in the resolution of the oedipal crisis and the relinquishing of infantile objects. Rochlin (1965) stresses that in depression there is a dread of abandonment and isolation, and a continual attempt to conserve the object. The level of object relations, internalization, and object representations determine in large measure vulnerability to depression.

TYPES OF DEPRESSION

Depression has been conceptualized either as a unitary phenomenon involving a decrease in self-esteem (Fenichel, 1945) or as the ego's affective reaction of helplessness to a difficult reality (Bibring, 1953). Fenichel considered the major issue in depression to be a loss

---

[1] Abraham was apparently most excited about these formulations of the development of object love proceeding from narcissism to full object love. He believed that this was a most important contribution to the understanding of neuroses. He wrote to Freud on April 1, 1923: "I myself feel it is an important addition to the theory of sexuality and, at the same time, my best work to date" (H. Abraham and E. Freud, 1965, p. 335). Abraham apparently discussed his ideas of object love with Freud during a summer visit in 1923, so there is no written record of Freud's reactions to these ideas. But in a subsequent letter (October 7, 1923), Abraham again commented on stages of object love and stated that partial incorporation as a stage of object love was also important in understanding paranoid and related psychoses (p. 340).

of self-esteem, either because of the feeling that the world was empty and barren or the belief that one did not deserve anything. According to Fenichel, the inferiority feelings in depression are frequently rooted in disappointment and humiliation, which result from failures to resolve the oedipal conflict:

> The content of the "injuries to infantile narcissism," which precipitate the primary depression, may vary. These injuries may be extraordinary experiences of abandonment and loneliness, or they may, in especially predisposed individuals, consist in the usual and unavoidable disappointments such as the birth of siblings, experiences of minor humiliations, penis envy, or the frustrations of the Oedipus longings [p. 404].

The depth of the narcissistic regression in depression, according to Fenichel, is based on the degree to which object relations are replaced by "relations within the personality" and a regression to an objectless phase (p. 402).

In an attempt to understand archaic regulation of self-esteem, Fenichel summarizes the developmental stages of guilt feelings as follows:

> In the life of the infant, the stages of hunger and satiety alternate. The hungry infant remembers having been satisfied previously and tries to force the return of this state by asserting his "omnipotence" in screaming and gesticulation. Later on, the infant loses belief in his omnipotence; he projects this omnipotence onto his parents and tries to regain it through participation in their omnipotence. He needs this participation, the feeling of being loved, in the same way that previously he needed milk. Now the succession of hunger and satiety is replaced by the succession of states in which the child feels alone and therefore experiences a kind of self-depreciation—we call it annihilation—and states in which he feels loved and his self-esteem is re-established. Still later, the ego acquires the ability to judge by anticipating the future. Then the ego creates (or rather uses) states of "minor annihilations" or small "diminutions" in self-esteem as a precaution against the possibility of a real and definite loss of narcissistic supplies. Still later, the superego develops and takes over the inner regulation of self-esteem. No longer is the feeling of being loved the sole prerequisite for well-being, but the feeling of having done the right thing is now necessary. Conscience

develops its warning functions; "bad conscience" again creates states of minor annihilations or small diminutions in self-esteem to warn against the danger of a definite loss of narcissistic supplies, this time from the superego [p. 388].

In this description, Fenichel articulates at least two ways in which self-esteem is markedly diminished: an early stage in which "annihilations" and "diminutions" are caused by the unavailability of the object and its supplies; and a later stage at which the feelings of annihilation and loss of esteem are caused by the superego judgment of having done something wrong. Thus, Fenichel seems to be describing at least two developmental levels of depression. The first is primarily oral in nature, where the emphasis is upon the direct availability of the object and of narcissistic supplies. Fenichel states that this "receptive orality" is often accompanied by a "receptive skin eroticism" and that in the last analysis the need for narcissistic supplies is the need for a union with an omnipotent mother. The second level of depression is developmentally more advanced and involves the loss of self-esteem as a function of the vicissitudes of the resolution of the oedipus conflict. The failure to experience appropriate approval and acceptance of assertive strivings results in feelings of inferiority and a loss of self-esteem from guilt.

Bibring (1953), like Fenichel, also saw depression as a unitary phenomenon. Bibring, however, viewed depression as the ego's awareness of helplessness in regard to its aspirations. These feelings of helplessness derived from several sources: (1) the oral level "of not being loved or not being independent"; (2) an anal level in which the failure to achieve mastery over one's body and to find adequate means of self-assertion results in feeling dirty, unworthy, guilty, and having no control over aggressive and libidinal impulses; and (3) a phallic level in which the competitive oedipal struggle results in feelings of helplessness about being reduced, defeated, or punished. Although similar feelings of helplessness may be experienced as an ego reaction to dependency and guilt or failure, these feelings of helplessness and depression derive from two different developmental stages in which there are differences in ego development, object relations, and the representation of the self and others. Although Bibring and Fenichel both view depression as a unitary phenomenon, their formulations suggest that a differentiation of the predominance of dependency or guilt in depression may provide a meaningful basis for more refined and precise study of the complex and perplexing phenomena of depressions.

Grinker et al. (1961), in a factor analysis of psychiatric descriptions of depressed patients, identified several independent factors in depression, two of which differentiate a depression which focuses on feelings of guilt and restitution from a depression which is primarily concerned with feelings of deprivation and attempts to manipulate the world to obtain nutrients. Anthony (1970), discussing masochism in adolescents, briefly comments on two types of depression. The first type is "mainly preoedipal" and "based on a marked symbiotic tie with the omnipotent, need-satisfying mother" and involves feelings of "shame, humiliation, inferiority, inadequacy, and weakness," narcissistic object relations, orality, and dependency. The second type is more oedipal in nature with a great deal of guilt and moral masochism associated with a punitive superego (p. 849). Schmale (1972) differentiates two types of depressive affect—helplessness and hopelessness. Helplessness is the depressive affect associated with separation and the loss of gratification, and hopelessness is "associated with the castration experience" and an awareness of "unachievable acceptance" in a "wished for relationship" or in attaining a specific goal (p. 331f.). D'Afflitti (1973) studied feelings of depression in normal female college students, and found highly consistent indications of two relatively independent factors of dysphoric feelings: (1) concern about dependency and seeking support and comfort, and (2) concern about failure to live up to expectations and the assumption of responsibility.

While types of depression are probably interrelated on a continuum, a simple or "anaclitic depression" can be differentiated from an "introjective depression." The term "anaclitic depression" is used somewhat more broadly than initially proposed by Spitz and Wolf (1946) but is consistent with Freud's use of the term to describe an infantile type of object choice in which the mother is sought to soothe and provide comfort and care. This type of depression results from early disruption of the basic relationship with the primary object and can be distinguished from an "introjective depression," which results from a harsh, punitive, unrelentingly critical superego that creates intense feelings of inferiority, worthlessness, guilt, and a wish for atonement (Freud, 1917, 1921, 1923; Cameron, 1963; Jacobson, 1966). The term "introjective depression" is used to express the relationship of this type of depression to superego formation and the predominant psychological processes at this developmental phase. Jacobson (1954), for example, discusses introjection as a mechanism which is part of the process of building up identifications. Jacobson speaks of an "introjective identification" with a bad object which the patients set up in themselves and in which the superego becomes "punitive through reanimation of a powerful, severe, aggressive" bad object (p. 251).

Anaclitic Depression

Several authors have discussed a "simple" form of depression in which the concerns are primarily focused on the basic relationship with the mother, where there is relatively little guilt, but there are dominant fears of abandonment and of being unloved. A simple, primary or endogenous form of depression has been characterized as primarily oral in nature and related to early childhood reactions to narcissistic injury, loss of love, and the fear of impoverishment and starvation (Abraham, 1911, 1924; Freud, 1917, 1926: Rado, 1928; Deutsch, 1933; Weiss, 1944; Jacobson, 1971). Engel and Reichsman (1956), for example, in a study of an infant with a gastric fistula, noted a phenomenon they called a "depression-withdrawal reaction" which "occurred when the infant was confronted alone by a stranger and was characterized by muscular inactivity, hypotonia, and sad facial expression, decreased gastric secretion, and eventually a sleep state. It vanished as soon as the baby was reunited with a familiar person" (p. 428f.). Jacobson (1971, p. 171f.) reports a large group of patients with "simple depressions," relatively free of guilt, but with intellectual and motor retardation, feelings of being dejected, detached, weary, inferior, worthless, empty, and apathetic, and having numerous physical and psychosomatic complaints.[2]

---

[2] Recent reports of biological factors in depression, particularly around the presence of manic symptoms (unipolar and bipolar depression), raise questions

The primary feelings in anaclitic depression are helplessness, weakness, depletion, and being unloved. There are intense wishes to be soothed and cared for, helped, fed, and protected. There are cries for love and of hunger, oral cravings, difficulty tolerating delay and postponement, and a desperation to find satisfaction and peace (Freud, 1917; Abraham, 1924; Rado, 1928; Lewin, 1950). There are fears and apprehensions of being abandoned, and there is a sense of helplessness in being unable to find gratification and comfort (Fenichel, 1945; Jacobson, 1953). Object relationships are primarily incorporative (Freud, 1917; Abraham, 1924; Rado, 1928; Klein, 1934; Fenichel, 1945), consuming, relatively undifferentiated, based on need gratification, and at the symbiotic and early substages of separation and individuation (Mahler, 1968). The object is valued only for its capacity to provide need gratification. A sense of well-being derives from a continual supply of love and assurance. When an object is unable to provide these supplies, feelings of being unloved and helpless are stimulated. With support and need gratification, a temporary sense of comfort is achieved, but satisfaction and gratification are experienced as emanating only from the object (Jacobson, 1971). Thus, there is an inordinate fear of abandonment and an excessive vulnerability to object loss (Rochlin, 1965)[3] and a difficulty expressing anger and rage for fear of destroying the object as a source of satisfaction. Weiss (1944) described this simple form of depression as "less awake" and less involved in the external world because of the libidinal fixation on an object which is rejected but cannot be relinquished.

---

about the complex interactions of biological, psychological, and social factors in the etiology and course of depressions. Further investigation of these and other issues requires increasingly precise clinical differentiations of types of depression.

[3] As Spitz and Wolf (1946) and Spitz (1965) indicate, anaclitic depression usually occurs with severe deprivation around 6–8 months of age when the infant begins to consolidate a differentiation between the primary need-gratifying person and others, but before the development of object constancy (A. Freud, 1952, 1965). The difference between severe infantile and narcissistic character disorders and schizophrenia is, in part, a function of the degree to which self-object differentiations are maintained. Severe infantile character disorders have intense symbiotic involvement but without a loss of the basic differentiation between self and nonself (e.g., Jacobson, 1954, 1964, 1966; Mahler, 1968).

The representations of the object express a preoccupation with frustration and gratification. There is a quality either of narcissistic blissful union or of utter depletion, which is primarily a function of the immediate and direct availability of the object. But there is relatively little internalization of the experiences of gratification or of the object providing the satisfaction. There is a constant demand for the visible and physical presence of objects, and separation and object loss are dealt with by primitive means, such as denial and a frantic search for substitutes. Abraham assumed that depression early in infancy, a basic depression with oral erotism, was a prototype for later melancholia (H. Abraham and E. Freud, 1965, p. 339).

Introjective Depression

Rado distinguishes two routes to depression: a sequence of hunger and deprivation, wakening rage, in which there is little self-object differentiation, like during satisfaction at the breast; and another characterized by themes of guilt, atonement, and forgiveness. Beres (1966) and Guntrip (1969) restrict the concept of depression to patients with severe conflicts with guilt. In the developmentally more advanced introjective depression, there are feelings of being unworthy, unlovable rather than unloved, guilty, and having failed to live up to expectations and standards (Jacobson, 1946, 1953; Jarvie, 1950; Zetzel, 1953, 1960). There are exceedingly high ideals (Jacobson, 1953), an overly harsh superego, a keen sense of morality and commitment, and a constant self-scrutiny and evaluation. There is guilt over temptations or thoughts of transgression (often related to oedipal issues) or the sense that one has failed to live up to expectations and will be disapproved of and criticized. There are extensive demands for perfection, a proclivity to assume blame and responsibility, and feelings of helplessness to achieve approval, acceptance, and recognition. Intense, overstated standards are often attributed to external figures, and there is a constant concern about disapproval and punishment. Ambivalent and hostile feelings toward the object are difficult to express because of fears of losing the object's love. There are struggles to compensate by overachieving in order to win approval and recognition, but there is usually little lasting satisfaction. The presence of an object is important, not so much to provide need gratification, but to offer approval and acceptance. Libidinal concerns are primarily at the phallic-oedipal level and related to the development of the superego, the processes of sexual identification, and the beginning phases of the oedipal conflict. The parents' conscious and unconscious attitudes and feelings about themselves and their child (Cohen et al., 1954) have important effects on the child's conscious and unconscious feelings about himself and his strivings. Zetzel's (1965) observations of major sexual identity confusion in patients with guilty depressions offer some support for the formulation that introjective depression evolves during the phallic phase. Depression develops at this stage, not from abandonment and neglect, but rather from markedly ambivalent, demanding, depreciatory, and hostile parent-child relationships. In contrast, affectionate relationships with parents enable the child to develop positive self representations and to express competitive strivings in the oedipal struggle with confidence.

The type of person described by Freud (1916) as "wrecked by success" is likely to have an introjective depression in which there is guilt over phallic strivings and symbolic oedipal triumphs. But success can also precipitate an anaclitic depression when the success involves the loss of a supportive relationship. The disturbances in both types of depression can be relatively mild or reach psychotic proportions. Hypomanic reactions can also occur in both types of depression; but in anaclitic depression this would consist of intense seeking and clinging to objects, while in introjective depression there would be frantic attempts to demonstrate strength, material accomplishments, power, physical attractiveness, intellectual capacity, or creativity as a way of seeking recognition and avoiding punishment and criticism. Compensatory and restitutive hypomanic reactions in introjective depression do not require direct and physical contact with the object, but rather involve more symbolic derivatives such as recognition, approval, and material possessions.

In introjective depression there is a higher level of ego development, and object relations are at the later stages of separation and individuation. The major defense, rather than denial, is introjection or identification with the aggressor, with a proclivity to assume responsibility and blame and to be harsh and critical toward the self. Object relations extend beyond need satisfaction, and the cathexis of and involvement with the object persist independent of frustration and gratification. There are concerns about receiving love and approval from the object, and there are also concerns about the object's response to and acceptance of one's feelings of love for the object. The relationship is highly ambivalent, and the person is unable to resolve and integrate the contradictory feelings. There are attempts to retain the object and its potential love and approval through introjection, and the struggles which originally were between the person and the ambivalently loved object come to exist primarily within the person (Freud, 1917). The representations of the object are more differentiated, but are based on repetitive, drive-laden interactions with the object and on distorted, exaggerated, and contradictory part properties and features of the object. Since these representations are usually based on the ambivalent, hostile, and aggressive aspects of the object relationship, the internalizations result in feelings of doubt, self-criticism, and guilt. The continual negative self-judgments and guilt, as well as the exaggerated and overstated representations, serve to maintain contact with the object in a vivid and hypercathected way. Object and self representations are at a somewhat higher developmental level in introjective depression, as indicated by the fact that guilt requires some sense of self, a capacity to be self-reflective, and some appreciation for sequences of causality, both in assuming responsibility for an act and in considering alternate modes of atonement and reparation. While introjective depression involves phallic-oedipal conflicts and more advanced ego development, regression can revive earlier conflicts and levels of organization.

It is only with the internalizations associated with the resolution of the oedipus complex that there is full separation from love objects, with individuation, emancipation, and the development of the capacity to seek new and enduring relationships (Loewald, 1962; Schafer, 1968). Object loss can then be experienced and accepted because adequate levels of representation have been established in the internalizations achieved in the resolution of the oedipal crisis and the relinquishing of infantile and oedipal objects.

The importance of object relations and object representation in depression has also been discussed by Klein (1934).[4] Klein, according to Segal (1964), believed that "the structure of the personality is largely determined by the more permanent of the fantasies which the ego has about itself and the objects that it contains" (1964, p. 9). While Kleinian theory emphasizes the content of fantasies, it is more likely that the structure and level of organization of the "more permanent" fantasies (or representations) play a major role in structuring personality. According to Segal, the move beyond the splitting of the paranoid position to the depressive position is determined by "a predominance of good over bad experiences." The depressive position is that phase of development in which the infant recognizes the whole object and relates himself to that object. This is a major step because the child now recognizes mother and perceives her as a whole object with diverse and even contradictory features. In the move to the depressive position, there is a growing differentiation and integration of the object, and anxiety in the depressive position stems from the ambivalent, hostile, and destructive impulses toward the object. In the depressive position, "introjective processes are intensified" as the child attempts to integrate, remember, and retain the good internal object. He is exposed for the first time to the depressive experience, that the object can be lost.

Segal (1964) comments that "symbol formation" is an outcome of the resolution of the depressive position and the "assimilation" of the good object. "Where the depressive position has not been worked through sufficiently . . . and its capacity to regain good objects internally and externally has not been firmly established . . . the ego is dogged by constant anxiety of the total loss of good internal situations, it is impoverished and weakened, its relation to reality may be tenuous and there is a perpetual dread of, and sometimes an actual threat of regression into psychosis" (p. 67f.). "It is the wish and the capacity for the restoration of the good object, internal and external, that is the basis of the ego's capacity to

[4] Klein's formulations about depression, and the developmental sequences leading to it, can be considered independent of her formulations about specific developmental timetables, the nature and role of infantile fantasies, and the centrality of the death instinct.

maintain love and relationships through conflicts and difficulties" (p. 79), and to restore and retain, in symbolic form, the lost internal objects. "Through the repetition of experience of loss and recovery . . . the good object becomes gradually better assimilated into the ego, because, in so far as the ego has restarted and recreated the object internally, it is increasingly owned by the ego and can be assimilated by it and contribute to its growth" (p. 80). Segal describes how this is achieved by "real separation" and results in "the acceptance of the idea of separateness—the differentiation of one's own self from one's parents," and "allowing one's objects to be free, to love and restore one another without depending on oneself" (p. 89).

From a number of theoretical positions there appears to be considerable support for the basic thesis of this paper that there is an evolving development of object representations and that impairments in the development of this capacity create a particular vulnerability to object loss and depression. In addition, there are different levels of impairment of object representation in anaclitic and introjective depression. Because of these impairments in object representation there are struggles in both types of depression to maintain contact with the object, either directly or in an intensification of the processes of introjection. It is only with adequate resolution of the oedipal crisis that symbolic representations of the objects are achieved; these allow for the object to be retained internally as it is relinquished externally. Sandler and Joffe (1965), Beres (1966), Rubenfine (1968), Roth and Blatt (1974) mention the possibility that in depression there may be a failure to achieve object constancy and adequate levels of object representation. Two clinical cases are presented to illustrate the differences between an anaclitic and an introjective depression and their vulnerability to object loss because of impairments in the development of object representation.

CLINICAL EXAMPLES

Helen H., a young married woman, entered analysis because of recurrent and intense feelings of depression, tension, and anxiety. She was in the process of obtaining a divorce and was frightened that she would become lonely, old, and crazy like her mother, or that she would commit suicide. Her mother had made a serious suicide attempt when Helen was in latency and her outstanding memory of this event was of being left behind, alone, frightened, and screaming as they rushed her mother to the hospital. This reminded her of her own hospitalization for a tonsillectomy at age 5 and her feelings of being "left alone" in the darkness of the anesthesia and her fear that she would die.

Helen was never able to sleep away from home as a child, and as an adolescent she was unable to take trips out of town. She married in an attempt to extricate herself from a consuming and destructive relationship with her erratic, labile, and probably psychotic mother; but after her marriage she rented an apartment within view of her mother's home. The mother called several times each day, frequently berating Helen. Although Mrs. H. was very upset by these endless calls, she could never place limits on them. She was convinced that she would be free of her mother only after the mother's death.

After Helen's birth, her mother was confined to bed because of severe back pains and was unable to care for her. The mother was unable to lift and cuddle Helen and the father assumed primary responsibility for her care and feeding. As an infant she had exzema and in her early teens, as she tried to leave home for camp, she developed psoriasis. Her parents were divorced when she was an adolescent, and she felt abandoned by her father in the divorce and earlier in his frequent absence from home during her childhood. She believed that she had never had a childhood and a chance to play, and that she had to work for anything she wanted. She maintained that she had never seen warmth, love or tenderness at home and that her family never had done anything together. She always became very upset when she saw a family together. For example, she abruptly ran out of a friend's engagement party in tears because she became upset by the warmth, closeness, and affection expressed by the family members of her friend. She went to her apartment and slept for more than 12 hours. At her own wedding her parents fought and her mother cursed her father.

Mrs. H. had great difficulty tolerating feelings of loneliness.

Shortly after she separated from her husband, she became intensely involved in a long series of brief relationships, most of which lasted only a few days. She ran frantically from one brief affair to another, each time convinced that this was "the real thing," "the perfect relationship," and that she would marry again. She felt little conscious guilt or embarrassment about these affairs, only disappointment and feelings of having been used and abandoned. Almost without exception she chose depreciated men from lower socioeconomic and educational levels. The men were of such a nature that she was convinced that if her parents found out about these affairs, her mother would commit suicide and her father would die of a heart attack. The promiscuity had stopped several months before she began analysis with me, and she did not report any of these incidents in the screening interviews.

Almost immediately on starting analysis, Mrs. H. seemed to have difficulty with the demands of the analytic process. Beginning in the third hour of the analysis, she began to doze when painful issues came up. The drowsiness increased in frequency and intensity; although she struggled to stay awake so she could "benefit from analysis," she was often unable to control her falling sound asleep. When awake she often played with her glasses, and it became apparent only later that she was using her glasses as a mirror to keep the analyst in sight. In the course of her analysis there were other indications of an association between object loss and an emphasis on vision. For example, she was very proud of having earned the money to buy contact lenses; yet on the day after the assassination of President Kennedy she confused which lens was for which eye and never wore her contact lenses again.

She had difficulty with separations in analysis. Weekends away from work and analysis were empty and painful. She seemed unable to tolerate the loneliness and she had frequent visitors and numerous phone calls each night. During the first extended separation from analysis for a month-long summer holiday she feared she would go crazy and would have to be hospitalized. She requested to "keep in touch" by mail. During the summer vacation she again became frantically involved in a series of brief affairs. Each affair lasted a few days and each time she again felt intensely in love. After being abandoned, she felt used, abused, and angry. She was aware of, and frightened by, her temptations to become a prostitute.

Her sleep in analysis also seemed to be in response to the feelings of loneliness and abandonment she experienced in my silences in analysis and her inability to keep me in sight. Her sleep in analysis had a peaceful, restful quality; she seemed to want to be held and enveloped. During the second extended separation from analysis, a two-week Christmas holiday, she joined her new boyfriend on a trip—the first time she ventured out of town. On her return she reported that she had once again fallen in love and that she was planning to get married. After a few days she abruptly announced that she had decided to interrupt her analysis because her boyfriend objected to it. It was only upon reviewing the case record that it was noted that her interruption of the analysis occurred exactly nine months to the day of her first meeting with the analyst (Rose, 1962). The interruption also occurred immediately after the Christmas-New Year holiday, when themes of birth and the start of a new life are prevalent in society as a reaction to the emptiness, barrenness, and darkness of the winter solstice.

Mrs. H. reported several brief dream fragments during the analysis. In one dream there was a knock on the door and when she answered the door, there was no one there. She also had frequent nightmares of being attacked and raped, but she would not elaborate on these in any detail. She briefly mentioned a dream she had had shortly before her marriage in which she awoke screaming, "Catch the baby, catch the baby before it falls from the shopping cart." In a current dream a rat bit her hand, and in another a boyfriend turned her over to other men for them to have intercourse with her. She was unable to associate to any of these dreams. She also commented that she often felt tempted to assume "a fetal position" when masturbating, but she was frightened by the implications of this. An image of her mother was frequently present in her masturbation fantasies, but she was unwilling to elaborate on this. At one point in analysis, while following a series of thoughts about her mother, she abruptly stopped and said she felt like she was "in quicksand, being sucked in." She often expressed the thought that her mother had cast a spell over her and she was frightened that she would eventually commit suicide or at least never remarry and become "lonely, old, and crazy" like her mother.

Diagnostically, Mrs. H. seemed to have an anaclitic depression in a basically infantile narcissistic character disturbance with possibly borderline features. Her depressive concerns focused on her feelings of being unwanted, unloved, and abandoned, which she defended against by seeking direct physical and sensory contact with objects. She had a desperate need to be close to people, to have direct contact with them, and to keep them in view. Her sadomasochistic fantasies and activities were ways of seeking intense sensory stimulation as well as expressing her rage about deprivation and abandonment. She had to seek substitutes for the loss of a need-gratifying object, yet she constantly provoked abandonment in her indiscriminate search for objects who would provide some sense of contact and need satisfaction. In numerous ways the clinical material illustrated her impaired object representations and her attempts to cope with potentially dangerous and frightening experiences of object loss and abandonment by maintaining direct, immediate, sensorimotor contact.

A second patient, George L., sought analysis because of intense feelings of depression and concerns about his increasing inability to function effectively. His colleagues and friends considered him to be quite successful; he had achieved genuine recognition in several high positions that most people felt required much more experience than he possessed. While he found little meaning and satisfaction in these accomplishments, he was driven to succeed and win recognition, and he worked endlessly to the point of exhaustion. Several years prior to his seeking analysis, on the eve of the completion of a long, complex, and highly responsible task, he began to feel faint and panicky while sitting in a barber's chair. The barber tissue around his neck seemed very tight and he felt choked by it. As he got up he was unable to walk, he felt that his feet were not touching the ground and that he was about to topple over. For several years after this incident his functioning continued to decline and he was barely able to concentrate and work when he finally sought analysis.

When Mr. L. was a preadolescent his mother died from an overdose of sleeping pills and he assumed that she committed suicide. The mother had been hospitalized at least once several years earlier when he was a young child, for what seemed to be a severe depression. He remembered her lying on the couch completely covered with a blanket, wearing sunglasses, and being unresponsive. He had a personal myth of himself as being simultaneously rich and poor because he was from a wealthy family which refused to provide him with funds or support. In part, however, this myth also reflected his early childhood experiences with his mother—her gaiety, laughter, and singing, which alternated with her periods of despondency and depression.

Shortly after Mr. L. sought analysis his father was killed in an accident and he became disorganized and acutely depressed. He was in analysis for $4\frac{1}{2}$ years, which, in retrospect, he described as consisting of four phases. The first phase he described as helping him hold on to life, preventing further disorganization and possible suicide. The second phase was a time of stabilization in which he gained strength and security. He characterized the third phase as the beginning of a will to live, and the belief that there was a future and that it was worth working toward. The fourth phase of analysis was a period in which he struggled with very painful issues and began the difficult process of change. Although he described his analysis in somewhat dramatic fashion, it accurately portrayed his precarious balance when he began analysis and his progressive integration.

Many hours in the first year of analysis were devoted to feelings of despair, anguish, guilt, and anger over the death of his parents and the tragedy of their lives. He had numerous images of death such as seeing himself on a marble slab, being trapped, abandoned, breathless, and choking, and a dream in which he felt like a cold mechanical octopus. He was intensely interested in Hamlet and Dostoyevsky, particularly in *Crime and Punishment,* and in fact he began his analysis with the announcement that he was Raskolnikov. He had intense feelings of guilt about his responsibility for the death of his parents, much of it associated with oedipal strivings. He believed that love killed his mother because his parents were sleeping together when she died. He felt sexually attracted to "older women" who were about the age of his mother when she died, and he was particularly interested in older women who needed help. He was excessively altruistic, unable to say no for fear of hurting, rejecting, or offending someone.

Throughout the analysis he spoke of something inside, vague and unspecified, which had to come out if he was to improve. On leaving each analytic session, he automatically stated the time of the next appointment. He was frightened that there would be no tomorrow and that the analyst would not be there. In his automatic phrase he sought to cope with his intense feelings and apprehension that life and people were unpredictable and unstable.

During the last year of analysis just after he began to consider the possibility of termination, he began "hearing" a voice inside, a male voice, not unlike his father's, saying emphatically, "Die boy, die." He heard this voice as he increasingly felt tempted to jump in front of a train or truck or out a window. In the analysis he spent considerable time working on his intense depressive feelings, his self-destructive impulses and behavior, his wish to die and rejoin his parents, his negative introjects such as the voice, and his anguished feelings that somehow his sexuality had caused his mother's death. He felt empty, impotent, listless, defeated, like a zombie or Dorian Gray because people were so impressed with him, while inside he felt disturbed, corrupt, and evil. While he felt that he had made considerable progress in his analysis and that his work was progressing well, he told a joke about a patient who died from improvement. Suicide seemed a serious possibility.

Throughout the analysis he sought information about the circumstances of his mother's death. He visited the home in which they lived when she died, he went to the local newspaper to read the death notice, and later in the analysis he actively considered for the first time trying to locate her grave. He often found it pleasant on a nice afternoon to walk through the local cemetery. Throughout his adult life he maintained an interest in a subject matter in which his mother had been actively interested and, while in analysis, he began to develop this avocation into a career. His interests were in the same specific area as his mother's, but he went even further than that: he became particularly interested in the development of this topic during the period of his mother's life. Thus, he was simultaneously involved in the area of his mother's major interest as well as in the era in which she lived. He made a major contribution in this area and eventually achieved considerable success and recognition. From an analytic point of view, one of the major functions of these interests was an attempt to reconstruct more reality-adequate representations of his mother by coming to know more fully her interests and many aspects of her life. But he also worked to establish a differentiation from her as well. He began to explore his fears that he might be psychotic like his mother, and he wondered why he had been accepted for analysis, since it seemed unlikely that he would ever improve.

His depression lightened after he began to express his anger toward his parents and as he began to elaborate aspects of his negative introjects, such as his identification with his severely depressed mother and his hearing the voice say "Die boy, die." He completed a major project in his new career and began to develop a confidence in the future. This was vividly expressed one hour when he reported seeing a sign with the comment: "Today is the beginning of the rest of your life." He began to feel that he had been through the depths of his depression and that "things inside had come out." As he worked through his ambivalence about his parents and aspects of the termination, he began to establish a more mature basis for identification. In a letter subsequent to termination he wrote, "I miss you very much and will always think of you with fondness and tenderness. Your courage, steadfast refusal to abandon your faith in me at a time when I virtually had given up hope for myself has helped me regain some measure of self-confidence and self-respect."

Mr. L.'s character structure was obsessive in nature. His depression was primarily introjective in quality, with major antecedents in his difficulty resolving oedipal issues. His depression focused around issues of guilt, blame, responsibility, and self-worth. He struggled with object loss in an intense and profound way. In analysis, he struggled to achieve a stable representation of his mother by attempting to reconstruct parts of her life and by coming to know her major area of interest and by building his new career around this interest. His progress in analysis closely paralleled his development of more conceptual and symbolic and less ambivalent, literal, and concrete representations of her.

In contrasting the two cases, Mrs. H.'s concerns were more oral in nature and involved struggles around individuation and separation from a mutually devouring, consuming, and destructive relationship with her mother. Her concerns focused on feelings of being unloved and abandoned, and, while there were no conscious feelings of guilt, there was considerable sadomasochistic activity and fantasy. Her object relationships were unstable and on the level of need satisfaction. Her object representations seemed insufficient to enable her to tolerate separation and object loss and she struggled to maintain direct physical and sensory contact with people. Mr. L., in contrast, had formed identifications and was struggling with superego issues and aspects of the oedipal crisis. He experienced profound feelings of guilt over his phallic strivings. While driven to succeed and win recognition and approval, he was unable to derive much satisfaction from his accomplishments. He was continually besieged by feelings of self-doubt and fears of castration and he dreaded criticism and disapproval. Like Mrs. H., he had traumatic experiences of object loss, but he struggled to maintain the relations to his objects on a developmentally more advanced level. Rather than trying to establish direct physical contact, he sought to develop consistent and integrated representations of the object. Initially, his object representations were ambivalent, somewhat concrete, and depictive; as his analysis progressed, his representations became more differentiated, abstract, symbolic, and integrated. While Mrs. H. and Mr. L. sought analysis primarily for intense feelings of depression related to their traumatic experiences of object loss, the two cases illustrate some of the differences between an anaclitic and an introjective depression.

In a discussion of depression in adolescence, Anthony (1970) presents case illustrations of two types of depression. This clinical material includes observations which are consistent with the hypothesis of this paper—that there are different levels of object representation in anaclitic and introjective depression. Anthony says of one patient, "Following the session, she would go home and try and continue the session on the telephone. She would 'shadow'

me from my home to my office, and even followed me round a
supermarket on one occasion" (p. 852). She approached the end of
each session with "anxiety, depression, anger, demandingness, and
a refusal to leave. . . . It was difficult terminating any session
without generating a miniature depression" (p. 854). The second
type of patient "mentioned that she did not need to be here all the
time since she carried a picture of me in her mind and was able to
discuss her problems equally with this picture. It's even better
because when you're inside me like that you don't interrupt" (p.
857).

On the basis of these and other clinical observations and on a
number of theoretical considerations it appears that at least two
major types of depression can be distinguished and both involve
impairments in object representations. In an anaclitic depression
representations are based much more on direct sensorimotor
experiences associated with drive satisfaction. Introjective depression evolves at a higher developmental level; psychosexual development is at the phallic and oedipal stages, there is greater
object-subject differentiation, a more complex affect structure with
the capacity for guilt, and a more highly developed ego with object
representations based on concrete perceptual characteristics and
specific part properties of the object. Careful consideration of the
development of object representations in psychoanalytic theory and
cognitive developmental psychology may extend our understanding
of the processes of object representation and their impairment in
psychopathology, particularly in the complex phenomena of depression.

THE DEVELOPMENT OF OBJECT REPRESENTATIONS

DEVELOPMENTAL PSYCHOLOGY

The two major statements on the development of object representations in developmental psychology come from the work of Piaget
and Werner. While there are important differences between the
observations and formulations of developmental psychologists and
psychoanalytic theorists, the work of Piaget and Werner can
provide important observations and conceptualizations which can

serve to enrich and elaborate psychoanalytic theory. It should be stressed that Piaget, in particular, based his formulations on the study of childrens' responses to inanimate objects, which are much less complex than human objects. They do not move of their own right, they are not responsive to the child, they are invariant, and they are not directly need-gratifying. Despite the important differences between the observational conditions of Piaget and psychoanalytic investigators, Piaget's work has an important contribution for understanding developmental sequences reported by psychoanalytic investigators, even though the specific time schedule may vary somewhat because of the differences between an inanimate stimulus and a human, need-gratifying object (Wolff, 1960).

Piaget investigated the development of object representations as a general cognitive process. While Piaget distinguished between object and person permanence, he views these two types of representations as developing simultaneously. Research by Décarie (1965) and by Bell (1970) supports this assumption, and also indicates that person permanence usually precedes object permanence. According to Piaget (1937, 1945), object representations develop throughout the entire developmental sequence ranging from sensorimotor activity to formal operations. The first level of object representation is achieved at the end of the sensorimotor stage, and in subsequent developmental sequences (the preconceptual, intuitive, and operational) higher levels of object representation are attained. Through processes of assimilation and accommodation, schemata are revised to include new perceptual, extraperceptual, and social stimuli, and each of these revisions of schemata achieves equilibrium in the establishment of a new level of object representation. In a "vertical décalage" representations are extended and reorganized at successive stages of development and at the higher stages earlier and current levels of representation are available. Thus, object representation is an evolving process established over several succeeding developmental sequences, each sequence serving to integrate prior sequences and to extend representations so they have greater generality and constancy. According to Piaget, the development of the concept of the object is "an actual constructive deduction" (1937, p. 93) and representations occur as a function of this accommodation. Representation is used by Piaget in a broad sense as identical with thought—as a system of concepts or mental schemata and, in a narrow sense, as a mental image or symbolic evocation of an absent reality. The two definitions are interrelated, however, since the mental image expresses the level of the cognitive schemata. Representation is a union of a "signifier" with a "signified." The "signifier" is a product of the process of accommodation, which is expressed in imitation ranging from sensorimotor action, to images, to "interiorised imitations." The "signified" is the product of assimilation which integrates the current experience of the object with earlier schemata and gives it meaning. Representation involves an interplay of assimilation and accommodation leading toward increasingly stable cognitive representations with greater equilibrium (1945, p. 273).

Initially, in the sensorimotor stage, the child responds to the action of objects and eventually separates the object from its action. The representations at this stage are immediate, direct, and have only minimal permanence. The memory of the child is still a "medley of disorganized reconstructions" and lacks a capacity for evocative recall. The representations link successive perceptions and movements as if they were "static images" and there is no overall representation of the situation. The child recognizes an object or person "in so far as he is able to react to them as he has done in the past, and it is these sensorimotor [or action] schemas which become memory-images" (1945, p. 188). The representations of the sensorimotor schemata form the nucleus for subsequent constructions. "The sensori-motor mechanisms are prerepresentational, and behavior based on the evocation of an absent object is not observed until during the second year" (Piaget and Inhelder, 1966, p. 52). Although true representation does not exist in the sensorimotor stage, there is signification, but the signifiers are perceptual and are not yet differentiated from the signified—they are more an "indicator" than a sign or symbol.

Imitation and play contribute to the introduction of symbols and to the development of representation. Representation begins when there is a simultaneous differentiation and coordination between "signifiers" and "signified." The first differentiations are provided by imitation and the mental images derived from it. Symbolic functioning is only possible as a result of the union between actual or mental imitation of an absent model and the "meaning" provided by assimilation. In early stages of imitation, the child imitates movements or sounds already known to him. Later on the child imitates new and complex movements and slowly the external model is replaced by an internal model—an evocative memory or representation of the object. Early forms of imitation in the sensorimotor stage are the "prefiguration of representation" and as imitation becomes less a direct perceptual copy and increasingly more symbolic, a transition from representation in action to representation in thought takes place (Piaget and Inhelder, 1966). The acquisition of language rapidly increases the capacities for representation in thought (Wolff, 1967).

According to Piaget (1945), the preconceptual stage (extending from the appearance of language to 4–4½ years) is the "first form of conceptual thought," which as a result of language is superimposed on the sensorimotor schema. There is a shift from the proprioceptive, sensorimotor experience to an apprehension of the surroundings (Cobliner, 1965). Objects at this stage are not general classes or relations, but are "merely signified by the image and by semi-individual verbal expressions" (Piaget, 1945, p. 282), and the representations contain only momentary situations and partial elements and lack constancy outside of the immediate field of action. Correspondence is achieved "between pairs or small sets of objects and there is no seriation or serial correspondence"—the representations are of "semi-individual, semi-general relations," but lack the anticipation of the whole figure or situation (p. 286). Piaget and Inhelder (1966) discuss two types of images: reproductive and anticipatory. Reproductive images are limited to things previously perceived and the preoperational child has, almost exclusively, static reproductive images.

The preconceptual stage is followed by the stage of intuitive thought (ages 4 or 5 to 7) which serves as a transition to the stage of operations. Gradually in the intuitive stage, the child moves beyond the simple semi-individual image and begins to construct a representation of a total structure or configuration. Representations are no longer based on a comparison between pairs or small sets of objects but rely on schemata of the entire series or configuration. But the representation is still linked to an image and an operational schema is still lacking. "Intuitive thought is intermediary between the image and the concept" (Piaget, 1945, p. 211).

In the fourth developmental stage, operational representation, adapted thought reaches a stage of equilibrium on a level of concrete operations (age 7–8) and later in formal operations (age 11–12). With the development of concrete operations, the child has reproductive images of movement (changes in position) and trans-formation (changes in form) and anticipatory images (things not previously perceived). Thus representations are no longer tied to certain configurations and to specific and static images, but are now concerned with symbolic transformations. The period of concrete operations is an "unfolding of a long, integrated process that may be characterized as a transition from subjective centering in all areas to a decentering that is at once cognitive, social, and moral. This process . . . reproduces and develops on a large scale at the level of thought what has already taken place on a small scale at the sensori-motor level"—the representation of an absent reality. The "decentering [is] based on the general coordination of action, and this permits the formation of operatory systems of transforma-tions and constants or conservations which liberate the representa-tion of reality from its deceptive figurative appearances" (Piaget and Inhelder, 1966, p. 128). The child becomes capable of distinguishing different points of view and is able to recognize his own perspective from that of others. With the full development of representation, it is possible to have evocative memory of objects and events outside the perceptual field by means of images, signs, thoughts, and symbols. Objects are experienced as having stable and consistent properties despite variations or changes of context, and the self becomes an independent object, among many, which has enduring properties. It is only with the development of formal operations that children have abstract concepts such as a "native land, social justice, and rational, aesthetic or social ideals."

For Werner (1948) and Werner and Kaplan (1963), cognitive development is a process of increasing differentiation and hierarchi-cal integration within an interpersonal matrix which proceeds through a sensorimotor, perceptual, and conceptual stage and culminates in the achievement of symbol formation. These three stages are three modes of experiencing and representing objects, with the higher levels providing for greater diversity of object relationships.

In the sensorimotor stage, relationships are immediate and involve reflexlike physical reactions, which can be motoric or affective and are often directed toward satisfying biological needs. Some aspects of an object or situation impel particular stereotyped reactions on the basis of which the object or situation becomes known. Self and object are fused and there is no mental representation of the object independent of the concrete and immediate reaction. The object is defined by the affective and motoric reactions and has no special identity other than the specific sensations of need satisfaction.

The perceptual phase involves a "shift in emphasis from the incorporation of a thing into one's body, to a holding and beholding of something out there" (Werner and Kaplan, 1963, p. 69). There is an awareness of objects as something distant from the body, an increasing differentiation of self and nonself. With increased distance between subject and object there is a shift from "things of action" to "objects of contemplation," and the relationship between subject and object becomes more deliberate and mediated than reactive and immediate. There is a shift from outward reactions to reflection upon objects through the internalization of sensorimotor patterns. Objects, like all elements of the visual field, however, are still perceived as a total configuration of a concrete natural situation. This total visual configuration, which is primarily pictorial, concrete, and fixed, cannot be broken down into separate components. These perceptual, depictive configurations are the precursors of true symbolic representation. The grasping and reaching of the sensorimotor stage move toward touching, looking at, and contemplating, and then eventually become pointing. This pointing is a communicative function and a sharing of experiences, which has its earliest paradigm in the nonreflexive smile of the infant in response to the mother's smile. This communicative sharing, however, becomes most manifest when the infant begins to share contemplated objects with the mother. Within this primordial sharing situation child and mother begin to contemplate objects and touch and look at things together. The child develops gestures such as pointing at an object and thereby shares the contemplation of an object with mother.

The communicative function of referential pointing still remains dependent upon the physical presence of the object or referent. The object is defined in literal and concrete terms as a perceptual totality within specific contexts; there is little abstraction or symbolic representation of the object. The context may be as important as the qualities of the object and serves as a partial substitute for it. With greater familiarity, objects are experienced as more articulated and their separate parts are differentiated and reintegrated within the framework of the whole object. Similarly, objects are differentiated in relation to other objects and the context surrounding them. This differentiation allows for a more stable concept of the object so that it is now experienced as having continuity despite variations in appearance or in context. There is the possibility for "exemplificatory representation" where a concrete object illustrates a concept or the "symbolic vehicle" (e.g., verbal pattern or gesture) presents a meaning, but these are still not full symbolizations. In gestures and vocal utterances there is a progression from affective reactions to objects, to sounds and gestures which are direct imitations of the object, to iconic representations that depict the object, to iconic representations in which the depiction is less literal, to truly representational forms in which the sharing of contemplated objects is achieved through symbols such as names which represent the object. The pointing which was an indication or denotation of a concretely present object develops into a symbolization which both refers to and represents an object. Pointing refers to a specific object in a given situation, but in symbolization the characteristic features of the object are abstracted and placed in a symbolic vehicle (words). This sequence involves the gradual differentiation and separation of aspects of the symbolizing situation—the symbolizer, the symbolic vehicle, and the referent or object.

Initially, in the conceptual stage, the symbolic vehicles are related to concrete situations (iconic representations), but the advanced levels of symbolization require a greater distance and autonomy among the components of the symbolizing situation. This is achieved only by an increased differentiation of external and inner forms of the components of the symbolizing situation. With the appreciation of inner form, objects are no longer perceived as particular entities but are considered more abstractly as exemplifications of general concepts. The referent, perceived as possessing an inner structure which is quite removed from perceptible features, becomes characterized in terms of properties far removed from ordinary nonreflective perception. Even when perceptual features are focused upon, they are understood as exemplifications of abstract concepts, rather than as isolated things in themselves. As the external and inner form of both symbolic vehicle and referent become differentiated, relationships between vehicles and referential objects come to be based upon inner form. This relative autonomy of vehicle and referent (representation and object) and the establishment of relationships based on inner rather than external form permit stable, relatively permanent representations of objects. Repeated encounters with the actual object are no longer necessary for the representation to be maintained. In fact, the physical or perceptual presence of the object has little relevance for its representation, which is now based upon a correspondence of inner form rather than outward appearance.

PSYCHOANALYTIC THEORY

The concept of mental representations has been a fundamental issue in psychoanalytic theory beginning with Freud's (1900) detailed consideration of the processes of representation in dreams. Mental representations (*Vorstellung*) were the images associated with drive discharge and gratification (either as a hallucinatory gratification or as an accurate image of the sought-for object) and, more generally, the memory, image, or idea of any experience or object. Freud discussed primary process representations in dreams and psychosis and reality-oriented representations of the higher level mental organization of the secondary process. Thinking in pictures ("thing representation") was differentiated from thinking in words ("word representation") and related to the progression from primary process to secondary process thought. The replacement of image representations by word representations was a basic aspect of the development of conscious (1916–17) and secondary process (1923) thought. Schafer (1968) also distinguishes between primary process and secondary process representations. The former are characterized as inaccurate, unstable, indeterminate in space, unreflective, and with little distinction between self and nonself. Secondary process representations are relatively accurate, stable, and reflective, with temporal and spatial references and self and object differentiation. But, as Schafer points out, these are only extreme positions and representations can occur at a variety of points on this continuum.

Object representations have also been considered as the mental schemata of objects encountered in reality (Novey, 1958; Sandler and Rosenblatt, 1962; Beres and Joseph, 1970). These schemata evolve from the internalization of object relations; as relations develop and mature, the mental schemata become increasingly differentiated. As Hartmann et al. (1949) put it:

> Every step in the formation of the object corresponds to a phase in psychic differentiation. That differentiation itself is determined by the maturation of the apparatus, which later come under the control of the ego, and by the experiences that structure the psychic apparatus. Hence both processes, differentiation of psychic structure and relation of the self to external objects, are interdependent [p. 26f.].

Object representations express the nature and level of object relations, the processes of internalization, and the degree of organization of intrapsychic structures. Sandler and Rosenblatt (1962) and Jacobson (1964) consider the building of representations a *sine qua non* for ego development and adaptation. According to Jacobson (1964), one of the major developmental achievements is the building of stable object representations and the establishment of enduring object-libidinal cathexis. Object representations are vague and variable at first and they gradually expand and develop into consistent, relatively realistic representations of the self and the object world. Based initially on pleasurable and unpleasurable experiences of frustration-gratification, concepts of the object world and the self emerge with advancing psychosexual and ego development. Initially the child cannot differentiate his pleasurable sensations and the object from which they are derived. Subsequently, the experiences of frustration and gratification become associated with the object. Based on "early reciprocal affectomotor identifications" (p. 42), the child imitates the mother's gestures, behavior, and action. The experience of merging with the love object gives way to partial identification with the object.

Rapaport (1950) points out: "From developmental psychology we know that the original experience of the need-satisfying object is a diffuse, undifferentiated experience in which visual, acoustic, tactile, thermal, cutaneous, kinesthetic, and other stimulations are fused. Discrete objects do not as yet exist, and thus the need-satisfying object itself is not differentiated from the context in which it appears, nor even from the experiences immediately preceding or following it" (p. 262). At this earliest level, the self, the object, and the sensory event and experience all constitute one undifferentiated unit. The representations are preobjectal (Spitz, 1965) and not of any particular object, but rather are a diffuse, affective, sensorimotor experience of pleasure and unpleasure. Mahler (1968) discusses this early phase as a symbiotic stage in which the infant is exclusively attached to and dependent upon the mother in an undifferentiated state in which I and not-I and inside and outside are fused. Slowly the infant begins to perceive need satisfaction as coming from the need-satisfying object. The infant begins to learn to anticipate need satisfaction (Spitz, 1965), and there is a shift from the internal experience to the external perception and from the cathexis of the satisfying experience to a cathexis of the need-satisfying object. As discussed by Rapaport (1950, p. 262), the diffuse image "differentiates into discrete objects and experiences, all of which are still related to instinctual drives in the same fashion as was the original undifferentiated image of the need-satisfying object." The discrete objects are experienced initially as part properties which have a function in need gratification. In the beginning subphases of the separation-individuation stage, the child slowly becomes able to separate and to differentiate primitive self and object representations (Mahler, 1968). Separation involves the emerging from the symbiotic fusion with the need-gratifying object and the development of object representations. Individuation involves the differentiation of the self and the development of self representations. For Mahler (1968), the development of object and self representations are inextricably intertwined with the development of object relations and ego functions. With the development and increased stabilization of object and self representations, there is the beginning of object constancy and identity. Object constancy is an important aspect in the development of mental representations.

Object constancy has been used in several ways in the psychoanalytic literature. Hartmann (1952, 1953, 1956) first discussed object constancy in psychoanalytic theory as an aspect of ego development—as part of the development of "objectification" in reality testing and "the building up and structuring of the object" and the inner world (1953, p. 188). Anna Freud (1965, 1968) and Beres and Joseph (1970) consider an inner image or representation of the object as essential for the development of a constant libidinal attachment to an object—for object constancy. Hoffer (1955) used object constancy to define an advanced and mature stage of development at which attachment to the object is maintained independent of momentary satisfaction. In the absence of the object and its satisfactions, the object is "longed for and not rejected." Anna Freud (1952, 1965, 1968) considered object constancy to be the capacity to maintain libidinal cathexis of an object independent of any positive satisfaction or gratification, and it is the constant libidinal attachment to the object which is the essential component of object constancy and not the mental representation of the object. Kris (1950) also maintained a distinction between the image of the object and the libidinal attachment to it. He discussed the danger of "losing the love object" as compared to "losing the object's love." The fear of losing the object represents "anaclitic needs," while the fear of losing the object's love represents a more integrated type of object relationship. Mahler (1968) considers the loss of the object (fear of abandonment) as occurring in the symbiotic and early separation-individuation phases, and the loss of love in later separation-individuation subphases. Hartmann et al. (1949) also commented on the important transition from the concern about maintaining the object to a concern about maintaining love.

While many psychoanalysts stress the libidinal attachment to the object as the essential feature of object constancy, others (e.g.,

Mahler, 1965) define object constancy as a stable level of mental representation. Mahler (1965) believes that the attainment of full object constancy occurs between 2 and 3 years of age, and it is this capacity which enables the child increasingly to tolerate separation from the mother. Fraiberg (1969) attempted to resolve some of the contradictions in the psychoanalytic concept of object constancy by distinguishing two levels of constancy—a libidinal level at which the child is able to "recognize" and have "a mental registration" of the need-gratifying object, and a representational level at which the child can "evoke" a memory of the object. Burgner and Edgcumbe (1972), in a review of the psychoanalytic literature on object constancy, were concerned that object constancy was frequently confused with the concept of perceptual constancy in academic psychology. They propose the term "capacity for constant relationship" for the ability to establish a "specific level of object relationships to animate objects" (p. 327). They distinguish "capacity for constant relationships" as a stage which succeeds the earlier "need-satisfying type of relationship," and as having several elements including "perceptual object constancy; the capacity to maintain drive investment in a specific object notwithstanding its presence or absence; the capacity to recognize and tolerate loving and hostile feelings toward the same object; the capacity to keep feelings centered on a specific object; and the capacity to value an object for attributes other than its function of satisfying needs" (p. 328). Burgner and Edgcumbe define perceptual constancy as the maintenance of an internal representation of the object, independent of its presence, or a primary need directed toward the object. In contrast, they consider the most important aspect of object constancy to be the maintenance of "a permanent investment of energy (be it libidinal or aggressive in its feeling tone) in the representation of a specific object" (p. 329). Burgner and Edgcumbe's emphasis on the uniqueness of libidinal constancy is appropriate, but it is important to note that while the concepts of perceptual constancy and object constancy in academic psychology are interrelated, they are different processes which occur at different points in development. Perceptual constancy is the capacity to recognize the object independent of its context; object constancy is the capacity to evoke an image of the object in its absence. Libidinal constancy is another dimension which intertwines and develops simultaneously in complex interaction with the mental representations of perceptual constancy and object constancy. Libidinal constancy depends, in part, on the formation of some mental representation of the object. While it is important to include the development of the capacity for a constant affective relationship in any formulation of the development of object representations, the various levels of object representation achieved in the development of perceptual and object constancy, as viewed in academic psychology, have important implications for understanding the development of the representational world.

INTEGRATION OF PSYCHOANALYTIC THEORY
AND DEVELOPMENTAL PSYCHOLOGY

Psychoanalytic and developmental psychology assign different importance to the affective and cognitive dimensions in the development of the concept of the object. Also, as Wolff (1967) points out, Piaget assumes an equal intensity for all actions regardless of the state of the organism, whereas psychoanalysis assumes a hierarchy of motivations often based on an epigenetic series of hierarchically organized organ modes (Erikson, 1950; Kestenberg, 1971); these frequently determine some of the categories of experience in which the development of representations occurs. Despite these and other differences between psychoanalytic and developmental psychology, each makes a considerable contribution to a fuller formulation of the sequences leading to the development of stable representations of the object.

With development, object representations become increasingly differentiated, integrated, and accurate. They proceed from amorphous, global representations, to a somewhat differentiated emphasis on part properties, to representations which are highly articulated and integrated, and closely correspond to reality. Representations can range from images of objects immediately present in the perceptual field to symbolic evocation of absent realities. Earlier forms of representation are based more on action sequences associated with need gratification, intermediate forms are based on specific perceptual features, and the higher forms of object representation are more symbolic and conceptual.

Initially, there is a prerepresentational, preobjectal stage in which the infant cannot differentiate his pleasurable sensations from the object providing the satisfaction. The need-satisfying object is not differentiated, but is part of a diffuse, global, affective, sensory, physiological experience. Slowly, the infant begins to perceive that need gratification comes from a particular source, and there is a shift of investment from the satisfying experience to the need-satisfying object. There is a shift from the pleasurable experience of being fed to a discerning of the source of the pleasure (Anna Freud, 1946). This is the first level of representation, a level of *sensorimotor representation*, in which the object is cathected at the moment of need gratification. The object still remains relatively undifferentiated and is cathected and represented primarily, if not exclusively, in its function of providing gratification. Although there is an awareness of the object, the object is still not fully separated from the context of the experience and the event. At this level the object is experienced in terms of its activities, its representation being an extrapolation of the action pattern. The object is recognized and valued only in the specific limited context of need gratification, and it has little meaning or existence beyond providing comfort and alleviating pain. The first representations of the object are indicated by the infant's capacity to search for the object, first after visible, and later invisible, displacement and by the imitation of the object's sensorimotor actions.

With repeated experiences of the object disappearing and reappearing, particularly at moments of considerable discomfort, the representations of the object become more defined. As the need-gratifying object is encountered in a variety of contexts, the object is articulated as separate from the specific experience of pleasure-pain, and the child is able to recognize the object despite variations in the surrounding situation. This stage can be characterized as *perceptual object representation*, which is an aspect of the general phenomenon discussed in the psychological literature as perceptual constancy. The child has formed some conception of the object and has developed the capacity to recognize the object independent of its action or of the specific context. The object is recognized as an entity in its own right with a variety of functions and actions, and a constant libidinal cathexis for the object is maintained independent of frustration-gratification. The representation of the object is indicated by the fact that the child recognizes the object in a variety of contexts and attempts to imitate the object. But the representation of the object is a concrete, literal, fixed, perceptual totality which is not broken down into separate components. There is perceptual recognition, but the child still lacks the capacity to evoke a representation of the object in its absence. Also, the child can be confused by extremely contradictory experiences with the object. But the child has consolidated his perception of the object and, as discussed by Cobliner (1965), the development of a permanent memory of the object "is founded on the consolidation, on the constancy, of its corresponding percept" (p. 347).

With experience, objects become more articulated and separate part properties and functions are differentiated within the framework of the whole object. The child begins to use these part properties as signs and symbols for the object. First they are used as concrete signs and later the child uses symbols such as a name. The symbols increase in their level of abstraction and begin to shift from being depictive to assuming a truly representational function. Imitation is first based on manifest perceptual aspects of the object such as mannerisms and gestures, and later it becomes increasingly symbolic and internal. There is the capacity for evocative memory, initially in pictorial form, later in signs, and finally in more symbolic modalities.

The conceptual stage of object representation can be subdivided into two subphases. In the first subphase, the representation is based on a concrete sign rather than an abstract symbolization of the object. This phase of *iconic object representation* is a transitional stage leading to conceptual representations in which the representation of the object is complex, integrated, and abstract. Iconic representations are partially symbolic and conceptual in that the representations are based on a part property or attribute which signify the object. But the qualities and attributes in iconic representations are based on relatively specific, concrete, manifest part properties, functions, and interests of the object. The qualities and attributes in these representations may reflect an appreciation of an inner state or form to some degree, but they are primarily linked to specific manifest features. They are limited in scope and range and, initially, at least, they are based on extreme or vivid part properties or features of the object. They often contain hostile, aggressive, and overidealized, idyllic features. Thus the representations at this level are denotative, depictive, concrete, fragmented, and overstated with considerable contradiction and ambivalence.

With development, the apparent contradictions between part properties and features are resolved, and the separate parts are reintegrated in a representation of the whole object, which becomes increasingly diverse, integrated, conceptual, and abstract. *Conceptual representations* are based on inner form and structure and are removed from ordinary nonreflective perception of manifest aspects of the object. The object is represented as a fully independent entity with specific and enduring characteristics, functions, values, and feelings, only some of which are relevant in any immediate situation or relationship. Object representations at this level have greater stability and continuity, and there is no longer any need for contact with the actual object in order to maintain the representation. It is now possible to have evocative memory of objects and events outside the perceptual field by means of images, signs, thoughts, and symbols, and to have anticipatory representations of things not previously perceived or experienced. The development of conceptual or symbolic representations is achieved in the later stages of separation-individuation with the resolution of the oedipal crisis and the relinquishing of infantile and oedipal objects. Identification is in part based on conceptual representations, and with this achievement the child is now capable of empathy and of taking the perspective of others. The full development of object representation is finally achieved in adolescence (Piaget, 1945; Werner and Kaplan, 1963; Jacobson, 1964).

Thus object representations can occur on a sensorimotor, perceptual, iconic, and conceptual level.[5] Bruner (1964) and Horowitz

[5] Various stages in the development of object representation can also be considered as stages of object constancy (Kaplan, 1972), but for clarity, the concept of object constancy is used in this paper for the libidinal attachment to an object irrespective of frustration and gratification. The various levels of object representation are aspects of the development of the concept of the object and of object permanence (Piaget, 1937).

(1972), in similar fashion, discuss enactive, image, and lexical modes of representation which develop epigenetically and have their own intrinsic properties and levels of organization. Representations at the sensorimotor level are based primarily on particular action sequences in specific contexts. Changes in need satisfaction, in the action pattern, or in the context can disrupt the infant's experience of the object. Representations at this level lack stability and flexibility. At the perceptual level, the object is recognized in a variety of contexts and is experienced as a unique entity. But the representations are concrete and literal and have little differentiation within the perceptual totality. Representations at the iconic level are more differentiated, but they are based on more manifest part properties and features and they often lack an integration of contradictory elements. Representations at the conceptual level are more symbolic and they transcend the manifest, the immediate condition, and the momentary experience; they have greater continuity and stability; and they integrate diverse, separate, and apparently contradictory images into a consolidated representation. The later stages of representation are based on an integration and extension of earlier stages; thus at the highest level of development, the earlier as well as the more complex levels of representation are available (Piaget, 1937, 1945). Aspects from earlier levels can vivify and enrich the total representation by adding affective dimensions.

Progress in the development of object representations, the achievement of more accurate, complex, differentiated, integrated, and stable representations, is the end result of each developmental sequence. A new level of representation evolves from the complex interactions between the individual's prior developmental achievements and the patterns of the environmental responses to the child's emerging needs, capacities, and strivings during that specific developmental sequence. Initially, the first representations emerge within the mother-child relationship, in the repeated experiences of frustration and gratification with a consistent and need-gratifying object. Later stages of representation emerge out of the increasingly differentiated parent-child interaction. The nature of the object relations determines the level of representations, and the establishment of more differentiated and stable representations provides a new organization for experiencing object relations. There is constant interaction between object relations and the development of representations. Representations emerge out of the affective relationship between mother and child and, in turn, serve to organize the future experiences of that relationship, leading to the next stage of representation. The level of representations indicates the level of ego development, the object differentiation that has been achieved, and the quality of the object that can be cathected (Hartmann et al., 1949).

There has been much discussion in the psychoanalytic literature about the relationship of libidinal object constancy and the concept of the object as defined by developmental psychologists. The development of libidinal constancy and object representations are inextricably intertwined. As described by Anna Freud (1946), libidinal attachment shifts from the pleasurable experience, to the part property of the object providing the satisfaction such as the breast or bottle, and eventually to the object itself. There must be some libidinal attachment to motivate the articulation of an object, and there must be some representation (recognition) of the object in order to develop libidinal attachment. Stages of representation both emerge from, and in turn facilitate, the development of libidinal constancy. The libidinal relationship and the levels of representation continually cause and affect one another. Without some representation of the object there can be little libidinal investment, and without libidinal investment there is likely to be little progress on the development of representation. The two processes develop simultaneously in a complex transaction.

IMPLICATIONS FOR OBJECT LOSS AND DEPRESSION

The distinction between types of depression in adults on the basis of a developmental model of object representation is independent of any consideration of the issue of whether depression occurs in childhood. Formulations of the etiology of psychopathology, however, raise the complex issues of regression, fixation, and how and why developmental disturbances in childhood become apparent only later. Subsequent life events, such as the surge of adolescent sexuality, cause a recrudescence of unresolved oedipal conflict. The midlife crisis, with the reemergence of concerns of strength, virility, fertility, and attractiveness, may revive and intensify earlier developmental struggles with sexual identification. And the same is true with levels of object representation: developmental disturbances in object representation may become apparent only later when the actual object is no longer readily available to provide the reality support and structure which serve to compensate for and minimize the impaired representations. These developmental impairments may become apparent only when the object representations must assume a major role in directing and organizing behavior.

The consideration of the development of levels of object representations is essentially a model of the progressive development of ego structures which regulate and direct behavior. These structures evolve out of a complex biological-psychological-interpersonal matrix. Higher levels of object representation are less contradictory and ambivalent and increasingly differentiated, complex, and integrated.[6] They provide higher levels of organization with the potential for more effective interaction with reality. Higher levels of representation provide the structures necessary for greater modulation and transformation of drives, affects, and impulses, and for the capacity to transcend the immediate environment. The development of the higher levels of object representation also contributes to the capacity to deal with object loss. Informal observations of children suggest that until early adolescence, children are often unable to develop a vivid mental image of a missing object or place. During periods of absence from home for either clearly pleasant or unpleasant purposes, children report difficulty recalling what their parents, close friends, their home, or their room look like. The capacity to evoke a vivid mental image of an absent object appears to develop fully around the age of 11 or 12, the age at which Piaget finds the development of formal operations.

The important role of mental images and representations in coping with loss or absence of an object is also suggested by the frequent emphasis on mementos and souvenirs as a way of maintaining the memories of times past. Mementos can range from

[6] Research by Roth and Blatt (1974) demonstrates that spatial and temporal features are important dimensions of object representations and provide a valuable way of assessing their level of organization.

direct and concrete parts of the object such as a lock of hair, to photographs, to more symbolic items which were important to the person. These items can serve as a replacement of, or as a support for, a limited capacity to establish mental representations of the object. At the developmentally more advanced levels, a wide range of memories and representations of the object can exist independent of any external sensory support. One of the primary differences between nostalgia and depression may be the capacity to evoke meaningful representations of the object.

There is considerable evidence (Freud, 1917; Abraham, 1924; Klein, 1934; Anna Freud, 1952; Rochlin, 1965) which suggests that impairment in object representation creates a particular vulnerability to depression. The predisposition to depression is determined by the failure to establish adequate levels of object representation. But even further, the level of representation is related to the specific type of depression. In anaclitic depression, the object representations are primarily within a specific drive-laden and action sequence (at a sensorimotor level) and there is a need to maintain direct physical, sensory, need-gratifying contact with the object. The danger is the loss of the object and the need satisfaction it can provide. There is often a desperate need to deny the loss of the object and to seek immediate and direct replacement. In introjective depression, the representations are primarily at a perceptual and iconic level; they are fragmented, isolated, static, and ambivalent, and there is little resolution of the contradictions between separate images or part properties. The danger of object loss at this level is related not to a fear of the loss of the object and its capacity to provide need gratification, but rather to the apprehension of the loss of the object's love, acceptance, and approval. There are attempts to win the object's love by striving for excessive achievements and perfection. Constant self-criticism and guilt and overstated representations of part properties of the object are means of maintaining contact with the object.

The integration of separate and isolated perceptual images and the resolution of contradictory and fragmented part properties result in the development of more conceptual and symbolic representations. At the lower developmental levels of object representation (sensorimotor, perceptual and iconic), there is a vulnerability to object loss and to feelings of depression. Conceptual representations, however, provide stable, diverse, integrated, and symbolic representations of the object so that object loss can be experienced without prolonged and severe depression. Successful mourning is partly a process of establishing and consolidating consistent, nonambivalent, symbolic representations of the object which facilitate the full acceptance that the object is no longer physically available. Likewise, mature acceptance of one's own eventual death can be achieved with the capacity for full representation of the self—with a sense of satisfaction with one's accomplishments and with the realization that one can continue to exist in symbolic and abstract form independent of one's physical presence. It would seem that the level of self representation develops in parallel with object representations. Thus, one would also expect impairments in the representation of the self in depression. Depressed patients lack a consistency of self representation since momentary events often have a disproportionate influence and effect on their self-esteem. Frustration or gratification, success or failure, acceptance or rebuff, approval or criticism of the moment— all have a major impact on current feelings about the self because of a lack of a consolidated and sustained self representation. While there is a predominant dysphoric and depreciated tone in the self representations of depressed patients, these often alternate with more grandiose images. Momentary events often dramatically affect self representations, both in a positive and negative direction. In depression there is no full sense of the self as having continuity and constancy over time. There is little sense of a differentiated past and little sense of a potential future—the moment is often the extent of the temporal field. There is no trust or belief in the future, for, as Loewald (1962) points out, a true sense of the future develops only with full superego formation in the resolution of the oedipal crisis.

Conceptual representations have achieved an integration of contradictory and ambivalently perceived part properties and attributes. They are based on inner form and structure and on abstract enduring qualities of the object. Therefore, these representations have continuity, they transcend time and are independent of the physical properties or presence of the object. The role of conceptual representations in dealing with object loss and depression is probably best illustrated by Freud's response to his friend Ludwig Binswanger on learning of the tragic death of Binswanger's eldest son. Freud wrote:

> We know that the acute grief we feel after a loss will come to an end but that we will remain inconsolable, and will never find a substitute. Everything that comes to take the place of the lost object, even if it fills it completely, nevertheless remains something different. And in fact it is a good thing that it should be so. It is the only way of perpetuating love, which we do not wish to give up [Binswanger, 1957, p. 84].

SUMMARY

Object representation is an evolving developmental process. New levels of object representation are achieved as the result of a consolidation (equilibration) of each developmental sequence. The development of object representation occurs through successive epigenetic stages including the sensorimotor, perceptual, iconic, and conceptual levels of development. At each of these levels, object representations become less literal and direct and more abstract and symbolic. Impairments in the development of object representation can occur at each of these levels, and each can have an important role in the potential vulnerability to depression. Actual, apparent, or fantasized object loss is often a major precipitant of depression because impairments in the development of object representation leave the individual vulnerable to object loss and to depression.

Based on a review of the theoretical, clinical, and research literature on depression and a formulation of levels of object representation derived from developmental psychology and psychoanalytic theory, an anaclitic and an introjective depression were differentiated. An anaclitic depression is characterized by feelings of helplessness, weakness, and depletion, and by wishes to be cared for, loved, fed, and protected. There are intense fears of being abandoned, oral cravings, and an urgency to fill an inner emptiness. In contrast to the oral quality of an anaclitic depression, the primary characteristics of an introjective depression derive from a harsh, punitive, and critical superego, resulting in intense feelings of inferiority, worthlessness, guilt, and a wish for atonement. There are concerns about having failed to live up to expectations, and there are struggles to win approval and recognition, but there is little lasting satisfaction.

In both anaclitic and introjective depression, there is impairment in the processes of internalization and in the development of object representations. In anaclitic depression, the representation of objects is primarily based on action sequences, and there is a need to maintain direct physical, sensory, need-gratifying contact with the object. Because of this impairment in object representations there is a vulnerability to profound feelings of loneliness. In introjective depression, there is a somewhat greater capacity for object representations, but the concept of the object is still usually at a perceptual or iconic level. Representations are fragmented, pictorial, concrete, and contradictory. They are limited in scope and range, and literal and depictive, and contain intense ambivalent, hostile and aggressive, overidealized and idyllic features. Because of the somewhat higher level of object representation in introjective depression, there is not the intense need for immediate and direct physical contact with the object. But there is a need for continued experiences with the object, or aspects of the object, to provide the stimulation necessary to maintain representations of the object. The presence of guilt, however, indicates that object representations are on a somewhat higher level because guilt requires some differentiated and reflective sense of self and some appreciation of causality both in assuming responsibility for an event and in considering ways of atonement. In addition, there is a struggle in introjective depression to resolve the contradictions and ambivalence inherent in the separate and fragmented representations which are based on extreme and overstated features.

At the highest developmental level, object representations are based on a complex, differentiated, and integrated articulation of the object and are experienced in conceptual and symbolic form. Objects are represented as consistent and stable, with a temporal dimension of both past and future and with complex and diverse properties. The representations are based on inner form rather than on manifest features of the object; therefore there is no longer a need for the physical or perceptual presence of the object to support the representations. There is relatively little vulnerability to severe and protracted depression associated with object loss. The consideration of levels of object representations facilitates a fuller appreciation of some of the mechanisms of depression and aids in the differentiation between two types of depression—an anaclitic and an introjective depression.

BIBLIOGRAPHY

ABRAHAM, K. (1911), Notes on the Psycho-Analytical Investigation and Treatment of Manic-Depressive Insanity and Allied Conditions. *Selected Papers on Psycho-Analysis.* London: Hogarth Press, 1927, pp. 137–156.

———— (1916), The First Pre-Genital Stage of the Libido. *Ibid.,* pp. 248–279.

———— (1924), A Short Study of the Development of the Libido. *Ibid.,* pp. 418–501.

ABRAHAM, H. C. & FREUD, E. L., eds. (1965), *The Letters of Sigmund Freud and Karl Abraham 1907–1926.* New York: Basic Books.

ANTHONY, E. J. (1970), Two Contrasting Types of Adolescent Depression and Their Treatment. *J. Amer. Psychoanal. Assn.,* 18:841–859.

BECK, A. T. (1967), *Depression.* New York: Harper & Row.

BELL, S. (1970), The Development of the Concept of the Object As Related to the Infant-Mother Attachment. *Child Develpm.,* 41:291–311.

BENJAMIN, J. D. (1961), Some Developmental Observations Relating to the Theory of Anxiety. *J. Amer. Psychoanal. Assn.,* 9:652–668.

BERES, D. (1966), Superego and Depression. In: *Psychoanalysis—A General Psychology,* ed. R. M. Loewenstein, L. M. Newman, M. Schur, & A. J. Solnit. New York: International Universities Press, pp. 479–498.

———— & JOSEPH, E. D. (1970), The Concept of Mental Representation in Psychoanalysis, *Int. J. Psycho-Anal.,* 51:1–9.

BIBRING, E. (1953), The Mechanism of Depression. In: *Affective Disorders,* ed. P. Greenacre. New York: International Universities Press, 1966, pp. 13–48.

BINSWANGER, L. (1957) *Sigmund Freud: Reminiscences of a Friendship.* New York: Grune & Stratton.

BLATT, S. J. (1966), Review of *Neurotic Styles* by D. Shapiro. *Psychiatry,* 29:426–427.

———— (1971), Object Representation in Psychoses. Presented at the meeting of American Psychological Association.

———— & RITZLER, B. A. (1974), Thought Disorder and Boundary Disturbances in Psychosis. *J. Consult, Clin. Psychol.,* 42:370–381.

———— & WILD, C. M. (1974), *Schizophrenia: A Developmental Analysis.* New York: Academic Press (in press).

BRUNER, J. (1964), The Course of Cognitive Growth. *Amer. Psychologist,* 19:1–15.

BURGNER, M. & EDGCUMBE, R. (1972), Some Problems in the Conceptualization of Early Object Relationships. *This Annual*, 27:315–333.

CAMERON, N. (1963), *Personality Development and Psychopathology*. Boston: Houghton Mifflin.

COBLINER, W. G. (1965), The Geneva School of Genetic Psychology and Psychoanalysis. In: R. A. Spitz, *The First Year of Life*. New York: International Universities Press, pp. 301–356.

COHEN, M. B., BAKER, G., COHEN, R. A., FROMM-REICHMAN, F., & WEIGERT, E. (1954), An Intensive Study of Twelve Cases of Manic Depressive Psychosis. *Psychiatry*, 17:103–137.

D'AFFLITTI, J. (1973), Dimensions of a Depressive Character Structure. Dissertation for Degree of Doctor of Philosophy, Yale University.

DÉCARIE, T. G. (1965), *Intelligence and Affectivity in Early Childhood*. New York: International Universities Press.

DEUTSCH, H. (1933), The Psychology of Manic-Depressive States, with Particular Reference to Chronic Hypomania. *Neuroses and Character Types*. New York: International Universities Press, pp. 203–217.

ENGEL, G. L. & REICHSMAN, F. (1956), Spontaneous and Experimentally Induced Depressions in an Infant with a Gastric Fistula. *J. Amer. Psychoanal. Assn.*, 4:428–452.

ERIKSON, E. H. (1950), *Childhood and Society*. New York: Norton.

FENICHEL, O. (1945), *The Psychoanalytic Theory of Neurosis*. New York: Norton.

FRAIBERG, S. (1969), Libidinal Object Constancy and Mental Representation. *This Annual*, 24:9–47.

FREUD, A. (1946), The Psychoanalytic Study of Infantile Feeding Disturbances. *This Annual*, 2:119–132.

——— (1952), The Mutual Influences in the Development of Ego and Id. *This Annual*, 7:42–50.

——— (1965), *Normality and Pathology in Childhood*. New York: International Universities Press.

——— (1968), Panel Discussion. *Int. J. Psycho-Anal.*, 49:506–512.

FREUD, S. (1900), The Interpretation of Dreams. *Standard Edition*, 4 & 5. London: Hogarth Press, 1953.

——— (1914), On Narcissism. *Standard Edition*, 14:67–102. London: Hogarth Press, 1957.

——— (1916), Some Character-Types Met with in Psycho-analytic Work. *Standard Edition*, 14:311–333. London: Hogarth Press, 1957.

——— (1916–17), Introductory Lectures on Psycho-Analysis. *Standard Edition*, 15 & 16. London: Hogarth Press, 1963.

——— (1917), Mourning and Melancholia. *Standard Edition*, 14:243–258. London: Hogarth Press, 1957.

——— (1921), Group Psychology and the Analysis of the Ego. *Standard Edition*, 18:69–143. London: Hogarth Press, 1955.

——— (1923), The Ego and the Id. *Standard Edition*, 19:12–59. London: Hogarth Press, 1961.

FREUD, S. (1926), Inhibitions, Symptoms and Anxiety. *Standard Edition*, 20:77–175. London: Hogarth Press, 1959.

GRINKER, R. R., MILLER, J., SABSHIN, M., NUNN, R., & NUNNALLY, J. (1961), *The Phenomenon of Depressions*. New York: Hoeber.

GUNTRIP, H. (1969), *Schizoid Phenomena, Object Relations and the Self.* New York: International Universities Press.

HARTMANN, H. (1952), The Mutual Influences in the Development of Ego and Id. *Essays on Ego Psychology*. New York: International Universities Press, 1964, pp. 155–181.

———— (1953), Contribution to the Metapsychology of Schizophrenia. *Ibid.*, pp. 182–206.

———— (1956), Notes on the Reality Principle. *Ibid.*, pp. 241–267.

———— KRIS, E., & LOEWENSTEIN, R. M. (1949), Notes on the Theory of Aggression. *This Annual*, 3/4:9–36.

HOFFER, W. (1955), *Psychoanalysis.* Baltimore: Williams & Wilkins.

HOROWITZ, M. J. (1972), Modes of Representation of Thought. *J. Amer. Psychoanal. Assn.*, 20:793–819.

JACOBSON, E. (1946), The Effect of Disappointment on Ego and Superego Formation in Normal and Depressive Development. *Psychoanal. Rev.*, 33:129–147.

———— (1953), Contribution to the Metapsychology of Cyclothymic Depression. In: *Affective Disorders*, ed. P. Greenacre. New York: International Universities Press, pp. 49–83.

———— (1954), Contribution to the Metapsychology of Psychotic Identifications. *J. Amer. Psychoanal. Assn.*, 2:239–264.

———— (1964), *The Self and the Object World.* New York: International Universities Press.

———— (1966), Problems in the Differentiation between Schizophrenic and Melancholic States of Depression. In: *Psychoanalysis—A General Psychology*, ed. R. M. Loewenstein, L. Newman, M. Schur, & A. J. Solnit. New York: International Universities Press, pp. 499–518.

———— (1971), *Depression.* New York: International Universities Press.

JARVIE, H. F. (1950), On Atypicality and the Depressive State. *J. Ment. Sci.*, 96:208–225.

KAPLAN, L. (1972), Object Constancy in the Light of Piaget's Vertical Décalage. *Bull. Menninger Clin.*, 36:322–334.

KESTENBERG, J. S. (1971), From Organ-Object Imagery to Self and Object Representations. In: *Separation-Individuation*, ed. J. B. McDevitt & C. F. Settlage. New York: International Universities Press, pp. 75–99.

KLEIN, M. (1934), A Contribution to the Psychogenesis of Manic-Depressive States. *Contributions to Psycho-Analysis*. London: Hogarth Press, 1948, pp. 282–310.

KRIS, E. (1950), Notes on the Development and on Some Current Problems of Psychoanalytic Child Psychology. *This Annual*, 5:24–46.

LEWIN, B. D. (1950), *The Psychoanalysis of Elation.* New York: Norton.

LOEWALD, H. W. (1962), Internalization, Separation, Mourning, and the Super-ego. *Psychoanal. Quart.*, 31:483–504.

MAHLER, M. S. (1965), On the Significance of the Normal Separation-Individuation Phase. In: *Drives, Affects, Behavior*, Vol. 2, ed. M. Schur. New York: International Universities Press, pp. 161–169.

────── (1968), *On Human Symbiosis and the Vicissitudes of Individuation*. New York: International Universities Press.

MENDELSON, M. (1960), *Psychoanalytic Concepts of Depression*. Springfield: Charles C Thomas.

NACHT, S. & RACAMIER, P. C. (1960), Depressive States. *Int. J. Psycho-Anal.*, 41:481–496.

NOVEY, S. (1958), The Meaning of the Concept of Mental Representation of Objects. *Psychoanal. Quart.*, 27:57–79.

PIAGET, J. (1937), *The Construction of Reality in the Child*. New York: Basic Books, 1954.

────── (1945), *Play, Dreams and Imitation in Childhood*. New York: Norton, 1951.

────── & INHELDER, B. (1966), *The Psychology of the Child*. New York: Basic Books, 1969.

PROVENCE, S. & LIPTON, R. C. (1962), *Infants in Institutions*. New York: International Universities Press.

RADO, S. (1928), The Problems of Melancholia. *Int. J. Psycho-Anal.*, 9:420–438.

RAPAPORT, D. (1950), On the Psychoanalytic Theory of Thinking. In: *Psychoanalytic Psychiatry and Psychology*, ed. R. P. Knight & C. R. Friedman. New York: International Universities Press, 1954, pp. 259–273.

────── (1953), On the Psychoanalytic Theory of Affects. *Ibid.*, pp. 274–310.

ROCHLIN, G. (1965), *Grief and Discontents*. Boston: Little, Brown.

ROSE, G. (1962), Unconscious Birth Fantasies in the Ninth Month of Treatment. *J. Amer. Psychoanal. Assn.*, 10:677–688.

ROTH, D., & BLATT, S. J. (1974), Spatial Representations and Psychopathology. *J. Amer. Psychoanal. Assn.* (in press).

RUBENFINE, D. L. (1968), Notes on a Theory of Depression. *Psychoanal. Quart.*, 37:400–417.

SANDLER, J. & JOFFE, W. G. (1965), Notes on Childhood Depression. *Int. J. Psycho-Anal.*, 46:88–96.

────── & ROSENBLATT, B. (1962), The Concept of the Representational World. *This Annual*, 17:128–145.

SCHAFER, R. (1968), *Aspects of Internalization*. New York: International Universities Press.

SCHMALE, A. H. (1972), Depression As Affect, Character Style, and Symptom Formation. In: *Psychoanalysis and Contemporary Science*, ed. R. R. Holt & E. Peterfreund. New York: Macmillan, pp. 327–351.

SEGAL, H. (1964), *Introduction to the Work of Melanie Klein*. London: Heinemann.

SMITH, J. H. (1970), On the Structural View of Affect. *J. Amer. Psychoanal. Assn.*, 18:539–561.

SPITZ, R. A. (1965), *The First Year of Life*. New York: International Universities Press.

—— & WOLF, K. M. (1946), Anaclitic Depression. *This Annual*, 2:313–342.

WEISS, E. (1944), Clinical Aspects of Depression. *Psychoanal. Quart.*, 13:445–461.

WERNER, H. (1948), *Comparative Psychology of Mental Development*. New York: International Universities Press, 1957.

—— & KAPLAN, B. (1963), *Symbol Formation*. New York: Wiley.

WINNICOTT, D. W. (1954), The Depressive Position in Normal Emotional Development. *Brit. J. Med. Psychol.*, 28:89–100.

WOLFF, P. H. (1960), *The Developmental Psychologies of Jean Piaget and Psychoanalysis* [*Psychological Issues*, Monogr. 5]. New York: International Universities Press.

—— (1967), Cognitive Considerations for a Psychoanalytic Theory of Language Acquisition. In: *Motives and Thought*, ed. R. R. Holt [*Psychological Issues*, 18/19:299–343]. New York: International Universities Press.

ZETZEL, E. R. (1953), "The Depressive Position." In: *Affective Disorders*, ed. P. Greenacre. New York: International Universities Press, pp. 84–116.

—— (1960), Introduction to the Symposium on 'Depressive Illness.' *Int. J. Psycho-Anal.*, 41:476–480.

—— (1965), Depression and the Incapacity to Bear It. In: *Drives, Affects, Behavior*, Vol. 2, ed. M. Schur. New York: International Universities Press, pp. 243–274.

Current Status of the Concept of Infantile Neurosis

Implications for Diagnosis and Technique

SAMUEL RITVO, M.D.

PAST AND PRESENT PSYCHOANALYTIC FORMULATIONS
OF INFANTILE NEUROSIS

THE CONCEPT OF THE INFANTILE NEUROSIS HAS BEEN AN INTEGRAL
part of psychoanalysis since Little Hans and the Wolf-Man (Freud,
1909, 1918). Anna Freud (1971) points out that in these early years
of psychoanalytic discoveries the focus was on the neuroses of adult
life and not on infantile psychopathology. The infantile neurosis,
whether directly observed or reconstructed, was studied mainly for
the light it could throw on the genetic and dynamic aspects of the
adult neuroses and on differentiating their diagnostic characteristics
from other types of psychopathology.

Infantile neuroses and the relevance of childhood experiences for
the formation of adult disturbances were new findings. Those early
studies also demonstrated the concordances between infantile and
adult disorders in their motivation by conflict, their construction,

Clinical Professor of Psychiatry, Child Study Center and Department of
Psychiatry, Yale University School of Medicine. Faculty, Western New England
Institute for Psychoanalysis and New York Psychoanalytic Institute.

Parts of this paper were presented at a panel of the Association for Child
Psychoanalysis, Paris, July 22, 1973. Also presented as the Freud Lecture at the
Psychoanalytic Association of New York, May 20, 1974.

the mechanisms employed, and the function of symptom formation. These and other basic formulations regarding the infantile neurosis have stood the test of time very well. The infantile neurosis as defined by the steps involved in the formation of neuroses—"conflict, followed by regression; regressive aims arousing anxiety; anxiety warded off by means of defense; conflict solution via compromise; symptom formation" (A. Freud, 1971, p. 80)—is still regarded as coming to a peak in the phallic-oedipal period. Only then has mental development and personality organization reached the degree of differentiation which makes possible the formation of a neurosis that structurally and dynamically resembles the adult neuroses. The leading factors responsible for this development are the phase-specific conflicts of this period (castration anxiety, penis envy, oedipus complex) and the increased potential for intrapsychic conflict that arises with the beginning formation of the superego.

In contrast to the past, Anna Freud sees psychoanalysis engaged at present in an effort to construct a detailed description of infantile mental difficulties and in an understanding and explanation of those factors which interfere with optimal growth and development. This trend was already strongly in evidence at the Arden House Conference on Problems of Infantile Neurosis (E. Kris et al., 1954), where the term infantile neurosis was used in the two senses defined by Greenacre: "one, meaning the outbreak of overt neurotic symptoms in the period of infancy, i.e., approximately before the age of six; a second, meaning the inner structure of infantile development, with or without manifest symptoms, which forms, however, the basis of a *later neurosis*" (p. 18). Most of the contributions to this discussion dealt with infantile neurosis in the latter sense.

In earliest infancy the prime factors in development are the constitutional characteristics of the infant and the mothering care as they reflect or convey the attitudes, fantasies, anxieties, and conflicts of the mother in relation to the child. The satisfaction-frustration experiences which are primarily centered on the infant's bodily needs take on their uniquely individual qualities via the interaction between the child and his human environment. On the child's side we can attempt to identify, describe, and roughly quantify such features as the manifestations of the infant's intrinsic drive rhythms, his patterns of discharge, the qualities of his stimulus barrier, the presence of unusual sensitivities. The care the infant receives is a major factor in the balance between satisfaction and frustration, pleasure and unpleasure. We can conceptualize the earliest conflicts as being mainly between the instinctual drives of the infant and the ability of the human environment to satisfy them. It is in this context that the differentiation of the ego and id begins to take place.

Loewald's (1971) recent studies on motivation and instinct in relation to the object afford us a new dimension from which to view the early development of the child. Loewald reexamines the psychoanalytic concept of instincts, which he defines as "psychic, motivational forces, [which] become organized as such through interactions within a psychic field consisting originally of the mother-child (psychic) unit" (p. 118). He regards the instincts as representational psychic forces which become transformed and organized through interactions within the mother-child psychic field. In this view, the neonate's behavior becomes organized into instincts with aims by activities and responses coming from the environment. This emphasis on the psychological development of instincts is useful in understanding both the normal range of variation in infant mental development and the disturbances of development arising from failures or excesses of the environment which have a damaging effect on the organization of normal and healthy psychic structures and the specific qualities of object relations. This view of instinct is also helpful in understanding what appears to be a lack of instinctual drive in deprived infants who have never experienced the organizing and excitatory influence of a consistent, interested, central love object. Furthermore, the fact that so many of the child's earliest neurotic symptoms involve anxieties and fantasies about his own body can also be explained in terms of the continuous concern, interest, protection, and care of his body by the adult.

The object gains its great significance for the developing infant at first via its function in the satisfaction of needs and its relation to shifts in the balance of pleasure-unpleasure. The relationship to the object then has an expanding function in the maturation of id and ego and therefore enormous significance for future development, both normal and pathological. Such important features of the personality as the tendency or disposition to conflict; the preference for particular defense mechanisms; the quality of anxiety and the capacity of the ego to tolerate anxiety and conflict—all these are strongly influenced in a formative way by the early interaction between primary apparatus factors and the mothering care experienced by the infant.

The frequency and variety of mental disturbances in children are great because of the child's vulnerability to external and internal stresses. Because the child's internal bodily needs and rhythms are not from the beginning in time with the patterns of the adult environment, he is liable to developmental disturbances involving bodily functions (A. Freud, 1965). How the bodily needs are managed by the mother is significant for later personality development and psychopathology. The child's ego will take an attitude toward the instinctual drives which is similar to that of the mother. The ego may be lenient or may oppose and deny satisfactions, attitudes that result in a tendency to conflict. Fluctuations in the quantity and quality of the instinctual drives in relation to the shift from one developmental phase to another also are accompanied by developmental disturbances, for example, the orderly and meticulous behavior of some children in the anal phase, and the castration anxiety and death wishes of the phallic-oedipal phase. Even though the external manifestations of these disturbances often resemble neurotic symptoms, they subside when the child enters the latency period.

Although we might have difficulty pinpointing the earliest age at which neurotic symptoms can make their appearance, we can outline the mental capacities the child must have to do so. The first requirement is the presence of conflict, which in the young child can be between his wishes originating in the instinctual drives and the external world which exists most cogently in the persons to whom the child is attached, whose love and approval he seeks to gain or retain, and who are necessary for his survival. Another essential is that the wish related to the conflict be capable of transference onto another thought which can give expression to one or more aspects of the conflict. This can occur only if memory traces and mnemic images exist.

The neurotic disturbances in childhood employ the same basic mechanisms in their formation as are used later in the construction of adult neurotic illness. Recent studies have emphasized that isolated symptoms do occur in younger children prior to the phallic-oedipal phase (A. Freud, 1965, 1971; Nagera, 1966). Actually, children are capable of forming neurotic symptoms as soon as they are capable of dreams which go beyond simple wish fulfillment and involve dream work. Regression is involved in the process in two ways: first, the use of sensory images as a mode of representation in what Freud (1900) called "the shortest path to wish fulfillment" (p. 566); and second, the regression to earlier forms of gratification.

The earliest neurotic symptoms usually involve basic body functions such as eating and sleeping and appear most frequently in reaction to the usual childhood traumas—separation, loss, bodily injury, awareness of anatomical differences, the birth of a sibling. They can be treated, often with dramatic success, by the correction of a child's distorted fantasy or inadequate understanding of an experience. The treatment draws upon the analyst's knowledge of how the displacements, transferences, and symbolizations operate in the formation of the neurotic symptom. The analyst then attempts to reconstruct the trauma. Aided by the verbalizations of the analyst or the parents under the guidance of the analyst, the therapeutic effect lies in the child's ego being able to master the anxiety connected with the trauma and the symptom itself. Providing opportunities for the child to play out actively what he has experienced passively contributes to his mastery of the trauma.

The universality of neurotic symptoms in childhood and the high frequency of more complex and structured neuroses in the phallic-oedipal period are a consequence of the basic primary process mechanisms which are relatively predominant over the less developed cognitive, synthetic, and reality-testing functions of the ego in early childhood. The progressive involvement of these ego functions in the formation of neurosis is reflected in the greater complexity, more intricate structure, and elaborate compromise formations of the neuroses arising in the phallic-oedipal period and thereafter. With the formation of the superego, the locus of the conflict shifts to the intrapsychic, intersystemic conflicts of the latency period.

Although early ambivalence conflicts and anal-sadistic regression have a large share in the formation of obsessional neurosis, the latter also reflects the progressive development of the ego as the symptoms are more predominantly mental and involve abstractions rather than the more bodily rooted symptoms of the preoedipal period.

Implications for Diagnosis and Technique

In the past several decades the direct observational studies and the longitudinal studies of infants and children, in some instances combined with child analysis, have extended our knowledge of the early, severe, developmental disturbances arising from constitutional and environmental factors and have sharpened our capacity to diagnose them. We are better able to distinguish between the child who is regressed or retarded on a broad front and the child who develops an isolated neurotic symptom which may include regressive manifestations. We have also become aware that a wide range of recovery is possible. This may occur spontaneously, for example, when the child enters a new phase of development which elicits a response from the mother more syntonic with the child's developmental needs for reasons of the mother's own internal conflicts or life circumstances (Coleman et al., 1953; E. Kris, 1962). The extension of our knowledge has also led to a broader spectrum of interventions. More refined developmental diagnosis makes possible the application of specific therapeutic measures in the preoedipal period. Identified conflicts can be verbalized or interpreted in the manner and setting judged most appropriate. This can be done by the analyst individually or in cooperation with the teacher in nursery school, or by the parents under the guidance of the child analyst. When an arrest or deviation in the child's development is due to an incompatibility between the parents' personality characteristics and the child's needs at a particular period, the therapist can function as a new object who may be more available to the child for the satisfaction of inner needs and enable the child to reach a higher developmental level.

Our greater appreciation of the wide variations and fluctuations within the normal range over the course of individual development affects our concepts concerning diagnosis and technique in border-line conditions and neuroses. We are less likely to be doctrinaire in regarding imprecise clinical entities such as the borderline condi-tions as being completely distinct from the neuroses. What we can observe directly are clinical pictures in which the child has such early lags and deficits in the development of ego functions, frequently aggravated by disturbances in the mother-child relation-ship, that they raise the diagnostic question of organic impairment or psychosis. Yet, the same child may also have isolated neurotic symptoms in the prephallic period and then go on to develop elaborately structured neuroses in the phallic-oedipal period. The phase-specific conflicts of the phallic-oedipal period exert a strong influence on the ideational content and imagery of the symptom (castration anxiety, penis envy, the wish to have a child). With such children the analyst may even gain the clinical impression that their phase-specific anxieties and conflicts have had a stimulating and organizing effect on the ego.

The normal developmental crises of childhood such as weaning, separation, sphincter control, and the phallic-oedipal rivalry, which are crucial for later development, are points of fixation, regression —and progression. They can constitute a stimulus or a barrier to ego development. In these crises, aptitudes and abilities become more available to the personality at the same time as susceptibilities and vulnerabilities may be heightened. New modes of adaptation and defense may make their appearance, or established modes may become more structured and through change of function make important contributions to the personality.

The menarche is an example of a normal developmental crisis which can precipitate regression and psychopathological reactions or mobilize the ego for progression. The initial reaction frequently includes an element of disgust and revulsion followed by reaction formation, because it is conceived and experienced as an excretory function on the model of the old and familiar anal and urinary functions. The most severe psychopathological reactions are likely to occur in two groups, one of them being girls in whom the menarche occurs very early, at 8 or 9 years. These very young girls usually have not had a sufficiently long period in latency to consolidate the various attempted solutions of their preoedipal and oedipal conflicts and to establish and strengthen appropriate defenses before the pubertal crisis. In the other group are girls whose intense penis envy, feelings of castration and inferiority, coupled with ambivalence conflicts toward the mother, have predisposed them to react to the menarche, the physical confirmation of their femininity, with anger, depression, and severe body-image problems. On the other hand, in many girls the menarche is accompanied by increased self-confidence and assurance, pride in its significance, a firmer and more satisfying sense of identity as a woman, and much greater activity and assertiveness in the pursuit of interests and goals about which they have hitherto been diffident or discouraged. In any case, the outcome of the menarche as a normal developmental crisis is determined by its relation to the earlier infantile neurosis.

Whether the ego of the child is strengthened by a normal crisis or not is partly dependent on the parental attitude and reaction to the child's behavior during a particular phase or critical period. The child's conflict or distress may threaten to aggravate the parents' own neurotic conflicts, or increase their vulnerability to regression and intensify their defenses against it. In contrast, just as some parents function best when the child is ill, others may be most supportive to the child when he is in a developmental crisis, with its attendant anxieties and symptoms, and thereby contribute to the development of his ego.

Similarly, in the analytic situation, the child may use the analyst not only as a transference but also as a new (or real) object in his attempts to reach a higher level of organization and integration. This use of the analyst may be facilitated by the unique nature of the analytic situation, in which the child is encouraged to reveal and express the very thoughts and feelings that in other life situations he is required to conceal. Thus, in a very real sense, the analytic situation offers the child a new relationship. In his role as a new object the analyst functions as a protector of the child's progressive development. The attitudes of the child's parents may further contribute to the fact that the analyst frequently finds himself in the position of safeguarding the child's development. Rather than viewing the analyst as being in competition with them, the parents, very much out of their own guilt, desire the analyst to mitigate or undo what they feel is their harmful effect on the child.

The vulnerability to neurotic conflict is rooted in the differentiation of ego and id and the ego's inability to protect itself from the internal sources of conflict without resorting to repression and neurosis, which in turn result in impairments of the ego. The wide variation of clinical pictures presented by the neuroses on one end of the continuum and the so-called borderline conditions on the other end is a consequence of the ego modifications resulting from the early interaction of the constitutional factors in the infant and the qualities of the mothering care (Ritvo and Solnit, 1958). Mothering care which contributes to developmental disturbances because it is unsuitable for the needs of the child at that time may actually result in a premature or precocious distinction between inner and outer world. Although this may hasten the differentiation of ego and id, it may have a traumatic effect by exposing the infant to inundation by outside stimuli when the organism has no suitable defense against such inundation in the form of either flight or avoidance and is developmentally incapable of defense or flight via neurosis. In the borderline conditions or narcissistic disorders, this may result in such features as an intolerance of frustration, intense ambivalence conflicts, difficulty in mastering unusual intensities of aggression, and a rapid rate of ego regression. These vulnerabilities may persist despite superior functioning in other parts of the personality and high achievements in work and community. They may coexist with a complex and intricately structured neurosis, which may be largely elaborated in the phallic-oedipal and latency periods. The specific qualities of and the lacks in the object relations which arise make for special transference and technical problems in the analyses of such persons, both children and adults.

Many psychoanalysts have a pronounced tendency to regard neuroses and borderline conditions as quite separate diagnostic categories, usually considering the former as transference neuroses and the latter as narcissistic disorders (Kohut, 1971). Child observation, child analysis, and longitudinal studies would suggest that it is useful to formulate the problem differently.

Frankie, analyzed as a child by Bornstein (1949) and by myself as an adult (1966), is a case in point. The child analyst found a similarity between the temper tantrums in latency when his wishes

were not satisfied and his screaming for hours for food and
comforting as an infant when the night feeding was stopped. In
latency, this analogy was the most telling part of the interpretation
given him: the demanding, omnipotent qualities were linked, in a
defensive manner, with longings for passive gratification. When as a
child his passive desires increased in intensity, Frankie had violent
attacks of panic in which he seemed unable to distinguish between
fantasy and reality. These wishes and these ways of defending
against them were present in the transference in the adult analysis.
His ego retained an infantile quality, which had its oldest roots in
the early interaction of the drives and the mothering care. A degree
of sameness persisted as the ego evolved in subsequent development.
The severe distortions in the ego remained closely linked to the
memories of the old conflicts and to their repetitions in the present.
Their severity and fixity, however, did not prevent the formation of
a transference neurosis along the lines of the basic mechanisms and
intrapsychic processes detailed earlier. The point of view that the
presence of severe ego distortions or extensive ego regression at a
time of acute conflict makes an individual like Frankie a borderline
case and incapable of developing a transference neurosis (Blos,
1972) is not in accordance with the observations in the psychoanalytic situation, where the "borderline" and "transference" phenomena are found to exist side by side. Thus, the problem may be
better conceptualized by asking: what has remained the same?
What has changed? How have these changes affected the old
constellations? And how do they mutually influence each other at
the present time?

The new findings concerning early development have influenced
our thinking about psychoanalytic technique with both children
and adults. Our newer knowledge of the environment, our fuller
understanding of the symbiotic mother-child relationship, and the
steps by which separation and individuation from the primary
object take place (Mahler, 1971), have led child analysts to new
attempts at influencing early deviations and retardations in ego
development as part of their technique. For children in whom
imbalances and ego defects exist Weil (1973) proposes preparatory
educational therapeutic help, which has the aims of making up for
early interactional failures and of stimulating ego growth and better

integration prior to analysis. New techniques may involve elements of gratification for a child who has been severely deprived so that in the opening phase the analysis may be conducted less in abstinence than we might have done in earlier times. We may feel freer to permit the child to use the analyst as a positive, supportive, and stabilizing adult when one or both parents have been unable to function that way with the child, or when the excessive and protracted aggression of the parents has compromised the child's capacity for libidinal attachments. In fact, in long analyses where such conditions prevail, the child analyst may be pressed into the role of an alternate parent by the child whether he intends it or not.

The recognition that a greater degree of instinctual gratification, albeit aim-inhibited, may be necessary in the analysis of children who have extensive or severe ego modifications again raises an issue referred to earlier—the analyst as a new object. Anna Freud (1965) points out that for children the analyst has a significant function as a new object in enabling the child to reach a new level of development.

The analyst becomes a significant object to the child in a number of ways, some of which have been mentioned earlier. The parents may regard the analyst as necessary for the child's well-being, a view which immediately makes a strong impression on the child. This facilitates the child's making his own transferences from the primary objects to the analyst, a process also impelled by the child's own need to find relief from anxiety and distressing symptoms. All these forces together with the regressive pull of the analytic situation contribute to the child's cathecting the analyst as a new object for the inner developmental needs and strivings which are an integral part of a current phase of development or an earlier period of development. The analyst's interest and attention which are part of the caring, supportive, "diatrophic" attitude of the analyst (Spitz, 1956), no matter what the age of the patient, further induce transferences and the cathexis of the analyst as a new object.

Although more pronounced in child analysis, the analyst as a new object is a significant element in adult analysis as well. Bibring (1937) spoke of the push to complete development as a dynamic force in the psychoanalytic process and spoke of the analyst and the analysis as new experiences enhancing the maturational process. In his study of the opening phase of analysis Gitelson (1962) drew the analogy of the mother-child relation to the analytic relationship. Via the basic transference (Greenacre, 1971) the analyst is cathected as an object who then can potentiate the individual's thrust to complete his development. All patients come to analysis seeking to redo large portions of their lives and their development. Through the transference they look to the analyst to be the father or mother they always wanted. In the "average expectable" psychoanalytic situation, we rely on the analyst's interest, attention, and understanding, and on his trained skill in establishing and maintaining the psychoanalytic situation to insure that the analyst will be available to the patient as a new and different object for the reexperiencing of old relationships which have been powerful etiological factors in childhood disturbances and in the structure of the infantile neurosis. However, specific personality traits, countertransferences, and insufficiently analyzed or unanalyzable conflicts in the analyst may result in a relationship to the analyst which tends to repeat the old disturbed or neurotic relationship to the parents to such a degree that the analyst cannot become the sought-for and needed new object. The analysis is then severely compromised or impossible.

Other problems arise when the child analyst, after the termination of a child's analysis, continues to maintain contact with the child. A clinical illustration is the case of Frankie. In the analysis as an adult it became abundantly clear that the child analyst who had analyzed him for nearly five years between the ages of 5 and 9 and who had been consulted by Frankie and his family for many years thereafter had become, emotionally and psychologically, a surrogate and alternate parent for him. She had also functioned as a significant real object in a subsequent developmental crisis which she analyzed and lived through with him. When he was considering analysis as an adult, he knew that he could seek her advice and recommendations—indeed, he would not embark on a new analysis without her specific recommendations—but he was also aware of his wish to *spare her* the trials and tribulations that his transference in a renewed analysis with her would cause her.

A second clinical illustration is again a longitudinal observation.

Evelyne was followed from birth in a longitudinal study of child development[1] for the first five years of her life and then in a psychoanalytic family study to the age of 11. I also saw her in follow-up interviews throughout her adolescence and as a young adult up to the age of 22, when she had a brief period of psychotherapy. The long period of analytic treatment and the repeated follow-ups provide an unusual opportunity, as in the case of Frankie, to make observations on the transference and the relationship to the analyst as a new object. I shall focus on the oedipal and latency periods.

When Evelyne began her analysis at the age of $3\frac{1}{2}$ years, she had lost the special position she had enjoyed as the welcomed first child who had established the new couple as parents and constituted a new nuclear family. The birth of two younger sisters had altered Evelyne's relationship to her parents. She no longer had the exclusive relationship with her mother, which had been such an important factor in her precocious ego development and in the remarkably early sublimations which she developed on the basis of an identification with her mother (E. Kris, 1955; Ritvo and Solnit, 1958). Her father's wish for a son, frustrated by the birth of two more daughters, persisted and found partial gratification in his identifying the physical activities and skills of the younger sisters with boyish qualities. Evelyne did not lend herself to this because of her awkwardness, which annoyed both parents. She tried doggedly for a long time to develop skills in order to please her father. Another severe obstacle in her efforts to win over her father was the fact, substantiated in his own analysis, that he unconsciously identified Evelyne with his own older sister for whom he had an intense antipathy because she had blighted his relationship with his father and had been the cause of severe disappointments and frustrations in his aspirations and opportunities for a professional career.

This virtual absence of love from her father was coupled with her mother's growing disappointment in Evelyne. Thus, in early latency, Evelyne presented the picture of an intellectually inhibited

---

[1] Various aspects of Evelyne's development have been reported elsewhere (E. Kris, 1955; Ritvo and Solnit, 1958; Ritvo, 1972; M. Kris, 1972).

and physically awkward child whose feminine libidinal development was blocked. Nor did she show any significant masculine strivings or envy of the male, tendencies which might have led her to active mastery and gratification. She wanted to please and be loved, but could find no certain or promising way. Periodically, the vicissitudes of family life brought a shift in her fortunes. When her father immersed himself in adding a room to the house and she could be helpful, he reacted positively to her for a short time. Evelyne's response to his interest in her was evident in the analysis: she became more lively, but also more messy and regressive in her play, and once again displayed her capacity for sublimation in drawing and painting. Another temporary improvement in her relationship with her father occurred after a summer at the shore where she could share her father's enthusiasm for boating and swimming, whereas the middle sister, whom the father identified more closely with himself and regarded as the wished-for son, was afraid of the water and had further fallen from favor because of her unruliness.

In the analysis Evelyne transferred her wishes to be recognized and accepted by the father. She also transferred her provocative and masochistic strivings toward both the father and the mother in the anal-erotic, messy, smearing play and the messy accidents caused by her awkwardness. The transference was an essential part of the effort to analyze the childhood neurosis. However, one of the benefits to Evelyne from the analysis derived from the relationship to the analyst as a man who, unlike her father, maintained his attention and interest in her despite her provocations and despite her presenting herself to me in the same ways which turned her father away.

When Evelyne returned as an adolescent she recognized quite openly that her father had very little warm interest in her. At 22 she was able to look at the relationship with her father objectively and to verbalize spontaneously that her father had begun to respect her achievements toward a professional career but had little affection for her because she was too much like his own older sister. She had warm memories of the analysis as a relationship in which she felt comfortable and free to do anything she wanted, even things that were not allowed at home. She recalled comparing notes with her sister and all of them agreeing that Evelyne's doctor was the best. This probably reflected the mother's positive attitude toward me since I was the one she consulted when she had a family problem. Evelyne had a lasting identification with the analyst and even with his analyzing function. She chose a career in the health professions, a preference she first expressed at the age of 6 when it was in identification with her mother's older sister to whom the mother had been strongly attached. During her training and in her professional career, she was most interested in what the client was feeling and thinking and how to allay his anxiety, whereas she could easily have gone along with the prevailing attitude of her fellow students and colleagues and paid attention only to the immediate practical needs of the persons in her charge. Among her friends she was regarded as the understanding person who kept the group together and helped each one with his or her crisis.

The long-term follow-up indicated strongly that the analyst had functioned as a new object during the course of the analysis of a childhood disturbance and that the identification with the analyzing function of the analyst was a lasting influence on the mental life of the patient.

In fact, this first became apparent when in adolescence Evelyne herself initiated contact with me. She felt troubled about her need to establish her independence and assert her own wishes in relation to her parents. She turned to me because in the past I had been a person with whom she felt free to express both positive and negative attitudes and who understood her, but did not tell her what to do.

While the case of Evelyne may appear to stress the advantages of continuous contact, I want to add a caution. The analyst has to be aware of the transference aspects of the earlier analytic relationship, even though the patient may in subsequent contacts use him primarily as a "real" object. This may preclude the possibility of resuming an analysis if it is indicated, or it may perpetuate an insufficiently analyzed dependence on an idealized transference figure. These are just some of the possibilities; others may exist. The interrelations between the transference and "new object" aspects in the analysis of children and adults, and in contacts between analyst and patient after the termination of an analysis, are so intricate that they require a great deal of further study.

The Relationship of Childhood to Adult Neurosis

That every child forms some isolated symptoms in the course of his growing up is an accepted fact. It is an inevitable consequence of the differentiation of ego and id and the immaturity of the ego in relation to the intensity of the drives, the ease with which the child reverts to primary process modes of thought, the inescapability of phase-specific conflicts, and the universality of the psychic phenomena of repression, regression, and transference. However, not all children manifest permanent neurotic formations which reach psychopathological proportions, lead to extensive and lasting regression, and represent a threat to the progress of their development.

A related question is whether every individual with a childhood neurosis suffers an adult neurosis later in life. There are two ways of attempting to answer this question—one theoretical, the other empirical. Theoretically, it is not difficult to envision that a benign life situation and absence of undue external stress, together with a fortunate balance between drive, conflict, and defense could combine to avoid or avert an adult neurosis. The greater maturity of the adult ego and the maturation of the drives may give the ego greater tolerance of anxiety and greater resistivity to regression. The establishment of defense mechanisms and character traits which have a high degree of automaticity enables the ego to deform itself in fixed and structured but also adaptive ways. The ego can then tolerate more internal conflict without being weakened further through the outbreak of neurosis.

Empirically, we would have to draw on longitudinal studies which would focus on the correlation of childhood and adult conditions. Very little of this type of information exists in the literature. It would have to be obtained by pooling individual case reports from a number of analysts. In the case of Frankie, extended analysis in childhood did not prevent the outbreak of neurotic illness in the adult. Although the predominant form of the adult neurosis was obsessional, the phobic childhood neurosis reappeared repeatedly at times of intensified conflict and anxiety. The formation of the obsessional neurosis started in latency.

Jerry, one of the children in our longitudinal study who was analyzed because of a complex phobic neurosis (Ritvo et al., 1963), had no manifestations of neurosis on follow-up with periodic interviews to the age of 15. In fact, we had feared a delinquent, sociopathic outcome for him on the basis of intense and protracted stimulation of his aggression by both parents and an identification with a sociopathic father and psychotic grandfather. The feared outcome did not occur, in large part because of a remarkable consolidation of the family during Jerry's latency under the driving leadership of the mother. The father remained the chief provider and became a firmer figure for identification and superego formation. In this case, as with Evelyne, the transference to the institution in which the services connected with the study were provided— well-baby and sick-baby care, social casework treatment for the mother, nursery school education, and psychoanalytic treatment for the child—was a significant factor in influencing the outcome. In addition to the analyst, the nursery school teacher was important as a new or alternate object in lending the support of her ego and offering a consistent object for gratification and identification at a time when the turmoil in the lives of the parents made it impossible for them to function adequately as parents.

Thus, both Jerry and Evelyne, who also was analyzed because of phobic symptoms, did not develop clinical neuroses. However, Evelyne did suffer from inhibitions and restrictions. Moreover, she experienced acute conflicts, especially in establishing relations with young men, whom she distrusted as much as she had come to distrust her father. Yet, while as a child she had tried to please her father, she did not carry this pattern over into her relations with boys.

The question of the shift of the form of neurosis, e.g., from phobic to obsessional, can be studied both prospectively in a longitudinal manner as with Frankie or retrospectively by reconstruction as in the Wolf-Man. The appearance of obsessional neuroses in latency following an earlier phobic neurosis is a frequent occurrence. In one sense the obsessional neurosis presents a paradox. On the one hand, as stated earlier, its appearance requires the development of thought processes to the level of the capacity for mental operations based on abstractions. On the other hand, the ego and instinctual regression may be deeper than in phobic neurosis, with regression to the level of ambivalence, sadism, and magic omnipotent thought. This suggests that the disposition to obsessional neurosis may be linked to early, intense stimulation of aggression on the instinctual side. On the ego side it may be rooted in early ego modifications, possibly in a premature differentiation of ego and id, which is caused by some undue environmental stress (such as illness or inadequate mothering). The result may be a weakening of the ego in the form of a greater vulnerability to regression, which paradoxically may manifest itself in a defensive or restitutive precocity of the ego. What I have in mind is analogous to the effect of "out-of-phase" overstimulation on instinctual development.

In considering the relationship of the childhood neurosis to the adult neurosis we should also bear in mind the importance of child analysis technique for adult technique. Whether the child analyst works with adults differently than the analyst who has had no experience with children is an intriguing question. The child analyst may be able to achieve a greater accuracy in attributing fantasies to a particular developmental phase because of his greater familiarity with the developmental timetable and norms of the child. He may have a greater facility for placing current behavior and relationships in their childhood contexts. A more intimate knowledge of the affects, fantasies, and behavior of children at various ages may be an aid in distinguishing when an adult patient in analysis, e.g., a parent talking about his child, is projecting or externalizing a thought or feeling of his own. Knowledge of children may be useful in judging when a parent's expectations of the patient as a child were age- and phase-appropriate and when they were not. All these should contribute to a greater accuracy and completeness of reconstruction, which was one of the benefits analysts expected from direct observational and analytic studies of childhood (E. Kris, 1950).

Child analysts may also be in an advantageous position in being able to offer interpretations in what I would call a developmental mode. For example, a woman in analysis had suffered great pain and anxiety over repeated separations and loss as a child. She reexperienced these in the transference at a time when she was having difficulty leaving her son in nursery school. His remonstrances stirred up her own anxiety and guilt. His objections subsided and she was able to leave him without distress after I pointed out that she was behaving as though she had to find a way to make the separation absolutely painless and as though the child, suitably prepared, had no resources or capacity of his own to tolerate the pain of this brief separation. The interpretation was given as one would guide a parent with a child in a normal developmental crisis, namely, one would support the child's ego in evolving suitable defenses and in its efforts at mastery. The interpretation did not take the place of analyzing the patient's own conflict. It merely established the conditions for doing so, because it brought a recognition and sense of conviction. In fact, by restoring to the ego some of its lost powers to tolerate anxiety and by strengthening the self-observing function of the ego, analysis and mastery of the patient's own infantile conflict were facilitated.

However, all the advantages are not with the child analyst. If he has never analyzed adults, the child analyst may take a more ominous or even alarmist view of childhood disturbances, losing sight of the great variety of ways in which very severe childhood problems can be resolved.

The concept of infantile neurosis as employed in relation to adults merits our attention here. It has recently been the topic of a study by Tolpin (1970). She argues that the concept of infantile neurosis should be confined to its special meaning as a metapsychological concept that is fundamental to the understanding of the transference neuroses. She restricts the definition of the infantile neurosis to the repressed conflicts of the phallic-oedipal phase in an individual who has progressed in his libidinal and ego development along more or less normal lines, so that he can experience the complex conflicts of the phallic-oedipal stage and has the intrapsychic task of mastering them. The repressed, unmastered conflict constitutes the central fixation point to which regression may later occur.

In this view, the infantile neurosis is not a clinically manifest entity but an unconscious configuration which may exert a pathogenic influence by virtue of transference. She recommends that the term be reserved for the metapsychological concept designating these repressed oedipal conflicts and that clinical disorders in children be referred to by other names. Diagnosis of such an unconscious configuration by the psychoanalytic method would be an indication for classical psychoanalytic treatment because the analyst could expect to find a classical analyzable transference neurosis.

This definition of the infantile neurosis in terms of normal maturation of the instincts and the normal development of the ego implies that the more normal or healthier the development of the individual, the more suitable are his disturbances for treatment by the method of psychoanalysis. But what about people with less normal development who express even more acutely the conflicts of the oedipal phase?

As a schematic presentation of a conceptual model Tolpin's propositions have a classifying function. At the same time she indicates her awareness that the infantile neurosis as a central unconscious conflict in an adult with more or less normal libidinal and ego development is a rare situation, if it exists at all in that form in patients coming to analysts for treatment. Not only conflicts of the oedipal period exert a continuing psychic influence, but so do preoedipal conflicts which have also undergone repression and find escape via the phenomenon of transference. The ego modifications in preoedipal disturbances may be extensive, but the mechanisms of the formation of neurotic phenomena remain basic. Eissler (1953) has noted that the same neurotic symptomatology can occur in widely divergent ego configurations. In the case of the Wolf-Man, which has remained the classic example of the analysis of an infantile neurosis, the oedipus complex was distorted by the preoedipal conflicts and their pathological outcome. What contributes so much to making the oedipus complex the nuclear complex of the neurosis is not that the phase-specific conflicts belonging to it have a special affinity or relationship to repression and transference, but that the psychic apparatus is more capable of maintaining structured neurotic formations. Furthermore, the oedipus complex remains nuclear because, in a hierarchical sense, it is the most recent of the psychosexual developmental phases and the one whose outcome has the greatest adaptational and developmental significance to the subsequent life of the individual.

In a recent paper Blos (1972) put forward the view that the

infantile neurosis, existing as a central unconscious conflict in Tolpin's sense, acquires delineation and structure at the time of the formation of the adult neurosis. In his view, the definitive adult neurosis is formed only with the achievement of the consolidation phase of late adolescence. What I take Blos to mean by the definitive adult neurosis being formed at that time is that in adolescence a revised or updated version of the central unconscious conflict (infantile neurosis) is formed which reflects the reworking of the oedipal and other infantile conflicts. With the shift of power to the ego in the psychic restructuring which normally takes place at the end of adolescence, the ego is again capable of the structuralized neurotic formations which provide elaborate pathways for the strivings and conflicts to escape from repression via transferences. Blos assigns great importance to this formulation for analysis in late adolescence because of his conviction that the establishment of a transference neurosis and the analysis of the transference are not possible until the definitive adult neurosis has been established.

This formulation raises once more the question of which conditions of the ego are necessary for the formation of a workable transference neurosis in the analytic situation. It is the ego, after all, that gives final form to the transference neurosis and communicates it in the psychoanalytic situation. For the analysis of the transference neurosis to be effective at all, certain qualities in the ego are essential. For example, the ego must have sufficient autonomy from intersystemic and intrasystemic conflict so that a diacritical form of self-observation can be maintained, and the ego's functions enlisted for the analytic work. In some people this becomes possible with the consolidation of the personality which occurs at the end of adolescence.

From the point of view of enlarging our knowledge of the relationship of childhood neurosis to adult neurosis, the cases of Frankie, Evelyne, and Jerry impress on us the rich potential of viewing neurotic disturbances longitudinally and developmentally rather than cross-sectionally at any one time.

BIBLIOGRAPHY

BIBRING, E. (1937), On the Theory of Therapeutic Results. *Int. J. Psycho-Anal.*, 18:170–189.

Blos, P. (1972), The Epigenesis of the Adult Neurosis. *This Annual,* 27:106–125.

Bornstein, B. (1949), The Analysis of a Phobic Child. *This Annual,* 3/4:181–226.

Coleman, R. W., Kris, E., & Provence, S. (1953), The Study of Variations of Early Parental Attitudes. *This Annual,* 8:20–47.

Eissler, K. R. (1953), The Effect of the Structure of the Ego on Psychoanalytic Technique. *J. Amer. Psychoanal. Assn.,* 1:104–143.

Freud, A. (1965), *Normality and Pathology in Childhood.* New York: International Universities Press.

——— (1971), The Infantile Neurosis. *This Annual,* 26:79–90.

Freud S. (1900), The Interpretation of Dreams. *Standard Edition,* 4 & 5. London: Hogarth Press, 1953.

——— (1909), Analysis of a Phobia in a Five-Year-Old Boy. *Standard Edition,* 10:3–149. London: Hogarth Press, 1955.

——— (1918), From the History of an Infantile Neurosis. *Standard Edition,* 7:3–123. London: Hogarth Press, 1955.

Gitelson, M. (1962), The Curative Factor in Psycho-Analysis: I. The First Phase of Psycho-Analysis. *Int. J. Psycho-Anal.,* 43:194–205.

Greenacre, P. (1971), *Emotional Growth,* 2 Vols. New York: International Universities Press.

Kohut, H. (1971), *The Analysis of the Self.* New York: International Universities Press.

Kris, E. (1950), Notes on the Development and on Some Current Problems of Psychoanalytic Child Psychology. *This Annual,* 5:24–46.

——— (1955), Neutralization and Sublimation. *This Annual,* 10:30–46.

——— (1962), Decline and Recovery in the Life of a Three-Year-Old. *This Annual,* 17:175–215.

——— et al. (1954), Problems of Infantile Neurosis: A Discussion. *This Annual,* 9:16–71.

Kris, M. (1972), Some Aspects of Family Interaction: A Psychoanalytic Study. Freud Anniversary Lecture, New York Academy of Medicine.

Loewald, H. W. (1971), On Motivation and Instinct Theory. *This Annual,* 26:91–128.

Mahler, M. S. (1971), A Study of the Separation-Individuation Process. *This Annual,* 26:403–424.

Nagera, H. (1966), *Early Childhood Disturbances, the Infantile Neurosis, and the Adult Disturbances.* New York: International Universities Press.

Ritvo, S. (1966), Correlation of a Childhood and Adult Neurosis. *Int. J. Psycho-Anal.,* 47:130–131.

——— (1972), Outcome of Prediction on Superego Formation. In: *Moral Values and the Superego Concept in Psychoanalysis,* ed. S. C. Post. New York: International Universities Press, pp. 74–86.

——— McCollum, A. T., Omwake, E., Provence, S., & Solnit, A. J. (1963), Some Relations of Constitution, Environment, and Personality As Observed in a Longitudinal Study of Child Development. In: *Modern Perspectives in Child*

Development, ed. A. J. Solnit & S. A. Provence. New York: International Universities Press, pp. 107–143.

RITVO, S. & SOLNIT, A. J. (1958), Influences of Early Mother-Child Interaction on Identification Processes. *This Annual*, 13:64–86.

SPITZ, R. A. (1956), Countertransference. *J. Amer. Psychoanal. Assn.*, 4:256–265.

TOLPIN, M. (1970), The Infantile Neurosis. *This Annual*, 25:273–305.

WEIL, A. P. (1973), Ego Strengthening Prior to Analysis. *This Annual*, 28:287–301.

Current Status of the Concept of Infantile Neurosis

Discussion

HANS W. LOEWALD, M.D.

MY DISCUSSION IS BASED ON THE RECONSTRUCTION OF THE INFAN-
tile neurosis in the psychoanalytic treatment of adults. Not being a
child analyst or investigator of child development, I cannot speak
from experience about infantile neurosis in the sense of clinical
neuroses or neurotic manifestations seen in childhood. I speak from
the vantage point of what adult patients report about their
symptoms or more diffuse disturbances, which are remembered with
more or less reliable accuracy and sophistication from their own
childhood or of which they have gained knowledge from parents
and other adults. On the basis of such reports it is at times possible
to come to the conviction that the patient indeed suffered from a
neurotic syndrome, such as a school phobia, or hysterical vomiting,
or periods of depression of pathological porportions. In such cases it
is often possible to reconstruct convincingly the psychological
setting in which these events occurred, to relate them to pathogenic
relations with important environmental figures and/or to phase-
specific psychosexual conflicts. Transference manifestations in the
analysis often give important clues as to the likely etiological factors

Clinical Professor of Psychiatry, Yale University Medical School, New Haven,
Connecticut. Faculty, Western New England Institute for Psychoanalysis.
Presented at a panel of the Association for Child Analysis, Paris, July 22, 1973.

involved in the development of these syndromes during childhood, in mutual elucidation of the transference neurosis and the infantile neurosis.

In many cases it is possible to detect layers from various developmental levels which have contributed to the formation of these syndromes, and one gains the impression that the syndrome reported from childhood is merely the most definitive or structured expression of earlier disturbances often going back to preoedipal times. The reported syndrome or symptom would then be comparable to a screen memory, not so much in the sense of a defensive formation against remembering the earlier conflicts or traumas, but because the traumatic experiences could assume structured psychic representation only at a later stage of psychic development.

Should preoedipal disturbances be seen as expressions of neurotic conflict? All depends here on our definition of neurosis and of neurotic conflict. The psychoanalytic concept of neurosis arose in the context of the treatment of adult hysteria, phobias, obsessions and compulsions. They were explained as compromise formations, compromises between instinctual impulses and the ego's defenses against them, i.e., as expressions of intrapsychic conflict. We can begin to speak of intrapsychic conflict only when danger situations can be discriminated by the psyche as external or internal. In other words, we can speak of intrapsychic conflict once there is enough psychic organization of ego and id as more or less distinct substructures of the mind, so that dangers arising in interaction with—for an observer—external objects may be transformed into internal dangers: instead of an external danger or conflict with the environment (from an observer's standpoint), there now exists an internal danger, a conflict between inner agencies which have come to oppose each other. Only when id and ego are opposed to each other does an inner conflict arise. Such a conflict has a pathogenic potential, but it does not have to lead to pathology: not every intrapsychic conflict has an outcome which is neurotic in the clinical sense. We should speak of a neurotic solution, a neurotic compromise if either id or ego or both give up something vital to their functioning, something that damages and not merely changes or modulates their functioning.

In this sense, repression, in contrast to a higher integration or taming or modulation of id tendencies, is neurotic, and the unconscious conflict persisting between repressed impulses and the ego, despite or rather because of the neurotic compromise, is a neurotic conflict. Since repression or other unconscious defenses are ubiquitous, although more or less prominent and pervasive in psychic life, human beings are neurotic by nature, as it were. Insofar as the oedipus complex is the culmination of the differentiation of id and ego, and its resolution always at best a mixture of repression and internalization or narcissistic transformation of its instinctual currents, the oedipus complex is the nucleus of neurosis. Before its ascendancy it seems best to speak not of neurosis but of developmental deficiencies or arrests which affect the undifferentiated or hardly differentiated psyche as a whole. These would interfere with the clear differentiation of ego and id in certain areas of the personality. In these areas id-ego differentiation has not taken its normal course and *intrapsychic conflict* would be absent in them, although discrepancies or discontinuities between more and less developed personality sectors would be present.

It is useful to remind ourselves of the three factors which Freud (1926) described as being involved in the causation of neurosis: a biological, a phylogenetic, and a purely psychological factor. The *biological* factor refers to the long period of dependency and helplessness of the human infant which "is sent into the world in a less finished state," intensifying the "influence of the real external world" upon the infant and thereby promoting an early differentiation between ego and id, as well as increasing the importance of the external world's dangers so that the value of the protecting object is "enormously enhanced." The *phylogenetic* factor refers to the biphasic development of psychosexuality. Due to the early differentiation of ego and id most instinctual demands of infantile sexuality are treated by the ego (which mainly represents the demands of the external world, including of course the parental objects) as internal dangers to be fended off, and later sexual impulses run the risk of "following these infantile prototypes into repression," of not being ego-syntonic. This Freud called the most direct cause of neurosis. The *psychological* factor consists in that "imperfection[1] of our mental

---

[1] Freud used the term *Unvollkommenheit*, which Strachey translated as "defect."

apparatus," the differentiation into an id and an ego, ultimately due to the influence of the external world, insofar as the dangers of external reality make the ego guard against certain instinctual impulses and treat them as dangers. It fends off these inner dangers by restricting its own organization and "acquiescing in the formation of symptoms" (p. 154ff.).

Clearly, these three factors are intimately interrelated. We find here the notion that the differentiation into id and ego, especially at a stage so early as to render that differentiation premature, is an imperfection of the mental apparatus; human development in childhood is then bound to lead to neurosis, a tendency which only later, under favorable circumstances, may to a certain extent be overcome, namely, at a time when the ego is stable enough not to have to rely so much on defenses against the id. Neurotic development in childhood, in this perspective, is inevitable, although its consequences for adult life vary. Here, then, would be a view of infantile neurosis according to which it is a ubiquitous phenomenon by virtue of the imperfection of the mental apparatus, which imperfection ultimately is due to the premature separation of infant and mother. We have the view of man as the neurotic animal, inasmuch as he is characterized by inner conflict and a degree of damaging inner compromises. This would be the norm for the human species.

I think the problem of infantile neurosis, as posed by Freud, must be seen against this background. It explains why we vacillate between considering the infantile neurosis as pathological or as normal, and it makes it clear that for Freud neurosis is the result of id-ego differentiation. To the extent to which this differentiation, which presupposes or implies the differentiation of internal and external, of subject and object, does not take place or has not yet taken place, we should not speak of neurosis in a strict psychoanalytic sense.

The "severe lags and deficits in the development of ego functions" of which Ritvo speaks, while they may be and often are in good part due to conflicts between instinctual impulses and the external world, are not expressions or consequences of *inner* conflict. They rather tend to interfere with that id-ego differentiation which leads to inner conflict. Ritvo points out that "We are better able to distinguish between the child who is regressed or retarded on a broad front and the child who develops an isolated neurotic symptom." Similarly, I think we are better able to distinguish in our adult patients between lags and deficiencies in ego development and neurotic conflict, i.e., inner conflict. It is true, however, that these deficiently developed sectors of the personality, especially in the so-called narcissistic personality disorders, come into conflict with the more mature sectors. Thus they may *cause* inner conflict, but they are not the result of inner conflict.

I agree with Ritvo's view that the sharp distinction between the classical neuroses and borderline conditions or narcissistic disorders, from a clinical standpoint, is not justified. One might say that neurosis and developmental deficiencies of ego are intermingled, with a preponderance of neurotic conflict in the classical neuroses, and a preponderance of developmental deficiencies in the narcissistic disorders. I would suggest that both components have to be taken into account in both forms of disorder, necessitating considerable flexibility on the part of the analyst in regard to transference-countertransference and technical problems. I believe our impression, that we see fewer classical neuroses than we used to, is in good part due to the fact that our eyes and ears have been sharpened so as to recognize ego deficiencies far more clearly than in earlier times when we did not have the benefit of analytically informed child observation, child analysis, longitudinal studies, and analytic work with psychoses, as well as of a more refined theoretical understanding of ego development. This understanding at the present time includes not only the role of unconscious defenses and of anxiety as signal anxiety located in the ego, but most importantly also the role that the earliest interactions with the environment play in the organization of the drives themselves and in the formation of the ego.

To return to the concept of infantile neurosis. I believe Marian Tolpin (1970) in her recent paper on the subject, referred to by Ritvo, is correct in saying that Freud did not clearly distinguish between the infantile neurosis as the underlying motive force and the clinically manifest disorders of the oedipal phase. Perhaps more important, to my mind, is that Freud did not clearly distinguish between the underlying motive force, the nuclear complex of neurosis, and the different possibilities of conflict solution. The oedipus complex is neurotogenic because in humans the oedipal attachments inevitably lead to inner conflict. To the extent to which this inner conflict undergoes repression, it is apt to lead to neurotic manifestations in the adult. To the extent to which the complex is not repressed but internalized, it leads to superego formation. This further differentiation of the mental apparatus, similar to id-ego differentiation, may also be seen as an imperfection of the mental apparatus, if we follow Freud, and this may entail more complexly structured neurotic developments (the problems of unconscious guilt, etc.). But superego development itself should not be understood as a neurotic solution of inner conflict—it is an unconscious solution of a different order.

Let me close with one further comment. The infantile neurosis, not as a manifest illness in childhood, but as a reconstruction on the evidence of the adult neurosis and the transference neurosis, may be considered as an analogue to the latent dream thoughts as reconstructed from the manifest dream content in dream interpretation. I believe Tolpin has something similar in mind when she speaks of the infantile neurosis as a "metapsychological concept," implying, if I understand her correctly, that the infantile neurosis, as reconstructed from the manifest neurosis, partakes of an order of psychic reality which can be discovered only in a psychoanalytic investigation. Peter Blos (1973) considers the infantile neurosis in the same light and speaks of the latent and manifest state of the neurosis, the latent state being the infantile neurosis, as "a specific potential." It is this quality of a potential state that the infantile neurosis has in common with the latent dream.

BIBLIOGRAPHY

BLOS, P. (1973), The Epigenesis of the Adult Neurosis. *This Annual*, 27:106–135.
FREUD, S. (1926), Inhibitions, Symptoms and Anxiety. *Standard Edition*, 20:87–172. London: Hogarth Press, 1959.
TOLPIN, M. (1970), The Infantile Neurosis. *This Annual*, 25:273–305.

ASPECTS OF NORMAL AND PATHOLOGICAL DEVELOPMENT

Distortions of the Concept of Fetishism

ROBERT C. BAK, M.D.

THIS PAPER REEXAMINES THE ROLE INANIMATE THINGS PLAY IN THE maturation of the infant, child, adolescent, and adult perversions, such as fetishism. I have placed the emphasis on a possible dynamic continuity or discontinuity in the use of inanimate things in the attempt to highlight their changing function during the interplay of maturational and developmental forces.

In 1963, Parkin commented on the increased interest in fetishism evident in the psychoanalytic literature during the preceding two decades. He attributes this phenomenon to the further insight that a study of fetishism can give into infantile manifestations and their possible formative role in later pathology.

In my view, this increased interest has not yielded further or deeper insight into the subject, but has led to a dilution of the clinical concept and a wide misapplication of it, together with a confusion as to its genetic background. One of the bases of this overextension consists in the description of "inanimate thing" attachments under the heading, or in relation to, fetishism when their metapsychology does not warrant it (Greenacre, 1955). Later authors have therefore tended to include "transitional objects" as "infantile fetishes," disregarding their essential function and the phase specificity of the fetish in the phallic phase (Wulff, 1946; Greenacre, 1970, 1971; Roiphe and Galenson, 1973a). Once this

From the Psychiatric Division, Montefiore Hospital and Medical Center, New York City. Faculty, New York Psychoanalytic Institute.

phase specificity was loosened and taken out of the genital context—or once a young child's overtly "fetishistic" behavior was equated with the corresponding adult manifestations (A. Freud, 1965)—the way was opened to the inclusion of women and girl infants among fetishists (Hug-Hellmuth, 1915; Spiegel, 1967; Sperling, 1963; Greenacre, 1970; Dickes, 1963; Roiphe and Galenson, 1973a).

The case material that will be discussed clearly validates A. Freud's view on the unpredictability of "pseudo fetishism in childhood." Whereas the "early origin" of fetishism in adult cases is beyond doubt, she refers to the fact that there are many more childhood fetishes than true fetishists in later years. In childhood the fate of such an attachment to things is hard to predict. "There is no certainty about its ultimate fate before adolescence" (p. 212). One may add: before they become prerequisites to genital functioning. This paper is therefore also concerned with the differentiation between the phase-specific quality and use of inanimate things and their changing functions.

Finally, the pregenital aspects of fetishism were emphasized. Quite early, Gillespie (1940) pointed to oral factors, which led Weissman (1957) to such distortions as the statements that fetishism attempts an ego identification with a "good breast" and that castration anxiety is quite secondary. Although Greenacre (1953) and I (1953) described a disturbance in the early mother-child relationship and an unusually strong separation anxiety in the cases observed, I did not consider the pregenital aspects as determinants of the fully developed fetish but only as contributors to it. In "The Phallic Woman: The Ubiquitous Fantasy in Perversions" (1968), I reemphasized the crucial role of the phallic phase.

In retrospect, I think we may surmise rather plausibly that this "dilutional" development was due to the papers of Bak, Greenacre, and Winnicott, all published in 1953. Wulff's (1946) contribution already contained a description of the transitional object, but not being able to differentiate it from the "fetish object," he failed to discover its essential significance in the process of separation-individuation (Mahler, 1961). It was left to Winnicott not only to give an accurate description, but to place it in the proper maturational-developmental frame. Winnicott issued a warning against the use of the term "fetish object" in infancy lest we lose some of the value of the term if we include normal phenomena and proposed that the concept of fetish be reserved to the "delusion of a maternal phallus" (p. 241).

Under the circumstances, I believe it may prove advantageous and clarifying to give an overview of fetishism and its related problems. It seems necessary to restate the obvious and review the more or less well-established body of psychoanalytic observations and theory.

This critical review of the literature has necessarily been confined to a consideration of the main discrepancies and does not do justice to the authors who have nevertheless contributed a great deal to problems somewhat related to fetishism and, more specifically, to the disturbances of object relations, especially in connection with separation.

FETISHISM

According to a strict definition of the clinical concept of fetishism, it is a male sexual perversion and belongs to adulthood. *Formes frustes* may appear in childhood from the age of 4 or 5, with experiences of diffuse sexual excitement, but they do not necessarily lead to adult fetishism.

In the adult, the fetish appears in concrete form or fantasy, as a condition for sexual arousal and the performance of the sexual or masturbatory act. The form can be varied; it can be—

1. an inanimate thing in the presence or absence of the sexual object;

2. a body part of the object not directly connected with the sexual act, such as foot, hand or earlobe;

3. an obligate ritualistic procedure introducing or completing sexual intercourse (e.g., hair cutting) (Romm, 1949).

Freud (1940) observed that one finds fetishism in various degrees, from its fully developed state down to a "hint." I understand this statement to mean that so-called "fetishistic" manifestations can contain the same genetic-dynamic and symbolic meaning, but the quantity of the investment and the defensive need are almost reduced to those characteristic of preference. "Preferences" may, however, have a totally different metapsychology from that of fetishism. That would exclude a number of inanimate-thing attachments, surviving transitional objects, sexual rituals, bizarre though fixed object choices, etc. "Fetishistic" should then be used only when the aforementioned dynamics are discernible. Fetishism can also be latent and reappear fully under castration stress. Stewart (1972) questions the existence of such latent perversion. Yet there can be a childhood—but not an infancy—fetishism that is transitory, later showing displacements or "sublimations" and residues in object choices that have some fetishistic quality and develop again to full-fledged fetishism under castration stress. In the same way, there can be a single homosexual phase in a lifetime under the impact of separation-castration trauma.

The function of a fetishistic perversion is to defend against castration anxiety through the illusion of the female phallus. It should not be necessary to reemphasize this specific defense against castration and it is done with the understanding that even though it serves primarily as defense against castration, fetishism also serves as defense against losses or threatening losses (separation) before the fully developed phallic phase (the biphasic defense [Bak, 1953]).

Genetically, the *sine qua non* of fetishism is its phase-specific castration anxiety during the phallic phase in an oedipal setting. It is predicated on the experience established during this phase of the high narcissistic value of the penis through conscious sensations of tumescence and detumescence, some form of masturbatory activity, size differences, castration threats, and the *uncertain* awareness of the absence of the penis in the mother and women in general.

Fetishism thus crystallizes around the idea of the maternal phallus by overinvesting the ubiquitous, dominantly male fantasy of the phallic woman. Whatever precedes the phallic phase is nonspecific to the development of fetishism.

It is absolutely necessary to emphasize the phase-specific position of fetishism in order to clarify its relation to aggression. The destructive and castrative wishes of the male child reach their peak at the phallic-oedipal phase with their consecutive retaliatory fantasies of heightened castration anxiety. In contrast, the so-called

pregenital fetishes defend against separation, object loss, deprivations, and total loss of body integrity, at a phase when the
destructive wishes toward the parental objects play a different and
less important role.

As to prephallic contributions to fetish formation, one may state
that "Perversions generally imply the dominance of pregenitality in
sexual function. This regressive feature is common to all perversions
and involves the denial of heightened castration anxiety and
marked bisexual identifications" (Bak, 1956). In fact, fetishism may
represent a higher developmental phase in propping up *genital*
function, partly integrating earlier fixations (Bak, 1968). The fetish
can be regarded as an externalized form of pseudogenital primacy,
condensing the pregenital elements.

The choice of fetish is often, though not invariably, influenced by
pregenital contents. Although the fetish can be determined quite
independently of a transitional object, vicissitudes in the status of
transitional phenomena in psychoanalytic theory have led to
theories that transitional phenomena constitute an earlier origin of
fetishism than was permissible under the original definition.

DISTORTIONS OF THE TRANSITIONAL OBJECTS

COMFORTERS, INTERMEDIARY, AND PROSTHETIC OBJECTS

About the transitional object, after Winnicott's description and
Greenacre's (1970, 1971) evocative elaboration, there is little to say.
There is a fair consensus that it is a nearly universal and healthy
phenomenon in infancy. It appears among the sequelae of weaning
and the separation from the mother's body. It is "transitional"
between the thumb or fist in the mouth and the blanket or teddy
bear. It primarily represents the breast, and substitutes for oral
pressures and the caressing skin sensations around the mouth and
nose that went along with feeding. The transitional objects'
warmth, fluffiness, and softness simulate not only the mother's
breast and skin but her total ambience and provide satisfaction of
the need for clinging. They may be separate from, or adjunct to, the
night bottle, which may be' the transitional object *par excellence*

(personal discussion with M. Mahler). The transitional object is *chosen* by the infant. It is important that the transitional object should *not change,* but remain the same in a changing world. It can be enriched and worn, and is the recipient of tender care and hostile aggression.

In the maturational process, the transitional object may acquire elements of substitute satisfaction for anal-olfactory and genital needs, depending on developmental factors and certain aspects of the object. In this context, I would rather speak of maturational stages of the transitional object than those of the fetish, as does Spiegel (1967).

Briefly, the transitional object belongs to early infancy. It is a near-universal phenomenon in a general atmosphere of good or good-enough mothering and is "relegated to limbo" (Winnicott) in the process of individuation and extending interests. It symbolizes the breast and skin-mouth aspects of feeding. Finally, its function consists of the attenuation of the trauma of weaning-separation.

In the 1953 paper, I described an "infantile fetish" in the case of an adult jodhpur fetishism. The patient, as a little boy, had difficulty in sleeping alone and generally in being separated from his mother. He took to bed a piece of velvet which he stroked and put to his cheeks before falling asleep. "This fetish of infancy underwent a change into interest in fabrics." Similar tactile sensations were created by the stroking of hair, about which he remembered his mother's long hair and his own blond silky hair from childhood pictures. I considered the piece of velvet as reappearing in the suede patch of the adult jodhpur fetish and also characterized it as a "prephallic" fetish that represents the mother's skin and smell. Winnicott's paper in the same year called for a correction of my formulation. Obviously, in the piece of velvet I had described a transitional object.

Winnicott (1953) gives an example of the distorted use of the term "transitional object" in the case of a little boy who, weaned at 7 months, had "nothing to fall back on"—no bottle, finger, or thumb-sucking. At 12 months, he adopted a rabbit which lived until he was 5 or 6 years old. He sustained an interest in live rabbits. Winnicott characterizes this object as a *comforter* against depressive anxieties (p. 234f.).

A woman patient of mine, a writer of children's books, basically homosexually oriented, was an unusually sensitive child. Her mother suffered a postpartum depression after her birth. She adopted as a comforter a woolly lamb that substituted for the mother's initial physical and later emotional absence. Her sensitivity to abandonment and sense of deep loneliness endowed her with particular empathy. At 4 to 5 years of age, she regularly woke up to wave at the milkman from her window "because the milkman came when nobody was there to greet him." Later she adopted a series of woolly dogs. It took considerable interpretive effort, and no little amount of persuasion, to separate her—at least for the analytic session—from the woolly beast. I need not emphasize that the dog also served a prosthetic function.

This is in contrast to the soothing effect of the transitional object, the cuddling and sucking of which help the baby lose his anxieties. It also reflects a need of the total mother (mother fixation), in contradistinction to the evolving separation and partial (breast) substitution. It may be that in the choice of these comforters, *tactile* needs predominate.

Intermediary Objects

The intermediary object (Buxbaum, 1960) is not found by the infant but *is given by the mother* or her substitute, i.e., the therapist, with the clear, but probably unspoken agreement that it substitutes for the mother *in toto*. The "magic blanket" (Wulff, 1946) and the gifts described by Buxbaum are typical examples. These objects, because of incomplete separation and establishment of psychic representation (internalization), may later acquire superego functions.

Prosthetic Objects

In the use of the original transitional object there is no noticeable difference between boy and girl infants. Gradually, the infants go over to the use of soft and hard toys. According to Winnicott, boys tend to progress toward the use of hard objects. From these hard objects, the prosthetic object[1] may develop out of the transitional object, but more frequently appears later than or in exchange for the transitional object, and may linger on, with variations, until the phallic phase and well beyond it. It seems to be less in the service of undoing separation and fulfillment of object-libidinal needs than for the narcissistic maintenance of body integrity and the reinforcement of phallic or clitoral representations. Leather belts or thongs as prosthetic objects may contribute later to the development of belt and whip fetishes mixed into sadomasochistic rituals (Bak, 1968). At an early stage, they are more involved in the aggressive drive; the objects stand for durability and hardness, and almost always belong to phallic paraphernalia. Wulff's little boy with the chamber pot and Greenacre's (1960) patient with the stone amulet are examples (see also Furer, 1964).

For adults, such objects may become fetishes for men, fulfilling both prosthetic and fetish functions (Bak, 1953) and illusory penis substitutes in women. Their function would range from defense against body dissolution to lessening of castration anxiety by reinforcing phallic and clitoral aggression. They may indeed be forerunners, intermediates of true fetishes, or contributory parts of the fetishes, if they become involved in the sexual function and especially in subject-object exchange, without which they remain only props of the phallic self image in both sexes.

THE "INFANTILE FETISH"

The "infantile fetish" came into the literature, I believe, with Wulff's observations. They were commented on by Winnicott and recently worked through by Greenacre (1970) and Roiphe and Galenson (1973a). Earlier Sperling (1963) had taken issue with Winnicott's findings. Disregarding the significance of terms, she finds transitional object and fetish interchangeable, a sort of "manner of speech," while at the same time she allots to the fetish the symbolic meaning of the breast.

Sperling's case material is varied. However, in three of the cases

---

[1] Greenacre (1970) explains the development of toys and tools as evolving from prosthetic elaborations of the body or its parts.

that she describes in detail, the inanimate objects were *given by the mother* and not *chosen* by the infants as transitional objects, as in Winnicott's definition. In both cases and in that of one adult woman (the use of pillow and mother's robe), they correspond to what Buxbaum called "intermediary object" offered by the mother to substitute for her absence. In the case "Martin," the mother, having tired of the child's play with her blouse buttons, provided a button which the child carried and sucked; and when lost, it could be replaced satisfactorily only by the mother's giving him another button. Later, *the mother* replaced the button with a blanket, which the boy carried and took to bed. With the mother's growing acceptance of the child's weaning and separateness, the boy gave up his attachment to the intermediary object. At the age of 10, he showed normal development. Sperling regards the function of the intermediary object as a defense against separation anxiety "due to a loss of the preoedipally gratifying mother." According to her, the accepted symbolism of the maternal phallus *does not seem to apply* fully to childhood fetishism.

Buxbaum presents two cases of little girls, who started to pull their hair around the age of 18 months. The first case, Beryl, came into treatment at age 6. She was a happy baby until her younger sister was born when she was 18 months old. She attacked the baby and pulled her hair, but stopped doing it when repeatedly slapped, and started to pull her own hair. The mother was far from "good enough" and the little girl acted out in doll play the caressing mother's role. The therapist gave her a doll. The child pulled out the doll's hair. But, when left alone by the mother or the therapist, she started to pull out her own hair again. She also manifested coprophagic tendencies of eating her hair. Through a series of suggestive questions, Buxbaum established the "fact" that the little girl saw the mother's bleeding genitals in the bath tub or blood in the toilet.

Buxbaum's second patient, Ann, started treatment at the age of 3. The parents "moved innumerable times" and quarreled in front of the baby. At the time the baby started to pull her hair, she also began to awake crying. This lasted for 6 months. This phase corresponded to *their moving twice in 4 months,* during which time the father had a genital operation and the grandfather, to whom the baby was very much attached, *died.*

By very sensitive handling, good mothering, and giving "intermediary objects" to both little patients, Buxbaum succeeded in eliminating the symptom of hair pulling. She attributes the resolution of the symptom to the discussion of castration traumas. The great improvement in the mothers' acceptance of their children and the establishment of an "intermediary object," [2] representing the mother or the therapist, are seemingly considered secondary in significance.

To me, it seems that the hair pulling shows a severe castration-anxiety disturbance in the separation process and belongs to the pathological sequelae of care-object loss. One may tentatively hypothesize that it dramatizes a painful tearing away from the mother's body, while the eating of the hair symbolizes a reunion with her, i.e., with the lost object.

At the time of their treatment, both children were 6, when they might well have had problems with their castration complexes. The evidence is far from satisfactory for retroprojection to the 18th month.

A compulsive, autoerotic, or autodestructive ritual or habit, coexisting with an ever-present castration complex, can be misleading if discussed under the heading of fetishism. Sperling is in accord with this view in her discussion of two other cases of hair pulling, which indicate traumas of separation and self-directed aggression. Both girl children (it seems more frequent in girls) developed the symptoms immediately after the birth of a sibling. Sperling does not consider hair pulling "true fetishistic activity," and I believe that the symptom could be studied more fruitfully as one of the pathological outcomes of the separation syndrome—if it is not forced into the category of fetishism.

Harry, at the age of 6½, "always carries a strip of silk stocking in his pocket to school and takes it to bed with him. Watching television, he fingers the strip and sometimes puts it into his pajama

----

[2] "Intermediate" and "intermediary object" are terms coined by Buxbaum. In Winnicott, I could find only "intermediate area" of experience, giving it an entirely different meaning.

leg and rhythmically rubs his scrotal region." The mother dated this attachment to his 18th month, "when she used to lie down with him on the bed when he drank his bottle. *He liked to stroke her legs"* while taking the bottle. As a substitute for herself the mother then offered him a silk stocking, which she later reduced to a strip (Sperling, 1963, p. 383; my italics).

In Harry's case, we may be following the development of an intermediate object into a childhood fetish. It may be (1) that the silk stockings, together with the mother's legs for which the child showed marked attachment, already had a phallic significance, in addition to representing the mother's total ambience, but functioned mainly as a defense against separation; (2) that with progressive development into the phallic phase, the stocking acquired increasingly clear phallic significance and its *function changed* in defense against castration.

THE EQUATION OF INFANTILE AND
ADULT MANIFESTATIONS

Another distortion of the transitional object is evident in the work of Dickes (1963), who considers the distinction between transitional object and childhood fetish and adult fetish artificial. He looks at these as various stages of development which in most cases are eventually resolved; only in the adult fetishist does the need for a special "thing" continue. He describes several cases with "fetishistic" symptoms.

1. An orally deprived child as a 3-year-old became attached to a "baby pillow" which the *mother gave her*. The pillow served as a comforter and friend at bedtime, and during stressful situations. The pillow was preceded by a small rubber doll which was in her crib and with which she recalled having masturbated. As an adult, she still caressed her pillow. This case combines a transitional (doll) and intermediary object (pillow) in the ambience of poor mothering and later overstimulation. While I agree that these substitute "things" represent parts of the mother's body, especially the breast, and thus signify substitutes for the need-satisfying object, the fetish has different symbolic meaning and function.

2. A man in his 20s remained attached to an undershirt that was

"first given to him by his mother in his earliest years to aid him in going to sleep" (p. 319). He would hold it and suck it. He recollected lying on his mother's breast and fantasied fusion with her. The shirt also acquired anal qualities and masturbatory functions. It was not obligatory for the sexual act. The case illustrates an intense breast attachment and the use of a surviving intermediary object (mother substitute). At puberty, this patient masturbated in front of a mirror in this undershirt, *wearing his mother's high-heeled shoes* (p. 322). This illustrates my point clearly: the undershirt is a relic of the maternal breast and fusion with her, whereas a thing of phallic significance had to be added in the form of high-heeled shoes in order to represent the phallic mother. *This* is the fetish.

3. A woman patient, "lacking determinants for forming permanent fetishistic behavior, nevertheless had as a childhood *fetish* a teddy bear" (p. 319; my italics). When she was about 4 years old, she masturbated with the teddy bear. (See below for comments on early masturbation with transitional and prosthetic objects.)

THE "PSYCHOTIC FETISH"

The attachment to inanimate things is present even in psychotic children. Furer (1964) "colloquially" calls it psychotic fetish.[3] Furer considers these as favorable signs toward a growing self-nonself differentiation in that the psychotic fetish contains "some residue of gratifying mothering experience" (p. 457).

The 3½-year-old Malcolm was first preoccupied with prosthetic objects, such as boxes and furniture. (As an infant he had a hernia, but surgery was postponed. On at least three occasions, unsuccessful attempts were made to reduce the hernia, causing intolerable pain, until he was operated on at 5½ months.) Furer cautiously interpreted the preoccupation—I believe correctly—as an attempt to fuse "his self-image with a form of object image" (p. 457). In the

---

[3] It is not rare for deteriorated schizophrenics, after decades of institutionalization, to carry a bag with (for us) worthless pieces of leather, buttons, etc.—lost remnants of object relationships. It is also possible that the word salad and verbigeration of old schizophrenics contain some elements of infantile "transitional babbling" (personal communication, Walter A. Stewart).

anal-sexual phase of preoccupation, the little boy considered the mother's feces as her phallus, remarking, "Mommy has a penis in her tushy." Finally, he became mainly preoccupied with a flag—preening it, building a flagpole outside the building, "wrapping his body in it and seeming to fall asleep" in states of distress. He held the flag in front of the lower part of his body and watched it in the mirror going up and down. At this stage, oedipal feelings and castration anxiety appeared, and the role of the flag at least seemed to assuage or resolve his castration anxiety.

For us it is important to note that the function of the inanimate thing, as well as the thing itself, changes in the course of development and may even come to condense several functions, especially if "the thing" itself is suitable. The flag could therefore act at times as a comforter, wrapping the patient in something akin to the soothing maternal milieu, while the flagpole, as a prosthetic object derived from the phallic phase, served as defense against castration. I would agree with Furer that the flagpole is a fetish *de novo*—prosthetic object in my terms—from the phallic phase.

THE QUESTION OF FETISHISM IN WOMEN

The literature on fetishism in women exemplifies both the clinical extension of the concept and a misevaluation of the vicissitudes and defensive functions of transitional objects. According to Fenichel (1945), the theory of fetishism does not apply to women. He considers female fetishists "very rare," and confuses the "illusory penis" with fetish. Referring to "cases that have been studied" (p. 344), his only reference is the Hug-Hellmuth case, a nonanalytic one, which Greenacre (1960) dismisses most accurately and which by now should be relegated to the realm of historical curios.

While Greenacre (1960) states that fetishism is inherently a male disturbance—but only at a clearly genital level (1955)—she adds that the "persistent use of a fetish may occur in women" (p. 192). In the latter it is supposed to appear in a less obvious but very persistent form and "represents an extremely severe form of the deviation" (1970, p. 447).

Among the three cases illustrating "pill fetishism," "amulet fetishism," and "the secret" (1960), the second case is that of a woman who as a child carried a stone in her pocket for a period of years, probably from the time she started school until the age of 9. The stone lost its significance for years while she was absent from school and was reinstated when at puberty she returned to school. The stone-carrying changed into clutching mannerisms, which appeared at anxious moments and also were evident in the transference.

The lucky stone was preceded by a blanket "fetish," which she carried until the age of 4. Greenacre interprets her need as a protection against separation anxiety and the stone as symbolizing a magic and degraded fecal phallus. It seems that in this case, between the use of the transitional object (blanket) and that of the stone, a great deal of sexual exploration took place and the soft object was exchanged for a hard prosthetic one as a safety measure against physical injury and castration, in terms of a hidden, indestructible phallus. It is noteworthy that in the discussion of the three cases, Greenacre *contrasts* them with fetishism. While one can completely agree with her interpretation of the genetic factors involved, one is perplexed by the characterization of the symptoms as "fetishistic." In contrast to the situation in well-developed perversions, such fetishistic symptoms are not so intimately and clearly connected with sexual functioning, but serve more *exclusively* to support and reinforce phallic (or clitoral) value as part of a general body safety and *so defend against bodily and separation anxiety.*

If we omit the word "fetishistic," we have a splendid description of surrounding ritualistic defenses and the use of prosthetic objects against separation and bodily injury by magic ingestions or by the anal-phallic variant of the illusory phallus—but not fetishism.

Nancy Spiegel (1967) described a young woman who had a compulsive habit of manipulating a shoestring. According to the patient's mother, the baby started shortly after having been *weaned from the breast* to twist a string of beads and stare at it unblinkingly. Her more extensive use of the string—a shoestring from her mother's shoe—started *with the birth* of her brother when she was $2\frac{1}{2}$ years old. When she grew older, she surreptitiously removed shoelaces from women's shoes. In adolescence she received some sexual excitement from stealing shoelaces as well as sweaters from big-breasted girls.

As a child she was most envious of her brother's being on the breast and suffered severe separation anxiety on entering nursery school. Without the string she felt empty, "nothing." She did not feel her lower part at all. At about the age of 6, she asked girls to give her enemas. Later she had scatological fantasies; anal masturbation imitated the childhood enemas administered by her mother. During young adulthood, the string was used as a ritual *against* masturbation.

According to Spiegel, it differed from our concept of a fetish in two ways: (1) manipulation of the string did not lead to orgasm; (2) it had a defensive, undoing, anti-masturbation quality. In addition, the string was given up at puberty—at a time when fetishism usually crystallizes. The shoestring seemed to have represented the breast at the beginning, serving as a transitional object. Later it acquired the qualities of an illusory phallus (probably representing both the male and female phallus). Finally, by virtue of its presence and "observing" functions, it acquired qualities of an externalized superego.

Winnicott (1960) describes a boy who suffered three separation traumas between the age of 3 and $4\frac{1}{2}$ years. Among other compulsive symptoms, he became obsessed with strings, with which he tied pieces of furniture together. He also put them around his sister's neck. The string served to *deny separation*—and also went through a twist into sadistic fantasies with the possibility of a later perversion.

Sperling (1963) describes a woman who, strongly attached to her mother, had since early childhood preserved a small head pillow. Because of her severe separation anxiety as a baby, her mother put her on the little pillow next to her. Later she gave the pillow to her daughter, who continued using it, carrying it, and remade it several times during adulthood. She remembered that while sleeping with her mother, she actually held on to her breasts. In adulthood, when sleepless or depressed, she put on her mother's robe, which she had also preserved. Sperling terms both objects fetishes, the pillow representing the breast and the state of being wrapped in the mother's robe representing the primal scene. Thus even in adulthood, this patient, quite incompletely separated from the mother, carried with her a transitional object of the "intermediary" type, which she used to soothe her anxiety and depression by undoing the separation from her mother; and by wearing her mother's robe, she reevoked her total ambience.

THE PRODROMAL PHALLIC PHASE

Greenacre (1970) scrutinized the existing literature on the infantile fetish. She accepted the concept of infantile fetish and hoped "to indicate the essential ways in which the transitional object differs from the fetish" (p. 455). "They are . . . at two ends of a spectrum" (p. 450), with transitions between the two phenomena. She found that in contrast to the "uncomplicated transitional object," the infantile fetish is more concrete and less plastic; originates in severe deprivation and frustration, i.e., not "good enough" mothering; and is more frequently given by the mother than "created" by the infant. She does not consider the infantile fetish to be "as circumscribed a substitute for the penis as is true in most adult situations, [it] rather seems to represent a replacement of a combination of breast and penis, in which the wish for the breast may predominate" (p. 451).

Just as in the cases she reviewed in Wulff's paper, she concludes that these "fetishes" came into existence at a time when transitional objects are adopted but "represent the feeding function even more strongly than is true of the transitional object" (p. 448).

It is likely that in these cases we are dealing with distortions of transitional phenomena, where the objects fulfill oral needs that are due to inadequate mothering and unsupported weaning, but there is insufficient evidence of their phallic significance. Only in a case like Idelsohn's (cited by Wulff), where a transitional object is carried to the age of $4\frac{1}{2}$, with progressive use from mouthing to genital stimulation, could we even consider with some plausibility a *childhood* (not infantile) fetish.[4]

There is more clinical evidence (Lorand, 1930) of childhood

---

[4] In her presentation (1970) Greenacre combines this case with that of the little boy who carried his chamber pot, as his most precious possession, in the orphanage. There is no indication in the case description that the chamber pot's use followed such a progressive development from mouth to genital.

fetishism around the age of 4. While there is neither clinical nor theoretical objection to the assumption of fetishism within and after the phallic phase, it is advantageous to keep fetishism and the distortions of the transitional object apart.

Roiphe and Galenson (1973a) base their deduction on nursery observations. Direct child observation—the main tool of developmental psychology—has perhaps made the most important contribution to psychoanalytic theory in the last decades. The trailblazing investigations of Mahler led to a systematic presentation of the *general* laws of early development and provided us with the baseline for some aspects of later pathology as well.

Interpretation of the behavioral data was safeguarded by the investigation, comparison, and follow-up of fairly large and homogeneous groups. The repetition of observations, their consistency, and their time sequence parallel to some extent the psychoanalytic method in which the continuity and convergence of many id derivatives enable the observer to interpret phenomena with high plausibility.

However, when it comes to the investigation of specific individual pathology, many difficulties arise. To establish convincingly by direct observation the existence of a fetish in a preverbal infant—a condition that in my view is based on the highly complex defensive function of partial denial through symbolic displacement of a unique meaning, namely, that of the maternal or female phallus for the purpose of the safety of the genital—such an attempt may prove to be an insurmountable task.

But let us assume in the light of the Roiphe and Galenson research that the phallic phase occurs earlier, or at the least that it has long forerunners, and that during this stage the inanimate object *does serve as defense against castration anxiety, without the meaning of the maternal phallus* that has not yet crystallized. With all this in mind, let us look at their clinical evidence.

Suzy, at 15 months, after being exposed to nursery experiences, developed intense sexual curiosity. When at 16½ months she received the uncanny gift of a walking, talking doll of her own size, and when its batteries fell out, she became terrified and did not want to have anything to do with the doll. When some 6 weeks later *the family moved into a new apartment*, she asked for the doll and a soft coverlet and maintained an attachment to them both for the next 5 months.

We may reconstruct that in this child the move from the accustomed milieu renewed separation and castration anxiety, following which she regressed to the protective mother-child environment, reestablished a mother-child unity through the doll, which represents the damaged self, and resorted to the safety of the transitional object of the coverlet.

Ruth is a rather complicated case because of the congenital hip injury. Again, it seems likely that the child was confronted with anxiety about body integrity and castration. The "boy doll" would thus serve to dramatize a conflictless mother-child relationship and possibly a phallic alter ego. I would regard her dolls as intermediates between a transitional and a prosthetic object.

Billy was 13 months old when, during a phase of an "expanding separation reaction" that reached a peak at 16 months, *his mother left him for 2 weeks*. The sexual arousal observed during the following period consisted in frequent clutching of his penis while rocking on his mother's legs, and the development of a sleep ritual in which he pressed the night bottle to his penis which he simultaneously clutched. Perverse penis-breast activities in the adult breast fetishist may have a similar history (Bak, 1968).

Roiphe and Galenson's interpretation of the ritual is that the bottle stands for the object and the penis-clutching expresses fear of the loss of the penis (perversion breast-nipple). Neither of these manifestations, separately or combined, would qualify as a fetish, but they can be regarded as a transitional phenomenon in which the token presence of the object or part-object breast is linked to genital stimulation.

OBJECT LOSS AND CASTRATION ANXIETY

The importance of the object has been one of the basic tenets in psychoanalysis. Object loss was regarded by Freud as the foremost precipitant of pathological development. Today we may say that the ego's capacity to resist or tolerate regression as a consequence of loss is one of the facets of ego strength. Through further understanding of the paramount significance of the early mother-child relationship, the object acquired a central role, not only in pathology, but also in normal development. The importance of the object in the differentiation of psychic structure and its role in the integrative functions and secondary autonomy (Hartmann) have received increasing recognition. The maturational sequence of loss of object followed by loss of love as precursors of castration anxiety (Freud, 1926) has an axiomatic place in psychoanalysis. This may explain why the genetic link between object loss and castration anxiety has not been critically explored and firmly established.

Clinically, the link has been a banal observation. In adult analyses we are all familiar with the type of person who cannot sustain the loss of a love object and has to replace it without delay. In some individuals, their sexual identity is strongly dependent on the *presence* of the object. When patients regressed and fell ill, we accepted without much further questioning that the object loss proved to be inseparable and indistinguishable from castration. At the other end of the spectrum are men whose potency disturbance is resolved by *one* particular object on whom they become overdependent and to whom they develop an attachment reaching the intensity of thralldom. In these types, the concrete presence of the object supports sexual identity and genital functioning and improves the capacity for reality testing.

I have previously examined the link between separation from the mother[5] and castration anxiety in psychosis. Theorizing about schizophrenic regression and the role of temperature orientation in the fused dual unity of mother and child, I suggested the following genetic proposition: At birth, the catastrophic cooling of the infant's body temperature constitutes the *prototype* of castration anxiety. The "loss" of the mother is simultaneous with marked bodily change or "loss" in the infant. I regarded this as a physiological model and did not speculate on its mental representation. Nevertheless, granting a number of later developmental factors, the love of the object will remain intimately connected with warmth, just as loss and abandonment are equated with coldness, emotionally, symbolically, and metaphorically (Bak, 1939).

---

[5] See Bak (1968) in which I considered the state of being in love, which is often triggered by object loss, as a regressive wish to relive the early mother-child relationship.

Wulff (1946) concludes from his material that the boy identifies with the "fetish object." He felt that this throws light on the process of object choice, namely, "that the first genuine libidinal tie to a strange object takes place along the path of an identification of this object with the individual's own penis. This perhaps explains why it is that rejection on the part of the object is felt as a very severe narcissistic injury and is experienced by many neurotics as a direct castration" (p. 468).

The genetic hypothesis that I shall tentatively propose crystallized on consideration of two papers by Roiphe and Galenson (1973a, 1973b). In "Object Loss and Early Sexual Development" (1973b), they describe the little boy Billy (previously discussed), who, at around 16 months of age, repeatedly put his mother's hand on his penis and started rocking in a state of excitement.

In "Phallic Passivity in Men," Loewenstein (1935) postulated two stages in the phallic phase, first a *passive* one, with the aim of being touched; and a much later and *active* one, with the aim of penetration. He also described his own observation of a 5-month-old boy who "used to bend himself back into an opisthotonic attitude, and, so to speak, present his penis to his mother, whenever she was attending to his toilet and her hand approached the region of his genitals. At the same time he uttered little grunts of pleasure" (p. 336). Loewenstein considers as an intermediate between the passive and the active aim the rubbing of the penis on or with inanimate things. (See also Ruth Mack Brunswick, 1940.)

It seems from the above observations that sporadic genital arousals (phallic or clitoral) are more frequent in the first year of life than has hitherto been described. It is easy to imagine that both mothers and nursery personnel may, on the basis of various motives, disregard these phenomena. Between 1 and 2 years of age, the arousals may even be more frequent, but still too incidental and unstructured, with diffuse fantasies, to correspond to our phase concept. But it may well be that with increasing frequency and the endogenous erotogenicity, and the assistance of the average expectable environment's maternal care and ministrations, the manifestations of the passive phallic phase begin to emerge, albeit with oral and anal elements. It is then precisely the maternal care that *promotes* the genital schematization. Roiphe and Galenson point out that during the phase of incomplete self-nonself differentiation, there may be an indistinct or fused representation of the infant's whole body and the breast, especially nipple and genital and the localization of the genital sensation.

During the later phase of solidifying object and self representations, the experiential connection between the object's care and the genital sensations seem to become established. It is perhaps more than a metaphor that in *this stage the infant's sexuality (or genital schematization) is in the mother's hands.* This specific phase vulnerability may also be contingent on the emerging representation of the dominantly *single object.*

From these assumptions, some further hypotheses can be derived:

In the earlier phase of self-nonself differentiation, object loss may lead to the infant's grief, described by Bowlby and discussed by others.

Physical traumas, actual dangers, surgical interventions, etc. (Greenacre, 1953) may constitute the bases for later severe pathology, such as the feelings of emptiness, disintegration and dismemberment, contents that appear in psychotic depressions and schizophrenia. These problems are beyond the scope of this paper.

In the later phase of genital schematization, which seems to take place at about 13 to 20 months, even a temporary absence of the maternal object may create the loss of genital sensation and even some sense of loss of the genital itself, as if the mother, by removing herself, takes along with her the infant's genital.[6] In this I hypothesize the genetic core of the "indissoluble" connection between object loss and castration anxiety.

The consecutive penis-clutching[7] and sometimes frantic mastur-

---

[6] Eissler (1958) mentions the fetishist's fantasy that the genital is a detachable thing. (See also the first case in my 1953 paper.)

[7] Dr. Robert J. Kabcenell called my attention to a Letter to the Editor on "Penis Clutching," in which Ward (1972) reported eight cases of male children, ranging in age from 2½ to 9 years, "with the obvious and embarrassing symptoms of penis-clutching. Penis-clutching in these cases indicated the presence of a meatal stenosis. None of these children had urinary tract infections." The symptoms of penis-clutching disappeared immediately after an adequate meatus was established. I think this little item indicates that there is some real danger in the penis-clutching on the part of some boys.

batory activity reinstate the presence and the stimulation of the maternal object by clinging to the genital and reproducing, now autoplastically, the sensations provided by the object. Inanimate things from the transitional phase usually serve this purpose. They are the token representatives of body parts of the caring object (part object) and usually derive from the various distortions of the transitional objects.

This phase-specific trauma of abandonment by the object may be responsible for the increased castration anxiety in the full-fledged phallic phase and may play an important role in the development of later pathological syndromes—*among them* fetishism. However, it has yet to be proven that these early masturbatory things before the phallic phase, or even within it, determine in any way the development of the adult fetish.

Summary

1. The literature contains a widespread confusion in the use of the concepts "transitional objects," "infantile fetishes," and childhood and adult fetishism. I have attempted to clarify these concepts in terms of their essential phase specificity.

2. Attachments to inanimate things in childhood and adulthood have a different metapsychology and serve different defensive functions. In the adult they usually function as defenses against separation and object loss.

3. (*a*) In infancy the inanimate thing serves as a "transitional object" and functions primarily to attenuate the trauma of weaning and separation.

(*b*) The prosthetic object may develop later and may continue to function against dangers to body integrity, especially castration.

(*c*) The intermediate object serves as a representative of the mother or mother substitute in a child who has progressed to a need-satisfying object relationship.

4. "Infantile fetish" is a misnomer before the phallic phase, irrespective of its eventual masturbatory aspects.

5. Fetishism is a defense against castration anxiety, in which the inanimate thing represents the maternal phallus and its symbolism crystallizes specifically in the phallic phase.

6. There is, for the time being, insufficient evidence to assume fetishism in women.

7. Object loss, or even temporary abandonment by the mother or her substitute during genital schematization (prodromal phallic phase), may establish an indissoluble link between loss and castration.

BIBLIOGRAPHY

Bak, R. (1939), Regression of Ego-Orientation and Libido in Schizophrenia. *Int. J. Psycho-Anal.*, 20:64–71.
——— (1953), Fetishism. *J. Amer. Psychoanal. Assn.*, 1:285–298.
——— (1956), Aggression and Perversion. In: *Perversions*, ed. S. Lorand. New York: Random House, pp. 231–240.
——— (1968), The Phallic Woman. *This Annual*, 23:15–36.
Brunswick, R. M. (1940), The Preodipal Phase of Libido Development. *Psychoanal. Quart.*, 9:293–319.
Buxbaum, E. (1960), Hair Pulling and Fetishism. *This Annual*, 15:243–260.
Dickes, R. (1963), Fetishistic Behavior. *J. Amer. Psychoanal. Assn.*, 11:303–330.
Eissler, K. R. (1958), Notes on Problems of Technique in the Psychoanalytic Treatment of Adolescents. *This Annual*, 13:223–254.
Fenichel, O. (1945), *The Psychoanalytic Theory of Neurosis*. New York: Norton.
Freud, A. (1965), *Normality and Pathology in Childhood*. New York: International Universities Press, pp. 207–222.
Freud, S. (1914), On Narcissism. *Standard Edition*, 14:67–102. London: Hogarth Press, 1957.
——— (1926), Inhibitions, Symptoms and Anxiety. *Standard Edition*, 20:77–175. London: Hogarth Press, 1959.
——— (1927), Fetishism. *Standard Edition*, 21:149–157. London: Hogarth Press, 1961.
——— (1940), An Outline of Psycho-Analysis. *Standard Edition*, 23:141–207. London: Hogarth Press, 1964.
Furer, M. (1964), The Development of a Preschool Symbiotic Psychotic Boy. *This Annual*, 19:448–469.
Gillespie, W. H. (1940), A Contribution to the Study of Fetishism. *Int. J. Psycho-Anal.*, 21:401–415.
Greenacre, P. (1953), Certain Relationships between Fetishism and the Faulty Development of the Body Image. *This Annual*, 8:79–98.
——— (1955), Further Considerations Regarding Fetishism. *This Annual*, 10:187–194.
——— (1960), Further Notes on Fetishism. *This Annual*, 15:191–207.
——— (1969), The Fetish and the Transitional Object. *This Annual*, 24:144–164.

GREENACRE, P. (1970), The Transitional Object and the Fetish. *Int. J. Psycho-Anal.*, 51:447–456.

HUG-HELLMUTH, H. (1915), Ein Fall von weiblichem Fuss-, richtiger Stiefel-Fetischismus. *Int. Z. Psychoanal.*, 3:111–114.

LOEWENSTEIN, R. M. (1935), Phallic Passivity in Men. *Int. J. Psycho-Anal.*, 16:334–340.

LORAND, S. (1930), Fetishism *in Statu Nascendi. Int. J. Psycho-Anal.*, 11:419–427.

MAHLER, M. S. (1961), On Sadness and Grief in Infancy and Childhood. *This Annual*, 16:332–351.

PARKIN, A. (1963), On Fetishism. *Int. J. Psycho-Anal.*, 44:352–361.

ROIPHE, H. & GALENSON, E. (1973a), The Infantile Fetish. *This Annual*, 28:147–166.

—— & —— (1973b), Object Loss and Early Sexual Development. *Psychoanal. Quart.*, 42:73–90.

ROMM, M. E. (1949), Some Dynamics in Fetishism. *Psychoanal. Quart.*, 18:137–153.

SPERLING, M. (1963), Fetishism in Children. *Psychoanal. Quart.*, 32:374–392.

SPIEGEL, N. (1967), An Infantile Fetish and Its Persistence into Young Womanhood. *This Annual*, 22:402–425.

STEWART, W. (1972), Personal communication.

WARD, G. A. (1972), Penis Clutching: A Cause and Its Cure. *J. Amer. Med. Assn.*, 219:1338–1339.

WEISSMAN, P. (1957), Some Aspects of Sexual Activity in a Fetishist. *Psychoanal. Quart.*, 26:494–507.

WINNICOTT, D. W. (1953), Transitional Objects and Transitional Phenomena. *Collected Papers*. New York: Basic Books, 1957, pp. 229–242.

—— (1960), String: A Technique of Communication. *Maturational Processes and the Facilitating Environment*. New York: International Universities Press, 1965, pp. 153–157.

WULFF, M. (1946), Fetishism and Object Choice in Early Childhood. *Psychoanal. Quart.*, 15:450–471.

Dimensions of the First Transitional Object

FRED BUSCH, PH.D.

WINNICOTT'S (1953) ORIGINAL ARTICLE ON TRANSITIONAL OBJECTS makes it clear that he did not consider his to be the final word on the subject. Yet many analytic authors have written about the transitional object as if there was nothing more to learn about or discover from it. An exception is Tolpin (1971) who linked the transitional object to Kohut's (1971) concept of "transmuting internalization." She argues that the transitional object becomes a "soother" via innumerable minute internalizations of maternal functions with which the transitional object has been endowed, and evolves into a structure which allows the child to soothe himself—a process which greatly enhances separation-individuation. Tolpin's discussion thus places the transitional object into a developmental framework that is the most concise and heuristic to date.

Our own study of the transitional object (Busch et al., 1973) took a different road. On the basis of data derived from extensive interviews with mothers and observations of normal nursery school children and toddlers, we explored how the attachment to transitional objects develops and some of the discrete functions they serve. We have found it necessary to define carefully some of the

Assistant Professor of Psychology, Department of Psychiatry, The University of Michigan Medical Center. An earlier version of this paper was presented to the Michigan Psychoanalytic Society on February 14, 1974.

This research was carried out under the auspices of the Child Psychoanalytic Study Program, Director: Humberto Nagera, M.D., of Children's Psychiatric Hospital, The University of Michigan Medical Center.

properties of what we were studying. Thus, before going into a discussion of our findings, it will be necessary to take a detour into some of the definitional limits that we feel are necessary in studying transitional objects.

FIRST AND SECOND TRANSITIONAL OBJECTS

Reports in the literature (Stevenson, 1954; A. Freud, 1965) suggested, and our own observations confirmed, that there are two distinct times in a child's life when attachment to an inanimate object may appear. The first is in the first year of life; the second is around 2 years of age. In our sample, the children who developed an intense attachment to an inanimate object at 6 months did not usually develop a second attachment to another object at 2 years.

In the literature on transitional objects the specific time when a child forms an attachment to an object has largely been ignored, all objects eventually being labeled as "transitional." Tolpin (1971) does point to the fact that differences in the timing of the development of the transitional object may account for the duration and intensity of the attachment to the transitional object, but she adds that these "have not yet been studied" (p. 326). It is our belief that it is not useful to refer to attachments to inanimate objects made by the child at two very different stages of development simply as "transitional objects." Lumping the two object attachments together obscures important developmental issues for each, because the enormous differences in the development of drives, ego, and object relations during the two phases are ignored.

We have chosen to call the object to which the child becomes attached in the first year of life the *first transitional object,* and the object attachment which appears approximately at age 2 the *second transitional object.*[1] This classification is a provisional one insofar as it

---

[1] In earlier publications (Busch et al., 1973; Busch and McKnight, 1973), these first and second transitional objects were identified as "primary" and "secondary" transitional objects. However, for a variety of reasons I have abandoned this terminology. In the psychoanalytic literature, the terms "primary" and "secondary" generally imply a genetic sequence. No such sequence was intended. More commonly, as noted above, the child who develops an attachment to a first

remains to be shown that underlying the attachment at different ages is a similar process, and/or that the resulting attachment serves equal or near-equal functions. Our initial observations have led us to include the attachment to an inanimate object at around age 2 under the generic heading "transitional objects," since in its use and importance it shows similarities to what we have labeled the *first transitional object*. In our present work the focus has been the development of attachments to objects within the first year of life (first transitional objects).[2]

DEFINING THE FIRST TRANSITIONAL OBJECT

In our investigations into the first transitional object it became clear that certain definitional limits would have to be placed on what we would consider a true first transitional object. This was necessary for two reasons. First of all, a distinction had to be made between the "blanket" and the vast array of objects[3] which either comfort the child or to which he becomes attached in the first year of life. It also seemed important in a beginning study of this complex phenomenon that the ambiguities which have invaded the literature on this topic be avoided. Two classes of objects have been separated out from the first transitional object. The first type is to be differentiated from the first transitional object either because of the time of its development, or the transitory nature of its soothing properties. Objects of the second class serve a soothing function for a

---

transitional object does not develop an attachment to a second transitional object and vice versa. The terms I am currently using also reflect more accurately the fact that the psychologically important element is not the object but the attachment.

[2] In the interests of simplicity and readability I have adopted Tolpin's (1971) "people language," and the term "blanket" will appear interchangeably with first transitional object. However, as our previous research has shown (Busch et al., 1973), blankets are not the only type of first transitional object.

[3] The word "objects" here is used in its dictionary sense of something seen or felt. What is being distinguished from the first transitional object are not strictly "things" or "pre-objects" (Spitz, 1965), but rather a variety of objects meeting differing narcissistic and libidinal needs. These do not lend themselves easily to classification, and thus I have opted for the common usage of the word "object."

longer period of time, but by their very nature are likely to have different representational values for the child than the "blanket." Thus in order to distinguish the first transitional object from other objects to which the child may become attached, we defined a number of criteria that had to be met before the object is considered a first transitional object (Busch et al., 1973). These will be presented in summary form here.

The attachment to the object should be manifested within the first year of life, and it must be of *lasting duration*. By lasting duration we mean approximately one year or longer.

The first transitional object should be distinguished from the fetishistic object to which it has been compared (Fintzy, 1971; Sperling, 1963; Wulff, 1946). Greenacre (1969) has elaborated a number of dimensions on which one can differentiate these phenomena. Among these are the differences between: the sets of experience from which they develop; the maternal imagos which each represents; and the function of each in adaptive development. We would agree with Greenacre's formulations in this area, and add that the fetishistic object increases excitation while the "blanket" decreases excitation.

A distinction should be made between the first transitional object and those objects which directly meet an oral, libidinal need (breast, bottle); objects which are provided by parents for comfort (pacifiers); parts of the infant's body which may also bring comfort. In the first case ("blanket" compared to bottle), it is just this difference which makes the first transitional object worthy of study. It does not meet an oral, libidinal need, yet in the first year of life attachment to it is exceeded in intensity only by attachment to the primary object. The main distinguishing characteristic of the "blanket" when compared to objects given to the child by the parents is the *origin* of the object. The first transitional object is created by the child, while the pacifier is first accepted and only later may it be re-created for different purposes. The *locus* of the object is the major difference between the "blanket" and parts of the infant's body which may bring comfort: the "blanket," by being outside the child's body, would have to lead to a series of qualitatively different soothing experiences than bodily parts. We would also assume a different discovery process for each.

THE FIRST ATTACHMENT TO AN INANIMATE OBJECT

In our sample, attachment to the first transitional object was always seen in the second half of the first year of life, and most commonly around 6 months of age. The object is usually soft, malleable, and has been an integral part of the child's life since birth.[4] By far the most frequent first transitional objects are blankets that have always been in the infant's crib. The attachment process is a silent one, with the parent usually becoming aware of it only after the attachment has reached an intense level.

Tolpin suggests that movement toward the first transitional object is based upon frustration stemming from the alteration of the symbiotic unity between mother and infant. According to her, the infant's physical growth disturbs the equilibrium established in the symbiotic dyad in such a way that movement toward the first transitional object is encouraged. The child turns to his "blanket" in order to recapture the soothing qualities found in the symbiotic unity. The infant attempts to merge with the first transitional object as he once did with the primary object in the symbiotic state.

Our own observations have led us to delineate two sets of factors in the infant's attachment to the first transitional object: (1) the general ones which involve the movement of the child from symbiosis toward the first transitional object; (2) the specific experiences which lead to the attachment to a particular object.

In terms of the infant's movement from symbiosis toward the first transitional object, it seems likely that the infant's physical growth, which leads to a difference in the mother's handling (Tolpin, 1971), is only one of many contributory factors. One important variable in the progression from the symbiotic phase has, we feel, been

---

[4] At this point in the paper I shall disregard the variations in the development of the first transitional object which we reported in our previous work, and focus only on the prototypical first transitional object. As an illustration of the type of variations in this extraordinarily rich and complex phenomenon, I briefly mention those children who use a series of objects which all serve as a single first transitional object. Thus, Andrew appeared to be attached to four blankets which were dissimilar in color and texture. However, they all had a satin edge, and this was the single factor in Andrew's attachment to them.

neglected, namely, the many subtle changes in what the mother expects of the child as a number of physical milestones are reached. As the child starts to sit up, roll over, crawl, smile, babble—in fact, does all of those things that lead parents to talk of their child developing a "personality"—more demands are made of him for independent functioning. These would include such expectations as that he amuse himself for longer periods of time, and show a capacity for delay in the face of need.

Another factor in the progression from the symbiotic state is the contribution made by ego development. For example, as perceptual and memory functions develop, the stable image of an object outside of the infant in the form of "recognition memory" (Fraiberg, 1969) occurs. By 6 months when the mother appears within the infant's perceptual sphere, she is recognized with pleasurable affect. The development of structures leading to representation of the primary object as external would seem to make it more difficult for regressive merging to take place with that same object. With increasing ego development, the mother, even if cathected as a self-object, is increasingly recognized as being outside the infant's control, while the first transitional object always remains subject to the infant's control and a willing partner in his omnipotent narcissistic state.

In summary, it would appear to be somewhat simplistic to hypothesize, as Tolpin does, a single causative factor (physical growth) as a major determinant in the move from the symbiotic state to the first transitional object. There probably are numerous factors, internal as well as external ones, which play a role in this movement. While I would agree with Tolpin that the movement from the symbiotic dyad is a crucial variable in the development of the attachment to a "blanket," it is not the only one. There appear to be many specific factors which influence whether the child develops an attachment to a "blanket" at all.

In all of the children studied by us the first transitional object had been an intimate part of the crib since birth. Clearly, then, the inference can be drawn that certain experiences around the crib are crucial in the formation of an attachment to the first transitional object. In attempting to explain this phenomenon two factors appear to be significant.

The first variable is the mother's absence from the child at bedtime.[5] Two recent studies (Caudhill, 1971; R. and E. Gaddini, 1970) found that in those cultures where the mothers stayed with their infants at bedtime (either lying down with them or sleeping in the same bedroom), the great majority of infants tended *not* to develop an attachment to a first transitional object. Therefore, the .mother's absence at bedtime appears to be one significant factor in the tendency to become attached to a first transitional object. Absence here is used in a general sense to denote the infant's awareness of the mother's absence (does not feel, see, or hear her).

A second factor in selecting the "blanket" from the crib is the "experience of bedtime," which I would see as stressful for the child. It seems likely that bedtime is the first regressive experience that the infant, in many Western cultures, is expected to adapt to on his own. The cathectic change in the movement toward sleep is a regressive process when compared to the wakeful state even for the 4- to 6-month-old child. While most mothers tend to mediate the regressive process by various activities, such as feeding, rocking, and singing, the infant, even in a semiwakeful state, must eventually be left alone to deal with his discomfort. I would assume, then, that the stressful state before falling asleep and the mother's absence at bedtime are two significant factors in the infant's forming an attachment to an object usually found in the crib.

The question must be asked why out of the totality of objects available to the child, a particular object is chosen from among those in the crib. Being unable to search for objects, it is reasonable to assume that he will choose an object with which he is most familiar and one which is readily at hand. Given the amount of time he spends in his crib during the first 6 months of his life and considering the fact that at most other times he is usually involved in some interchange with the human object, it is not surprising that the first inanimate object chosen for special attachment is connected with the crib.

In addition to familiarity and ready availability, the choice of the specific object is also determined by its having certain qualities. In

[5] Included here are all those times when the child is put in his crib to go to sleep, which at 6 months may be as many as 3 to 4 times a day.

our sample, the most important attribute was softness. One little girl whose first transitional object was a diaper would refuse it after it had been washed and dried outside (making it stiff and hard, according to the mother). She would not accept it again until it had been "handled," thereby restoring its soft texture. The materials most common among our children's first transititional objects were cloth, silk, and terry cloth; there were no examples of plastic, rubber, or vinyl objects. This seems to give support to Harlow's (1970) work with infant monkeys which indicates something inherent in softer textures that leads to more effective comforting and a greater preference for these materials in infancy. The objective qualities, then, of the object chosen as the first transitional object would be: that the object is a part of the infant's crib since birth and it must be soft.

There are certain other factors which seem to aid, but which do not appear necessary for, the formation of a special attachment to an object. In some cases the object which eventually became the first transitional object had been an intimate part of soothing mother-child interactions since birth. In the case of one infant who had become attached to a diaper, the mother had used it during feeding and also put it under the infant's head while sleeping. Another mother reported that her child had become attached to a blanket with a particular binding that had the same texture as the pajamas she had worn while nursing. In other cases there were no such observable intimate links to soothing mother-child interaction. However, when an object has always been part of the crib, and was also used in some soothing mother-child interactions, the probability that it will become a first transitional object is increased.

FUNCTION OF THE FIRST TRANSITIONAL OBJECT

While Tolpin has spoken convincingly of the metapsychological aspects of the first transitional object as a soother, I believe we are in a position to give a more specific dissection of the first transitional object. Certain prototypical situations highlight important, observable functions which the first transitional object serves. The first of these situations is when the young child is under stress and needs his "blanket." When the "blanket" is given to him, he will take it and literally bury his face in it. One has the impression of a struggle to get as close to it as possible. The second situation is when the child goes to sleep, and the "blanket" is immediately brought up to the face area. The most common experience is to see the sleeping child with his "blanket" shoved under his face in what seems like a most uncomfortable position. However, during restless sleep if the "blanket" happens to stray accidentally to a different area of the child's crib, parents can be sure they will be awakened to fetch the lost object, which is often just a few inches away from its usual position.

What I would like to highlight in the situations cited above is that the first transitional object seems to be used mainly in a tactile fashion. While various authors (Greenacre, 1969; Winnicott, 1953) suggest the importance of the smell of the first transitional object for the child, our own data do not support this. In our sample of children the first transitional object was not rejected when it was washed (thus obviously changing the smell), but in the one case where the texture of the first transitional object was changed regularly it was rejected until its original texture was restored.[6] Most striking though is the mode in which the first transitional object is used in certain prototypical situations. In these situations the infant relates to the object via contact perception, using the oral cavity (Spitz, 1965), which includes the tongue, lips, cheeks, and nasopharynx as its mode of reception. This perceptual mode, which is characteristic of the very young infant, speaks elegantly to the temporary regressive nature of the child's use of the first transitional object with its roots in early experience.[7]

---

[6] Greenacre (1969) has pointed to the biologically based importance of smell in the first months of life. I cannot rule out the possibility that smell may be an important factor in the infant's initial attachment to a "blanket," but that later on its smell may lose significance.

[7] While pointing to the regressive nature of the child's relationship to the first transitional object, one must also speak to its adaptive qualities. It is to the point that it is the "blanket" rather than the mother herself which is related to in this regressive manner. Here one can see the growth potential in the child's use of the first transitional object. I would disagree with Tolpin's assertion that the transitional object cannot be more important than the mother herself. Our own records are filled with innumerable examples indicating that the first transitional

Behaviorally one can see the "blanket" used by the child in a regressive, perceptual mode, while attempting to merge himself as much as possible with it. Here I think we can see the relationship of the first transitional object to the symbiotic tie to the mother, with the first transitional object representing the soothing, affective, experiential components of that relationship.

While I have focused on the prototypical first transitional object, its complexities also need to be stressed in order not to miss its function throughout development. I shall therefore briefly discuss some variations in the form in which the first transitional object is used and the different functions it serves as the child grows older.

Observation teaches us that not all children use the first transitional object via the oral cavity on all occasions. At various times the special object may be draped over the shoulder, carried in a ball under the arm, put on a table or chair at arm's length and fingered, or used to rub a part of the body other than the oral cavity. In all of these instances the soothing function of the "blanket" remains uppermost, while the overt method of using it is less regressive. We do not understand all the variations in the use of the "blanket." However, two important factors that seem to be specific to the manner in which it is used are the degree of psychical stress that the child is under at the moment, and the degree of internalization of the soothing process which has occurred. I would hypothesize that, at any one particular time, the less acute the stress and the more internalized the soothing properties of the first transitional object, the less intense would be the regressive use of the object. Thus, while the tired 18-month-old who has had a bad fall might immediately use his "blanket" via the oral cavity, the 3-year-old going to nursery school for the first time might be satisfied to carry his object over his shoulder for the first few days and then put it aside. In looking at a child's use of the first transitional object, then, one might well expect to see wide variations. I have singled out only two variables; others still need to be investigated.

The first transitional object, while always serving a soothing

---

object was clearly more important than the mother at times of stress, and this was a source of bewilderment and hurt for many mothers.

function, may temporarily also serve other purposes in the child's life. Our records contained many descriptions of children who, during the toddler stage, used the "blanket" as one of the many vehicles for expressing their ambivalent, anal-sadistic tendencies to their mothers. A typical example told us by several mothers was a 2-year-old who, having hurt himself slightly, demanded that mother get his "blanket" for him and then fell apart when this was not fulfilled. He would yell, scream, and pull at the mother until his demand was met.[8] Another example of a first transitional object serving not only a soothing function was seen in one boy who used a blanket as part of a compulsive ritual in going to sleep. He had three objects (a pacifier, a blanket, and a teddy), to which he had become attached at different times and which had to be in their special place when he went to sleep. In short, while looking over the wide usage of the first transitional object, one should note these different uses but not be misled into mistaking temporary usage with necessary functions.

DISCUSSION

The prototypical attachment to the first transitional object seems to be formed as a result of a complex set of experiences in the developing infant. First of all, there is the movement from the symbiotic tie to the mother. This in itself is a complex movement that involves libidinal shifts in relation to developing ego functions and demands from the external environment. However, the stress of progression from the symbiotic stage seems a necessary but not sufficient cause for the child to develop an attachment to a "blanket." We discovered that the attachment to the first transitional object develops from a particular experience, that of going to sleep. I hypothesized that two factors involved in the sleep process contribute to the infant's forming an attachment to the first transitional object: (1) the absence of the mother at bedtime, which

---

[8] Here it is of interest that when the child finally received the desired object, he could use it to soothe himself, although he remained ambivalent toward the mother. This demonstrates the adaptive qualities inherent in the child's use of the first transitional object.

the 6-month-old infant experiences cognitively as a disappearance (Fraiberg, 1969); and (2) the particular type of regressive experience involved in going to sleep. Under the impact of this twofold stress, the infant figuratively (and later literally) reaches for a comforting object which must be familiar, at hand, and soft. This object seems to have representational qualities of the symbiotic relationship to the mother.

The child thus creates a self-object which does not mete out the innumerable, slight narcissistic disappointments which are characteristic of the "good enough" mother (Winnicott, 1953). Here we come upon one of the contradictions inherent in the first transitional object. While the object is inevitably turned to because of the disappointments in the mother, the qualities of soothing with which it becomes endowed can occur only within the "good enough" mother-child relationship. I would surmise that if the early mother-child relationship was not satisfactory for the infant, or if the move from the symbiotic state was experienced as too disruptive, the infant would not be able to cathect the first transitional object with soothing qualities. In our sample of children the "blanket" was never created in an ambivalent manner. In its inception it is a unidimensional phenomenon—its one dimension being soothing. While this may be modified to a slight degree at a later time, the first transitional object is rarely handled in an aggressive fashion.

The regressive perceptual mode with which the first transitional object is used is clear. Contact perception via the oral cavity is characteristic of the very young infant and, in the case of the first transitional object, seems to be an important method of recapturing the symbiotic relationship to the mother. While there are variations in the manner in which the first transitional object is used as the child grows older, the primary method of use appears to remain one of contact perception.

While Tolpin's hypothesis regarding the function of the first transitional object is clearly the most heuristic to date, a crucial question must be answered to test the validity of her hypothesis. If the soothing properties of the special object are internalized so that a structure is formed, leading the child to more self-sufficient soothing and the demise of the object, one might expect significant differences in the development of self-sufficient soothing in those children who did not have a first transitional object. Leaving out the case of the child who did not have a "good enough" mother (because of the many other psychological consequences in such a case), and focusing on those children whose mother remained the primary soother (e.g., because of bodily contact at sleeptime), one might wonder what other routes are followed or what complications occur in the development of self-soothing and object constancy in the separation-individuation process. Tolpin (1971) hypothesizes that the first transitional object may be an important determinant in the child's development of object constancy:

> . . . transmuting internalization of regulatory functions mediated by the "good enough" mother of the separation phase (the narcissistically perceived maternal imago and its functions) and the "assistant" (the transitional object) gradually leads to psychic structure which enables the child to satisfy some of his own needs; the freedom from exclusive dependence on the need-satisfying object conferred by this structure is indispensable for the achievement of object constancy [p. 332].

Would we then expect children who do not have an attachment to a first transitional object to show deviations in the development of object constancy and separation-individuation? Would we also expect significant differences in the means and timing of self-soothing in those children whose mother serves as the primary soother? Our own data do not provide clear-cut answers and further study is required. However, our initial impression is that we do not see very obvious differences in some of the variables noted above between those children who do and those who do not have first transitional objects. It is more likely the child can use a variety of mediating "assistants" which lead to psychic structure and self-soothing, and that the first transitional object is not the royal road to adaptive self-soothing. Thumb sucking, pacifiers, ear rubbing, as well as subtle means where the mother appears to be the primary soother, all appear to be possible routes to self-soothing. The crucial factor is that each method of self-soothing (including the first transitional object) is likely to have its unique effect on self-soothing and result in a variety of developmental consequences.

A final word must be said on the issue of transitional phenomena which are lumped together with transitional objects by many analysts (Coppolillo, 1967; Tolpin, 1971; Winnicott, 1953). It seems worthwhile to differentiate these on a number of bases. The first question is whether the transitional phenomena really have the importance in childhood that has been attributed to them. Our records contained no examples of transitional phenomena, and I have yet to see in the literature a report of a transitional phenomenon having the same permanence as a first transitional object. Certainly, the transitional phenomena are not seen as providing soothing at times of stress (except at bedtime) in the same way as the first transitional object. Even if transitional phenomena did show the same objective uses as the first transitional object, the particular perceptual mode with which the first transitional object was used would lead to a very different set of soothing qualities. However, my own hypothesis is that the transitional phenomena are most often transitory in nature and serve a time-limited function that is superficially similar but qualitatively very different from the function served by the first transitional object.

BIBLIOGRAPHY

BUSCH, F. & McKNIGHT, J. (1973), Parental Attitudes and the Development of the Primary Transitional Object. *Child Psychiat. Hum. Develop.*, 4:12–20.
——— NAGERA, H., McKNIGHT, J., & PEZZAROSSI, G. (1973), Primary Transitional Objects. *J. Amer. Acad. Child Psychiat.*, 12:193–214.
CAUDHILL, W. (1971), Personal communication.
COPPOLILLO, H. P. (1967), Maturational Aspects of the Transitional Phenomenon. *Int. J. Psycho-Anal.*, 48:237–246.
FINTZY, R. T. (1971), Vicissitudes of the Transitional Object in a Borderline Child. *Int. J. Psycho-Anal.*, 52:107–114.
FRAIBERG, S. (1969), Libidinal Object Constancy and Mental Representation. *This Annual*, 24:9–47.
FREUD, A. (1965), *Normality and Pathology in Childhood.* New York: International Universities Press.
GADDINI, R. & E. (1970), Transitional Objects and the Process of Individuation. *J. Amer. Acad. Child Psychiat.*, 9:347–365.
GREENACRE, P. (1969), The Fetish and the Transitional Object. *This Annual*, 24:144–164.

HARLOW, H. F. & SUOMI, S. J. (1970), Nature of Love—Simplified. *Amer. Psychologist,* 25:161–168.

KOHUT, H. (1971), *The Analysis of the Self.* New York: International Universities Press.

SPERLING, M. (1963), Fetishism in Children. *Psychoanal. Quart.,* 32:374–392.

SPITZ, R. A. (1965), *The First Year of Life.* New York: International Universities Press

STEVENSON, O. (1954), The First Treasured Possession. *This Annual,* 9:199–217.

TOLPIN, M. (1971), On the Beginnings of a Cohesive Self. *This Annual,* 26:316–352.

WINNICOTT, D. W. (1953), Transitional Objects and Transitional Phenomena. *Int. J. Psycho-Anal.,* 34:89–97.

———(1954), Preface to O. Stevenson's "The First Treasured Possession." *This Annual,* 9:199–201.

WULFF, M. (1946), Fetishism and Object Choice in Early Childhood. *Psychoanal. Quart.,* 15:450–471.

Conditions Promoting Creativity in Group Rearing of Children

CHARLOTTE KAHN, ED.D. AND
GERALDINE PIORKOWSKI, PH.D.

Wer keine Kraft zum Träumen hat,
Hat keine Kraft zum Leben.
(He who has no strength to dream,
Has no strength to live.)
　　　　—ERNST TOLLER, quoted by Elon (1971)

IN RECENT YEARS, GROUP CHILD-REARING PRACTICES HAVE BEEN vying for acceptance as an alternate to child rearing within the nuclear family. Communal care of children, as illustrated by the kibbutz in Israel, the day-care program as practiced in China, and as advocated by the women's liberation movement in the United States, is considered to be more effective and practical in many respects. However, while group rearing of young children, including infants and toddlers, is advantageous in freeing women from certain repetitive chores, some of the disadvantages described by Bettelheim (1969) and others need to be evaluated.

Bettelheim pictures the kibbutz-educated generation as conforming, secure, noncreative, intensely loyal persons who have few

---

Dr. Kahn is a Faculty Member of the Training Institute, National Psychological Association for Psychoanalysis in New York, and Associate Professor of Psychology, Kean College of New Jersey, Union, New Jersey. Dr. Piorkowski is Clinical Psychologist with the Adolescent Program of the Illinois State Psychiatric Institute, Chicago, Illinois.

resources for coping with the outside world. He further maintains that they have achieved neither a high degree of individuation nor the potential for creativity. Concomitant with these shortcomings, he sees the compensatory absence of psychopathic behavior. Bettelheim writes: "While such people do not create science or art, are neither leaders nor great philosophers nor innovators, maybe it is they who are the salt of the earth without whom no society can endure" (p. 320). Thus, Bettelheim advances the hypothesis that communal rearing of children results in security at the expense of creativity.

Confirmation of Bettelheim's view can be found in the writings of Freud (1910), Eissler (1967), Greenacre (1957, 1958), and Rosen (1953), all of whom suggest that an important, motivating factor in creative production is the creator's early special relationship with his mother. Intimacy with and disappointment in a doting mother, fear and idealization of a withdrawn or absent father, identification with and yearning for the creative mother, and conflict between pressing impulses and puritanical prohibitions are described as important features in the development of the personalities of creatively gifted individuals (McClelland, 1961).

The well-publicized research on the ordinal position of unusually successful people lends further support to the idea that a very intimate, special relationship with parents must exist for such development to take place: first-borns and only children, who have been found to succeed in far greater proportions than middle children, occupy a position within the family which lends itself to the forming of "special" relationships (McArthur, 1956; McClelland, 1961; Altus, 1966).

Indeed, it would seem that the conditions favoring development of creativity are more likely to arise in the setting of a small nuclear family than in any situation where the parent-child relationships are diffused—and defused—whether this be in a primitive clan, a large extended family, or a commune located in the U.S. (Noyes, 1937), Israel (Spiro, 1965; Bettelheim, 1969), or China (Sidel, 1972). The question of ultimate interest to us is whether, in a group setting, such child-rearing conditions could be replicated as would offer similar opportunities for the development of a creative personality.

In the attempt to answer this question we shall first examine some of the factors which in the psychoanalytic and psychological literature have been correlated with artistic or scientific creative abilities. Rather than reviewing all the literature on creativity, we have selected those items which appear to have relevance for the development of creativity and its environmental contingencies.

In the context of this discussion, creativity denotes the ability to produce unique syntheses in reality-oriented, communicable forms. Creativity is not synonymous with productivity but refers to a particular kind of productivity, namely, that which is both original and integrative in nature. Creativity, viewed as an aspect of normal development, is heightened by innate perceptual sensitivities and the ability to synthesize sense data into Gestalten. The first overt manifestations of the creative abilities seem to occur in the toddler stage.

The strength, quality, and forms of creativity vary with the interaction between the cultural influences and the intrapsychic processes in the course of maturation. Any kind of new or unique reorganization of data can be considered creative, regardless of the impact on a given field. Creativity is possible not only in art and science, but in any field of endeavor.

PERSONALITY CHARACTERISTICS OF CREATIVE INDIVIDUALS

An examination of the studies of personality characteristics of creative individuals reveals that, for obvious reasons, psychoanalysts quite often address themselves to the relative stability or pathology of creative artists (Freud, 1910; Eissler, 1967; Kubie, 1958; Niederland, 1967; Slochower, 1967; Wolman, 1957). Psychologists, on the other hand, list personality attributes such as "preference for intuitive perception" in contrast to "sense perception," flexibility, and "openness to experience on the fringes of ordinary consciousness" (Barron, 1969, p. 77f.). Frequently, however, psychologists make no serious attempts psychodynamically to account for the characteristics which they discovered to have a high correlation with creativity. Yet, on the basis of these personality characteristics, it is possible to speculate about the parent-child relationships which would tend to produce an organization of personality that facilitates creative expression of fantasies and novel efforts to satisfy needs.

One psychological study, cast "in the context of psychoanalytic theory and ego psychology" (Myden, 1959), compared two groups of successful individuals: professionals and creatives. In contrast to the professionals, the creatives exhibited a greater capacity for using the primary process without experiencing an increase in anxiety. Another study, using creative children as subjects (Weisberg and Springer, 1961), found a tolerance for anxiety as well as "ease of early recall." This finding is referred to as "less repression" by Myden. In Kris's words (1952, p. 25), "The capacity of gaining easy access to id material without being overwhelmed by it, of retaining control over the primary process, . . . suggest[s] psychological characteristics of a definite but complex kind." Combined with this is a "strong fantasy life" and "energy" which effects a translation from fantasy into creative productions.

THOUGHT PROCESSES

Weisberg and Springer (1961) define a creative mind as "one in which a problem stimulus easily evokes material from various experiential areas" (p. 564). Following Guilford et al. (1951), these authors list the requisite thinking abilities for the creative mind: ideational fluency, flexibility, irrelevance, fantasy, and originality; hypothesis development and curiosity are additional factors, which seem to be of a slightly different order.

In Weisberg and Springer's study, *ideational fluency* refers to the number of responses an individual can produce to a stimulus within a given time limit; *flexibility* has to do with the "shifting from idea to idea," that is, with the variety of ideas. *Irrelevance* refers to a lack of logical connection between the stimulus and the subject's response, while *fantasy* may be logical yet unrealistic. Fantasy, as defined by Weisberg and Springer, is in accord with Noy's (1969) theory of the primary process, insofar as it is related to the gratification of inner needs and wishes, rather than based on reality-oriented feedback.[1]

---

[1] In the primary period of organization, "input is processed and memories stored according to programs which put together all the perceptions and actions belonging to the same affective state. As no differentiation exists between any of the elements put together, they are condensed and treated as a single element, i.e. the program operates according to the process of *condensation*. . . . But as these elements

Irrelevance might fit the concept of condensation insofar as neither depends upon logical connections for establishing relationships between input and memories, stimulus and response. "Irrelevant" elements are linked according to an order determined by affective states rather than according to logical organization of attributes inherent in the perceived object. Probably, in flexibility and fluency, displacement is operating. It may be the process of substitution, of representing one element by several others belonging to the same affective state, which results in the greater number and variety of ideas. Thus the "thinking abilities" which Guilford et al. and Weisberg and Springer deem important to creativity can be seen as expressions of primary process activity.

Curiosity, the desire to know, as it serves a need to "integrate new experiences into the existing self-schema" (Noy, 1969, p. 161), falls within the realm of an ego function which is probably not carried out exclusively by means of primary processes (see footnote 2). Curiosity involves the encounter with reality, conscious acquisition of objective data (secondary process) as well as the subjective integration of the data (primary process). Similarly, *hypothesis formation*, "solutional guesses about the environment" (Weisberg, 1961, p. 555), depends in part on primary process type of operations: the inductive process brought to bear on the environmental stimuli may avail itself of displacement and condensation. Nevertheless, such guesses are checked against a more objective view of the environment by means of the secondary process in which "input and memories have to be processed and stored according to the relation between the perceived elements, not according to their effect on the self" (Noy, 1969, p. 171). Thus, following Noy, hypothesis formation and curiosity illustrate the continuum of which primary process and secondary process are the extremes, the first organized in terms of the self, the second "according to the relation between the perceived elements." [2]

---

still have no meaning of their own, but only in terms of the affective state they are related to, they are treated as equal: any single element can stand for all the others, and can be replaced by any other . . . the process changes from condensation to . . . *displacement*" (Noy, 1969, p. 167f.).

[2] ". . . all mental processes are regarded as one system; from it a group of functions is differentiated. . . . The assumption presented here is that this

Weisberg and Springer also speak of extremes in the creative individual, albeit in terms of the "primitive-mature" continuum. According to their observation, creative children can have simultaneous "interests in Shakespeare and dolls." We have heard of a preteen girl describe herself as a "responsible baby."

ORIGINALITY

Originality is the essence of creativity. The thinking processes described so far may lead to a re-creation of previously discovered solutions, an aesthetic appreciation of someone else's work of art, or comprehension of another's scientific discovery. Only uncommon ideas or unique syntheses of previous knowledge are truly creative productions.

Koestler (1961) differentiates between the more common, habitual ways of thinking and creative thinking. He states that habit is based on associative thinking; it takes place in a "single matrix." A matrix might be compared to a mold, or to a pattern or program in communication theory (Peterfreund, 1972). Creative thinking, according to Koestler, is an attempt to solve conflict by means of "bisociation"; that is, finding hidden analogies in multiple matrices. The bisociative process might be seen as moving from primary to secondary process organization; from one program to another; from kinaesthetic, sensorimotor to conceptual methods of dealing with disequilibrium-producing stimuli (Inhelder and Piaget, 1964).

---

differentiation of the secondary process is achieved by the constant monitoring influence of feedback" (Noy, 169, p. 161). It should be noted that, according to Noy, both primary and secondary processes are normal adult processes, although developmentally they become effective at different ages. Noy differentiates primary from secondary process thinking in terms of function. The primary has as its main task the assimilation and integration of new experiences into the self, that is, to maintain the sameness and identity of the self, whereas secondary process thinking has as its main task the monitoring of reality. Noy, following Holt (1967), assumes that the primary processes have a synthetic function which serves the ego's integrative endeavors.

While Noy's revision of the concepts of primary and secondary processes differs considerably from Freud's and others', Freud along with Hartmann, Kris, and Loewenstein emphasize "that *there are no strict delineations in our mental life; that* Freud's concept of a *continuum* is the only valid one to apply" (Schur, 1966, p. 117).

Sonnenfeld (1972, p. 124), without referring to matrices, programs, or primary and secondary processes, speaks of transformations in the perceptual process ("stimulus to . . . reality-attuned response in consciousness") by means of various cognitive strategies. One strategy is a transformation from the abstract to the concrete, or vice versa, with the use of "optical" or "conaesthetic images" as an intermediate step. Presumably, the abstract ideas belong to secondary process, the concrete to the primary process. Therefore, he writes that creative spells begin with regressive moves, but are carried out by nonregressive moves: "two igniting sparks . . . below and above." Similarly, according to Adorno (1970), art—and we would include any other creative products—is not simply a purely subjective private language. Rather, the estrangement from reality which accompanies the unconscious or regressive moves must be joined with awareness of reality.

Images, as used in the transformation of the perceptual process, states Sonnenfeld, are not pure replications of remembered perceptions. Images take on semantic relations with thought. However, these meanings do not have to be understood consciously or necessarily in secondary process terms. As Langer (1948, p. 71) put it, "in this physical, space-time world of our experience there are things which do not fit the grammatical scheme of expression. But they are not necessarily blind, inconceivable, mystical affairs; they are simply matters which require to be conceived through some symbolic schema other than discursive language." Some languages are cast in presentational form;[3] the languages of music and art; the languages of dream and poetry. ". . . unconscious appreciation of forms is the primitive root of all abstraction . . . so it appears that

[3] Noy uses "representation" by word or image. Langer distinguishes presentational from discursive symbols because words may be used for both purposes: presentational as in metaphor and poetry; discursively as in a scientific treatise. Visual symbols also may be used in presentational form as in the Mona Lisa, or discursively as in a graph or in pictographs. "In the non-discursive mode that speaks directly to sense . . . there is no intrinsic generality. It is first and foremost a direct presentation of an individual object. . . . Language in the strict sense is essentially discursive; it has permanent units of meaning which are combinable into larger units; it has fixed equivalences that make definition and translation possible; its connotations are general" (Langer, p. 78).

the conditions for rationality lie deep in our animal experience—in our power of perceiving, in the elementary functions of our eyes and ears and fingers" (Langer, 1948, p. 72). "Metaphor fuses sense experience and thought in language," says Sharpe (1940, p. 155).

That presentational forms can be categorized as primary process may be deduced from Langer's description: "Artistic truth . . . has logical peculiarities that distinguish it from propositional truth: . . . presentational symbols have no negatives, there is no operation whereby their truth-value is reversed, no *contradictions*. Falsity [is] . . . not a function of negation . . . but inexpressiveness" (p. 212). However, she explains further that "the distinction between discursive and presentational symbols does not correspond to the difference between literal and artistic meanings" (p. 211). Certain presentational symbols are easily translatable into words, into discursive symbols, though this is not true of artistic symbols whose sense is bound to their form and whose meaning is implicit (see footnote 3). Yet, the recognition that some presentational forms are easily translated into discursive forms indicates a recognition of the interrelationship and continuity between primary and secondary process functioning (see footnote 2). Furthermore, we can find confirmation here of the common origin of scientific and artistic creativity (Sharpe, 1935). The idea, artistic or scientific, takes shape at first as "isolation or 'centering' of an essential element from a data set and the relating of this element, and hence its correlative set, to other elements and so to other sets, in new, yet effective relationships" (Shouksmith, 1970, p. 202). Or, to quote Bruner et al., "Science and common sense inquiry do not discover the ways in which events are grouped in the world, they invent ways of groupings" (1956, p. 7).

These statements, too, indicate switching from matrix to matrix, among groups of perceptions or Gestalten. We know that such shifting is efficiently accomplished by primary process through displacement and condensation. It is, therefore, more likely to involve presentational symbols, images, or perceptions which are more easily retrieved "by image than recall" (Klein, 1959, p. 23).

One would expect, then, that the creative process, particularly originality, is dependent on: (1) an ability to use the primary process comfortably; (2) retreat from commonly established configurations; and (3) a wealth and variety of sensual and intellectual experiences, the raw materials for presentational forms. If these are the intrapsychic conditions for creativity, what are the environmental factors which help to spawn them?

PERSONALITY CHARACTERISTICS OF PARENTS OF CREATIVE CHILDREN

Weisberg and Springer (1961) selected their sample of gifted children and rated them according to the above "thinking abilities." They then examined the parental attitudes of the most creative group.[4] Three factors emerged as highly significant: (1) expressiveness of parents coupled with a lack of domination of children; (2) acceptance of regressive tendencies in children; and (3) father's occupational autonomy.

It should be stressed that expressiveness alone does not differentiate the high creatives. In fact, expressiveness in parents produces either very high or very low creatives. One might speculate that expressive parents who dominate their children, instead of providing a model for identification, would tend to establish a situation in which children feel forced to accept passively what parents emit. In order to desist from dominating children, parents probably must develop a reliable feeling of self-worth and absorbing interests in addition to the raising of children. The parents, by extension, will harbor respect for their children as individuals who have a right to pursue their own goals in their unique fashion.

Some supporting evidence for this notion emerges from the Weisberg and Springer study. Generally, in their families of creatives, there prevails a lack of interdependence, each member being an individual in his own right, "with the better defined personality of the two tending to be that of the parent of the same

---

[4] The 50 third-graders of 7,000 public school children who achieved the highest scores on the Kuhlman-Anderson group intelligence test were chosen to participate in the study. To determine high and low creativity, a portion of the Torrance battery of tests was administered. Information regarding the child's personality and his relationship to his family was derived from Rorschach tests, Draw-a-Family tests, and interviews.

sex as the child" (p. 563). The characteristic "defensive techniques" of each of the parents of high-ranking children also seem to differ more from that of the other parent than is true of parents of the low creative group. Undoubtedly, this offers exposure, from a very early age on, to a variety of means of dealing with the disequilibrium imposed by life on each organism. It is an implied permission to be divergent, an important ingredient of originality (Hudson, 1966). Since variety is perceived at first in sensorimotor and affective terms, there are available from the beginning more varied raw data for the organization of symbols. We expect that both the disequilibrium and the availability of various methods to reestablish balance will be experienced more keenly by children with unusual perceptual or intellectual endowment, provided the level of anxiety aroused by the disequilibrium is not overwhelming. In this regard, too, the family has an important function. To quote Bergman and Escalona (1949, p. 349), "We may regard an infant as protected from the onslaught of stimuli in two different ways . . . by the constitutional factor of the protective barrier . . . by the mother who both keeps stimuli from him, and provides them in the right dosage."

The perceptually sensitive children in Bergman and Escalona's study were overwhelmed by the force of the stimuli impinging upon them; yet, this is not the inevitable outcome, as the authors indicate. Myden (1959) and Weisberg and Springer mention anxiety as a factor in creativity. The one notes the absence of anxiety during primary process activity; the others state that "Oedipal anxieties were closer to the surface in the high-ranking than the low-ranking children as judged by fantasy, content of early memories, and dream material" (p. 72). One wonders whether these children had easy access to oedipal feelings or whether the authors of the article truly found anxiety. We would be inclined to make the former interpretation of the statement on the basis of Greenacre's work (1957), our own observations, and other psychological studies which indicate that anxiety interferes with creativity. In this connection Rokeach's work is quite illuminating. What ultimately differentiates his subjects is the degree of anxiety. Those with "closed" minds were the more anxious subjects. According to Rokeach (1960, p. 211), "childhood experiences . . . can reasonably account for such differences in anxiety." The result, a "closed" mind, makes it exceedingly difficult for a person to accept "new belief systems contradicting old ones." Those with a closed mind rely on the support of an authority and on defenses of isolation. Evidently there is a need to stay with the familiar, the accepted, the "convergent," thus precluding the new, the unique, the divergent ideas. How, then, can originality be expected? Whereas the rejection of new ideas can be seen as a counterpart to repression, the mechanisms of introjection and projection seem to be more useful in the creative process (Rosen, 1949); whereas isolation and dissociation are practiced by the "close-minded," negation or denial is more useful in the furtherance of divergent thinking.[5] Thus, a nondominating, yet optimally protective environment seems to be of crucial importance.

In two other related connections the nondominating, optimally protective environment is of importance: the development of superego and ego ideal and the management of aggression.

According to Torda (1970), parental attitudes which foster creativity include a rejection of mediocre standards and efforts to minimize children's anxiety during early attempts at accomplishment. In other words, while demands for achievement are made on children, parents support, enable, and protect from failure. Thus, children are at first shielded from feelings of utter helplessness and worthlessness which would discourage later attempts to tackle creative tasks. Coupled with these attitudes is the subsequent encouragement of reliance on the child's own resourcefulness, skills, and efforts toward fulfillment of the special needs to which he is entitled. Thereby, the path is prepared from dependence to independence.

IDENTIFICATION WITH THE PARENT

Identification with a parent who upholds ideals and derives satisfaction from his own pursuits is undoubtedly of great impor-

---

[5] "With the help of the symbol of negation, thinking frees itself from the restrictions of repression and enriches itself with material that is indispensable for its proper functioning" (Freud, 1925, p. 236).

tance. However, identification with the powerful parent who protects against instinctual demands (Weissman, 1971) and who also permits and facilitates gratification is probably more directly related to creativity. Identification with the gratifying parent offsets the punitive, critical superego which makes demands for self-provision rather than creation; that is, demands for practical reality-oriented activity rather than playful fantasy. Conversely, identification with punitiveness and strict demands are often projected, resulting in crippling expectations of severe criticism. Such crippling might be avoided by an accepting parental attitude; an attitude more likely to prevail in families of low interdependence where individuation and individuality as expressed by the children might less likely be viewed as hostile rejection of the imperfect parent. According to Kleinschmidt (1967), the creative act is an angry act, an expression of dissatisfaction with imperfection, ultimately parental imperfection. Understood as such, the creative act of reorganizing divergently, with originality, and the development toward individuality are easily and often severely hampered by fear of retaliation and abandonment. This was the case, for instance, with Sonnenfeld's patient (1972), a scientist whose hostile fantasies relating to senior colleagues interfered with his creative work.

Arieti (1966) addresses himself to the individual's resourcefulness and reliance on himself by postulating that the creative individual has to have a conviction that there is an order in the world and that he has the power to find that order. We think that such an attitude must necessarily rest on self-confidence arising from early acceptance and a sense of success. Frequently the sense of success flows from an ability to redress narcissistic hurt or to deal with feelings of grandiosity.[6] Anxiety about the ego's capacity to survive onslaughts from within and to achieve mastery over the world without is more likely to lead to defensive, "close-minded" conformity than to a

---

[6] While the relinquishment of narcissistic claims is not absolute, a patient's "archaic exhibitionism and grandiosity must be gradually transformed into aim-inhibited self-esteem and realistic ambitions; and his desire to merge . . . has to be replaced by attitudes which are under the control of the ego, e.g., by his enthusiasm for meaningful ideals" (Kohut, 1972, p. 388).

breaking down and subsequent reorganization of Gestalten into original, unique productions. Arieti sheds further light on the self-dependent attitude. He speaks of it as the ability to be alone and the opportunity for daydreaming. The importance of privacy becomes apparent when being alone is seen as a partial, temporary removal of the feedback necessary for the maintenance of secondary process functioning. Privacy opens the door to primary process just as it may close the door between the daydreamer and the people in his environs. Dulling reality-oriented feedback disinhibits the affectively organized primary process programs.

REGRESSION

The second highly significant parental attitude in Weisberg and Springer's group is that of acceptance of regressive tendencies. While the authors distinguish between acceptance and encouragement of regressive tendencies, they do not elaborate the idea. We wonder whether encouragement leads to infantile organization? In acceptance, is there an implied demand that the regressive tendencies be expressed in what might be labeled good presentational form, instead of seeking direct, unsymbolized outlets for infantile wishes? Perhaps so, because the research data show that parents of this group of creatives do not favor them in the sense of overvaluating their abilities, the implication being that standards of performance are upheld.

FEELING "SPECIAL"

In the limited sense (overvaluation of abilities) that Weisberg and Springer mention parental favoring of children, we can accept their findings. However, by virtue of the fact that the children in the sample were "often" elder siblings, did they not in some way feel special? Nearly every other report on creatively gifted people indicates that, during their childhood, either the parents did indeed accord them a special position (Eissler, 1959; Ehrenwald, 1967) or the children felt "special" for other reasons. Frequently, the feeling of being special derives from the child's recognition that input from his especially sensitive perceptual apparatus is somewhat different from other people's in quality or intensity. Sometimes an unusual ability to create form, to synthesize sense data into a Gestalt, becomes evident very early. For example, a 3-year-old stopped suddenly during a walk along city streets, pulled his mother several paces back, pointed to the cracks in the pavement, and said, "Do you see the cow?" Mother and older sibling saw cracks but not a cow. Only when the little fellow traced the line of the cracks according to his organization did a picture of a cow emerge, with well-drawn parts of bovine anatomy. Another example is a patient's report of feeling special—specially unhappy and deserted—because he knew by age 4 that he was much more intelligent than his parents. He felt that his mother in particular was unreliable, inasmuch as she could not be counted on to protect him from himself. His aggressive schemes were sufficiently clever to remain a mystery to her until some damage had obviously been done. Unfortunately, this patient developed compulsions and mild psychopathic tendencies instead of creative tendencies, because in his family none of the environmental conditions which could have promoted creativity seemed to prevail (Deutsch, 1955).

The feeling of being special can be produced in yet another way, namely, by being on the periphery of a social, ethnic, or cultural group. This is not a comforting feeling. To the contrary, it produces conflict in the form of two or more different, internalized, attitudinal, value, or defensive systems. If the resulting disequilibrium does not reach proportions of immobilizing conflict, it can stimulate curiosity. Furthermore, under favorable circumstances, the differences in value systems which a person brings to an environment and the variations in symbolizations, presentational and discursive, might facilitate a new perspective on standard organization. A series of matrices become available, encompassing secondary and primary processes developed on diverse cultural input and superimposed on greater or lesser perceptual sensitivity. Reestablishing equilibrium by means of successful synthesis might under fortuitous circumstances result in truly idiosyncratic ideation which, when transformed into communicable, socially shared thought or artistic form, may turn out to be a great original contribution.[7] "A

---

[7] Sir Isaac Newton, born to a widow who sent the son, age 3, to live with relatives when she remarried; Marie Curie, who struggled with Polish identifica-

somewhat different value system and an unrealistic non-acceptance of partial solutions" seem to provide the content and motivation for a search for original solutions, while "frequent attempts at memory retrieval . . . resulting in easy accessibility of primary process type thinking" become the enabling process (Torda, 1970, p. 111).

GROUP REARING AND CREATIVITY

Es ist Menschenrecht sich nicht abzuquälen,
sondern lieber sich geistig zu entfalten.
(It is man's right not to drudge and toil, but
rather to unfold himself spiritually.)
—THEODOR ADORNO (1962)

Can the environmental conditions which emerged as significant for creativity be provided for infants, preschoolers, and schoolchildren raised in groups? Is it possible that the group situation is more fertile ground than the nuclear family for the development of certain characteristics found in the creative personality? For example, the multiple mothering in the group brings with it the exposure to alternate defensive styles. Parents of children in groups are usually involved in pursuits unrelated to child rearing, a condition which reduces the likelihood of a too intense, dominating attachment between parent and child. On the other hand, does the group setting allow for privacy, regressive tendencies, and protection from failure during early attempts at mastery? To what extent can a young individual in a group develop the comfortable access to primary process, an ability to retreat from commonly established configurations, and the tolerance of ambiguity without debilitating anxiety?

In both family and group settings, a caretaker who has access to his or her own primary processes and views these processes as valuable means of gaining insight into current concerns as well as a source of creative resolutions to current dilemmas can promote a

---

tion under Russian domination, and who lost her mother at an early age; Marx, Freud, and Einstein, who had to reconcile their Jewish background with the surrounding, predominantly Christian culture; and, most recently, Chomsky (New York Times Magazine, December 3, 1972), are just a few obvious examples.

similar process in children. A caretaker who is flexible, open-minded, and therefore able to respect divergent perceptions in others, provides an appropriate model for identification. While not all divergent thinking is creative and not all primary process images represent new Gestalten, they serve an important function in providing affective links to earlier experiences, thus stabilizing the feeling of self-continuity. At the same time, a flexible, empathic caretaker reinforces idiosyncratic images and symbols among the children in his charge.

The encouragement of idiosyncratic perceptions and symbols can take many concrete forms. A caretaker may manifest an interest in those dreams, fantasies, and primary process ideations which reflect clearly a child's unique perceptions and experiences. The adult's attention to the unique aspects of a dream conveys the attitude that idiosyncratic images are meaningful. Furthermore, the responses subject the child's processes to the reality-monitoring feedback function of the secondary process. By both accepting and monitoring primary process activity, autistic thinking can be modified and creativity enhanced. Ultimately, a child might thus be able to achieve the state where "primary processes, rather than resulting from a change in the inner dynamic balance, such as weakening of the defense mechanisms, regression, or even inspiration, is . . . no more than one secondary cognitive function among the others" (Noy, 1966, p. 212).

The feeling of being special or unique is probably more likely to be fostered in a nuclear family, where an intense emotional relationship between parent and child conveys to the child that he is an important source of the parent's gratification. The resulting narcissism and grandiosity are often observed in successful artists and innovators; however, feelings of omnipotence are also observable in many forms of psychopathology. The ideal kind of feeling special would seem to be a self-confident awareness that one is important, though not solely important, to one's caretakers and that one's unique perceptions and skills are valuable means of resolving one's own dilemmas. In a group setting, this kind of feeling special can be instilled more easily in small groups of four to five children, a situation which enables the caretaker to establish a unique relationship with each child.

One of the authors observed a grandmotherly woman during bathtime.[8] The group of approximately 15-month-old kibbutz toddlers played under the supervision of the assistant while the metapelet (caretaker) in charge bathed each child individually. Her sensitivity to the children's different temperaments and current moods was amazing. The way she spoke to them, washed, dried, and dressed them was largely determined by her empathic understanding of their needs. Yet, she was not unaware of educational or psychological maxims. She asked questions regarding the meaning of the somewhat hyperactive behavior of an unusually well-coordinated little boy; she also wanted to know whether her method of play and discipline, her minimal use of restraints was appropriate. She seemed to be feeling just a trifle guilty that she derived so much pleasure from this child, who was obviously special and was special to his caretaker.[9] However, with the other group members no less than with him, she was supportive and facilitated their implementation of their own plans within the limits of safety. Is such interaction possible without adult responsiveness to children's idiosyncratic signs and symbolizations? Admittedly, this metapelet was unusually well suited for her work. It would be difficult to find mothers who could equal her. The point is that even within a group child-rearing setting, it is possible to establish an intimate relationship between adult and child; it is possible to become special.

In another kibbutz, a kindergarten teacher was observed responding to each child individually and providing variations of the general group experience in accordance with each child's need. One member of this group was physically retarded as a result of an incurable disorder; another required much structure and direction; another, the "professor," was given detailed answers to his many questions and supplied with stimulating materials and ideas. On

---

[8] C. K. spent three months in Israel during the summers of 1970 and 1971, observing in eight kibbutzim.

[9] Observation notes: Metapelet favored one 15-month-old boy. He brought a basin to climb on to reach the table from which he reached to the high tub; from the tub he swung and chinned himself; then he let himself down to the floor. Metapelet gave history of child with "unusual sensitivities." He has a larger vocabulary than any other child in the group. Responds to airplanes overhead while indoors.

the other hand, in a different group, a substitute for a metapelet on vacation stood rigidly as a toddler reached up to her, pulled on her skirts, asking clearly, though nonverbally, to be picked up.

In many subtle and overt ways, creative expressions can be facilitated in either the nuclear family or in the group-rearing setting. Privacy, a facilitating condition for primary process activity (see Arieti on the ability to be alone), is a more difficult commodity in a communal setting unless privacy is valued and insured in that setting. In a nuclear family, the child can more easily retreat to his own bedroom or another unoccupied room in the house to engage in fantasy activity. In many households, solitary activity is not criticized or interrupted unless the activity is noisy, or daydreaming is pursued for hours at the expense of more practical concerns (see Weisman on playful fantasy vs. self-provision). In a structured group setting, solitary activity is often seen as a rejection of the group or as unhealthy withdrawal from reality issues. The fantasy-prone youngster might more often be pressured into normative behavior in a group setting than in a nuclear family. Indeed, according to a report by Gerson (1970), kibbutz adolescent girls, especially at about 18, have expressed the feeling that the group pressure is slightly "oppressive" in spite of their attachment to the group. Nevertheless, in the preface to the new edition of *Kibbutz: Venture in Utopia*, Spiro wrote that "within the context of its present reality . . . the demand for privacy seems to have been recognized as legitimate" (p. xii).

While privacy is more difficult to insure in a group setting, it can exist. In the midst of—more accurately, on the periphery of—the activities in the main room of the kibbutz toddler house, a $2\frac{1}{2}$-year-old child was observed lying on a mat, nude, sucking to her heart's content. Privacy can be wherever reality ceases to demand intrusion.

While the development of creativity in children depends heavily upon the personality of the caretaker, the value placed by the society upon individuality as opposed to conformity is important. The importance to the society of individuality and creativity seems to be at least as much a function of economics as of ideology. Conformity is essential in times of crisis when a common effort, a united group, offers the sole escape from annihilation by economic failure or by enemy bullets. Moreover, during times of danger, labor is deployed in production, with the result that the caretaker-child ratio is reduced (see Weissman on self-provision). According to Sidel (1972), that seems to be the prevailing condition in China today. The same austere conditions prevailed in Israeli kibbutzim until recently, as well as in Russia after the Revolution and after World War II. Bronfenbrenner (1970, p. 87) quotes from Novikova's paper on collective upbringing in the Soviet Union (1967): "Relations in school are most often limited to the sphere of task-oriented relations . . . of mutual dependence, mutual responsibility, mutual control, subordination and commanding, and intolerance to persons interfering with the common tasks." Novikova continues, however, by suggesting that "By developing primarily the task-oriented aspects of human relationships in the children's collective and allowing other characteristics to develop as they may, we in the last analysis impoverish the personality of the child." She explains: "The function of the collective in relation to the individual in socialist society was expressed differently at different periods of socialist development." At one time emphasis had to be placed on "overcoming the difficulties connected with the war and the destruction of the economy." Now it becomes important to develop personalities who know "how to find a position in society which permits the realization of all their individual potentialities . . . abilities, talents, gifts." She concludes: "If earlier we were confronted with the problem of creating that type of collective which could insure the necessary conditions for the existence of all its members, then today we have to discover how to create the kind of collective which will insure the most full and many-sided development of each person."

Observations (C.K.) indicate that many kibbutzim share this opinion and have taken effective measures to achieve the goal. While in the Soviet Union it is still the practice to assign one caretaker to groups of 10 to 15 toddlers, the ratio in Israeli kibbutzim is one caretaker plus assistant to 8 to 10 toddlers. No longer do the conditions prevail which Spiro (1958) related to the character of the sabra and others related to the anxious dependence of kibbutz children on the approval of their group. No longer is a child promoted the moment he reaches a given age. Removal from his nurse is considered a serious matter; removal from his peer group is equally important. Each child's psychological, social, and medical background is reviewed before any change is initiated. Unforeseeable or unavoidable separations are carefully treated. Allowances are made for special situations. For instance, a preschooler was seen leaving his group, running toward the fence surrounding the playground in front of his house. He did this daily at a special time. The guidance counselor explained to the caretaker why the child should be permitted this freedom and that the behavior probably would cease before long. What occasioned the running? Mother was in the hospital giving birth to a sibling; father spent most workdays during the year away from the kibbutz because he was enrolled full-time at the university (all expenses paid by the kibbutz). During the summer months, father was making his contribution to the community: he drove the garbage truck (tractor). Daily, at about the same time, the tractor could be heard approaching the children's houses. Daily, the child ran out to greet his daddy.

In addition to the various factors seen operating in the relations between individuals, in the kibbutz a general feeling of "specialness" seems to pervade the community. By virtue of being a member or child of the kibbutz family, a special "different" status seems to accrue to the individual; this, within the larger community of the "chosen" people, who have been favored, according to biblical interpretation, by the gift of the Law and the promise of the Land, but who have been burdened with exceptional responsibilities and obstacles. Speaking of the coincidence of beneficial environmental factors in Goethe's life, Eissler writes (1959, p. 270): "The blending of the image of a benign, preoedipal father with that of a law-enforcing and prohibitive, oedipal father was a fortunate prerequisite for the relationship between ego and superego on whose proper cooperation in the adult personality largely depend the intensity and quality of creativity." Yet, having been "chosen," benignly and restrictively, by no means guarantees the "proper cooperation" between "ego and superego." The philosophical commitment to productive physical labor on the part of early settlers in Palestine and the necessity to defend the settlements against Arab attackers vitiated any serious professional interest in artistic creation. According to Spiro's original observations, kibbutzniks are avid consumers of art who permit themselves to be only amateur producers of art.

It is in this context of philosophy and threat to survival that one might consider the factors of varying defensive styles and matrices. Aside from the fact that children in group settings are exposed to the diverse defensive styles of their caretakers and their parents, they see each functioning in a variety of roles: vocational, familial, and communal. Moreover, while early settlers and present-day members of border kibbutzim require submission to group decision in times of crisis, leaving little room for diversity, they brought to their agricultural and military tasks a rich cultural heritage. Spiro refers to them as the "landed intelligentsia" (1956, p. 154). Therefore, although economically productive work is held in the highest esteem and although children are trained "to appreciate but not to create art, science, and scholarship," they nevertheless are exposed to adults who in their spare time compose, write, paint, and sculpt. Some of these kibbutz-reared children do develop into creative artists.[10]

---

[10] Zev Dorman, bassoonist; Jonathan Karmon, choreographer, for example. It is to be hoped that with generally greater security, affluence, and diversity in economic pursuits, kibbutz members will see fit to maintain creative artists and scientists whose chosen work requires that it be performed outside the confines of the kibbutz. In the past, both the communities and the individuals have had to suffer as a result of the limited choice confronting gifted young people: leave the intellectual or artistic work in order to contribute such labor as is required by the community or pursue the chosen work but resign from the community. Precedents exist for a compromise solution. For instance, one kibbutz, unable to maintain itself economically by agriculture alone, joined with two others in the building and operating of a plastics factory. This venture required that workers from the two communities leave daily to work "outside" in the factory located on the premises of the third.

Similarly, guidance teachers and psychologists serve more than one kibbutz and attend meetings at headquarters in Tel Aviv; often they work outside three days a week and more, nonetheless remaining full members of their kibbutz. Physicians have comparable schedules. A successful architect, whose services are hired by individuals and organizations all over Israel, has an office on the premises of his kibbutz. The kibbutz furnishes him with an automobile so that he may travel to inspect building sites. Payments for the architect's professional services accrue to the kibbutz. Such arrangements might be made for performing musicians, painters, research scientists.

Thus, first generation sabras were somewhat protected from the stultifying effects of rigidity, dogmatism, and isolation by their elders' variegated cultural background. Today's sabras need no longer be so isolated: there are some opportunities for travel; from all parts of the world, visitors and temporary workers are received in the kibbutz; finally, there is a limited number of television programs. Furthermore, today's kibbutzniks are no longer subjected to the rigidity with which philosophical principles were enforced during earlier periods. Still, sabras' exposure to alternate ideologies and life styles has been meager, indeed. And there is evidence that the feelings of being "special" and secure in the kibbutz coupled with the jealousy aroused by the realization that, unlike themselves, outsiders—American visitors or relatives from the cities—have greater freedom and more funds, causes many sabras to react defensively when confronted with novel ideas or life styles. Furthermore, they anxiously cling to the rebellious rejection of their image of a Diaspora Jew. On that basis, they can easily discredit unfamiliar approaches suggested by visitors; ideas brought by non-Jews can be discredited as irrelevant to Israelis; Oriental Jews are seen as backward (see Rokeach on closed-minded conformity).

It is possible that the children of religious, authoritarian, Oriental families brought into close contact with the philosophical naturalism of the kibbutz might finally be able to integrate and use the disparate Gestalten presented by the adults in their environment to create idiosyncratic, original forms. What the chances for such cultural cross-fertilization might be for Soviet and Chinese group-reared children is difficult to assess in view of the restrictions in those countries on travel and communication.

One question which must be raised in regard to the formation of diverse matrices and Gestalten is that of rate and timing of exposure to alternate systems. At what point in the organization of a personality is the introduction to a foreign culture and strange values experienced as an enrichment rather than a pathogenic disruption? "The problem is to have the child's ego develop in such a way that strains . . . will stimulate or energize ego functions, elicit the evolvement of new ones, or lead to the synthesis of already existing ones. [If the child's] ego has enough energy at its disposal to bind all the processes that are set into motion by the intruding potentially traumatic stimuli, then the resulting conflict can be used for creative purposes" (Eissler, 1959, p. 287). Too much exposure too early can create traumatic disequilibrium, confusion about values and identity. Too little access to alternate value systems tends to perpetuate the homogeneity, as all experience tends to be interpreted according to one introjected model. However, if the goal of child rearing is the development of individuals who can utilize themselves to create art, music, science, value systems, or an image of man in keeping with the demands of their era, then exposure to alternate value systems, at some time in the course of their development, would seem to be a vital component of the pedagogy of such a model.

In reviewing the characteristics of the creative person and the environmental conditions that promote creativity, it becomes apparent, then, that the conditions are not intrinsic to either the nuclear family or to the group-rearing model.

BIBLIOGRAPHY

ADORNO, T. W. (1962), Zur Bekämpfung des Antisemitismus heute. In: *Kritik: Kleine Schriften zur Gesellschaft*, ed. R. Tiedeman. Frankfurt: Surkamp Verlag, 1971, p. 112.

—— (1970), *Ästhetische Theorie*. Frankfurt: Suhrkamp Verlag.

ALTUS, W. (1966), Birth Order and Its Sequelae. *Science*, 151:44–49.

ARIETI, S. (1966), Creativity and Its Cultivation. In: *American Handbook of Psychiatry*, ed. S. Arieti. New York: Basic Books, Vol. 3, pp. 722–741.

BARRON, F. (1969), *Creative Person and Creative Process*. New York: Holt, Rinehart & Winston.

BERGMAN, P. & ESCALONA, S. K. (1949), Unusual Sensitivities in Very Young Children. *This Annual*, 3/4:333–352.

BETTELHEIM, B. (1969), *The Children of the Dream*. New York: Macmillan.

BRONFENBRENNER, U. (1970), *Two Worlds of Childhood*. New York: Russell Sage Foundation.

BRUNER, J. S., GOODNOW, J., & AUSTIN, G. (1956), *A Study of Thinking*. New York: Wiley.

DEUTSCH, H. (1955), The Impostor. *Psychoanal. Quart.*, 24:483–505.

EHRENWALD, J. (1967), A Childhood Memory of Pablo Picasso. *Amer. Imago*, 24:129–139.

EISSLER, K. R. (1959), Notes on the Environment of a Genius. *This Annual*, 14:267–313.

—— (1967), Psychopathology and Creativity. *Amer. Imago*, 24:35–81.

ELON, A. (1971), *The Israelis*. New York: Holt, Rinehart & Winston, p. 145.

FREUD, S. (1910), Leonardo da Vinci and a Memory of His Childhood. *Standard Edition*, 11:59–137. London: Hogarth Press, 1957.

——— (1925), Negation. *Standard Edition*, 19:235–239. London: Hogarth Press, 1961.

——— (1926), Inhibitions, Symptoms and Anxiety. *Standard Edition*, 20:77–175. London: Hogarth Press, 1959.

GERSON, M. (1970), The Family and Other Socializing Agents in the Kibbutz. Presented at the Seventh Congress of the International Association for Child Psychiatry and Allied Professions, Jerusalem, Israel.

GREENACRE, P. (1957), The Childhood of the Artist. *This Annual*, 12:47–72.

——— (1958), The Family Romance of the Artist. *This Annual*, 13:9–36.

GUILFORD, J., WILSON, R., CHRISTENSEN, P. & LEWIS, D. (1951), *A Factor Analytic Study of Creative Thinking: I. Hypotheses and Description of Tests*. Los Angeles: University of Southern California Press.

HARTMANN, H., KRIS, E., & LOEWENSTEIN, R. M. (1946), Comments on the Formation of Psychic Structure. *This Annual*, 2:11–38.

HOLT, R. R. (1967), The Development of the Primary Process. In: *Motives and Thought* [*Psychological Issues*, 18/19:344–383]. New York: International Universities Press.

HUDSON, L. (1966), *Contrary Imaginations*. Harmondsworth: Penguin Books.

INHELDER, B. & PIAGET, J. (1964), *The Early Growth of Logic in the Child*. New York: Norton.

KLEIN, G. S. (1959), Consciousness in Psychoanalytic Theory. *J. Amer. Psychoanal. Assn.*, 7:5–34.

KLEINSCHMIDT, H. (1967), The Angry Act. *Amer. Imago*, 24:98–128.

KOESTLER, A. (1964), *The Act of Creation*. New York: Macmillan.

KOHUT, H. (1972), Thoughts on Narcissism and Narcissistic Rage. *This Annual*, 27:360–400.

KRIS, E. (1952), *Psychoanalytic Explorations in Art*. New York: International Universities Press.

KUBIE, L. S. (1958), *Neurotic Distortion of the Creative Process*. Lawrence: University of Kansas Press.

LANGER, S. K. (1948), *Philosophy in a New Key*. New York: New American Library.

McARTHUR, C. (1956), Personalities of First and Second Born Children. *Psychiatry*, 19:47–54.

McCLELLAND, D. (1961), *The Achieving Society*. New York: Van Nostrand.

——— (1962), On the Psychodynamics of Creative Physical Scientists. In: *Contemporary Approaches to Creative Thinking*, ed. H. E. Gruber, G. Terrell, & M. Wertheimer. New York: Atherton Press, pp. 141–174.

MYDEN, W. (1959), An Interpretation and Evaluation of Certain Personality Characteristics Involved in Creative Production. *Percept. Mot. Skills*, 9:139–158.

NIEDERLAND, W. G. (1967), Clinical Aspects of Creativity. *Amer. Imago*, 24:6–34.

NOY, P. (1966), On the Development of Artistic Talent. *Israel Ann. Psychiat.*, 4:211–218.

Noy, P. (1969), A Revision of the Psychoanalytic Theory of the Primary Process. *Int. J. Psycho-Anal.*, 50:155–178.

Noyes, P. (1937), *My Father's House*. New York: Farrar & Rinehart.

Peterfreund, E. (1972), *Information, Systems, and Psychoanalysis* [*Psychological Issues*, Monogr. 25/26]. New York: International Universities Press.

Rokeach, M. (1960), *The Open and Closed Mind*. New York: Basic Books.

Rosen, V. H. (1953), On Mathematical "Illumination" and the Mathematical Thought Process. *This Annual*, 8:127–154.

Schur, M. (1966), *The Id and the Regulatory Principles of Mental Functioning*. New York: International Universities Press.

Sharpe, E. F. (1935), Similar and Divergent Unconscious Determinants Underlying the Sublimations of Pure Art and Pure Science. In: *Collected Papers on Psycho-Analysis*. London: Hogarth Press, 1950, pp. 137–154.

———— (1940), Psycho-Physical Problems Revealed in Language. *Ibid.*, pp. 155–169.

Shouksmith, G. (1970), *Intelligence, Creativity and Cognitive Style*. London: Batsford.

Sidel, R. (1972), *Women and Child Care in China*. New York: Hill & Wang.

Slochower, H. (1967), Genius, Psychopathology, and Creativity. *Amer. Imago*, 24:3–5.

Sonnenfeld, S. (1972), Psychoanalytic Observations on the Creative Spells of a Young Scientist. *Israel Ann. Psychiat.*, 10:123–136.

Spiro, M. (1956), *Kibbutz: Venture in Utopia*. New York: Schocken Books, new ed., 1963.

———— (1958), *Children of the Kibbutz*. New York: Schocken Books.

Torda, C. (1970), Observations on the Creative Process. *Percept. Mot. Skills*, 31:102–126.

Weisberg, P. & Springer, K. (1961), Environmental Factors in Creative Function. *Arch. Gen. Psychiat.*, 5:554–564.

Weissman, P. (1971), Superego in Creative Lives and Works. *Israel Ann. Psychiat.*, 9:208–218.

Wolman, B. (1967), Creative Art and Psychopathology. *Amer. Imago*, 24:140–150.

Impairment of the Freedom to Change with the Acquisition of the Symbolic Process

LAWRENCE S. KUBIE, M.D., D.SC.

THIS PAPER IS AN ATTEMPT TO MAKE CLEAR CONCEPTUALLY WHAT one of the central goals of research in child development must be; and it does this by singling out for emphasis a neglected problem in the development of human thought processes, which from early childhood links closely the creative and the neurotic potential.

The symbolic process is the unique gift and attribute of human mentation, and its most valuable. At the same time that it is essential for all that is creative in human thinking it also is most vulnerable to distortion. This is because it develops around a core of asymbolic or preconscious processing (what was called "imageless thought" by the Würzburg school). This preconscious processing begins in infancy to play an effective role through a process akin to conditioning; but if it is to continue to play an effective role in our adult thought processes, weighted and fragmentary samples must be drawn from this preconscious stream and must then be represented by symbols which are used for purposes of memory, rumination, coding and ordering, and communication. Thus the symbolic

This paper was presented at the Biennial Meeting of the Society for Research in Child Development in Philadelphia, March 30, 1973. It is published posthumously.

Dr. Kubie was Senior Associate in Research and Training, The Sheppard and Enoch Pratt Hospital, Towson, Maryland, and Clinical Professor of Psychiatry, University of Maryland School of Medicine, Baltimore.

257

devices are linked to samples of the preconscious stream; but these links to the preconscious referents are also vulnerable to distortion and when these links become distorted, they give rise to misrepresentation and obstruction, which in turn leads to the process known as "unconscious" processing. It is an effort at representation, but it leads to a misrepresentation or to no representation at all. This imprisons the preconscious stream between unconscious distortion on the one hand and pedestrian literal-mindedness on the other, and thereby limits its capacity to evolve and grow and change. This may start in infancy; but it is a process which is sorted out and resolved only slowly with the years. Thus the impairment of freedom begins with learning, yet it is a problem which has so far not been solved by any method of education which we have discovered.

The creative process depends for its freedom upon the play of preconscious functions which are balanced precariously between the rigidity of conscious processes at one end (with their anchorage in reality), and the rigidity of unconscious functions at the other end (with their anchorage in the stereotyped and repetitive symbolism of unconscious processes). It is a measure of the profound and tragic failure of our educational system that it does not accept the challenge of this problem; on the contrary, it tends to reinforce the imprisonment of preconscious function by its dependence upon drill and grill.

Let me recapitulate briefly this essential element in my story. Conscious anchorage to reality is chronological and logical. It is rooted in conscious representations of perceptions which are built out of exteroceptive, proprioceptive, and enteroceptive units. Of these the exteroceptive perceptions are readily checked and controlled because we can compare them, and when desirable in some measure shut them out. The proprioceptive contributions come next. Internal perceptions are the most difficult modalities to control, compare, and interrupt. In turn, this is why the three perceptual modalities play different roles in fantasies, symptoms, and dreams (Kubie, 1966).

At the other pole (the "unconscious" end) the symbolic process never represents current perceptual processes, but only memory traces of a past to which it is unalterably and rigidly anchored. Specifically this is because of the iron curtain which separates the "unconscious" symbol from that which it both represents and disguises. As long as that iron curtain separates the two, their relationship to each other cannot be altered either by experience or by imagination. It is for this reason that the symbolic process at the "unconscious" end of the spectrum is sterile, repetitive, noncreative, and incapable of communicating even its limited store of meanings.

In between come the preconscious functions with their automatic and subtle recordings of multiple perceptions, their automatic recall, their multiple analogic and overlapping linkages, and their direct connections to the autonomic processes which underlie affective states. The rich play of preconscious operations occurs freely in states of abstraction, in sleep, in dreams, and as we write, paint, or allow our thoughts to flow in the nonselected paths of free association. Yet preconscious processes are assailed from both sides. From one side they are nagged and prodded by rigid and distorted symbols of unconscious drives, which are oriented away from reality and which consist of rigid compromise formations, lacking in fluid inventiveness. From the other side they are driven by literal conscious purpose, checked and corrected by conscious retrospective critique. The uniqueness of creativity—its capacity to sort out bits of experience and put them together into new combinations—depends on the extent to which preconscious functions can operate freely between these two ubiquitous concurrent and oppressive prison wardens.

Here is where the neurotic imprisonment begins almost from infancy onward, not in strange and unusually traumatic circumstances but in the very process which we euphemistically call "education." Thereafter each neurotic symptom has its own distorting consequences; and in turn each such consequence tends to develop secondary symptoms, which in turn develop tertiary consequences which lead to new symptoms. As this tendency multiplies, it forms the self-perpetuating, reverberating chain reaction which constitutes neurotic illness, or the neurotic process. This occurs no matter what the symptom may be—whether it is inherently simple and innocent, or whether it is deeply distorted.

Actually many symptoms are even socially rewarded, but this does not make their consequences any the less destructive to an individual life.

Once a reverberating chain reaction is built around the central stream of preconscious processing, only weighted samples are given symbolic representation first by paralinguistic gestures and mimicry, then by preverbal sounds, and finally by verbal forms of symbolic representation. If the links between the symbolic representatives and their referents (whatever their nature) become strained, distorted, or disrupted, further distortions supervene; these then lead to the obligatory, unchanging, and unchangeable repetitive patterns which are the core of the neurotic process (Kubie, 1941, 1958a, 1963a, 1964). It is this which is at the heart of all neurotic processing. (Drugs such as alcohol or alcohol and marijuana, or alcohol and barbiturates, and also brain damage may intensify this, sometimes to a parapsychotic and lethal degree.) This is the imprisonment of the freely creative preconscious stream of analogic processing; and it challenges us to revise our entire educational approach to child rearing.

Contrary to ordinary preconceptions and assumptions, we do *not* think consciously. All actual thinking is done without the magic of images. Thought is imageless, as the Würzburg school pointed out many years ago. It is fortunate that this is so, because it achieves an enormous saving of time. Furthermore, the freedom which can occur in imageless thought could not be achieved with thought processes which are anchored either to reality or to unreality.[1]

Conscious thought carries on a pedestrian struggle to keep some measure of freedom, but it achieves very little. What we call conscious thought is really a slow and laborious, weighted sampling of the continuous preconscious stream, which thereby is given

[1] The first two chapters of my book on *The Neurotic Distortion of the Creative Process* (1958b) deal with this in great detail. See also my article on "Relation of the Conditioned Reflex to Psychoanalytic Technique" (1934) in which I pointed out that time relations in chains of free associations are as important to the technique of free association as are time relations in the development of the conditioned reflex. And in 1959 I again dealt with the mechanism by which preconscious functions come to play such a major role in the development of the stream of thought.

conscious symbolic representation. This goes on day and night, asleep and awake, in dreaming as waking fantasy and waking thought. There is a rigid relationship between the preconscious stream and those weighted fragments of it which are represented by conscious symbols. Where on the other hand the relationship of these conscious symbols to that which they are supposed to represent becomes distorted or severed, the thought process itself is subject to unconscious distortion—a result that is close to the roots of psychopathology. Instead of representing fragments of the preconscious stream accurately it hides them. This is what is meant by unconscious processing. Note that I do not say "*the* unconscious." There is no "*the* unconscious." That is only an abstraction. But where the links between the symbol and what it is supposed to represent are distorted or severed, fragmentary samples of the preconscious stream which form the core of all human mentation are disguised and distorted or hidden (Kubie, 1966). But this comes at the end of the line. This is what happens, for example, to the adult use of language, as a paralinguistic or linguistic form of representation of the preconscious stream. And this is what happens when the preconscious stream with its speed and extraordinary fluidity, its dependence upon analogic thinking becomes trapped.

I have previously (1958b) tried to show how it happens that this imprisonment occurs between two jailors—the conscious roots on the one hand and the unconscious distortions of the relation of the symbol to its referent on the other. This imprisonment of preconscious processing between pedestrian conscious sampling and its loss of linkages to the sampling process has many consequences. There is a loss of freedom of input, of intake, of representation, and of sampling. There is an impairment of freedom of expression. Most important of all is the impairment of the *freedom to change* and therefore to learn; because without change there can be no learning, and without learning there can be no therapy and of course no freedom to create (Kubie, 1968). This is the impairment of freedom which occurs whenever the preconscious stream becomes trapped between the conscious symbolic representation on one side and the encroaching neurotic process on the other side, with its distortions by the impairment of the linkages to the conscious sample.

In the early entrapment in neurotic illness there also is a carry-over of the affective imprisonment by a central affective potential. I dealt with this in a paper (1963b) I wrote in honor of René Spitz, who was the first to describe this process (1945). (See also Bowlby et al., 1965.)

These are the challenges which child rearing and child education face. There are no greater challenges to us as educators of successive generations. Yet instead of facing this, the "educators" (so-called) continue to depend on drill and grill which actually reinforce the obligatory repetition of the neurotic process and which are a confession of failure of education because they create an atmosphere in which a child cannot learn without reinforcing the neurotogenic processes. Obligatory repetition invades the picture as our educational hopes fail. What to do about it is another question. All I can plead for is that we face our failures and search for remedies.

BIBLIOGRAPHY

BOWLBY, J., AINSWORTH, M., BOSTON, M., & ROSENBLUTH, D. (1965), The Effects of Mother-Child Separation: A Follow-up Study. *Brit. J. Med. Psychol.*, 29:211–247.

KUBIE, L. S. (1934), Relation of the Conditioned Reflex to Psychoanalytic Technique. *Arch. Neurol. Psychiat.*, 32:1137–1142.

——— (1941), The Repetitive Core of Neurosis. *Psychoanal. Quart.*, 10:23–43.

——— (1958a), The Neurotic Process as the Focus of Physiological and Psychoanalytic Research. *J. Ment. Sci.* 104:518–536.

——— (1958b), *Neurotic Distortion of the Creative Process.* Lawrence, Kansas: University of Kansas Press.

——— (1959), The Relation of the Conditioned Reflex to Preconscious Functions. *Trans. 84th Ann. Meet. Amer. Neurol. Assn.*, pp. 187–188.

——— (1963a), Neurosis and Normality. In: *The Encyclopedia of Mental Health*, ed. A. Deutsch. New York: Franklin Watts, pp. 1346–1353.

——— (1963b), The Central Affective Potential and Its Trigger Mechanisms. In: *Counterpoint*, ed. H. S. Gaskill. New York: International Universities Press, pp. 106–120.

——— (1964), Research in Protecting Preconscious Functions in Education. *Trans. ASDC 7th Curriculum Research Institute*, Washington, pp. 28–42.

——— (1966), A Reconsideration of Thinking, the Dream Process, and 'the Dream.' *Psychoanal. Quart.*, 35:191–198.

——— (1968), The Nature of Psychological Change and Its Relation to Cultural Change. In: *Changing Perspectives on Man*, ed. B. Rothblatt. Chicago: University of Chicago Press, pp. 135–148.

SPITZ, R. A. (1945), Hospitalism. *This Annual*, 1:53–74.

CLINICAL
CONTRIBUTIONS

Some Unusual Anal Fantasies
of a Young Child

ANNE HAYMAN, M.B., B.Ch.,
M.R.C. Psych., D.P.M.

EVER SINCE WE LEARNED ABOUT LITTLE HANS AND HIS *lumpfen*, THE wealth of fantasy young children have about their anal products and activities has been one of the best known and uncontested pieces of knowledge psychoanalysis has contributed. Hans revealed the unconscious equation feces = baby, with childbirth understood as defecation, while the unconscious identification of feces with penis, with defecation seen as castration, was described by Freud (1918) in the Wolf-Man. Both of these fantasies have long been an inherent part of knowledge informing the psychoanalysis of adults, and both have appeared directly in the reports of analyses of children of both sexes. Berta Bornstein (1935) reported that Lisa, aged 2½, was constipated when she was occupied with problems of sex, and objected to the removal of her stool, as if she "hoped to make a penis" of it. Both Editha Sterba (1949) and Selma Fraiberg (1950) present case reports documenting the young child's equation of fecal loss with castration. Moreover, Sterba's 2-year-old patient George also believed that babies "come out of the poo-poo place" (anus). Liza, who was referred to Sara Rosenfeld (1968) when she was 4 years old, retained her feces because of the projected fear of

This paper forms part of a research project entitled "Childhood Pathology: Impact on Later Mental Health," conducted at the Hampstead Child Therapy Clinic, London. The Project is financed by Grant No. MH-5683-09, the National Institute of Mental Health, Washington, D.C. The analysis itself is financed through the generosity of the Freud Centenary Fund.

her wish to steal her mother's new baby, and dispose of it in the lavatory, where it "might get squashed . . . just like a bit of faeces" (p. 43).

A few extensions of the classic unconscious equation penis = feces = child have also been reported. Rosenfeld's Liza identified her stool with her mother, retaining it partly as a defense against object loss. Rosenfeld's other child case, Debbie, fantasied that she and her mother were twins, with the twin living inside her own body, as feces. The literature contains further examples of feces being cathected as an object. Anthony (1957) reports a child, aged $6\frac{1}{2}$, who spoke of feces as "asleep in my tummy . . . sometimes I'd like to cuddle them." (An adult patient of mine remembered an uncanny feeling in childhood on seeing human feces in a field; late in analysis, she "recognized" her own stool as an "old friend.")

It should not be surprising, in view of these reports, to come across a fantasy of feces which appears to have various other characteristics that a young child might easily attribute to a baby. In view of the fact that feces are essentially experienced as moving, a youngster might easily attribute to it means of perambulation. Yet when Simon, aged $4\frac{3}{4}$, said firmly that "jobbies" have feet, I believed I was hearing something I had never heard or read about. I was less surprised than I might have been because a few weeks earlier he had produced another unfamiliar anal, in this case anal-phallic, fantasy—namely, that his penis defecates.

At the time of writing, his analysis is still in progress; therefore it is not possible to describe the full nexus of impulses, defenses, and fantasies associated with these unusual ideas, and certainly quite impossible to "explain" how they arose and what their function is, in this child's past and present psychodynamic balance. It nevertheless seemed worth reporting briefly upon them: (1) as information; and (2) to invite other reports of similar, or similarly unusual, clinical observations.

BACKGROUND

At the age of 2, Simon somehow managed to dislodge a bucket of boiling water which was standing on a cooker or a kitchen dresser, and was rather badly scalded, mainly on his right shoulder and upper arm. For several weeks he was treated in the Burns Unit of a leading pediatric hospital, where he was strapped to his bed naked in a glass cubicle, as part of their technique of asepsis. This "crucifixion" also served to stop his interfering with his uncovered wounds. Skin for a graft was taken from one thigh, and while this area was healing his penis was strapped to the other thigh. Excretions were immediately visible to the nursing staff and cleaned up by them. In the several months of his gradual physical recovery, the severe symptoms emerged which led to his being referred for help at $3\frac{1}{2}$ years.

As a baby and toddler Simon was a "bouncing masculine *boy*," according to his father, who thought the feeding battles and food refusals, which started at about 12 months, were the only signs of disturbance prior to the accident. More detailed descriptions indicated that Simon might have been overactive, perhaps restless, against the background of his mother's being quite depressed. His accident did not reflect an isolated instance of her being withdrawn and inattentive to his concerns. I gained the impression that while she struggled hard to do everything necessary, despite her physical presence she was quite often "absent" by being locked in a book or paper, which was her way of trying to cope with her own inner concerns. She reported that toward the end of the second year, Simon, though not yet toilet-trained, was beginning to show signs of shame; when he defecated into his pants or onto the floor, he would cover himself with a little blanket which he had had on his bed since the age of 16 months. In the hospital, once he had recovered from the severe physical shock, he screamed for it whenever he defecated. Perhaps he was asking to be covered by this blanket. Because of the danger of sepsis he was not permitted to have it. This sign of rage or terror associated with defecation persisted. At the time of referral, he constantly refused to go to the lavatory to pass stool. If put there, he would scream, kick, bite his mother; and when he finally, reluctantly, passed the stool, he piteously began to cry and scream, "Save me, save me." This was often followed by the most worrying symptom of withdrawal. He would stand motionless with his eyes closed for up to half an hour, impervious to any attempt to reach him by talking to or touching him. His mother would carry him to his bed, and after a while he would "wake up"—that is, he would open his eyes and resume communication.

This was not the only symptom. His toddler "aggressiveness" expanded into what looked like attacks of wild rage. He was extremely clinging to his mother, usually not in a gentle way. He violently attacked anyone to whom she gave attention, especially his older brother. He shouted "little rat" at him as well as at his mother during toileting attempts and on other occasions when he would also suddenly and violently clutch, hit, bite or kick her, sometimes for no reason that she could determine. After messing or otherwise "misbehaving," he was frequently abjectly apologetic. He had regular nightmares and no night passed without his going or having to be taken into his parents' bed. He refused to sit at table for meals, usually walking around the room nibbling something or throwing food on the floor; he regularly took drinks, especially milk, from a bottle.

These food refusals, which had started as a sort of "faddiness" in his second year, were extreme in the hospital, where, according to his parents' belief, he lived on milk and vitamin injections; they expressed wonder at his later appearance of excellent physical health and vigor since he always seemed to eat so little. He was said to masturbate "only a little," and never to have sucked his thumb; but since he often clutched his penis during his sessions, and his thumb occasionally made abortive moves toward his mouth, it seems likely that these reports reflected his parents' ability not to notice or remember some things.

Simon also had difficulty in pronouncing some consonants, so that strangers often found him incomprehensible. His speech difficulties did not fit any well-known pattern; e.g., they did not indicate high frequency deafness.

Despite this picture of frantic, restless, violent anxiety, he was warmly appreciated for some quality of likableness, and had coped well with, and been well liked by, children and adults in a nursery group he was attending for two hours each day. He probably responded well to a far more structured environment than that offered by his mother. His main disturbance seemed to be centered on her, because generally he screamed and kicked only when she was present. The first time I saw her she hesitantly told me that somehow he seemed "less destroyed" than most of the other children she had seen in the Burns Unit; and the first time I saw him I, too, was struck by his warm and apparently partly intact personality.

Since this communication is focused upon Simon's anal fantasies, other aspects of his progress in analysis will be mentioned only very briefly. It was many weeks before he could face being in the room with me without his mother for even a few moments; but from the first week his true excellence as an analysand was obvious, in his responding to interpretations with attention and an immediate change of play. All his symptoms diminished in intensity within a few months, his eating problem vanishing abruptly on the first day he was taken into our nursery school five months after his analysis started; he also began eating perfectly well at home, confirming my impression that this symptom, a legacy from his second year, was almost entirely reactive to his mother's intense ambivalent pressuring.

He is still a faintly odd, though extremely likable little boy. He is now 5, and has just left the nursery to start at primary school. His play has tended to lag developmentally. He was more than $4\frac{1}{2}$ years before he became enough interested in other children to play spontaneously with them (and even vanish under the table with a little girl). Prior to this, he had been cooperative and friendly, but almost entirely in relation to the loved nursery teacher. Although he is clearly a very intelligent and knowledgeable child, he preferred rather unstructured pursuits, like racing and running around, long after his peers were ready for much more organized games and play with each other. Similarly, he had an enormous and mature vocabulary which was generally understood, although his speech is still somewhat unclear; yet it was not until he was more than $4\frac{1}{2}$ that he seemed to have any idea, even, of drawing things; and only in the last few weeks of his fifth year did he begin to show interest in letters and figures. Diminishingly, Simon gave an impression of tight, organized control, which seemed likely to crumble before an outburst that never actually happened. Indeed, his attempts at control had an obsessionallike quality that seemed quite well established. For example, although he never washed or attempted to dress himself, at referral his mother mentioned his hating to have sticky hands.

"Anal" Fantasies

Simon's concern with his "jobbies" (or "poohs" or "plops"—as his vocabulary soared, he also used many other nursery colloquialisms) has been a constant feature, and he seems to have portrayed some variant of just about every known childhood fantasy about them.

FECES AS VEHICLES OF ANAL AGGRESSIVENESS

In the early months Simon's frequent, sudden, anxious outbursts of aggressive behavior—he viciously threw large wooden blocks around, and often toward me, or suddenly pounded me (or his mother) hard—were understood mainly as "defecatory" attacks. Such aggressiveness was, of course, associated with correlating anxieties; for example, intense fears that the jobbies were, or would turn into, monsters which would attack him. This fear was one reason for his terror of sitting on the lavatory. He began to sleep more easily after a session in which he "played" at cowering under the bed, where he had thrown a banana skin. This was interpreted as the terrifying "jobbies" in bed with him. His defecatory fears were interwoven with fears of fire; e.g., he believed that aggressively expelled stool could burn. Naturally, his destructiveness was felt to operate against object and himself. It was not clear whether it was his objects or he himself who he believed would suffer when he thought of half-expelled stool as being "like a cigarette." Yet when he feared that, like his mother, he too would bleed into the lavatory, he certainly showed his terror that jobbies, hard and pointed like wooden blocks, would damage his "bottom" as they emerge.

FECES AS PRECIOUS POSSESSIONS

Simon soon declared his disbelief in jobbies really vanishing down the lavatory, thus expressing, among other things, his great wish not to lose them, a wish that was connected with his identifying jobbies with babies. After a few months in analysis he verbalized his wish to bear a baby. During the second half of his first year in analysis he often led with increasing knowledge into the matter of how males and females differ anatomically. When he really knew, intellectually, that only males have a "penis = weewee," and only females have a "baby hole" and can bear babies, he increasingly became able to express his contrary wish by saying determinedly or wistfully that "*Some* boys, *some* men can have babies."

The wish to retain or reclaim those precious baby-jobbies showed in a variety of fantasies, which indicated that some derivatives from all libidinal phases were involved. In the second year of analysis he spoke of "needing" a bookcase. This was understood as meaning a place where feces could be kept, stored, taken out, and put back again, as books are in a bookcase. He wondered if he could put his stools back again by eating them, "but," said Simon sadly and hesitantly, "they're poison." Perhaps they could reenter him anally, but this wish immediately stimulated the terror that "monsters" would invade him if he sat on the lavatory.

FECES ENDOWED WITH HUMAN ATTRIBUTES

Early in analysis Simon identified jobbies with his (also frequently vanishing) mother; but more significant and unusual was his subsequent deep concern for these jobbies-as-babies with whom he identified. (It seems likely that his former cries of "save me, save me" while defecating pointed to an identification with the feces that were being got rid of, but this has not been confirmed because this symptom vanished early in the analysis.) For example, he said that the jobbies might hurt themselves when they fell (and he played at falling and hurting himself); that jobbies would drown in the "lavatory sea" or would be eaten up by the lavatory shark (and he showed his fear by avoiding a plasticine shark he had made).

FECES = PENIS

The literature clearly documents that many children unconsciously connect the feared loss of the penis and the loss of feces; a common expression of the fantasy that penis equals feces is a confusion between "front" and "back." Simon eventually showed clear evidence of this fantasy when he said firmly, "Penis *is* jobbies." This phase was preceded by open castration anxiety made explicit when his mother, in half-joking irritation, threatened to cut off his tongue if he kept sticking it out. The subsequent confusion between that

which sticks out in the front (tongue, penis) and that which comes
out at the back (feces) was, not surprisingly, correlated with an
intermixture of excitement related to different erotic zones. On
many occasions he lay squirming on the couch, face down and then
up, often with one hand clutching his penis and the other at his
bottom. During a period when he appeared to get an erection the
moment he entered my room, he pulled his pants down for me to
admire his erect member, and the second time turned around at
once, wanting me similarly to admire his bottom.

This confusion between the zones produced what I regard as his
most unusual fantasy. I had been interpreting one aspect of an
undoubtedly fecal fantasy when he suddenly said, "But weewees
too" ("weewee" stood for both urine and penis). He tried to solve
this contradiction intellectually by reiterating that "Penis does
weewee and bottom does jobs," but this was ineffective and his
anxious uncertainty remained. Finally he resorted to a new game.
He leaned his two-foot-square blackboard against the couch and
began to roll cylindrical wooden blocks down the board. He was
momentarily relieved when I spoke of the "jobbies" rolling down
and collecting together on the floor, but then he picked up an
angular block that was shaped somewhat like a pistol. His
"rolling-down-the-jobbies" game was then interspersed with his
pointing the pistol at me, "threatening" to "shoot," but also looking
as if he might throw it at me at any moment ("a defecatory"
attack). This particular combination led me to interpret that he
believed that jobbies came out of his penis. He paused, very
thoughtfully, and then slowly and emphatically said, "That's JUST
what I was thinking. Jolly good, Anne!"

ORAL INVOLVEMENT IN FECAL CONFLICTS AND WISHES

Simon's question why one doesn't drink urine, which looks like
orange juice, long preceded his ideas of smelling and tasting feces
which look like sausages; child analysts are certainly familiar with
such phenomena. The rather less common variations of these
"polymorphously perverse" ideas appeared later. He believed that
feeding could take place per anum or that defecation could readily
occur through the mouth (he was very frightened of vomiting).

Thus, the 15 months of Simon's analysis have led to the emergence of an extended series of fantasies about feces and defecating, with oral and phallic concomitants. As his conflicts emerged, his anxiety progressively diminished. His attacking me, or changing the subject when I mentioned "jobbies," gradually gave way, so that after a few months he himself was able to "talk about jobbies." Recently, this insightful, hard-working little analysand sometimes introduced the subject by asking me first "not to talk about jobbies" and then, a few minutes later, "to talk about" them.

COMMENT

This small selection from Simon's fantasy life was presented to illustrate some unfamiliar versions of very familiar themes, and the question arises as to their provenance. How far are they specific to this child, and perhaps specific because of his accident? This seems very likely, when he identifies defecating with burning. His accident happened at a time when he had begun to show shame after dirtying himself, but he had not yet begun acquiring bowel control. He was interested in an interpretation that he thought his feces burned, because he believed he was burned as a punishment for wanting to defecate at and into people. Later he asserted that he would defecate "properly" when his burn scars vanished, which he hoped was happening. It is true that Melanie Klein mentioned fantasies about excrement as burning substances, and in one paper (1935) this seems to refer to feces. Joan Riviere (1936) states that "loose motions . . . are felt to be burning . . . agents" (p. 50). Generally, though, these authors linked "burning" fantasies with urination. Simon certainly sometimes confused the two excretory products (as an aspect of his confusing "front" and "back"). Whatever the sequence might have been, it is difficult not to believe that the accident played a most significant part in promoting this group of fantasies.

The fantasy that "jobbies" would drown in the lavatory is similar to one reported by Anthony (1957) in a 5½-year-old, who hated pulling the lavatory chain because the feces might get "stuck in the pipes and cannot breathe." But Simon's other fantasies, that jobbies have feet, or would hurt themselves if they fell on the floor, seem to be more unusual. His identifying himself with these mobile, hurt or drowning "jobbies" may appear to be only an extension of the expectable early identification of the subject with his products; but how often, in fact, are these particular elaborations reported?

There seems little doubt that the accident played a significant part in Simon's developmental lags; for example, he did not reach the oedipal stage and achieve age-appropriate relations with peers until well after he was 4½ years old. But a direct link between Simon's accident and his unquestionable idea of phallic defecation is by no means immediately obvious. At this stage of his analysis I can point to only two factors that may have some bearing on this issue. I can describe the sequence of themes and behavior that followed the emergence of that fantasy and some special personality characteristics that may generally have facilitated the expression and exploration of his fantasies.

The session in which Simon firmly said "Penis *is* jobbies" for the first time came a session or two after the one in which this fantasy of a defecating penis was revealed. In that same week he showed great curiosity about the various contents of bodies (food, feces, penis, baby) and pursued his ideas with great determination, including some ideas of oral impregnation. In the following weeks there was much further elaboration of such "classical" material. I have wondered about the possibility that the "defecating penis" fantasy is a common prelude to or concomitant of the well-known "penis = feces = baby" fantasy, but one that is generally not verbalized. After Simon had first expressed this fantasy, it rapidly gave way to the more usual versions of such fantasies. I therefore must ask again: what is special about Simon that he should so clearly indicate and so readily confirm it? He is by no means the only child in analysis whose problems center on severe conflicts about anal control.

In this connection I must stress, not just Simon's particular excellence as an analysand, but also his intelligence, and particularly his outstanding interest and involvement in words and verbalizable ideas. In the very first week of analysis, while he was bursting with anxiety and showing it in wild violent behavior, he understood the function of interpretations, and began asking me to "talk" if I lagged behind. A little later he managed to formulate the difference between speech in the everyday world and that in analysis, by calling the former "ordinary talk" and the latter "real talk." During his first months in the nursery, when his mode of play showed no forward development, his vocabulary, his knowledge of the world around him, and his ability to converse and describe things and ideas in very mature, sophisticated ways flowered at an enormous rate. He is very bright: he is seriously devoted to sorting himself out via psychoanalysis; and, perhaps like his writer-father, he is an especially verbal person.

As Simon's analysis has gone so well—indeed, unexpectedly well so far—I dare to hope that further analysis will contribute further toward understanding and resolving his remaining foci of anxiety and symptomatology. But however favorable the outcome, I cannot predict whether or not it will yield any new generalizable knowledge or understanding.

Summary

Material from the analysis of a boy in his fourth and fifth years is given to illustrate some unusual details of anal fantasies. These include extensions of the fantasy "feces = baby" to ideas of feces having feet, hurting themselves when they fall, or drowning in water. Many of these fantasies also indicated with unusual clearness the child's identification with his products. The most startling of his unusual fantasies was an extension of the common fantasy "penis = feces," which could be observed when the child emphatically confirmed the interpretation that he thought his penis defecated. Possible determinants to these fantasies are discussed briefly.

BIBLIOGRAPHY

ANTHONY, E. J. (1957), An Experimental Approach to the Psychopathology of Childhood: Encopresis. *Brit. J. Med. Psychol.*, 30:146–175.

BORNSTEIN, B. (1935), Phobia in a Two-and-a-Half-Year-Old Child. *Psychoanal. Quart.*, 4:93–119.

FRAIBERG, S. (1950), On the Sleep Disturbances of Early Childhood. *This Annual*, 5:285–309.

——— (1962), Technical Aspects of the Analysis of a Child with a Severe Behavior Disorder. *J. Amer. Psychoanal. Assn.*, 10:338–367.

FREUD, S. (1909), Analysis of a Phobia in a Five-Year-Old Boy. *Standard Edition*, 10:3–149. London: Hogarth Press, 1955.

—— (1918), From the History of an Infantile Neurosis. *Standard Edition*, 17:3–123. London: Hogarth Press, 1955.

KLEIN, M. (1935), A Contribution to the Psychogenesis of Manic-Depressive States. *Contributions to Psycho-Analysis*. London: Hogarth Press, 1950, pp. 282–310.

RIVIERE, J. (1936), On the Genesis of Psychical Conflict in Earliest Infancy. In: *Developments in Psycho-Analysis*, ed. J. Riviere. London: Hogarth Press, 1952, pp. 37–66.

ROSENFELD, S. (1968), Choice of Symptoms: Notes on a Case of Retention. *J. Child Psychother.*, 2:39–45.

STERBA, E. (1949), Analysis of Psychogenic Constipation in a Two-Year-Old Child. *This Annual*, 3/4:227–252.

Psychotherapeutic Assistance to a Blind Boy with Limited Intelligence

THOMAS LOPEZ, PH.D.

RONNY BEGAN ATTENDING THE CLINIC'S NURSERY SCHOOL FOR BLIND children at the age of 3½. Approximately one year later the staff decided that he should have individual sessions, primarily to supplement his regular nursery program, which by itself had not sufficiently furthered his development. It was also hoped that close contact with Ronny would contribute to a better understanding of him.

The focus of this account reflects the focus of the therapy: my efforts to communicate with Ronny, his to communicate with me, and the means which were devised in order to carry out this communication.

The nature of Ronny's limitations (combined, perhaps, with shortcomings on my part in understanding it) made it impossible for me to gain much insight into his inner life and into the effect of his blindness on his psychological development. These aspects will therefore be touched upon only briefly and tentatively.

The work with blind children is part of the Educational Unit of the Hampstead Child Therapy Course and Clinic and as such is maintained by the Grant Foundation, Inc., New York.

My gratitude to Mrs. D. Burlingham and to the members of the Group for the Study of Blind Children at the Hampstead Clinic for their help and encouragement.

The author is presently with The Center for Preventive Psychiatry, Inc., 340 Mamaroneck Avenue, White Plains, New York.

I saw Ronny in individual psychotherapy for a year and a half. During this time he made some progress, which came to a halt when his family moved away from London. Although the enduring gains made by Ronny must probably be judged to be minor, I nevertheless believe this account to be valuable for the following reasons:

First, while such attempts are common at the Hampstead Clinic, especially in its work with blind children (e.g., Burlingham and Goldberger, 1968), therapeutic efforts in which a prolonged and intimate relationship between child and therapist is central are, to judge from the literature (Robinson and Robinson, 1970), extremely rare with children as limited as Ronny. It is hoped, therefore, that the experience gained in the present attempt will be of benefit to others working with similar children, even if their approach is different.

Second, the material to be presented provides good reasons for feeling positive about the approach which was actually attempted. Ronny did in fact "come to life" in the time we met. He took some steps forward, even though these steps (for the time at least) depended on my presence for their stability. Most important, however, I am convinced that could we have continued meeting, he would have taken even more such steps.

BACKGROUND

Ronny was born blind; the result of Leber's amaurosis, a rare hereditary form of blindness transmitted to him by his parents, both of whom carried the gene recessively.

He was of medium build and height; light complexioned with loosely curled brown hair; and with a very handsome, very attractive face. He was quite adept motorically, capable of using his feet skillfully to feel his way as he walked. He could distinguish light from dark and often, therefore, the gross outlines of large forms.

At the time I began seeing him, Ronny's verbal capacities were limited largely to echoing what others said; his repeatedly uttering words and phrases clearly did not serve to communicate meaning, but had the purpose of hearing the sound of his own voice and that of other people responding to it. He was quite isolated from people and tended to engage in activities that excluded them. He either explored and manipulated inanimate objects, or, more often, occupied himself with monotonously repetitive activities such as rocking or jumping in place, pressing his eyes with his fingers, turning the water taps in the nursery's sink off and on, opening and shutting doors.

It was, and still is, most uncertain to what extent "inherent" factors (other than blindness)—such as primary mental retardation or organic brain abnormality—ought to be held responsible for the gross defectiveness of his personality; to what extent "environmental" factors have played a role; and, above all, how much potential for further development exists. With regard to the possibility of organic brain abnormality, part of an opinion submitted by Dr. P. Zinkin, Honorary Consultant at the Wolfson Centre, and Department of Developmental Pediatrics, Institute of Child Health, University of London, seems worth quoting.

> There are many children with Leber's amaurosis who do in fact have cerebral malformation, and air studies on these children have frequently shown some kind of developmental anomaly of the brain. Such studies were not undertaken in Ronny's case since it was felt that these were not justifiable clinically; since whatever brain pathology there might be, it would be most unlikely to be amenable to present methods of therapy. Nor was his clinical state such that dangerous investigations such as air studies would be justifiable. In other words, there is no evidence that Ronny does not have some cerebral developmental pathology.

With regard to environmental factors, the following seem especially relevant: Ronny's parents—both in their early 30s, both college educated and with middle-income occupations—almost certainly had their capacities as parents markedly diminished by the distress caused them by their son's blindness. Depression, attempts to deny the severity of Ronny's handicaps, and withdrawal from close involvement with him were clearly evident; they escaped into their jobs and employed multiple baby-sitters to care for him. To make matters worse, three years after Ronny's birth—despite medical forewarning—a daughter, tragically afflicted with the same condition as Ronny's, was born to them. With her birth, all of the negative elements inherent in the situation became intensified.

Thus, whatever the organic foundations, it seems very likely that the environment made a considerable contribution to Ronny's impeded development.[1]

TREATMENT MATERIAL

I saw Ronny in therapy for five terms. (At the Hampstead Clinic, the treatment year is organized into three terms of about $3\frac{1}{2}$ months each, interrupted by holidays of 2 weeks at Christmas and at Easter, and by 6 weeks in the summer.) In the first term we met for three sessions of about 40 minutes each week during nursery school hours; in subsequent terms we met four times.

Throughout, Ronny's parents showed only minimal interest in his treatment, viewing the nursery as little more than yet another place to leave him and gain relief from the psychic pain his presence caused them. It soon became evident that it was impossible to involve them in any substantial way. My contact (and the Clinic's contact) with them was therefore quite limited. In all, I had only three interviews with the mother and two with the father.

THE FIRST TERM (SPRING)

In the first two weeks I visited Ronny in the nursery, attempting to form a relationship with him, but generally I felt at a loss as to just how I would do it and often was quite pessimistic about my capacity to do so. My initial strategy was to try to make my presence felt to him in a way he would find enjoyable. When he walked about or did things, I loudly carried on a running commentary on his activities. When he moved about on his tricycle, I made sounds resembling those of a motorcycle motor. When he did anything even remotely worthy of it, I praised him and patted him on his back, head or stomach. Throughout, however, I had no sense that anything was happening. Ronny showed no sign of recognizing me. He continued to press his eyes or to explore his

---

[1] See Burlingham (1961, 1964), Omwake and Solnit (1961), Klein (1962), A.-M. Sandler (1963), Fraiberg and Freedman (1964), Nagera and Colonna (1965), and Wills (1970) for discussions of the effects of blindness on a child's development, and of the effects of a child's blindness on his parents' capacities to function as parents.

surroundings, the nursery school and its garden. His attention remained steadfastly and intently focused on whatever it was he was doing. There seemed no evidence that he was in any way interested in me.

In the third week, however, a change occurred. I became aware of being angry with Ronny because of his continuous eye-pressing. Here, in effect, was I, with great persistence and goodwill, trying to make contact with him, and whenever it struck his fancy—so, it seemed to me—he withdrew into the eye-pressing! It then struck me that possibly the eye-pressing had begun to annoy me because it had in fact become linked up with a relationship, which was developing between the two of us and represented, perhaps, its first glimmer.

My first thought was that the eye-pressing might be serving as a defensive measure against aggressive impulses directed at me, which perhaps were being stirred up in him by his developing feeling for me. The next time Ronny pressed his eyes, I took his eye-pressing hand and, making a joke of it, punched myself in the face with it several times. Ronny looked happy and seemed to enjoy the frolic.

Following this session, I rethought the matter. Whatever other meaning or purpose Ronny's eye-pressing had, it unequivocally had the result of excluding me. I decided to try to counter this exclusion by attempting to intrude myself into the activity. From then on, whenever Ronny pressed his eyes, I pulled his hand away, placed it on my own eyes, and then placed my hand on his eyes. After a few trials, I gained the impression that while Ronny seemed to like my hand on his eyes, he was indifferent to placing his hand on my eyes. I therefore eliminated the latter, and settled into simply removing his hand from his eyes when he was eye-pressing, substituting my own, and then saying something like, "Ah, that feels good!"

In the ensuing weeks, a new pattern began to emerge in the course of our sessions. At their beginning, Ronny typically would be especially preoccupied with some inanimate object such as a door, a toy, part of a fence or a wall. At the same time, he unwaveringly would exclude me. In their latter parts, however, while not really showing any interest in me, he did seem more willing to include me in his activities. For example, he started to allow me to take him on walks outside of the nursery area.

Then, in the fifth week, our relationship took a considerable step forward. Ronny and I found something which he truly enjoyed doing and which he did only with me. In the course of our walks, on Ronny's initiative, we started climbing to the top floor of one of the Clinic's buildings, to a room not in use at the time. From that time on, this room came to serve as our therapy room.

Once we regularly used the room, Ronny soon became involved in playing with a telephone he discovered in it. He would spin the dial a few times and then jiggle the receiver, duplicating the sounds, though, of course, not the actions of a sighted person making a phone call. I followed his lead by play-acting the part of a person at the other end of the line. Ronny easily picked up the idea, though in an extremely limited way. He would first say "hello" into the receiver—"Hello Mrs. Hayes" (the cook), or "Hello Lorraine" (I never discovered who Lorraine was); and then, after a while, he would say, "Good-bye, I have to hang up now." Between "hello" and "good-bye" he interspersed an assortment of comments. However, despite considerable efforts on my part, these comments never came close to the reciprocal exchange characteristic of ordinary conversation. In a short time it became clear that although Ronny's playing with the phone initially represented a definite progressive move, subsequently it became little more than yet another piece of repetitive autistic behavior which served to impede rather than to encourage his developing a more significant attachment to me. I therefore tried to frustrate it; to interfere with his becoming settled in it. When he said "hello," as if to start a phone conversation, I countered by touching him and saying we were both in the same room and could talk to each other without recourse to a phone. When he persisted—and he always did—I attempted to introduce another object (a doll, a chair, a toy), but Ronny invariably refused it. While my efforts did not result in Ronny's giving up his playing with the telephone and his engaging in another activity, they did result in his efforts at withdrawal not being as successful as they might have been had they gone unchallenged.

By the time the term ended, I had the impression that both Ronny and I enjoyed meeting together and that the rudiments of an emotional tie to me were definitely present in Ronny.

THE SECOND TERM

Upon his return from the summer holiday, however, Ronny impressed me (and Mrs. Curson, the head teacher in the nursery) as less accessible than ever. To his usual difficulties in communicating verbally was now added a substantial lessening of emotional responsiveness. My experience was one of being quite out of touch with a little boy who not only seemed out of touch with me and the other people in his life, but who also seemed quite content to remain so.

At times, Ronny monotonously repeated the phrases: "Is it the garage?" "Is it the gingers?" "Are these your gingers?" At other times he rocked back and forth from one foot to the other, or opened and shut the door of the therapy room. I could discern no purpose in these activities other than one of engaging in them for their own sake. I tried to turn what he was doing into a game in which I could participate; I asked him questions about what he was doing; I told him I did not understand; I engaged him in other activities—all to no avail. Ronny simply pursued his own course, more or less oblivious of my efforts.

In the third week of the term, however, an incident occurred which did make a difference. By accident, I partially closed the door of the therapy room on Ronny's hand. I realized what was happening only when I noticed that the door was not shutting. I looked down quickly and much to my dismay there stood Ronny: his hand stuck in the hinge side of the door, in complete silence and with large tears rolling down his face. Quickly, I opened the door. I saw that his hand was not hurt, rubbed it, hugged him and said: "Poor Ronny. Ronny hurt his hand. Ronny should scream when something hurts."

That this incident had psychological significance for Ronny soon became clear because in the next two sessions he often repeated the very words I had used in comforting him. Nevertheless, all my efforts to build on them, to carry them further, failed. I tried to get across to Ronny that when he was in pain, he should scream: if he screamed, I could help him. Ronny, however, only repeated my words in a parrotlike manner: "If your hand hurts, you should scream. Poor Ronny." I tried to demonstrate what I meant by screaming a bit myself, but Ronny merely became frightened at the loudness of my voice. I nevertheless felt encouraged. My efforts to comfort him when he hurt his hand seemed to have some impact on him. His becoming frightened at my raised voice indicated that at least he was listening.

My raised hopes turned out to be justified. Very quickly now Ronny began to show signs of increasing emotional attachment to me. Up to this point, for example, he often passed air during our sessions, but he never responded affectively in any way I could discern. In the last session of the fourth week of the term, however, Ronny apparently involuntarily passed a loud flatus. He then stopped short as if in anxious anticipation of my reaction. When I responded by jokingly saying, "Ronny made a . . . [imitation of flatus]," his face lit up in a broad smile. Then, also in a spirit of good humor, he repeated what I had said, at the same time jumping happily up and down.

Ronny's greater attachment to me soon led me astray, however. I felt that I could now discern some symbolic meaning in his behavior and action and, accordingly began to make verbal interpretations to him. Whenever I made such an attempt, Ronny stopped whatever he was doing, his face took on a serious expression, and to all appearances (at least to me) he seemed to be listening attentively and with understanding. The following material from one session is typical of our interaction at this time:

As the session began Ronny engaged in his now customary activity of opening and closing the door of the therapy room, while at the same time repeatedly uttering the phrases: "Is it the garage? Are these your gingers? Is it the taxi?" It occurred to me that in his activity with the door he was consistently keeping me on one side and himself on the other side of it. I interpreted: "Ronny doesn't want to be close to Tom." Ronny again shut the door. I remained silent. He opened the door and said, "You're angry." I replied: "You think I'm angry because I didn't talk, and maybe you get angry when your mum and dad shut the door on you." Again in a more or less random manner Ronny uttered the phrases mentioned above. I intervened with: "Maybe when Mum and Dad talk Ronny doesn't understand." Again he slammed the door, and I heard nothing from him for a few moments. I gently opened the door and saw him sitting on the floor, rubbing his penis with his hand. I said: "Ronny slammed the door because he thought Tom wouldn't let him rub his penis and bottom. But Tom knows that it feels good to Ronny and that when Ronny does it he doesn't need Tom as much. Ronny thinks Tom will get angry though." Each time I spoke, Ronny became serious in his demeanor and seemingly very attentive. At the same time he pressed his eyes with thumb and index finger and rocked gently from foot to foot.

I presented this and similar material to the Clinic's Group for the Study of Blind Children. Much to my surprise, the Group's opinion was that although some of my interpretations might be more or less correct, and although Ronny might have some vague notion of what a few of the more simple words I was using meant, his capacities were so limited that he could not possibly understand what I was saying. His seeming to pay attention to me when I spoke was attributed to his being interested in the sound of my voice, especially in its affective qualities.

I returned to Ronny to test those ideas out. I set out, at least provisionally, to view Ronny within the framework suggested by the Group, and quickly became convinced of its essential validity. My perspective altered, as a result of which I developed some new strategies in my approach to him. I now attempted to offer him my ego as an auxiliary to his very limited ego. For example:

1. I took special pains to make sure that Ronny really understood what I said to him. Immediately the amount of time we spent communicating to each other on the same "wave length" was greatly increased. I spoke only of specific actions he was performing or of specific objects—mostly parts of his own body—which he was touching or could touch. When Ronny touched a body part, I named it: "Ronny is touching his nose [leg, head]." Then I asked him to touch these and other parts of his body and found that he could do so correctly. Similarly, when Ronny turned the lights on or off, opened or shut the door, I verbally described what he was doing. I then asked him to carry out similar actions and again found he could do so correctly. At times I initiated this kind of interaction, at other times Ronny did.

Ronny showed himself capable of adequately carrying out

requests to open and shut the door; to hit the wall, floor, a chair, or parts of his body; and to shake a toy car he now called his "taxi" and carried about with him, seemingly at all times. He also was able to place his "taxi" in a small cupboard he called his "garage." (Mrs. Curson and I had attempted to tie the words Ronny repeated in an apparently meaningless manner—"taxi," "garage," etc.—to specific objects—a toy car, a cupboard, etc.)

In a variation of this approach, I asked Ronny what he was doing when he engaged in an activity. Often he replied with simple but accurate descriptions: "Ronny is touching his nose, slamming the door, banging the floor." When he did not reply, I provided the answer myself. In this way Ronny demonstrated that he was able to call all the major parts of his external anatomy by their correct names, including his penis and his "bottom." In fact, he seemed to be capable of more than that. Ronny sometimes touched his penis or his "bottom" and then smelled the fingers of the hand with which he touched it. I asked, "What is Ronny doing?" Instead of answering in a concretistic way, he answered, "Ronny is smelling his penis [or bottom]."

2. Ronny was obviously confused about the meaning of the pronouns "you" and "I." I therefore deliberately substituted "Ronny" and "Tom" with the aim of making the distinction between himself and me as graphic as possible to him. Occasionally I used "you" or "I" to test whether he showed any sign of understanding what these words meant. There seemed no evidence, however, that he did. (Although the idea occurred to me, it seemed pointless at this time to make any special effort to teach him their meaning, since Ronny seemed too far from being able to learn it.)

3. I made use of Ronny's liking to open and shut the door of the therapy room to try to convey to him some idea of what it means to be seen and not to be seen by another person, and in yet another way to try to enhance his sense of a distinction between himself and other people. When we were on different sides of the door, I said loudly, "Tom cannot see Ronny now. Ronny is on the other side of the door." When he opened the door and became visible, I said, "Now Tom can see Ronny." Then for a few moments I described his actions to him in some detail and sometimes touched him.

4. When I was doing something that did not directly involve

Ronny—for example, put on or take off my jacket, or draw the window shade (to make the contrast between the lights being on and their being off maximal)—I carried on a running narrative of my activities. Ronny soon got some sense for these routines and often called out what I was about to do ("Tom is taking off his jacket"), just before I either did it or described doing it. In this way I hoped to enhance his sense of the continued existence of, and his capacity to maintain a relationship with, another person, even when that other person was not close enough for him to touch (Burlingham, 1961, 1964).

5. I encouraged Ronny to shout, and played shouting games with him; activities in which he soon engaged with enthusiasm. In this I was mindful of his earlier inhibition with regard to shouting, especially when his fingers had been painfully caught in the door. In essence, I attempted to convey to him that shouting, in addition to being a good way of making other people aware of one's presence, is also an acceptable, safe, and even enjoyable activity to engage in.

During this time, Ronny also grasped the idea of "teasing" and began to enjoy teasing me. He would either run as if to enter a room he was not permitted to enter, or he would describe situations in ways opposite to what they actually were, all the while saying, "Ronny is teasing Tom." For example, when Ronny switched the lights off, I asked, "What are the lights?" He answered, "The lights are on." I, in turn, would respond with a dramatic show of frustration: "Oh! Ronny is teasing Tom!" Whereupon Ronny jumped up and down gleefully while repeating, "Ronny is teasing Tom," and then as if to comfort me in my misery, described the situation correctly ("The lights are off").

In order to enhance his awareness of me and to enrich our interaction, I found ways of "teasing" Ronny. When he did not want me to step outside the therapy room, for example, I pretended to strive mightily to leave, despite his objections. Then after a short "struggle," I would say, "Tom is teasing Ronny." Ronny invariably responded by laughing. He clearly appreciated the play-acting involved.

In the final two weeks of the term, Ronny spontaneously walked over to me, gently patting my face, at times gently pinching it (sometimes accompanied by the statement, "Ronny is pinching Tom"), and hugging me gently. I responded simply by putting into words what he was doing (patting, hugging, pinching). In these two weeks, Ronny occasionally spoke in sentences that were longer than any he had previously used: "Mummy goes to work." "Daddy puts his car in the garage." "Ronny took his [toy] clock into Gaye's room." (Miss Gaye McGilvery is a social worker, whose room was next to ours.) Upon hearing her leave: "Gaye left her room and went downstairs." Although the first two sentences may have been rote memories of something he had heard someone else say, the latter two surely were not. Furthermore, on some occasions Ronny clearly attempted to string phrases together. Then, apparently not having the necessary words available, he ended up mumbling with a rhythm resembling that of normal speech.

The term ended on a sad, but very positive note. In the final session before the Christmas holiday, for which he had been prepared by Mrs. Curson and me for some two weeks, Ronny cried quite touchingly as we parted. While his sadness quickly disappeared when his attention was distracted in the nursery, he had clearly experienced pain as a result of separating from me. I had become a person it hurt to say good-bye to.

THE THIRD TERM

In interaction with me, Ronny's affect became richer and more intense. He made a real effort to communicate meaning verbally, to understand what was communicated to him, and to reciprocate by saying something relevant himself. Finally, his inner experience began to show signs of greater continuity and constancy; of not being so strictly determined by the stimulus characteristics of his immediate environment. The emphasis in my own approach gradually shifted from the previously encouraging and prodding one to placing greater weight on understanding what was going on in Ronny and, on the basis of this understanding, attempting to respond to him in a therapeutic way. Two examples will illustrate this.

1. Ronny (who, as mentioned, could distinguish between light and dark) had been in the habit of repeatedly switching the

fluorescent light in our therapy room off and on. In the beginning of March, the light occasionally began to flicker prior to coming on; then sometimes it failed to come on at all; by mid-March it had broken down completely. Three issues seem worthy of being underscored in Ronny's reaction to the failure of this light.

The first concerns the sheer intensity of his affect. When the light flickered prior to coming on, Ronny stared at it in anxious anticipation, and when it finally did come on, he showed definite signs of relief. When it temporarily failed to come on altogether, he became quite agitated and rapidly manipulated the switch until it finally did come on. And on the day it did not come on at all, Ronny was truly beside himself. He cried desperately, jumped up and down frantically, and repeatedly bawled, "Ronny doesn't want the lights to be broken!" All of this was in very marked contrast to his earlier, relatively indifferent affective expressions.

The second concerns the fact that Ronny did not stop feeling badly as soon as he left the therapy room on the day the light broke. Up to this time, his affect had had a peculiar "stimulus-bound" quality. As was illustrated by his crying when he said good-bye to me before Christmas, when Ronny's affect was aroused, it had a very noticeable tendency to cease abruptly either as soon as he was removed from the situation that had elicited it, or as soon as his attention was diverted. In contrast, Ronny was inconsolable about the light, not only during his session in the therapy room, but also afterward while he walked down the stairs, and even during the car ride home. He remained inconsolable even though I showed him, and he verified, that the other lights in the building worked, and I attempted to reassure him that the light in our room would, in time, be fixed.

The third concerns the opportunity for therapeutic intervention. It also illustrates the use of an educational technique, which often seems very much called for in meeting the therapeutic needs of children as limited as Ronny. When the light was fixed, I discovered a way of tampering with it so that I could make it operational or nonoperational, "fixed" or "broken," as I wished. When I caused the light to be "broken," Ronny responded with distress as he had done earlier. At first, I simply attempted to verbalize his distress: "Ronny doesn't like the lights to be broken.

Ronny feels sad." As soon as these efforts had a calming effect, I "fixed" the light and put into words the idea that broken things can, in fact, be fixed. After four such sessions, Ronny's reaction to the light being first "broken" and then "fixed" became toned down to a simple verbal acknowledgment. At this point I gave up the routine.

2. Throughout the time I saw Ronny I repeatedly made attempts to introduce toys into his activities in the hope that he might use them in symbolic play and to encourage a displacement of his interest away from his body (Fraiberg et al., 1966; Wills, 1968). My efforts came to naught. Ronny simply rejected whatever I offered him. But there was one exception: Ronny readily accepted a Teddy bear. He felt it, hugged it, and spontaneously declared, "It's like Wanda" (his sister). From that time Teddy became a constant feature of our sessions. It was kept in a small cupboard: brought out at the beginning, and greeted; put away and said good-bye to. Ronny sometimes hugged, sometimes rejected and threw the Teddy down. I tried to use this to get the idea across to him that sometimes Ronny liked people (Wanda, Mummy, Daddy, me), sometimes he did not; sometimes he wanted to play or talk with them, sometimes he wished to ignore them. This use of the Teddy led to an interaction which not only shed some light on the nature of his inner life, but also reflected what, at the time, seemed to me to be Ronny's highest level of verbal communication.

Ronny began a session near the end of the term with his customary switching the lights off and on. Trying to interest him in something else, I said, "Ronny doesn't want to play with Tom. Poor Tom is sad." Ronny merely repeated my words and continued with the lights. I then pushed the Teddy into his arms and said, "Teddy wants to play with Ronny. Teddy likes Ronny."

Ronny hugged the Teddy for a moment and said, "Ronny doesn't want to hurt Wanda. Wanda shouldn't scratch. Ronny is afraid of Wanda." I said, "Ronny gets angry at Wanda when Wanda scratches Ronny. But Wanda doesn't know better. She's only a baby."

Ronny agreed, and then said, "Ronny doesn't want to hurt Tom." I replied that Ronny could not hurt Tom because Tom was big and strong, and that Tom would not get angry at Ronny because Tom was not afraid of Ronny.

At this point Ronny walked over to me and touched my face with his hand with great gentleness and caution. I picked him up, hugged him, swung him about, and once again told him he need not fear, for he could not hurt Tom. ·

THE FOURTH TERM

Ronny became even more responsive and was emotionally more "in touch" with me. I experienced his affect as especially rich, and at times actually believed he had the richness of affect of a normal child (!). His use of language, although still very rudimentary, improved vastly. He became much bolder; he left the therapy room on his own, often popping into offices and greeting their occupants; and occasionally he went to the toilet on his own (none of which he could or would have done earlier). Above all, he showed very clear signs of wanting to learn and to function more adequately. The following three examples convey this progress.

1. Ronny began the first session following the two-week holiday interruption by his customary switching the lights in the therapy room on and off. In an effort to enlist his interest, I asked him some simple questions. Ronny at first made quite visible efforts to find the words to answer me (mouth movements, a strained look on his face). However, despite his efforts, the words did not come; and so I said, "Words are hard to find sometimes." Ronny again withdrew into his repetitive activity with the lights and continued at it with no sign of letup despite my again saying to him, "Words are hard to find," and adding, "but Ronny must try."

Finally I said to him, "The holiday is now over. Tom and Ronny are meeting again." Ronny responded immediately by ceasing his activity with the lights and by repeating what I had said. He then uttered some phrases which I did not grasp. But then, with very appropriate affect, Ronny said, "Ronny was sad during the Easter holiday, because Ronny wanted to meet with Tom." I responded with, "Tom was sad too because Tom and Ronny didn't meet." Then, as if sorting the matter out in his mind by thinking out loud, Ronny went on repeating phrases such as: "The holiday is over now. Tom and Ronny are meeting again." This exchange indicates Ronny's capacity to reestablish our relationship and the degree of subtlety which our communication with each other had achieved.

2. Early in June I stopped avoiding pronouns and began to instruct Ronny in their use. Shortly thereafter Ronny was putting his Teddy in and out of a small cupboard, closing the cupboard door each time he put the Teddy in or took it out. Presently the cupboard door jammed, and the following dialogue took place:

> *Therapist:* Do you want me to help or do you want me to remain seated?
>
> *Ronny:* I want me [I corrected to "you"] . . . I want you to sit. [He struggled on.]
>
> *Therapist* [after a time]: Do you want me to help?
>
> *Ronny:* I want to do it by myself. I want to put Teddy in the cupboard. [Ronny managed to open the cupboard door and returned to his game, but soon the door jammed again.]
>
> *Therapist:* Do you want my help?
>
> *Ronny:* I want me [he then corrected himself] . . . I want you to get up and help me. [I did so and Ronny went back to playing. He put the Teddy in the cupboard and shut the door.] The Teddy bear goes away. I'm going in the cupboard!
>
> *Therapist:* Who said that?
>
> *Ronny:* The Teddy bear said, "I'm going in the cupboard." Bye, bye Teddy bear. "Bye, bye, Ronny" says the Teddy bear.

Clearly, Ronny was making purposeful, self-critical efforts to learn.

3. The following interchange, which took place late in the term, illustrates the progress in Ronny's use of language and in asserting himself.

At the start of each session just prior to entering the therapy room, I usually checked to see if Miss McGilvery was in her office by saying, "Hello Gaye! Are you in?" (I did so in order to prohibit Ronny's entering it if indeed she was in.) On this occasion, however, when we had reached the door to her office, Ronny stepped quickly in front of me and said sharply: "I want to see if Gaye is in myself. Hello Gaye! Are you in? [No answer.] Gaye is not in."

As we entered the therapy room, Ronny said, "I want to open the cupboard by myself." With a bit of help from me he unlocked the cupboard door. He then played for a while, putting his Teddy in and out of the cupboard, opening the door each time he took it out and closing it each time he put it in. Finally I asked, "What are you doing?" Ronny replied sharply and with a show of annoyance: "I don't want your questions!"

THE FIFTH TERM

Ronny returned from the summer holiday with little or no loss in the progress he had made. He recognized me as soon as he heard my voice, seemed very happy to be with me, and we set off to work straight away.

But within a week and a half Ronny's parents informed the Clinic that his father had been offered a better, higher paying job in another city and that the entire family, including Ronny, would be leaving London in the very near, but (unfortunately) indefinite future. I spoke with Ronny's parents at this time, tried to convey to them what I thought he and I had accomplished together, and advised them to do their best to communicate their impending move to him. They assured me they would.

Ronny was clearly affected by the situation, though it was impossible to say what and how he understood it. In his session he initially reverted to his former nonsense talk, eye-pressing, rocking, and repetitive activities. Once again he became quite inaccessible. I concentrated my efforts on telling him that I knew he was soon to leave and on conveying to him how very sad this made me feel. These efforts—and especially the latter, I think—soon got through to him: Ronny's facial expression changed, the nonsense talk decreased, and he again became accessible. Further, Ronny clearly demonstrated that he had some idea of what I was getting at—even if only a vague one—as he recited the name of the city he would soon be living in, and the names of relatives who would be living nearby.

Then an entirely new type of behavior emerged. Very cautiously at first, but with my encouragement soon more boldly, Ronny alternated between hugging me affectionately; slapping, pinching, and biting me; and pulling my hair. While he carried on in this manner, he would make statements such as: "Don't do it Ronny!"

and "You're a pig!" In answer to my questions, he volunteered that these were things his mother said.

Initially, I allowed Ronny to "act out" directly on me as the object, because he seemed unwilling, despite my efforts, to make use of dolls, his Teddy, or other toys for this purpose. When this became too painful for me to tolerate, I held him at arm's length while I verbally encouraged his openness: I tried getting across to Ronny that it was okay to want to do all the things he wanted to do to me, but when he actually did them they hurt, and that was why I was holding him off. Attempting to use his affect as a guide, I also tried to interpret to him. When I felt, for example, his biting urges primarily represented libidinal aims—using food he liked as an analogy—I would interpret accordingly. When I felt aggressive aims were predominant, I put these into words. Throughout, I tried to make links to our imminent separation. I stressed my sadness and, when it seemed appropriate, his biting, pinching, and clinging as evidence of his sadness.

It is difficult to assess what effect, if any, these efforts at interpretation had on Ronny. Three points, however, may be made: (1) I felt I maintained myself in emotional touch with him, since, by my efforts, what he was doing continued to make sense to me. (2) Throughout the time he hugged and pinched me, Ronny's functioning did not deteriorate in his sessions. (It did deteriorate in the nursery, however; a matter which is discussed below.) (3) After about three weeks Ronny himself began to say that it would "hurt Tom" if he bit, slapped, or pinched me or pulled my hair. To what extent he was merely parroting, however, remained unclear.

In early December, some six weeks after the new behavior had begun to emerge—without advising the Clinic ahead of time— Ronny was taken on a long car trip by his parents to a number of cities, for interviews at institutions for blind children where they hoped to enroll him. According to their later report, during the trip, Ronny became carsick, his functioning deteriorated, and he performed very poorly in the interviews.

When he returned to treatment one week later, Ronny once again was quite inaccessible and uncommunicative; he withdrew into garbled talk—in which one could discern, however, some vague reference to his having been carsick—and into his former rocking, eye-pressing, and repetitive activities. Furthermore, Ronny's nursery attendance now became quite irregular, probably because his parents were occupied with the problems of moving. Ronny and I never again achieved the quality of relationship we once had had.

In the final three weeks before he left, my principal means of making contact with Ronny was to sing to him. He seemed adamant about not wanting again to enter into a relationship with me in which we would talk to one another, but he did respond very attentively and warmly to my singing.

At this point there seemed nothing for me to do but to follow his lead. At the beginning of each session I asked Ronny whether he wished me to sing or to talk. Invariably he answered, "Sing." Invariably too, he refused to accompany me (saying "no" to my efforts to prompt him to). He never was able to ask for his favorite song, "Greensleeves," by name, but always chose it from a list of songs I offered him.

Although Ronny refused or was not able to converse with me in the manner he once had, he did converse with people we met on our walks together, and he talked as well as he previously had.

RONNY'S FUNCTIONING IN THE NURSERY

Ronny attended the nursery throughout the period he saw me in treatment. Particularly during the final four terms of treatment—a time during which Ronny so clearly improved in his functioning while he was with me—his functioning in the nursery just as clearly deteriorated. In the nursery he tended to withdraw more than ever into the repetitive activities mentioned earlier; his interest in relating to people and in exploring his environment decreased. Occasionally he attacked one of the other children, pulling their hair or attempting to strangle them. At other times he forcibly engaged in coitallike motions with one of the girls. Furthermore, quite unlike his behavior prior to treatment, he now at times openly rejected the nursery and his teachers. (An explanation of this discrepancy is offered in the next section.)

We also received reports from Ronny's parents about his

behavior at home. These consistently spoke of improved functioning. However, they were so vague that it was difficult to decide what stock, if any, can be placed in them.

DISCUSSION

Ronny's disturbance is best viewed as a massive developmental arrest, primarily at levels normally reached by children in their second year of life. The validity of this formulation can be demonstrated by focusing briefly on a number of the more central of the "lines of psychological development" (A. Freud, 1965).

In the realm of object relations, there was clear evidence that Ronny had achieved object constancy. This was demonstrated by the very definite attachment he formed to me as a person. His main level of relating was, in fact, well within the teasing, sadomasochistic mixture of affection and torture so typical of the toddler (A. Freud, 1965, p. 65). In the realm of psychosocial development (Erikson, 1950), there was evidence that Ronny had made definite moves toward greater autonomy (i.e., his independent jaunts away from the therapy room; his wishing to do things on his own) and that he derived considerable narcissistic gratification from these ventures.

In the realm of language development, there was evidence that Ronny was making some progress from using words as "things" (often playthings [Freud, 1915]) to using language to communicate meaning (McNeill, 1970).

In the realm of drive organization, there was evidence that Ronny's "center of gravity" was well within the oral-sadistic and anal-sadistic phases. This was demonstrated by the dominance of impulses to bite, pinch, hit, and strangle, but also to kiss, hug, and be tender. (The coitallike behavior he displayed in the nursery indicates that phallic drive aims might have developed as well, though only in a very primitive way. Clearly, very little neutralization, sublimation, or any kind of elaboration of drive aims—whatever their level of development—could be detected in Ronny.)

In the realm of "moral development" (A. Freud, 1965), there was evidence that Ronny functioned primarily or perhaps wholly) at the presuperego level at which the actual presence of the object representing authority is required for prohibitions against "forbidden" impulses to take effect. For example, when Ronny had impulses to bite, hit, pinch, or otherwise hurt me, he seemed to hear his mother's voice from within, admonishing him not to do so. However, this "inner voice" appeared to require my actual presence for it to be heard (or at least to be taken notice of) by Ronny, probably because I represented for him a substitute for his mother. When he was in the nursery, away from me (and his mother) he readily acted on these very impulses, with the other children as objects.

Ronny's defense organization also appeared rooted in a level of development normally reached by children between the first and second years of life. His primary means of coping with anxiety was withdrawal of attention or interest from involvement with people (at the same time, perhaps, denying their existence), and then displacing it onto repetitive activities and inanimate objects. This means of defending, while a very primitive one developmentally, also implies that at least the beginnings of a differentiation between self and object had taken place. The external object must, to some extent at least, first be acknowledged before it is rejected.

Ronny's level of development could, of course, be located on still other developmental lines, but those adduced above seem sufficient to warrant the hypothesis that an extremely serious disruption took place in the second year of Ronny's life. This disruption was undoubtedly caused by many factors, but chief among them were his blindness (A.-M. Sandler, 1963) and his parents' incapacities to help him cope with it.[2] Another contributory factor may have been an organic abnormality of his brain or primary mental deficiency.

However, whatever the precise etiology, Ronny's only chance of resuming development lay, on the one hand, in at least residual

---

[2] In discussing a draft of this paper, Mrs. D. Burlingham informed me that when Ronny first came to the nursery (and before I knew him), the phrases he repeated seemed very much to concern the topics of "nighttime" and sexual activities. They made those who were involved with him at the time think of the possibility that he had been severely traumatized between his first and second years, possibly by having been grossly exposed to his parents' sexual activities. This possibility seems to fit well with the coitallike activity and with the excitable aggression which Ronny displayed in the nursery.

"potentials for interaction" and, on the other, in the environment making "contact" with these surviving potentials and encouraging them to develop. This statement is based on Erikson's (1950) views of normal psychological development. In his terms, development involves the emergence in the individual of a "succession of potentialities for interaction" with the environment, which the environment must, in turn, "move" to meet half-way in order to safeguard and encourage the proper rate and the proper sequence of their unfolding. Optimal development depends on the joint capacities of the individual and the environment to initiate and sustain this process of cogwheeling with one another; deficiencies in the one (for whatever reason) require that they be compensated for by special efforts or capacities in the other. (See also Freud's [1916–17] concept of the "complemental series.")

These views also provided the rationale for the therapeutic approach, in which my sustained effort to meet Ronny "half-way" was central. At first I attempted to induce him to form and then to maintain a relationship with me—at whatever level he was able to make it. Once this relationship was established, I attempted to exploit, by whatever means devisable, every opportunity that might encourage further development.

The crucial development-promoting factor was Ronny's loving attachment to me, which in turn led to improvements in other areas. It caused the world of people, the "social world" (Erikson, 1950), to be more positively experienced and valued by him; for it was in this "social world" that I resided. This made it more difficult for him to withdraw from it; gradually his withdrawal became less complete, and especially since he also strove to develop the means "actively [to] improve his relationship" (Hartmann, 1939) to it. This process was most apparent in Ronny's efforts to learn to use language for the purpose of communicating with me; but it also was discernible in Ronny's efforts to cope with the affects and wishes that our relationship had reactivated in him. For these endeavors posed new tasks for his ego, especially for its organizing function. The gradual enrichment of affect, and the enhanced continuity of experience which clearly took place in Ronny throughout the time we met, may be taken as evidence that his ego was responding positively to the challenges posed by these new tasks.

The same growth-promoting factor also accounts for the apparent deterioration on Ronny's functioning in the nursery, at a time when he had definitely improved in his sessions with me. In the therapy room Ronny had my total attention; in the nursery he was forced to share his teachers' attention with the other children. The exclusive relationship Ronny had with me in our sessions exerted an organizing influence—even if a very imperfect one—on his reactivated affects and wishes. In the nursery, however, in the absence of this influence, the same reactivated affects and wishes probably created in him, not the means for an enrichment of his interaction with the environment, but rather the threat of inner chaos. Ronny's intensified and obviously defensive withdrawal in the nursery and the occasional breakthroughs in the form of acting on impulse are completely consistent with the contention that the exclusive, positive relation to me did, as long as it lasted, promote development.

BIBLIOGRAPHY

BURLINGHAM, D. (1961), Some Notes on the Development of the Blind. *This Annual*, 16:121–145.

——— (1964), Hearing and Its Role in the Development of the Blind. *This Annual*, 19:95–112.

——— & GOLDBERGER, A. (1968), The Re-education of a Retarded Blind Child. *This Annual*, 23:369–390.

ERIKSON, E. H. (1950), *Childhood and Society*. New York: Norton.

FRAIBERG, S. & FREEDMAN, D. A. (1964), Studies in the Ego Development of the Congenitally Blind Child. *This Annual*, 19:113–169.

——— SIEGEL, B. L., & GIBSON, R. (1966) The Role of Sound in the Search Behavior of a Blind Infant. *This Annual*, 21:327–357.

FREUD, A. (1965), *Normality and Pathology in Childhood*. New York: International Universities Press.

FREUD, S. (1915), The Unconscious. *Standard Edition*, 14:159–215. London: Hogarth Press, 1957.

——— (1916–17), Introductory Lectures on Psychoanalysis. *Standard Edition*, 15 & 16. London: Hogarth Press, 1963.

HARTMANN, H. (1939), *Ego Psychology and the Problem of Adaptation*. New York: International Universities Press, 1958.

KLEIN, G. S. (1962), Blindness and Isolation. *This Annual*, 17:82–93.

McNEILL, D. (1970), The Development of Language. In: *Carmichael's Manual of*

Child Psychology, 1:1061–1161. Third Ed., ed. P. H. Mussen. New York & London: Wiley.

NAGERA, H. & COLONNA, A. B. (1965), Aspects of the Contribution of Sight to Ego and Drive Development. *This Annual*, 20:267–287.

OMWAKE, E. B. & SOLNIT, A. J. (1961), "It Isn't Fair": The Treatment of a Blind Child. *This Annual*, 16:352–404.

ROBINSON, H. B. & ROBINSON, H. (1970), Mental Retardation. In: *Carmichael's Manual of Child Psychology*, 2:615–666. Third Ed., ed. P. H. Mussen. New York & London: Wiley.

SANDLER, A.-M. (1963), Aspects of Passivity and Ego Development in the Blind Infant. *This Annual*, 18:343–360.

WILLS, D. M. (1968), Problems of Play and Mastery in the Blind Child. *Brit. J. Med. Psychol.*, 41:213–222.

——— (1970), Vulnerable Periods in the Early Development of Blind Children. *This Annual*, 25:461–480.

Promiscuity in a 13-Year-Old Girl

WILLIAM THOMAS MOORE, M.D.

ALTHOUGH SEXUAL PROMISCUITY IN PUBESCENT GIRLS IS NOT RARE, it is a little understood form of delinquent behavior. Psychoanalytic case studies of this phenomenon are scarce in proportion to the frequency of its occurrence in our culture. The early analytic inquiries into delinquent behavior in promiscuous adolescent girls resulted in more questions than answers. August Aichhorn (1949) asked important questions about female juvenile delinquency: "What are the psychological determinants responsible for the tendency in young girls towards prostitution and for their actually becoming prostitutes? What measures are advisable in order to deal with this type of delinquent girls?" He further wondered whether the "infantile instinctual fixations" evident in juvenile prostitutes might also be present "in a certain type of neurotic women [and] under what conditions a certain infantile instinctual fixation will lead not to neurosis, but to prostitution or the danger of promiscuity" (p. 440f.). In other words, what is the difference between the girl who acts out her fantasies and the one who does not?

On one occasion Blos (1957) attempted to answer these questions by referring to Friedlander's (1947) statement that "the difference

Presented in an abbreviated form at the Congress of the Baltimore District of Columbia Society for Psychoanalysis, the Cleveland Psychoanalytic Society, and the Philadelphia Association for Psychoanalysis.

Director of the Division of Child Analysis of the Institute of the Philadelphia Association for Psychoanalysis; Associate Professor of Clinical Psychiatry, University of Pennsylvania.

in the psychological make-up of the delinquent and the non-delinquent are of a quantitative rather than of a qualitative kind" (p. 230). He further commented that delinquency in female adolescents, unlike delinquency in males, is actually quite limited because the girl steadfastly clings to pregenitality. Her "repertoire" of "wayward behavior is restricted to stealing of the kleptomanic type; to vagrancy; to provocative, impudent behavior in public; and to frank sexual waywardness" (p. 232). On another occasion, Blos (1963) stated:

> The realization that female delinquency is almost synonymous with sexual delinquency must, however, not blind us to the fact that we deal with cases of heterogeneous structure in the individual cases of female delinquency. In order to penetrate the riddle of female delinquency we have to isolate the differentiating genetic factors and arrive at types characterized by a specific trauma occurring at a specific time in the girl's development. Fixation points and constitutional factors always play an intrinsic part. For this formulation and analysis a detailed history and genetic data are indispensable in order to arrive at the delineation of different types of female delinquency [p. 545].

In her study of riots in a home for delinquent girls Ruth Eissler (1949) said:

> They were constantly in danger of being overwhelmed by and becoming conscious of their homosexual desires and strivings . . . whenever their desire was very close to consciousness, or at the point of being actively satisfied, they were on the verge of panic [p. 452].
>
> [She emphasized that] the delinquency of these adolescent girls represents essentially a defense against their homosexual impulses directed toward their mothers, but, simultaneously, it serves as revenge for the imagined or real rejection by their mothers. Whether this homosexual attachment is based on guilt feelings stemming from the oedipal situation, or is a regression to the pre-oedipal phase because the relationship to their fathers was either too tenuous or too traumatic, could not be definitely evaluated. Only psychoanalysis of a series of cases of this type would furnish an answer [p. 451].

In line with these suggestions, I shall give an account of the developmental history of one such case.

CASE PRESENTATION

HISTORY

Sandy S., a 13-year-old girl, came into analysis because of promiscuity which began when she was $11\frac{1}{2}$ years old. She had had sexual relations with Jeff, a 17-year-old friend of her older brother, Joe. A short time thereafter she began to walk in the city park and along lonely roads in order to be "picked up" by strange men. When she began her analysis she had a history of frequent sexual relationships with a number of men of various ages. Her parents had been only vaguely aware of her sexual activity until they became concerned over an increasing number of phone calls which Sandy received from anonymous men. Repeated staying out late at night, mysterious whereabouts on weekends, a gradual withdrawal from the close relationship with her mother, constant secretiveness, obvious lying, a progressive decline in academic performance, diminishing peer relationships, and frequent periods of irritability or depression, all contributed to the parents' decision to obtain professional help for their daughter.

Sandy's father, aged 54, a prominent architect, paid very little attention to his daughter; in fact, he was openly disappointed because he considered her unattractive and only of "average" mental ability. He showed Sandy very little affection; yet he was so demonstrative with his wife that his expression of affection bordered on exhibitionism. Much of the time the parents behaved as though they were adolescent "lovebirds." They held hands, stared into each other's eyes, and touched without restraint in the presence of the children, relatives, friends, and frequently in public places. Parental nudity around the house was the rule rather than the exception. Sandy frequently commented that a weekend at home was like living in a nudist camp. Mr. S.'s involvement in most matters concerning his daughter's rearing was minimal to nonexistent. Most decisions for Sandy were made by her mother, who was permissive, and even indulgent. As Sandy grew older, Mrs. S. treated her more like a younger sister or confidante than a daughter.

Mrs. S. was a short, slim, attractive woman who looked 10 years younger than her 45 years. She managed her own fashion boutique. Beneath an artificial, saccharine exterior, she was devious and deceptive in most of her relationships. With tears in her eyes, she told me how long she had been deeply troubled about her sexual attraction to other women, and then detailed three homosexual love affairs which she had never before disclosed to anyone. She often invited one of the women to her home for the weekend and "discreetly" made her available for a sexual relationship with Mr. S. Sandy became quite fond of this particular woman and referred to her as Aunt Ellen. Late in her analysis Sandy related that from her 10th to 14th years, Aunt Ellen slept in the same bed with her during visits to the family home at the seashore. She remembered awakening early and lying still so that she could stare at the sleeping woman's partially exposed breasts. She was often aware of a strong desire to touch them as she "bunched" her pajamas between her thighs in order to press them against her genitals.

When Sandy was 11 years old her maternal grandmother died, and Mrs. S. sank into a deep depression. She could not work for 6 months, stayed in bed most of the day, and became childish in her demands, especially those she made on Jessica, the housekeeper. Frequently while holding Sandy in her arms, Mrs. S. cried, repeating that she missed her own mother and was afraid she herself would soon die.

During this difficult period, Ruth, a 16-year-old cousin who had lived with the grandmother prior to her death, moved into the S. house for several months. Also at this time, Sandy began to menstruate at the age of $11\frac{1}{4}$ years. The girls became quite fond of each other, traded clothing, exchanged confidences, talked about sex and pregnancy, and compared notes on breast size and menstruation. Ruth slept in the same bedroom with Sandy. When Ruth became frightened at night, she crawled into bed with Sandy and often fell asleep in her arms. On the few occasions that they kissed and fondled each other's breasts, Sandy was aware of genital excitation, accompanied by feelings of fondness for Ruth. One day she commented, "This must be the way sisters love each other." When her own breasts began to develop, Sandy played with her nipples and masturbated at the same time. She frequently crossed her arms to make her breasts protrude over her forearms and seem larger than they were. She said she loved to "hug" herself in this way because it was sexually exciting.

Shortly after Ruth left the S. home, Sandy became interested in Jeff. Early in their relationship, she performed fellatio or he sucked at her breasts, but they did not have sexual intercourse until several months had passed. She denied having any feelings of love for Jeff as she had for Ruth, and stated that sexual intercourse had not been very enjoyable for her. After 18 months, Sandy abruptly discontinued her relationship with Jeff when she discovered that Ruth had had sexual relations with him during a visit. Sandy cried and begged her forgiveness for "taking Jeff away." On two occasions she picked up a young man and then "permitted" Ruth to take him away from her. She could not tolerate the thought that Ruth might become angry with her.

Jessica, an unmarried 37-year-old housekeeper who lived in the S. home, had the major responsibility for the care of the children. During Sandy's preschool years Mrs. S. worked in her office at home from 9 until 3 o'clock in the afternoon so that she would be available if needed and to prepare the daily meals. Both mother and Jessica were reported to be excellent cooks; both placed great value on good, well-prepared food and competed with each other for the family's praise of their cooking. Sandy alternately confided to Jessica or her mother that she preferred the cooking of one over that of the other. Often she ate all of the food each had given her until, to use her mother's words, "she looked like a stuffed goose." Sandy always carried her lunch to school; in fact, she refused to eat anything that had not been prepared by either her mother or Jessica.

When Sandy was 8 years old and again when she was 10, Jessica became pregnant out-of-wedlock. The first pregnancy resulted in a full-term delivery and adoption; the second was aborted. On each occasion, when Jessica indicated that she wanted to leave the S. home to start her own family, loud arguments ensued between the two women. Each episode ended after Mrs. S. cried hysterically and took to her bed; then Jessica relented and promised to "stay on awhile longer."

In earlier years, Sandy depended more on Jessica than on her mother and had a close relationship with her until she reached puberty. Jessica referred to Sandy and Joe as "my children" and generally cared for most of their physical needs. During a rather vaguely defined illness at age 5, Sandy refused to go to school for a period of 6 months because of chronic intermittent gastrointestinal upset characterized by abdominal pain, nausea, vomiting, and weight loss. This illness was chronologically related to a period of time when Jessica wanted to leave employment in the S. home to get married. Because Mrs. S. became depressed she worked only a few hours, then spent the rest of the day in bed or in the kitchen preparing special foods for Sandy. When Jessica's fiancé became discouraged about the possibility of marriage and moved to another city, both Sandy and her mother spontaneously recovered from their illnesses.

Joe, 2 years older than Sandy, resented and ignored her. The parents considered him to be the more intelligent of the two children; he usually did well academically. He was the "apple of his father's eye" and they frequently did things together. Mrs. S. showered Joe with physical attention along with ample helpings of praise over his cleverness and intelligence. Sandy's professed hatred and open envy of her brother were rather transparent disguises for her obvious desire to please him in order to be accepted by him. Roughhousing or teasing was the only common ground upon which the two children met until Sandy became involved with Jeff. During Jeff's visits, Joe was often present or in another part of the house, and frequently the three of them would go to rock concerts or the movies. Joe no longer teased; instead, he frequently discussed his hobbies or other interests with Sandy; yet, they never talked about her involvement with Jeff. As she terminated her relationship with Jeff, her brother withdrew his interest in her. She was hurt and angry with him and defensively said that she didn't care any more about Joe than she did about her "faggy father."

FRAGMENTS FROM THE ANALYSIS

After a period of intensified streetwalking Sandy's parents insisted that she enter analysis. During the early months of treatment, she was occasionally sullen and uncommunicative, complained about the time consumed by analysis, insisted she could not talk to a male analyst because of embarrassing sexual thoughts, claimed no one would believe her because of her lies, and thought she was hopeless. For several months she accused me of having no interest in her and tried to provoke termination of treatment. When Sandy became certain that I was not going to send her away or transfer her to another analyst (she insisted upon a woman analyst), she seemed relieved.

It was a new experience for Sandy to ask a man for help and not to be turned away, as her father had done in sending her to mother or Jessica. On occasion, he admitted his disinterest in and even disgust with her so that his attitude to Sandy was well known in the family. Sandy felt equally rejected by her brother, so that she had had little opportunity to feel accepted, let alone loved, by any of the men in her life. The first gratifying relationship with a man was her courtship with Jeff. The initial pregenital gratification with him followed by sexual intercourse set a pattern for her future encounters with men. In the early weeks of analysis she explained that she was embarrassed about her sexual thoughts in connection with me and was uncertain about what I might think of her. After I replied that they were probably an expression of her desire to gain my interest and help, Sandy volunteered that she did not find her sexual encounters with men very gratifying. Further discussions reflected her growing sense of trust in the analytic relationship and her desire to continue therapy. With the therapeutic relationship established, she settled into an analysis that continued for $3\frac{1}{2}$ more years.

During the first year Sandy talked in graphic and abundant detail about her numerous encounters with men. She alluded to the excitement of anticipation, mingled with a fear of rape, which she had already experienced during her streetwalking episodes. She felt that most of the fun was in the anticipation of what would happen when she met a man. Her usual approach was first to refuse a number of men before allowing one of them to pick her up, thereby prolonging the sensation of anticipatory excitement and pleasure.

Sandy also spoke of her hatred of men, her jealousy of her brother, and her feeling of satisfaction as she imagined her father's agony over her promiscuity. "It would serve him right if he only knew what a whore I am." In actuality, Sandy's father cared little about her late hours or her safety, and Sandy's conjecture about his dismay was largely her own wish. It was only her mother's concern that brought Sandy to treatment.

The more she talked about her past heterosexual activities and present fantasies, the less she found it necessary to act out sexually. She was able to identify the mixed fear and excitement as belonging to fantasies of prostitution, rape, and pregnancy, which were similar to daydreams she had had at an earlier age before she had started to act out. Even while she dated Jeff she occasionally had the fantasy that her brother brought several friends home to "ball" her. She also recalled fearing that prowlers would come into her room at night and rape her or her cousin Ruth. In the first year of analysis, Sandy did not go out in search of men as frequently as she had done before starting her analysis; but she masturbated while daydreaming of "exciting" sexual encounters. She felt that her promiscuity was dangerous because the "white slavers" might kidnap her and turn her over to a whorehouse where the "madame" would be "strict but kind to her girls" (an idea that is very reminiscent of the pubertal prostitution fantasy referred to by H. Deutsch [1944, p. 262]).

Sandy frequently expressed anxiety about contracting a venereal disease. She had purposely avoided the use of any kind of contraceptive because she wanted a baby. She had decided that if she became pregnant, she would refuse to have an abortion. She would then live at home so that her mother and Jessica could care for her and at the same time help her take care of her own infant "daughter." In her daydreams there were no provisions for a father for the child. Hopes of pregnancy and childbirth seemed to fulfill several wishes for Sandy. She could return to the women's world of her childhood in which she could concentrate her efforts on motherhood and infant care. She could even emulate Jessica in having an "illegitimate child" (on the unconscious level, her father's child). She remembered that when she was about 8 years old she believed for a while that she was really one of Jessica's illegitimate children and that Jessica had been her father's "wife" or "lover." She recalled "bunching up" a pillow or some "covers" between her legs while she was daydreaming. The excitement she felt during streetwalking was like the feeling she had "down there."

She also recalled that during a crying spell over Jessica's pregnancy, her mother wanted Jessica to bring the new baby home rather than leave the S. household. So it seemed that Sandy's delinquent behavior was an attempt to avert homosexual entrapment: the fantasy of pregnancy associated with it ultimately led back to her preoedipal wishes.

In the first 10 to 12 months of analysis, Sandy's only reference to conscious homosexual interests was related to her revulsion about masturbation. She could not remember a time during her childhood when she had not actively indulged in genital masturbation. She recalled that when she was small, she liked to rub her bottom as she sat on her mother's lap and pressed her head into her breasts. She also remembered lying awake for many nights trying to decide whether to rub herself or not. She tried to forget her repetitious nightly thoughts. "It wasn't so bad during the day because I was busy, but at night thoughts came into my head that were all bad—but worst of all, I would sometimes rub my bottom to make the bad feelings go away. It didn't always work. Sometimes I even rubbed when I didn't have any thoughts." She did not want to "ever" tell anyone about her thoughts and feelings, just as she did not want to discuss her masturbation. Her "worried thoughts" usually involved a concern about her mother or Jessica dying or going away. The "ooky feelings in my throat, good mixed with bad," were accompanied by thoughts about "pinching or biting" her mother's "soft skin or breasts." Sometimes she had "ooky feelings" about Jessica, Aunt Ellen, or Ruthie. She thought she was the only one who had the "rubbing habit" and was afraid to tell her friends because "then what would they say?" She knew of another girl who "rubbed," but "everybody knows there is something wrong with her. They all think she is queer." She said she did not like to masturbate anymore because it got too painful "down there"; "anyhow, it makes me think my lesbian thoughts." She added, "I do not see what anyone gets out of it. I would rather ball with men."

With this comment and under the pressure of great concern about homosexuality, Sandy contradicted an earlier statement denying that sexual intercourse was pleasurable for her. In an attempt to divest herself of homosexual masturbation fantasies that

William Thomas Moore

were present in one form or another during most of her childhood, Sandy tried to deceive herself by giving false testimony that touted a preference for heterosexuality. That she would be labeled a "lesbian" by her peers was a matter of grave concern to her. After a lifetime of autoerotic indulgence her attempt to relinquish genital masturbation obviously was aimed at avoiding the accompanying fantasies.

At the end of her second year of analysis, she began to ask questions about my secretary. Sandy recounted how she often hurried to her late afternoon appointment in order to catch a glimpse of her before she left work for the day. If she missed seeing her, Sandy was in a bad mood and frequently would not talk during her analytic session. She made no attempt to explain her behavior, even though she was fully conscious of the cause of her ill disposition. Once her homosexual thoughts and feelings were out in the open she asked endless questions about the secretary, such as, "Where does she live? How old is she? Why does she leave early some days? Is she a good cook? Does she have a daughter?" She spoke openly about her "crush" feelings and physical attraction to the secretary. This expression of interest was the starting point of her revelation about her lifelong homosexual attachments and thoughts.

Sandy spoke of her conscious interest in breasts that was directly related to her love of Ruth, Aunt Ellen, Jessica, and her mother. She remembered that as a child more than once she had held and comforted her mother when the latter was depressed or cried. Sandy often helped her mother dress and frequently peeped in on her as mother slept so that Sandy could watch mother's naked breasts rise and fall with her breathing.

Heterosexual fantasies were in the forefront during the first year of analysis, but were hardly mentioned during the second year. Sandy's revelations dealt almost exclusively with her thoughts about women. As she began to understand her relationships to them, her fears about homosexuality diminished. As she learned more about her true feelings toward her father, and was able to separate fact from defense and fantasy, her attitude toward him took a turn for the better. He began to show more interest in her as she improved in her academic work and personal appearance. He was especially pleased when she was accepted to an Ivy League college. Even though her resentment toward him lost much of its former bitterness, Sandy accepted the idea that she might never be able to have a very close relationship with her father; as a result, her expectations of men assumed more realistic proportions. She was able to realize a more gratifying relationship with her brother. She also established several selective friendships with young men who were college classmates. When analysis was terminated she was aware of her lingering attraction to women, but homosexual thoughts and interests seemed to fade into the background as she developed more intense object relationships with two young men, one of whom she was to marry a few years later.

DISCUSSION

Before a girl can achieve adult genitality, she must complete repression and sublimation of her infantile pregenital sexuality. The environmental circumstances of Sandy's life exposed her to continuous stimulation during the entire course of her development. Early preoedipal fixations contributed to her difficulty in repressing her pregenital sexual wishes and prevented adequate sublimation of pregenital aims. Continuous temptation and seduction encouraged her to act upon her pregenital impulses with preoedipal objects so that all phases of Sandy's development were inevitably influenced by the preoedipal model. At the end of "latency" the strong pull of regressive forces that usually are the hallmark of the onset of puberty proved to be overpowering.

Sandy's father, unable to hide his dislike for his daughter, was rarely involved with her and usually rejected her advances. This state of affairs made it quite difficult, if not impossible, for Sandy to make the important developmental transition in love object from mother to father. By the time she approached oedipal development, it simply had not been part of her life experience to perceive herself as being acceptable to her father. Therefore, of necessity, women remained the only source of gratification for her—a definite deterrent to negotiating the oedipal developmental tasks and a powerful incentive to permanent preoedipal fixation. The specific nature of this fixation was determined by the sustained pregenital overstimulation Sandy received from her mother and from Jessica, as well as that which she constantly perceived in the relationship of the two women. It can therefore be said that Sandy never underwent a satisfactory oedipal development. Nor can it be said that she experienced a latency period in her libidinal development. The pervasive polymorphous-perverse atmosphere in her home persisted, as did the sexual overexcitation, which Sandy attempted to discharge by her continual masturbation.

Sandy's history is replete with evidence of genital masturbation persisting uninterruptedly throughout latency and adolescence. In my clinical experience, however, such activity is not greatly reduced or nonexistent in most other girls during this period. In contrast to Sandy, most girls appear to be less open about the physical act of masturbation than they are about the accompanying fantasies. Sandy, by her own account, had always been conscious of both. Nevertheless, she experienced the same secrecy and shame about genital masturbation as most girls. She too tried to disguise her practices until she began her relationship with Ruth. At that time Sandy seemed to have alternated between masturbation and acting out with a homosexual partner.

One of the most important functions of what I have called the "masturbation fantasy complex" (1974) during adolescence is to provide the adolescent with a developmental laboratory in fantasy for testing transitions to other objects. This method of trial-and-error imaginary relationships enables the emerging young adult eventually to establish heterosexual relationships, thereby contributing to the formation of sexual identity, ego ideals, and character traits. This interaction of genital masturbation and fantasies involving a series of objects provides a safe transition from preoedipal and oedipal to heterosexual object love. By living out pregenital fantasies with her cousin and continuing primary object priority, it seems to me that Sandy had closed off this helpful route for object transition.

As was true in Sandy's earlier development, during the early school years she had no positive experiences with men. Sandy's relationship with her brother had been adversely affected by her father's attitude, so that by the time she had reached prepuberty, all relationships with men were approached with uncertainty, fear of rejection, and bitterness. Sandy thought of men as distant and enigmatic because they had never shown her any interest. At the onset of puberty, early rapid and complete physical development gave this child of 11 the quite attractive body of a young woman. Much to her surprise and confusion, within a short period of time, she found herself for the first time in her life the object of eager attention from men. She was quick to respond in kind. She reveled in the closeness and warmth of the embrace; and she was quite flattered by the attentions of grown men, but especially of those between the ages of 20 to 40. Psychologically, she was unprepared for and incapable of enjoying her numerous heterosexual encounters. In her own words, sexual relations were not pleasurable except for the pregenital aspects of foreplay. What seemed most gratifying to Sandy was the elation she felt while streetwalking and the pleasure she derived from the idea that rejection was her prerogative. In other words, her own fantasies and their partial acting out provided the most satisfaction.

Never having made the step from primary to oedipal object and being exposed to homosexual temptations and seductions, Sandy found continued gratification in her relations with Aunt Ellen and Ruth. It was only when Ruth left the home and Sandy was confronted with the loss of the homosexually loved object that she took drastic measures to cope with her mounting tensions. For release she turned to an acting out of sexual fantasies, which were, of course, conditioned by her life experiences: her father's nudity and his promiscuous sexual behavior with other women, as well as the unusual arrangements his wife made for him to sleep with other women. Coming from a family with a way of life characterized by sexual acting out, Sandy was bound to react according to the family character. She seemed destined to delinquent behavior, homosexual as well as heterosexual.

Feeling worthless and rejected by both men and women, Sandy began to walk the streets where she found some fulfillment of her primitive fantasies. But what appeared to be heterosexual interests were constantly threatened by her homosexual wishes. She gave up her relationship with Jeff after Ruth had had intercourse with him and then sought other men in order to hand them over to Ruth, as mother had made Aunt Ellen available to her father.

In summary, Sandy's delinquent sexual activity seemed to be an expression of a pathological development which in early adolescence resulted in the acting out of masturbation fantasies that were expressions of her instinctual drives, ego defenses, and superego-sponsored conflicts: (1) Her behavior provided her with an outlet for the unrestrained expression of her pregenitality, although it was transferred to men. (2) Her sexual delinquency with men acted as a defense against an overwhelming desire for homosexual activity that was repeatedly brought to consciousness by open seduction and stimulation. (3) Her behavior represented an attempt to master the rejection by her father; by identification with the aggressor, she acted out the role of the rejector. (4) As a "streetwalker" she acted out a fantasy of revenge on her father by behaving promiscuously as she thought he had done. (5) Through her sexual delinquency she felt desirable to men and at the same time was able to reassure herself that men were more desirable to her than women. (6) By identifying with mother and Jessica, Sandy acted out two separate impressions she had about each woman. Both had been mother to her; however, Sandy was also aware of their sexual acting out. She told me that both had behaved like "whores." Sandy's split image of mother and Jessica is reminiscent of the ego split which H. Deutsch (1933) described in the fantasies of adolescent girls: "The split in the love life of men has its parallel in the love life of women . . . the woman's own ego takes the place of the man's object. The woman is herself 'mother' or 'prostitute' " (p. 191). (7) The culmination of her "streetwalking fantasy" was to become pregnant. Then she would be able to return to her mother and Jessica and, in identification with her daughter, relive her own infancy and preoedipal childhood. In this way, her fantasy completed the full circle: she would be able to return to a preoedipal existence with her mother.

The case of Sandy thus bears out some of the earlier findings in the literature. Blos (1957) suggested that "Theoretical considerations tend to support the thesis that female delinquency is often precipitated by the strong regressive pull to the preoedipal mother and the panic which the surrender implies" (p. 237). The history of Sandy also lends support to Ruth Eissler's contention (quoted at the beginning of the paper) that delinquency in girls is essentially a defense against homosexual impulses. Moreover, Sandy's relationship to her father was tenuous and, in addition, she was exposed to many homosexual temptations. In Sandy's case, the homosexual attachment was based on these factors rather than on guilt stemming from the oedipal situation. Some of my other clinical experiences further support the finding that the existence of strong pregenital fixations and the dread of homosexual regression are the most important factors leading to promiscuity and sexual acting out in girls.

THE MASTURBATION-FANTASY COMPLEX IN ADOLESCENCE

As with most acting out, Sandy's delinquent behavior gave little satisfaction or comfort and resolved nothing. It only added to her ultimate frustration and provided additional psychological trauma. Sandy's self-esteem diminished further as she erected barriers that prevented her from ever making the important transition from primary love object to oedipal love object.

Usually, during early adolescence, the decathexis of primary and oedipal object representatives leaves the adolescent with a real object hunger that contributes to changing, superficial, and intense, but evanescent relationships so common in this age group. Transitory crushes are usually maintained in an active fantasy life and are developmentally functional for the following reasons: (1) They prevent object libido from being totally drained by concentration on the self. (2) They allow for a period of trial and error, which is helpful in establishing new ego techniques for developing object relationships, while at the same time the adolescent can become accustomed to the idea of heterosexual relationships on a genital basis. (3) The transient nature is predetermined by the rapid buildup of old conflicts around new objects (transference).

Because these conflicts are borrowed from incestuous objects, the process of decathexis of the original objects is repeated in each new relationship. By repeating the gain and loss of an object in fantasy,

the adolescent gradually achieves mastery over the loss of oedipal
and preoedipal objects. By giving up each new object and reliving
intense emotions, such as separation anxiety, object loss, and
depression, she is able gradually to decathect her original love
objects. The intense and stormy adolescent crushes which vacillate
between the extremes of self-sacrificing loves and violent hatreds
vividly portray and reenact the saga of the rediscovery of love for,
the separation from, and mourning over the loss of the original
objects. By repeating this process in fantasy many times before
putting it into action, the adolescent avoids the added trauma of an
actual sexual encounter with each new oedipal object. The
relationship to each new object, whether carried out in fantasy or
reality, retains a relatively high titer of transferred conflict over
incest with strong remnants of pregenital ambivalence. As in the
case of Sandy, if the adolescent engages in sexual relationships
before she has sufficiently decathected old incestuous objects, she
will be incapable of freeing herself from her incestuous bondage.
This can lead to any number of pathological solutions that result in
a highly disturbed young adult.

During the period of streetwalking, Sandy seemed to carry into
action a kaleidoscope of fantasies that ordinarily would have
remained a part of the masturbation-fantasy complex, which
includes fantasies of romantic love, revenge, prostitution, pregnancy, heterosexuality, and homosexuality. At first, but only
briefly, in early puberty, she indulged in regressive homosexuality,
then more extensively in defensive heterosexuality. In a sense, she
acted out conscious heterosexual masturbation fantasies in order to
reinforce denial and repression of more dreaded homosexual wishes
that were in danger of becoming acted out. Sandy's pathological
fixation had driven her to an extreme defensive position that was
fraught with additional developmental dangers and in fact, if
carried to conclusion, would have necessitated her return to
permanent attachment to her preoedipal love objects, Jessica and
her mother. By acting out a portion of her masturbation-fantasy
complex Sandy stood a chance of losing developmental benefits that
ordinarily accrue as a result of heterosexual masturbation fantasies
and the pathological behavior itself had a good chance of becoming
a fixed pattern in her permanent character structure.

A Clinical Postscript

During her analysis Sandy was able to work on her regressive wishes and the unsuccessful defenses opposed to them. By the time she had stopped analysis, the transition from primary homosexual object to heterosexuality was well under way. She was able to understand the significance of pregenital fixations and to incorporate them into a heterosexual orientation (sex change in object and partial change in aim). Through analysis Sandy experienced a measure of developmental progress that enabled her to achieve some degree of adaptation and maturity. She was able to analyze pregenital conflicts and to free herself from the hopeless attachment she had to her mother. Insight into her resentment toward her father and her desire for his acceptance paved the way for her to work through her oedipal conflict during her third year of analysis.

In a recent follow-up, 4 years after the termination of analysis, some old scars and remnants of fixation were in evidence. Sandy, 21, is married, has moved to another city, and is studying for her master's degree. She recognizes that at times she has some unrealistic concerns about her mother's health and that occasionally some aspects of her relationship with her husband are reminiscent of infantile desires. She looks up to and admires him for his stability and professional capability. Even though she feels loved and valued by him, she is at times unsure of his love and on these occasions becomes unreasonably demanding of his time and attention.

She does not want children right away because at times she feels she does not want to share her husband with anyone, a thought that causes her some misgivings about her ability to be a good mother. She is apprehensive that she will make the same mistakes her mother had made. She concluded the interview by expressing her intention to return some time in the future for more analysis in order to work through some of her lingering problems.

Sandy's fate illustrates and supports an idea proposed by Helene Deutsch in 1944: "A prepubertal attempt at liberation from the mother that has failed or was too weak can inhibit future psychological growth and leave a definitely infantile imprint on the woman's entire personality" (p. 21).

BIBLIOGRAPHY

AICHHORN, A. (1949), Some Remarks on the Psychic Structure and Social Care of a Certain Type of Female Juvenile Delinquents. *This Annual*, 3/4:439–448.
BLOS, P. (1957), Preoedipal Factors in the Etiology of Female Delinquency. *This Annual*, 12:229–249.
——— (1962), *On Adolescence*. New York: Free Press.
——— (1963), Symposium on Female Delinquency: Discussion. *J. Amer. Acad. Child Psychiat.*, 2:540–560.
DEUTSCH, H. (1933), Motherhood and Sexuality. In: *Neurosis and Character Types*. New York: International Universities Press, 1965, pp. 190–202.
——— (1944), *The Psychology of Women*, Vol. 1. New York: Grune & Stratton.
EISSLER, R. S. (1949), Riots: Observations in a Home for Delinquent Girls. *This Annual*, 3/4:449–460.
FREUD, S. (1931), Female Sexuality. *Standard Edition*, 21:223–243. London: Hogarth Press, 1961.
FRIEDLANDER, K. (1947), *The Psychoanalytical Approach to Juvenile Delinquency*. New York: International Universities Press.
MOORE, W. T. (1974), A Consideration of Some Economic Functions of Genital Masturbation During Adolescent Development. In: *Masturbation: From Infancy to Senescence*, ed. I. Marcus & J. Francis. New York: International Universities Press (in press).

Issues in the Analysis
of a Preschool Girl

KERRY KELLY NOVICK

THIS PAPER IS AN ACCOUNT OF THE FIRST YEAR OF TREATMENT OF A
4-year-old girl, who presented a complicated mixture of age-adequate functioning and quite severe symptoms which interfered with
her progress. The parents' main complaint focused on Rosa's refusal
to go to nursery school and her anxious clinging and tantrums
whenever the mildest separation from mother was threatened. Rosa
occasionally still wet in the daytime and had never been dry at
night. At referral, she was wetting two or three times every night,
but either denied this vehemently, or admitted it in an offhand way,
which reflected her mother's overtly casual attitude to the problem.
Rosa's chronic constipation was also played down by the parents at
this stage, but it emerged later that this had been a severe problem
since infancy; changes in this symptom proved to be a good
indicator of the progress of treatment during the first year. Mr. and
Mrs. T. reported Rosa's extreme sibling rivalry, which had taken
the form of dangerous physical attacks on Laura, born when Rosa
was 23 months old, and was still a source of turmoil in the family.

This paper is part of a study, entitled "Assessment of Pathology in Childhood,"
which is financed by the National Institute of Mental Health, Bethesda, Maryland
(NIMH Grant MH 05683). The study is conducted at the Hampstead Child-
Therapy Clinic, London, where the author is a member of the Staff. I would like to
acknowledge the work of the Well-Baby Clinic and the Toddler Group of the
Hampstead Clinic, and of Dr. A. Couch in relation to this case and to thank the T.
family for permission to use material from Rosa's treatment. This paper was first
presented at a Wednesday meeting of the Hampstead Clinic on February 23, 1972.

Although they were wearied by Rosa's behavior, they did not see this as quite so serious a problem as we did.

Rosa has been known to us since the age of 10 months, when the T. family first came to the Well-Baby Clinic. Rosa attended the Toddler Group from 1 year, 2 months, until she was 2½. After another year or so, the frequency of Mrs. T.'s attendance at the Baby Clinic decreased and we did not see the family for about six months. When Rosa was just over 4 years old, Mr. T. asked for advice about her sudden refusal to go to her nursery play group, and a referral for diagnostic assessment was made. Intensive treatment for Rosa was recommended at the diagnostic conference, with the reservation that Mr. and Mrs. T. might find it hard to support the child's treatment consistently, without help for themselves. Rosa has now been in treatment for a year; during the first term, the parents were seen together by a colleague; subsequently he saw each parent individually on alternate weeks, while I also had weekly interviews with the mother.

In presenting material from the first year of Rosa's analysis, I shall concentrate on the interaction between her ability to tolerate separation from her mother and the growing differentiation and complexity of her ego function of defense vis-à-vis instinctual impulses. Whenever possible I shall supplement the analytic material with the historical information that we have.

TREATMENT MATERIAL

Rosa was 4 years, 5 months old when she began treatment. She was a tall, well-built, active child, with a willful angry expression on her mobile face, which changed suddenly into a radiant charming smile at times when she was pleased or surprised. The tone of Rosa's emotionality is difficult to convey, but it has struck every observer since her infancy—she seems to carry an aura of intensity and activity, even at moments of distractible, disorganized behavior. The vivid quality of her involvement with other people is a very marked characteristic—one that is also important in assessing the kind and degree of her disturbance.

Rosa spent much of her first week in treatment in a state of sexualized excitement. Her instinctual impulses seemed very readily accessible; while she occasionally avoided painful or conflictual topics, it was difficult to discern the operation of defenses. She proudly presented me with primitive messy paintings and drawings which showed little evidence of sublimated impulses, but seemed almost direct expressions of pleasure in anal messing. At the same time, Rosa displayed considerable maturity in other areas of ego functioning, using her large vocabulary and wide general knowledge appropriately, perceiving details of my dress or demeanor and asking reality-oriented questions about them, telling me about her family in an organized way, and similarly asking about mine and Dr. Couch's. Sexual material from different libidinal levels appeared together; for example, Rosa both threatened and worried that a "snake like a penis would go in and eat up all my female eggs"; the same day she revealed her enjoyment in picking her nose and picking feces from her anus, then went on to talk about how nice it felt to "put fingers in my wee-wee." In the fifth week, Rosa spilled some water on the table and it then began slowly to spread along the surface; as it neared the edge, Rosa became almost frantic with sexual excitement and shrieked with tension, which appeared to be related to conflict between fear and pleasure at the idea of the water overflowing. She readily agreed that the water reminded her of urine.

Such incidents were a measure of how little her impulses were mediated by the ego in an age-appropriate way. On the other hand, there was evidence that Rosa was capable of exerting ego controls, even in areas of conflict, such as going to the toilet. In the third term of treatment, Mrs. T. told me that constipation had been a problem since Rosa's infancy: at 4 months Mrs. T. became so concerned about her baby daughter's evident discomfort and inability to defecate that she took her to the casualty department of the hospital where she had been born. Suppositories were prescribed, and Mrs. T. administered these intermittently throughout Rosa's first year. At 10 months, there was another crisis: Rosa cried with pain while she tried to defecate, and again the hospital recommended suppositories. When Mrs. T. mentioned this history in the Baby Clinic, Dr. Stross immediately advised against continuing suppositories with Rosa, who was by then 18 months old, and Mrs. T. began giving other forms of medication, which would provide less interference with Rosa's libidinal development. At referral, the parents only mentioned chronic constipation as a problem, but it soon became clear that Rosa effectively paralyzed the family and drew everyone's exclusive attention to herself by long sessions of sitting on the toilet, screaming with distress but refusing the assistance or management of an adult.

In the first few weeks of treatment, Rosa was very anxious about going to the toilet in the Clinic and, whenever she thought she might need to go, insisted on going downstairs to be taken by her mother. By the fourth week, more specific anxieties were coming into the transference; when Rosa passed wind, she became worried that this was dangerous to me. I could then take up how afraid she was of feeling more powerful than I and this led on to her fear that I would retaliate with fury if she soiled her pants and thereby "made everything be a mess." Again she had to run to check with her mother that this was all right and that she had not soiled her pants. Analytic work on these incidents allowed us to approach the pleasurable side of her anal preoccupations; by the following week, Rosa felt able to go quietly to the toilet on her own, insisting only that I stand in the hallway to ensure that she did not get lost on her way back to the room. Further progress in her ability to function independently in this area continued, so that after another two weeks Rosa simply excused herself from the session when she needed to go to the toilet.

At home, however, the same dramatic scenes continued to be played out every time, so that the analytic work on the association between anger, hostility, and separation and Rosa's sudden need to defecate seemed to have no effect outside the treatment. Evidently, Rosa actually had the ego capacities to control her functioning in this area, but used them only in the Clinic. The issue here is to understand what enabled her to behave more maturely in one setting than in the other, and to achieve in a few weeks the control over her bowel function that had never been reached at home. Similarly, although Rosa could both understand and use secondary processes in speech and was quite capable of constructing accurate, complicated sentences, in this area too there were often break-throughs of the primary process; for example, looking at a cartoon, she exclaimed, "Mickey Mouse, Pickey Mouse, Pickey Nose, Pickey kaka."

Thus, early in Rosa's treatment, I found myself wondering why this competent little girl who had so many well-developed ego functions appeared to have so few defenses consistently available. One aspect of her inability to control her impulses was directly linked with her upbringing and the parental standards. At the end of the first session I was struck by Rosa's apparent incomprehension of the idea of a limited time period. It was not so much that Rosa wanted to carry on playing, although this was a factor; rather, it seemed that nobody had ever insisted on a fixed time regardless of her wishes. In this Rosa did not give the impression of a spoiled child who, in effect, wins too many battles, but rather of a child who has not had demands made on her to conform to adult wishes.

Similarly, Rosa simply did not really understand my demand that she share the work of tidying up the considerable mess at the end of each session. This incomprehension rapidly changed to annoyance and frustration, however, when I insisted that Rosa participate, and she began to rage at me in just the same way that she did at her mother when threatened with separation. Her behavior became disorganized; she threw water and plasticine around the room in a wild, unfocused tantrum; she made indiscriminate attacks on me and the objects in the room—in short, Rosa changed suddenly from a child with whom it was possible to communicate into one who appeared to be severely regressed and disturbed, whose ego became inaccessible and submerged by overwhelming impulses.

Rosa's behavior illustrates Anna Freud's description of the effects of regressive moves which begin from the side of the ego and superego: "Ego and superego, if regressed, have less controlling power and this becomes manifest in a weakening of 'censorship,' i.e., in the dividing line between id and ego and the general efficiency of the defenses of the ego. The results are impulsive behavior, break-through of affect and aggressive tendencies, frequent breaches of id control, and irruptions of irrational elements into the child's consciousness and formerly rational behavior" (1965, p. 128). Anna Freud attributes such changes in the child's character to stress on the ego and superego from traumatic shocks or separations, among other happenings.

One clue to understanding Rosa's sudden regressions came from the circumstances in which they arose: she reacted with equal violence when demands were made on her and when separation from her mother for any length of time was threatened. This suggests that Rosa experienced these situations as similar, that both separation from an important object and demands for independent functioning made by an object had the impact on her ego of a trauma, with the resulting deterioration in her functioning. This hypothesis was provisionally confirmed by Rosa's reaction to my handling of her regressive outbursts. The first time it happened, in the fifth week of treatment, Rosa's tantrum was very startling, and it was important, both literally and figuratively, to stop her flinging herself and all the toys about the room, to get back in touch with her, and to impose a measure of control and structure on the situation. I grasped her firmly by the shoulders and made her sit down next to me on the couch; we sat together in silence until her breathing became calmer and then I quietly explained to her that I would not let her hurt herself, the toys, or me, because it obviously frightened her so much and therefore kept us from working together and understanding what was going on. Rosa reacted that day with rather sleepy relief, but the following day she produced, for the first time, an age-adequate drawing, a picture of me surrounded with X's for kisses, which she worked on carefully, insisting that I periodically count the kisses. She vacillated about whether to leave the picture with me or to take it home, but decided in the end to keep me with her by keeping the drawing. In the weeks which followed, I tried to grade my demands on Rosa. At first I asked her to stay in the room while I tidied up; then we progressed to her doing the last bit; eventually, we shared the work equally, while I stressed verbally the "togetherness" aspect of this.

This way of handling Rosa's panicky regressions apparently provided her with an alternative way of experiencing demands. They no longer implied that she had to be separate and apart from the object, but rather provided a way of staying with the object, but on a higher level. This understanding, however, still leaves us with the problem of why Rosa reacted so catastrophically to the threat of separation; why was her ego so vulnerable? What factors in her history and development had interfered with the formation of adequate defenses against the anxiety aroused by separation? On the other hand, what factors had enabled Rosa to develop as well as she did, functioning most of the time on an appropriate level, and presenting the impression of an organized, happy personality?

Rosa was not a wanted baby. During the first few months following Rosa's birth, Mrs. T. suffered intense anxiety lest Rosa be damaged or die accidentally, and often checked five or six times in the night that the baby was still breathing. The effect of Mrs. T.'s extreme fears and the influence of the many books on child care which she read combined to make her feel that Rosa must be the absolute center of her life if she was to be a good mother; accordingly, she *never* left Rosa alone: when it was time for the baby to sleep, the lights were put out and the whole family went to bed, rather than risk the psychic damage she feared would result from putting the baby to sleep in another room. Mrs. T. did not until recently express much conscious resentment of the effect such a regime must have had on her life.

If we look at this mother in her own right, it is clear that her attitude indicates the presence of disturbed elements in her relation to her baby; but the picture seems completely different if we try to imagine what Rosa's experience of her first year must have been. From the child's point of view the situation may have approached the ideal: Rosa was fed on demand, rarely made to wait, almost never left to cry alone or unattended—in short, her world was actually organized around her needs and demands to an unusual degree, which must have provided for an exceptionally high level of primary narcissism. The effect of this on Rosa comes across vividly in one of the early comments when Rosa began attending the Toddler Group at 14 months. An observer wrote: "Rosa continues to behave as if the whole world were hers to command and, because she is so friendly and does everything with such a happy smile, she usually achieves her end."

But reality soon intervened, as Mrs. T. became pregnant with her second child when Rosa was 16 months old. Rosa reacted to her mother's relative withdrawal of attention with moodiness and heightened sensitivity to incidents of physical hurt. For instance, in the Well-Baby Clinic, when Mrs. T. told the staff about a recent injection she had had, Rosa began to cry and then fell down, hurting her head on her mother's chair. Rosa "did not regain her usual cheerful competence" after this incident. It seems that Rosa became newly vulnerable at this time; her omnipotence had received a blow and, without her mother's total attention, Rosa could not cope with her impulses. She seemed both excessively identified with her mother and in danger of dealing with aggression by means of an instinctual mechanism, turning it against herself, rather than by developing defense mechanisms in the ego.

After Laura's birth, when Rosa was 1 year, 11 months old, Rosa reacted even more violently—she seemed a different child. There was a brief phase of head banging whenever she was "very frustrated." She regressed to demanding the bottle, and toilet training collapsed. Rosa became clinging and passionately demanding, making violent scenes and tantrums when Mrs. T. did not accede to her wishes. Rosa assaulted the baby frequently, hitting and scratching her, and she became more distractible. Mr. and Mrs. T. were at a loss to deal with this change in their child; they usually gave in to Rosa, often sacrificing Laura's needs to this end. For instance, the baby was put on the bottle at 5 weeks partly because of Rosa's furious reaction to her being breast-fed. Thus, for Rosa at the age of 2, the birth of Laura and the subsequent demand to share her mother with the new baby acted as a trauma, and her parents' handling of her reactions, rather than fostering ego controls to help her master the stress of the situation, contributed to her feeling that her ego was constantly in danger of being overwhelmed with her aggressive impulses. Over the next 2 years, Rosa gradually recovered her earlier high level of functioning, but areas of severe vulnerability remained, as in her symptoms of wetting, constipation, clinging, and school refusal, and in the swiftness with which her self-confidence fluctuated and her moods changed.

These data help to illuminate the factors that were operative in Rosa's disturbance. They also highlight the developmental steps she needed to take before she could begin to deal effectively with her impulses.

Earlier, I described the progress Rosa made in the early weeks of treatment toward better control of defecation. In the ninth week, when Mrs. T. knew that Rosa managed to go to the toilet in the Clinic and Rosa had also happily returned to the nursery, she sent Mr. T. to see me at Rosa's session time to say that she did not want to continue with Rosa's treatment. I spent an hour on the phone with Mrs. T. in the evening and we sorted out some of her feelings of being made guilty by her mother and friends who disapproved of Rosa's treatment, and even more guilty by her husband and me that Rosa should need treatment. But the clearest emotion which came through from this mother who was trying so hard to do whatever was the "right thing" for her child was her own sense of feeling bereft, that is, her own anxious reaction to Rosa's moves toward independence and separation as well as the sense Mrs. T. had that she was getting nothing to fulfill her own needs. At this point we dealt with the crisis by offering the family more involvement with treatment: Dr. Couch was to go on seeing Mr. T., and I offered Mrs. T. a weekly interview so that she could keep in closer touch with Rosa's treatment. Another measure designed to take pressure off Mrs. T., who was by now pregnant with a third child, was to move Rosa's treatment from the Clinic to my private consulting room, which is much nearer to the family home. We did not take up directly at this time Mrs. T.'s own separation problem, although it seemed clear to us by then that this must be a factor in Rosa's difficulties.

Rosa returned to treatment; for the remaining two weeks of term, the material concerned her anxiety over controlling her anger, particularly with her mother or me in the transference. She mistreated and scolded her doll impatiently; the doll became furious and spilled water, occasionally threatened to throw water at me, and generally wanted to make a vengeful mess. Rosa attributed panicky fear of retaliation to her doll and fiercely resisted my attempts to link this to her own feelings. When I broached the possibility that controlling anger was related to difficulties in controlling urination and defecation, Rosa simply switched off—she spent a great deal of time singing loudly to herself during this phase of treatment. Her other reactions were to deny flatly any connection—"I have no ideas about kaka! It doesn't matter, it doesn't matter, it doesn't matter!"—or to change the subject with an effort to charm my attention away from the distressing material. Gradually, however, she herself realized that she needed to leave the session and go to the toilet every time we mentioned anger. We worked on her fear of destroying and flooding her objects with anal aggression, and by the end of the term she was rarely constipated at home or at the Clinic, had one, or sometimes two, dry nights a week, and showed no difficulty over going to nursery school.

I mentioned earlier that Rosa had brought a messy, primitive painting to her first session. Throughout the first term she either brought with her or produced in the session page after page of wet, sticky, unintelligible pictures, which she made by using her saliva to attach to the paper a combination of paint, crayons, smeared plasticine, and bits of paper. Rosa expected and anxiously demanded my enthusiastic praise for these productions. While it appeared that the primary determinant of her need for my approval of the pictures lay in their derivation at no great distance from anal productions, there was another transference element, in that her parents lavished indiscriminate praise on her work in an attempt not to stifle her creativity.

At the beginning of the second term, however, the material changed slightly. Increasingly, it related to Mrs. T.'s pregnancy and Rosa's reactions to it, so that it became possible to understand the complicated background of Rosa's refusal to draw or paint as well as I knew she could. It was linked to Rosa's reaction of lowered self-esteem, which had at least three roots. The first was a direct reexperience of feelings relating to Laura's birth. Rosa felt her position with her mother threatened anew and feared that she was not good enough to hold her mother's love. This concern also appeared in the transference in a heightened anger and curiosity about my other patients and the thought that I had been seeing other children during the holiday. Secondly, Rosa's need for an adult's approval of her anal productions related to her comparing herself with her pregnant mother on the anal level. She again became severely constipated and refused to eat meat, identifying instead with her mother's vegetarian food habits. This too seemed linked to the events of Laura's birth when Rosa was nearly 2, because Mrs. T. had then tried forcibly to train Rosa quickly before the arrival of the new baby. The third aspect of Rosa's use of the drawings and paintings was linked to her moves toward the oedipal level, just at the time when her mother appeared to Rosa to be an unbeatable rival—she was really pregnant. This became apparent in a session when Rosa made one of her first age-adequate drawings. One day she drew a little girl, but could not finish, and said I should do it, because I could do everything better, and ended by scribbling all over it. Anything that augured well had to be destroyed during this phase.

Anna Freud (1936) discussed the differences between ego restriction and inhibition as follows: "In ego restriction, . . . disagreeable external impressions in the present are warded off, because they might result in the revival of similar impressions from the past. . . . the difference between inhibition and ego restriction is that in the former the ego is defending itself against its own inner processes and in the latter against external stimuli" (p. 101). It seemed that Rosa was restricting her ability to draw because it inevitably fell short of the adult's capabilities. Thus her narcissism was wounded again as it had been wounded during the anal phase, when her anal productions were not valued highly, but her mother produced a baby. At the same time, however, there were signs of an inhibition in that Rosa could not let herself try to compete with her mother or me in producing a person or a picture of a person for fear that she might win. This fear too was linked to her earlier confusion, in relation to both inner and outer world, about her own omnipotence.

When I took up these two reasons for not feeling good, Rosa's constipation again remitted and she simultaneously finished drawings more frequently without destroying them or scribbling all over them. The oedipal cast of the material shifted and appeared in an almost daily routine that had a teasing, competitive quality. Rosa began a drawing and asked whether I could guess what it was. Sometimes she seemed pleased when I did guess, and at other times she was annoyed and instantly changed her picture to something else. She refused to be mollified by my attempts to delay guessing until she had finished, but made an issue of my divining her intentions when there might be no more than a little mark on the paper. At the same time, she became much more attentive to my style of talking and working and often exclaimed, "Why do you always want *me* to talk about things?" or "Why do you always ask what *I* think?" I interpreted this material in terms of her feelings about whether I was omnipotent and omniscient, and the wish she displayed to be the one who was both and could control my knowledge about her. Sometimes I simply told her that I could not know her thoughts unless she showed them to me or told me about them. When I was able to guess what she was planning to draw, even when she was pleased, Rosa said, "How did you know?" Again I dealt with this by first interpreting her wish that I should know automatically, because then she felt that I was close to her, and secondly by explaining how I actually had figured out what she was doing.

The links between this material, separation, and her mother's pregnancy showed more clearly in Rosa's wistful remark one day, "I'm lonely because I've no babies in my tummy." This was her response to my suggestion that she might be worried about feeling lonely for me during the imminent summer holiday. Rosa felt that she would not be lonely if she, *like* her mother, were pregnant; i.e., she wished to identify with the object she felt in danger of losing. She began to ask questions about whether I had children and again displayed curiosity about my other patients. At that time, I felt that Rosa perceived her mother's use of the children in order not to feel lonely; she had the idea that adults are not sad and lonely if they have babies, and therefore she also wanted to be my baby for the holidays.

Returning from the summer holiday, Rosa marched into the room and announced, "I'm not four anymore, you know." She proceeded to mystify me for the next two weeks with her integrated, competent, grown-up manner, and her apparently unconflicted happy anticipation of starting "big" school very soon. In her sessions Rosa played well and happily with dolls and cars, painted pictures of her summer holidays, talked about events of the summer, and told me all about the preparations for the new baby, due in several weeks. Mrs. T. informed me, however, that at home Rosa was as bad as she had ever been—clinging, demanding, and horrid to Laura and her parents; badly constipated and wetting more than ever. On Monday of the third week, Rosa bounced in and told me excitedly all about her first day at school, including even her having had fish fingers for lunch. She spent the next few days telling me jokes she said she had heard at school, asking me if I knew any magic tricks, and wanting to wrap secret "surprise" presents for me. At the end of the week I learned from Mrs. T. that Rosa had not yet started school, and we were both astonished that she had managed to fool me so completely.

The clue to understanding Rosa's behavior in these weeks lay in the connection glimpsed before the holiday between guessing and omniscience on the one hand, and separation and loneliness on the other. Rosa's successful fooling of me represented in part a counterphobic reaction to the separation of the holiday break and the separation from her mother entailed in starting regular school; if she could confirm her grown-up separateness by knowing something I did not know, she could be the powerful one in control. This attitude carried her through the actual beginning of school and when, to her relief, neither mother nor I disappeared even though she had really started school, Rosa could begin to complain in an ordinary way about school meals, for instance, and she could begin to face in treatment some of the feelings she had had about the summer break and some of the turmoil around the impending arrival of the new sibling. Rosa's symptoms abated again; she easily went to the toilet at school and at my house, and even at home had less difficulty in this area.

There was a distinct change in the way Rosa brought material; for example, in the first week of treatment, she had named the little dolls for the members of her family, but had always used them to convey direct information; that is, there was very little distancing in her doll play. At this point, however, although she retained the family names, she insisted that the dolls were not actually the same people as her family and she sometimes allowed the dolls to have feelings and wishes that were denied in the real people. One day she used the dolls in further displacement and airily discussed the fighting going on between the anonymous "older children" and "younger children." When I ventured that some children might want to fight to get rid of each other, to have the mother to themselves, Rosa herself took the next step and said, "You're really talking about me, aren't you?" This sequence in the material—of work on the defensive maneuver followed by interpretation of the underlying wish—was a new feature and indicated the growth of new abilities of Rosa's ego to interpose itself between her impulses and their direct expression.

Rosa began to tell long stories in her sessions, sometimes illustrating them with interesting drawings. Their content was oedipal, as in her tale of a little girl who was a beautiful princess; she got lost in a forest and was found by a prince who married her. The stories clearly derived from fairy tales in which she had only recently become very interested. But the important point here is that Rosa always wanted to check on whether I believed what she told me. She entered into long discussions about what I would and would not believe, in relation both to the material she frankly presented as "stories" and to things she just told me in passing, such as that her teacher gave her two apples and a whole bag of sweets, two days in a row. Although I could interpret the specific wishes revealed in the manifest content of this material, for example, positive and negative oedipal strivings, and although I suspected that Rosa's intense need to know whether or not I believed her, or whether she had again fooled me, related in general to separation problems, it was difficult to find the direct link either to the present situation of a new sibling about to arrive or to her long-standing and overdetermined problems in this area. Meanwhile in her sessions Rosa brought more and more material in the same vein: she told jokes, she tried to do magic tricks, she clowned and giggled; she began for the first time to play games, usually hide-and-seek or tag; she told stories—and always there was the refrain of "do you believe me?" She was doing well at school and seemed genuinely to enjoy it, and this caused Mrs. T. great distress and guilt. Mrs. T. became aware of how much the reluctance to separate came from her side when she told me how unbearable she found it not to know every detail of Rosa's life and how she wished the teacher would write down a minute-by-minute account of the child's day.

Annabelle was born midway through the third term of Rosa's treatment. Rosa reacted differently at home and in treatment; at home, although she wet her bed more than usual, she was incredibly well-behaved and loving toward the new baby. Mrs. T. found this "too-good-to-be-true" behavior "horrible" and phoney and wished that Rosa would throw her familiar tantrums, but I felt that this "sweet big sister" act demonstrated that Rosa was at last developing some reaction formations to add to her relatively meager repertoire of defenses. In treatment, Rosa simply did not tell me about her new baby sister; she seemed to hope that we could together deny Annabelle's existence as long as she did not mention her or tell me her name. All Rosa said was, "Would you believe me if I told you I had a new Mummy?"

Anna Freud (1936) discussed denial in fantasy and denial in word or act as follows: "In his fantasies a child is supreme. So long as he does not tell them to anybody, no one has any reason to interfere. On the other hand, dramatization of fantasies in word and act requires a stage in the outside world. So his employment of this mechanism is conditioned externally by the extent to which those around him will fall in with his dramatization, just as it is conditioned internally by the degree of compatibility with the function of reality testing" (p. 91). Rosa's environment had always allowed her an unusual degree of freedom in acting out her impulses and wishes, that is, in avoiding resolution of conflicts autoplastically and colluding with her denial of demands for the development of internal controls. Her extended experience of omnipotence also had its effect on the development of reality testing. Rosa's parents did not present themselves as representatives of reality demands, thus affording Rosa little opportunity to develop this function at the appropriate rate. Her preoccupation with her own and my omnipotence-omniscience and her almost compulsive examination of what was believable, plausible, or real in relation to her wishes and their fulfillment appeared to be an attempt to order the limits which would be placed on her impulses from outside and to develop her own reality testing to serve as an internal control. The anxiety surrounding these developmental steps, however, was derived from their relation to the terror of separation, which mother and child shared, and the traumatic rejection Rosa experienced at the time of Laura's birth. When Annabelle was born, Rosa was in a transitional phase, on the one hand moving forward as a result of the progressive tendencies freed by the analytic work on her separation conflicts, on the other hand held back by the regressive temptation to deal with the threat of the new baby as she had dealt with Laura's arrival. Thus Rosa had begun to internalize controls and experience internalized conflict, but this tendency toward maturing was at this time only partially syntonic with either her own or her parents' ideals.

At this time Mrs. T. again experienced intense conflict about Rosa's treatment. There was another dramatic crisis, with Mrs. T. keeping Rosa at home and refusing to speak to me for several days. When we finally met, I could take up with her the similarities between this crisis and the last, both of which had occurred at moments when Rosa was making visible progress in independence from her mother, and when Mrs. T., for various practical reasons, had had less contact with me than usual. Mrs. T. managed to express her hostility to me and her withdrawal as a way of protecting me from the aggression she felt, because I was taking her baby Rosa away from her, and because she was a successful mother of three lovely daughters while I (as she knew) had miscarried earlier that year. This clearing of the air allowed us to go on to work directly on Mrs. T.'s confusion about her mothering role and her handling of the reactions of both Rosa and Laura to Annabelle's birth. In the weeks which followed Mrs. T. exercised her considerable sensitivity and intelligence to examine how to convey to Laura the difference between thought and action, and how she as a mother could help Laura tolerate her feelings about the baby while refusing to allow Laura to hit Annabelle. I feel sure that this work with the mother was important in setting the scene in which Rosa could make further forward steps.

In the eighth week after Annabelle was born, Rosa appeared for her sessions on Monday and Tuesday wearing a long, trailing, white ribbon tied around her waist. She explained in a dignified fashion that she had invented this belt herself and that it was her very own. When I remarked on its hanging down so far across her lap, Rosa began to talk about other things which ·hang down or stick out on bodies, and it soon emerged that her long ribbon represented a penis. She did not wear her ribbon the following day, but she talked about "long, wriggly white things" and mentioned in passing that she had seen a white worm that morning in her stool, just like the one she had seen once before when she was very small "right before Laura was born."

Rosa's symbolic representation of a baby contained elements

from the phallic level (baby = penis) and the anal theory that a baby is part of the feces and issues from the anus. Although this material appeared in the context of positive oedipal strivings, the continuing presence of earlier fixations could clearly be seen.

I had not previously heard that Rosa had worms, but I felt I ought to mention the matter to Mrs. T., in case the child really needed medical attention. The next morning, I could hear Rosa sobbing all the way from the end of the street up to my door. She sat herself down on the steps, refusing to come indoors at first, but came grudgingly when I said it was just too cold to stay outside. She resisted entering the room until I suggested that her Daddy come along with us. Although she kept her face averted from me, muttering that she did not like me and did not ever want to see me again, she took the tissues I offered her to dry her tears. After a moment I asked her whether she could give us some idea of what the trouble was, whereupon Rosa rounded on her father with an incoherent accusation that he had told something to a man. I suggested that I had told her mother about the wriggly white worm and that Rosa had not wanted anyone to know that she was thinking about making live things in her own tummy. Rosa nodded miserably and said, "It was my *secret* and you told!" She was feeling in-conflict about the content of the material, i.e., over her oedipal rivalry with her mother, but the aspect which had really so hurt her feelings and aroused a passionately angry reaction toward me was the betrayal of her secret, any secret, which she experienced as an attack on her integrity. I had shattered her denial in fantasy and, in effect, made a demand that she give up the comforting idea that she was making her own baby and face the reality of her inability to do so. There were hints that on the instinctual level my action also represented for Rosa a theft of her precious anal productions.

Thus, Rosa had moved from wanting me to be able to guess everything and know her thoughts, as a way of staying together, to a wish to have a secret. This secret, however, brought her close to her mother and me, because it cloaked her wish to be able to make a baby, as we could. The next step would be to have really different secrets. This betrayal of her secret threatened her emerging autonomy and she again felt in danger, even if only briefly, of being overwhelmed with aggressive retaliatory impulses. In the next few sessions, Rosa was able to talk about how disappointed she was and how my action made her feel, as she put it, "a confused girl." She repeatedly asked me why I told her mother and, after we had examined her feelings about this, I gave her a realistic explanation. I told her that we needed to understand her feelings and wishes when she thought of the worms; but if she had really had them, as she did when she was little, only the doctor would know exactly what was needed to make her better. Rosa accepted this explanation with relief, and I felt that her trust in me was restored on a more realistic basis.

Two currents in Rosa's emotional life again converged in the weeks just before the Christmas holiday; the coming break revived feelings about separation from me and my pregnancy was becoming too visible for Rosa to deny. Rather than expressing her sense of her own inadequacy in relation to me as an oedipal rival in the self-denigration we had seen six months earlier, when she destroyed her drawings, Rosa prosecuted an active search for ways to bolster her self-esteem. She tried to learn how to draw all sorts of things which earlier she had refused to attempt, and became excitedly involved in participating in the Christmas concert at school. Father Christmas became a central figure in the material, and Rosa told long stories about his bringing surprise presents to her and other children. Rosa wondered why he brought presents only to children, while grownups had to make do with gifts to each other, and concluded that this was because he liked children better. Many themes were involved here: Father Christmas as an oedipal object, gifts in relation to sexual intercourse and babies as surprise packages, sexuality as a private adult preserve. I could take up the elements of reversal of affect in Rosa's approach to my pregnancy, and she then intermittently allowed her wistful sadness to come through directly, but, in addition to this reactive concentration on how good it is to be a child and how much she herself preferred other children to adults, Rosa also began to make genuine moves toward peers. She had always resisted going to parties; although she still said she felt shy, she began to attend and enjoy parties and teas with school friends. Mrs. T. often saw her walking through the playground, her arms entwined with another little girl's, and in her sessions Rosa began to talk about games with friends at school.

Upon her return from the Christmas holidays, Rosa again seemed surprisingly more grownup, but this time she was the same at home and in treatment. She had not regressed to constipation during the break, and she was wetting only about twice a week at night. On the first day back, she drew pictures of my "big fat dresses," but withdrew into apparent deafness or singing when I tried to discuss directly her feelings about what was making me so big and fat. In the middle of the second week, Rosa began playing in a very concentrated way with several little cars, wanting to race them across the table. She made them bump into each other and wondered which cars were faster and stronger than the others, and then became quite distressed at the idea that the strongest might go all the way across the table, fall off, and crash into my boots. With a great air of discovery, Rosa took a little set of traffic lights out of the box and set these up to control the fast cars, but almost immediately began to worry that the traffic lights might not work. I verbalized her fear that her strong angry feelings might crash and hurt me, and we talked about the "traffic lights inside" which she feared would not keep her in control. Rosa nodded miserably when I observed that the difficulty was in loving and hating the same person, and in feeling that being angry would make her lose the ones she loved. Suddenly she leapt up and ran out to the toilet. When she returned, she told me with some relief that she had been able to get there in time, and we linked her feeling of precarious control of her body with the earlier material concerning her doubts of the effectiveness of her internal controls. Rosa sat quietly for a while and told me that she was remembering her mother bringing her a treat of some fresh hot bread one day and how she wished all the time to have treats from me, but felt she would never get them. I discovered from Mrs. T. that Rosa's memory dated from before she was 3, when she was sometimes fetched from the play group by her mother alone, without Laura. When Rosa mentioned this memory again, I could then link it with her wish to be my only patient and my only baby.

Since Christmas, Rosa had a new early morning session time; she was brought by her father and they usually missed at least one session a week because he overslept. Rosa was faced with real uncertainty about whether she would be able to see me or not, a

circumstance that led to an interesting sequence of reactions to
these unexpected separations. The first day after a missed session,
Rosa talked of magic and secrets and the witch or ogre in fairy
stories; we understood these to be adults who let her down—she
described with some bitterness that she and Laura did not
oversleep, only Mummy and Daddy. The disappointing grownups
also were the objects who did not keep Rosa as the only favorite
baby. In these sessions, Rosa drew pictures, made me guess what
they were, and seemed concerned that I should like them and
express my preferences for one or another object depicted. On the
second day, the material shifted to more distinctly oedipal themes,
but with a strong admixture of feelings of rejection stemming from
all levels. Rosa viewed me as the oedipal rival who could have a
baby while she could not and she was sure that I would prefer the
baby to her. Recently she imagined being a little girl who would
steal toast from me, which was equivalent to the hot bread her
mother had brought. This was understood in relation to both
wanting to steal away my baby and the earlier material about theft
of anal products.

I have described these recent events in some detail to indicate
how the form and quality of the material have changed after one
year of treatment. As Rosa has gained some awareness of the
internal connections between her various difficulties, she has begun
to devise more symbolic methods of dealing with them.

SUMMARY

In presenting material from the first year of Rosa's analysis I have
tried to trace the interaction between her developing sense of
autonomy and the development of internal controls and defense
mechanisms. This is comparable to the parallel development of the
differentiation of self and object and the differentiation within the
mental apparatus, i.e., between id and ego.

In Rosa's case, the abilities to fool and to have secrets were
central to this ongoing parallel development: until she could fool
me, she was unable to fool herself, as it were, to keep some thoughts
and feelings unconscious. Rosa's ability to have her own thoughts,

to think of a secret, was a sign that she had developed a sense of herself as an independently functioning person, separate from her mother; this ability in turn further helped to define her sense of separate selfhood.

Rosa's developmental difficulties can be understood in terms of the unduly long "omnipotent honeymoon" she had as a baby. Rosa was not given the opportunity to assimilate aspects of reality gradually; therefore, when Laura was born, Rosa's emerging ego was overwhelmed with anxiety, which stemmed from her feeling abandoned by her mother and her inability to control her own aggressive impulses toward her indispensable mother. The situation was further exacerbated by the collusive life style of the parents and Mrs. T.'s own difficulty in separating from Rosa and allowing the child to have a separate existence. Since the age of 2, every progressive move Rosa made toward individuation and autonomy evoked in her the threat of the pain she suffered when Laura arrived. Hence we can understand why this little girl did not develop differentiations within herself, particularly not the ego function of defense vis-à-vis the id. Giving up her instinctual wishes, her omnipotence, and the immediate mutual knowledge of thoughts and feelings meant, to Rosa, giving up her mother. She could begin to do this only when a change in the external demands from her parents and the environment and in the internal demands posed by the development of other ego functions, such as reality testing, provided her with different sources of gratification. Usually, she now receives approval and narcissistic supplies from her loved objects for independent functioning, and she heightens her own self-esteem by exercising ego-syntonic internal controls over her impulses.

In conclusion I offer the speculation that the aspect of good ego functioning seen in Rosa at referral represented a postive correlation between her high level of primary narcissism and the unfolding of the primary autonomous ego apparatuses, while the interferences in the development of the secondary ego apparatuses, specifically the function of defense, stemmed from the disruption of the normally gradual separation from mother and the delay in individuation.

BIBLIOGRAPHY

FREUD, A. (1936), *The Ego and the Mechanisms of Defense.* New York: International Universities Press, rev. ed., 1966.
———— (1965), *Normality and Pathology in Childhood.* New York: International Universities Press.

On the Concept "Borderline" in Children

A Clinical Essay

FRED PINE, PH.D.

THE DIAGNOSTIC TERM "BORDERLINE" IS A SPATIAL METAPHOR. IT is intended to convey something about the status of certain relatively severely disturbed children who lie "between" psychosis on the one hand and neurosis or milder forms of pathology on the other. It is a hazy area, but a few things can be said about the nature of the borders surrounding this domain; and a good deal can be said about the internal borders within this domain, about distinctions among the children who can be characterized in this way.

This paper sets out to pursue these two tasks: to discuss the attributes that differentiate this set of children from those with other forms of pathology which, in general, we see as either milder or more severe and, in so doing, to define some aspects of the borders "between" these children and the less and more disturbed; and, secondly, to describe a variety of syndromes found in such children, in so doing delineating borders "within" the domain of the borderline. While both approaches are intended to lessen the vagueness in the discussion of borderline children, the second has an

From the Department of Psychiatry, Bronx Municipal Hospital Center, Albert Einstein College of Medicine. This paper grew in part out of a discussion group with Drs. Katherine Dalsimer, Jan Drucker, Lisa Goldsmith, Jo Lang, and Nicholas Papouchis, and Ms. Doris Penman. I would like to express my indebtedness to them for their stimulation and contributions.

additional aim: it is intended to argue against a search for a unitary concept of "the" borderline child. Just as we aim for specification beyond the diagnostic term "neurosis," we can aim for specification within the borderline domain. While I place no value on the creation of new labels per se, I believe that the kinds of children to be described here are recognizable to most clinicians who work with children, and deserve to be identified by the attributes that distinguish them from one another; labels help in that task.

The metaphor "borderline" sounds descriptive of a surface terrain; but this is only true of the metaphor. The diagnostic view taken here is consistent with what Anna Freud (1970) espouses in her paper on the symptomatology of childhood. I shall attempt to outline common genetic and structural features that underlie divergent surface pathologies, and, contrariwise, indicate varying underlying features that point up differences in superficially similar presenting pictures.

The core idea to be developed is that genetic considerations, the presence of developmental arrest or aberrant development (principally in the spheres of ego function and object relationship), give unity to the divergent phenomena in the borderline domain. In her 1956 paper on the borderline child (as in her work in general), Anna Freud places developmental considerations at the center of our clinical thinking about child pathology. On the other hand, variations in these developmental phenomena, as well as variations in the structural and dynamic ones that proceed from them, permit, indeed require, diagnostic refinement within the broad borderline domain.

In what follows I shall proceed "downward" (to continue the spatial metaphor)—first discussing the "border" between neurosis and the borderline group of children, then describing various subgroups of children within this domain, and ending with a discussion of the (far vaguer) border between these children and the psychotic child. Throughout, I attempt to keep in mind that diagnostic labels and groupings are conveniences of our own making. Hence, I do not try to find out what the borderline child (or concept) "really" is; it is not "really" anything in that sense. Instead, I propose a set of phenomena to which the term (and subdivisions of it) can usefully be applied.

MAPPING THE BORDERS

ON THE "UPPER" BORDER

We usually think of the essence of neurosis as involving an unconscious conflict between drive and an opposing force that culminates in anxiety, unsuccessful defense, and symptom formation. Beyond this, diagnostic considerations stem from the "content" of the conflict—the drives involved and the extent of drive regression, and the defenses characteristically relied upon. Temporal considerations (transience or fixity), the "spread" of the neurotic conflict (involving wider areas of functioning or a range of character traits in addition to symptoms), as well as the ego syntonicity or dystonicity of the resultant behavioral signs (symptoms and character traits) are also relevant.

But this "essence," the unconscious drive conflict, clearly fails to define neurosis adequately. Take the following example:

A 12-year-old schizophrenic girl, Francesca, who had a variety of visual and auditory hallucinations (centering around monsters), a variety of symptomatic bodily phenomena centering around liquid flow (of tears, vomit, urine, blood), and an insatiable oral craving, evinced interest in bloodsucking vampires. In a session with her therapist, whose time and attention she had been craving, she became attracted to the therapist's neck—specifically to a necklace the therapist was wearing. The girl immediately became upset and reported the taste of blood in her mouth (gustatory hallucination). Soon thereafter she expressed fear that the therapist would turn into a monster if the latter left the room, and Francesca tried to block the door to keep her there.

Here we have an unconscious drive conflict and pathological defense. The essence of neurosis? Hardly. While the inner workings of the child in this clinical vignette cannot be fully explicated, they seem to include defense against the oral-incorporative drive first by displacement (to the necklace), then by hallucination formation in part disconnected from the (inferred) initial impulse ("I feel blood in my mouth"), and then by disguise (loss of specificity) of the content plus projection outward (the therapist will become a "monster")—a final turn which allows the child to hold onto the therapist after all, but in a new way (keeping her in the room). But these are not neurotic phenomena.

So the concept of the core conflict between drive and an opposing force as defining neurosis is insufficient—as above, it is seen in a psychotic child. It is far more widely present than in the neuroses alone. And well it must be. Waelder (1936), in his important paper on multiple function, makes clear that *all* behavior, to be fully described, must be looked at from the point of view of drive and defense as well as from the point of view of adaptation to reality, superego functioning, and the compulsion to repeat. Drive and defense, including varying degrees of conflict or coordination between them, are components of all behavior. In an earlier paper (Pine, 1970), I have tried to show how multiple function comes into being developmentally and gives order and permanence to the behavior of the child. For example, when we hear that an 8-year-old boy asks permission to take an extra piece of cake when his parents are out on a Saturday night, and to watch an extra (late) TV program, we may not be overly impressed by the psychodynamics of the situation. But when we learn that this is the final step in a stormy history of separation difficulties for this boy, and that he has gradually come to be able to give up his longings for the absent parent via displacement to alternative gratifications (cake and late TV show) and also to give up his fear of abandonment via a compensatory feeling of being "big" (eating more, staying up late), we see that such everyday behaviors, too, are constructed out of the history of conflict and accommodation between drive and defense. And this in the context of essentially normal development.

The unsuccessfully resolved unconscious drive conflict, which clinical work shows to be a core problem in certain patients (whom we call "neurotic"), is a necessary but not sufficient defining attribute of the neuroses. We actually define the neuroses as involving such a conflict *in the context of more or less normal development of the several sides of the personality,* though this latter clause is often only implicit, assumed rather than stated. And the several aspects of the personality are critical here. We speak of neuroses where (in addition to the neurotic conflict and pathology) ego development has proceeded to the point where secondary process thinking and reality testing are well established (though Freud [1924] points out certain secondary losses of reality focal to the neurotic conflict) and where some capacity for delay and at least some well-structured defenses have been attained. In addition, object relations have developed more or less normally through the early autistic (object-less) and symbiotic (undifferentiated) stages (Mahler, 1968); some degree of libidinal object constancy (Hartmann, 1952; Pine, 1974) and of specificity of object attachment have been achieved; and object relations have been subjected to the shaping influences of the drives at each of the psychosexual stages of development (receiving and taking, giving and holding, intruding [Erikson, 1950]); further-more, the triadic relations of the oedipal period have been experienced and dealt with in some manner. Superego development has proceeded to the point of at least some degree of internalization of standards—that is, with some experience of guilt for transgression and with some internally powered efforts at control and delay of impulses. Whether we add anything more by saying that drive development has also proceeded more or less normally (in the person who, for other reasons, is termed "neurotic"), or whether that is implied in the normal development of ego, object relations, and superego, is an arguable point. In any event, we usually think of neurosis as a focal drive conflict in the setting of more or less normal development of ego and superego functioning and of object relationship, though, of course, secondary regression may also have taken place. Hence we think of neurosis, from the standpoints of development and psychic structure, as a relatively "healthy" state—even though there can be much suffering and impairment of function.

By contrast, the group of children who are generally considered "borderline" or severely disturbed do not show this context of normal development of ego functioning and of object relationship. In particular, ego malfunction in them includes disturbances in the sense of reality and at times in reality testing, as well as a failure in the development of signal anxiety so that unpleasant affect readily escalates to panic instead of triggering defensive operations (Rosen-feld and Sprince, 1963). Object relations are characterized by their shifting levels, by too great a dependence of ego structure upon the object contact (Ekstein, 1966), and by regression to primary identification (Rosenfeld and Sprince, 1963). While superego forerunners are also likely to be impaired, these are not readily separable in their impact from failures of judgment and affectional attachment that are already implied by pointing to failures in ego function and object relationship. Final superego formation is likely to be secondarily interfered with by prior developmental failures.

The children to be discussed here all show *developmental arrest or aberrant development* in one or another aspect of *ego function or object relationship.* These are primary developmental failures rather than secondary regressions. I say this for two reasons: it seems to me that is what others imply when they write about such children; and it seems to me that this lends somewhat more conceptual clarity and clinical homogeneity to this domain.

But the line between developmental failure or aberration, on the one hand, and secondary regression on the other, is not always clear. Nor is the line between normal development and what is only a semblance of normal development. That is partly why the concept "borderline" came into use, and why it continues to be used. Indeed, the borders are fuzzy. But the absence of absolute clarity should not deter the search for some relative clarification in this area, and with this in mind I shall now describe a set of children who show severe pathology involving developmental failure, aberrant development, or both.

SOME INTERNAL BORDERS IN THE BORDERLINE DOMAIN

No hard and fast distinctions, no sharp and absolute boundaries, are implied in the following discussion. This is inevitably so, because diagnostic entities are our creations, intended to give order to the phenomena we observe. In part, the phenomena have their own order, and our diagnostic terms are searches after that order. For example, in the case of anal impulses and obsessional neuroses, there may be certain features of bodily experience (the physical separation of "higher" and "lower" parts, the alternation of being messy and being clean), certain features of societal controls (Erikson, 1950), and certain features of the learnings that take place simultaneously with the acquisition of bowel control (Greenacre, 1958) which make for a co-occurrence of anal impulses and the defenses of isolation, undoing, and intellectualization in obsessional neuroses. But such patterning in the phenomena only partially underlies diagnosis. Often it seems that all, or almost all, variations are possible. Our diagnostic terms are discontinuous, whereas human phenomena are continuous. It is in this sense that the following diagnostic subentities are given; they may flow into one another, or one may replace another over time, in the severely disturbed child.

Indeed, it may be best to consider the following not only as "diagnostic entities" but simultaneously as "aspects of the pathological phenomena." The difference is that the first implies *types of children,* more or less different from one another, while the latter implies *types of phenomena,* more than one of which may be found in any particular severely disturbed child. The two approaches are not contradictory; a particular child may show one aspect of the phenomena so predominantly that he well represents that as an "ideal type." I have attempted to select illustrative cases where one feature is predominant, but considerable overlap would often be evident if the full case material were presented.

Chronic Ego Deviance

I begin with this group because it has often been discussed in the literature. Weil (1953, 1956) and Rosenfeld and Sprince (1963, 1965) have reported on children with multiple disorders of ego functioning and object relation. While these children do not show hallucinations and delusions as central or persistent features, they nonetheless are very different from neurotic children. Weil refers to them as children of "deviant" development; Rosenfeld and Sprince refer to them as "borderline." I chose the former designation here because I view them as one subgroup of a larger category of borderline children.

These children are deficient in the "development of object relationship with all its consequences (giving up of omnipotence, of magical thinking, acceptance of the reality principle), in reality testing, in the development of the synthetic function, and in the proper use of age-adequate defenses" (Weil, 1953, p. 272). Additionally, Rosenfeld and Sprince (1963) point out their failure to establish phase dominance in drive development, such that drives of all levels appear in nonintegrated array, and the absence of fine ego-drive attunements reflecting coordinate development appropriate to specific stages. Each of these writers (and others) emphasize the failure in the establishment of the signal function of anxiety, so that any anxiety rapidly escalates to panic.

By no means every individual peculiarity of ego development warrants the diagnosis "borderline." There are variations that are stylistic or are matters of maturational lag or are peripheral to more basic developmental achievements. Central to the features of the more disturbed children are failures in the establishment of the reality principle, unreliability of the signal function of anxiety, and fluidity of object attachment. Thus, these children lack the basic *stabilizers* of functioning that other children acquire: a reliable anchor in external reality and in patterned object relationships that give the children shape, and an array of intrapsychic defenses reliably set into motion when anxiety is aroused.

Weil (1953) and Rosenfeld and Sprince (1963) give detailed case material. I shall briefly describe two other such children.

Alex, age 8, the youngest child of now-divorced parents, grew up in a home where the mother felt overwhelmed and where the longed-for father was irresponsible and unavailable. He was an odd boy. There was some minimal brain damage which contributed to this oddness (his bodily movement was peculiarly lacking in grace), but the oddness went beyond this. While he made contact with adults, it was in a somewhat too undifferentiated manner, and too passively, like a puppy dog with its master. No thought disorder was evident at first, but unrealistic ideas (people came at night and cut open his stomach) were soon revealed. A history of dangerous behavior (firesetting, knife throwing, an attempt to cut his penis), which at first seemed reactive to inordinate stress in his environment, soon came to be regarded more as an internal characteristic, the result of faulty judgment and the absence of more adequate defenses. When Alex was questioned about such events, his affect was bland, his judgment poor, and his sense of the reality of what he had done was minimal. In his fantasies, he was Superman, invulnerable, powerful; he claimed to know this was not real, yet much of the time he behaved (including dangerous risk-taking) as though it were.

Kurt, age 10, in spite of his characteristic glassy stare and affective blandness, related to his therapist as a truly reliable other person whom he could trust and lean upon. Yet, especially early in his treatment, the therapist frequently felt Kurt disappear from contact with her, much as Kurt's foster parents had reportedly found him to be when he first came to live with them. Frightening events, such as the severe illness of his father, would precipitate disorganization—mechanical body movement, word gibberish, and a sense of panic. The withdrawals and panics were short-lived, but even at his best, peculiarities of reasoning, a sense of "oddness," and a wide open vulnerability mixed with a defensive, paranoidlike suspiciousness were characteristic of him. His thought content flowed too easily from sexual wishes and confusion to primitive hunger, despair, and fears of and wishes for destruction. Today, three years later, the panics and withdrawals are rare, but the oddness is immediately evident.

These children show chronic and characteristic failures of object relationship, defense organization, and reality testing. While at times they function better than at other times, their deficits are "silently" present at all times, part of the child, shaping his reaction to experience. Hence the term "*chronic* ego deviance." They differ in certain respects from Ekstein's cases (discussed below) which show markedly differing levels of *overall* ego organization at different times; Ekstein's cases tend to show more of an all-or-none quality in their pathology, while these children are more consistently a mixed bag of varying levels of ego function, drive level, and object relationship. There is an important difference between these children and those whose pathology is more fully reactive to external disorganization (also discussed below); the latter children heal (rapidly, though only partially) in a benign environment, while the pathology of the chronically deviant group continues to peer through (or even to be revealed more fully) as a trusting relationship develops.

In some ways the phenomena of chronic ego deviance are the "parent" phenomena, diagnostically speaking, of all the others described in this paper. To some extent what I shall be doing henceforth is teasing out several specific varieties from this general category, leaving this group yet to be described more precisely. Weil (1953) suggests that such children grow up to be odd adults (perhaps borderline, schizoid, or worse). If one were to imagine what the childhood of the adult "process schizophrenic" might have been like, this would seem to be one of the varieties.

I now turn to some other kinds of borderline children (or other kinds of phenomena in the borderline child). Much of the clinical use of the concept "borderline" is somewhat fuzzy, it seems to me, because the phenomena are fuzzy, at least in some of the severely disturbed children under consideration. A geologist may describe the shape of a stone with precision; but not so a meteorologist, a cloud. Some of the children who have been described as borderline have a quality of changing shape, a fluidity, which is far less a characteristic of the neurotic child. The apparent imprecision in description may itself be a reflection of the "imprecision," i.e., the absence of clear structure, in some of these children. Three kinds of children seem to fall under this rubric: the child with shifting levels of overall ego organization, the child whose internal disorganization mimics or is reactive to external disorganization, and the child with incomplete internalization of psychotic mechanisms.

Shifting Levels of Ego Organization

This is one of the most dramatic of the syndromes in this domain and has been the subject of extensive study by Ekstein and his co-workers. Ekstein and Wallerstein (1954, p. 349) refer to the "fluid ego organization" in these children. They fluctuate back and forth from a reality-oriented, though often painfully troubled, world to a world of idiosyncratic fantasy. Near-autistic unrelatedness or symbiotic absence of differentiation on the one hand, and the appearance of true object relationship (though often at infantile levels) on the other, are seen in turn. The fantasy world gives way when the therapist makes contact as a benign object, only to reappear when the therapist is out of touch or when unknown inner or outer stimuli trigger the onset of the fantasying state (Ekstein, 1966). Drives from every level of personality development are seen, first one then another seeming to have primacy. Some of the cases reported by Rosenfeld and Sprince (1963) appear to be similar, as do the following two cases.

Junie was first seen at age 11. I knew from records covering years of prior professional contacts (as well as from my own observations) that she would periodically go off into what she called her "kooky" moods—states of primitive rage expressed in mock form, of remarkable access to normally unconscious material, of perceptual confusion about the office and outside, and of distorted and idiosyncratic fantasies about her body structure. This alternated with the functioning of a sensitive, though painfully suffering, young girl who was in good reality contact and formed a good therapeutic alliance. Only much later did the inner stimuli (feelings experienced as crazy which were handled by enactment of a crazy self) that touched off these states become clear.

Francesca, the child with the vampire fantasies who was discussed in the opening section of this paper, showed similar phenomena—though her pathology had developed to the point of including highly differentiated and persistent delusions and hallucinations. The variation between levels of overall ego organization was striking. She emerged from her world which was peopled with monsters to speak to her therapist in heartrending fashion of the "monstrous" way she was treated by the real people of her real world. And then, when her own inner monstrous feelings would arise (her rage and her gnawing neediness), she would again go back to her world of magic and unreality—a state in which, as she once said, "the world is dead."

These children differ from the first group described in the *totality* of the shift that takes place in their ego organization. Ekstein and Wallerstein (1954; and Ch. 4 in Ekstein, 1966) emphasize this fluidity of movement between ego states, the very tenuous hold on the more advanced states, and the differing degrees of primitiveness of drive expression in the differing ego states. They stress the relation between the shift in state and the child's being in contact or out of touch with the therapist.

I would add that, in these children, a true ego organization has been achieved, but at *at least two different levels.* The ego-deviant children described earlier are more likely to show a mixture of partial organization along with interruptions, failures, and sometimes panic. While these features may also be found in the children with shifting ego organization (they are, once again, not mutually exclusive "types"), the latter show a distinctive additional feature. My impression, from children I have seen, is that the more pathological ego organization in fact "works" (in those whom I am characterizing as children with "shifting levels of ego organization"). The total shift to a more psychoticlike state deals with anxiety "successfully," though in a highly maladaptive way (see also Ekstein, 1966). Thus I would emphasize the organized *defensive* function of the total shift to the more psychoticlike ego organization, a shift away from painful inner or outer reality to a world of magic and relative safety. This defense is, of course, unlike the defenses seen in persons with a neurotic structure in the degree of renunciation of ego achievement and object relationship that it entails. The defensive shift operates in the context of an already fragile ego and drive organization that has never fully moved beyond the more infantile position. But it serves to avoid panic.

I append a few general remarks about both groups, the chronic ego deviant children and those showing shifting ego organization. The two groups often overlap. The children who flow from one level or form to another of ego organization, of object relation, of reality orientation, and of drive primacy appear not to have established a stable hierarchy of organization in any of these areas. Stable phase dominance vis-à-vis drives seems not to have taken place and drives from all psychosexual levels coexist in their more or less infantile forms, not sufficiently moderated or altered by the subsequent prominence of later stages of drive and ego organization. While they have developed the capacity for object relationship—to a person experienced as "out there," as "other"—this seems neither to bind together the whole ("good" and "bad") object in one tempered whole, nor to replace fully a symbiotic undifferentiatedness, nor to guarantee against profound withdrawal. While children generally move back and forth from reality to fantasy more readily than adults, there is more slippage in these children—the fantasy being too idiosyncratic, too sustained, coming at wrong moments, not easily enough given up. For whatever reason, these children have failed to establish a solid hierarchy in their ego states and functions, their forms of object relation, and their drive organization. This shows in the ease of slippage from one level or form to another. Such is the characteristic of some kinds of "borderline" children.

Internal Disorganization in Response to External Disorganization

The children just described, at least by the age they are seen professionally, carry their pathology within them. They bring it into the treatment hour with a benign therapist. Although outer events may set off a change of state, the readiness for this change, the tendency to react in this way, is characteristic of the child. That is to say, he is predictably unpredictable, characteristically unstructured, or the like.

In the psychiatric ward of a large urban hospital, serving in part a population from deprived, impulse-ridden homes and neighborhoods, one also sees quite different pathology. Some children, when they arrive at the hospital, show destructive behavior (to self or others), sometimes with extreme uncontrollability, and are reported to have hallucinations, affectlessness, or inappropriate affect—multiple signs of serious disorder. But in the hospital they soon integrate very well, and one begins (superficially at least) to question why they are here. Although the ward (in our large city hospital) is far from idyllic, it is nonetheless, for many of these children, one of the first stable homes they have had—with three guaranteed meals each day; and with adults who are more or less consistently present and caring, and who demonstrate and assert reasonably firm behavioral controls.

These are often children from homes where child neglect or abuse, violence, psychosis, prostitution, addiction, and the like, usually in combination, are the setting of daily life. Judging from the rapid gains made by these children when they are hospitalized, one has to consider at least the grossest forms of their pathology as reactive—as massive stress reactions, as attempts to turn the passive-destructive life experience into an active one, as explosive releases of tension, or as despairing withdrawals. We conceptualize the traumatizing environment as leading to reactive disorganization and failure of consolidation, often culminating in repetition that produces mastery at the price of behavioral pathology. Moreover, the overstimulating environment further leads to repetition through imitation and interferes with the work of repression.

But these children often relate very well—and not indiscriminately—to kind adults. They are capable of some degree of trust and specificity of object attachment. Thus we see a failure of psychic integration, of adequate self-control, and even of realistic thought processes in a setting where, to some degree, these lie dormant and ready at hand if the surround elicits and permits them.

Jayne, a 10-year-old black girl, was hospitalized following an incident when she announced that she would leap out a window and made a move to do so. In the preceding days she had stayed out of school without her mother's knowledge, apparently spending the days crying in a hallway. At first there was some question about the intactness of her thought processes and her capacity for any self-control. In the hospital, she soon became a charming girl, a girl who actively wooed the adults' attention. And more and more there seemed no reason to keep her in the hospital, except that any move toward discharge precipitated self-destructive behavior, again raising the threat of suicide. Ultimately, we learned that Jayne had been grossly neglected by her mother who preferred all the other siblings to her, in a pattern that repeated how the mother had been treated by her own mother. Shortly before the suicide threat, a neighbor's child had fallen from a low window, had been hospitalized, and had received the loving attention of Jayne's mother. Jayne looked longingly on, and in a confused state sought this for herself. Only after Jayne and her mother, along with a supportive maternal aunt who nurtured them both, were seen together and these events discussed and worked through to some degree, was Jayne able to leave the hospital, safely we felt.

The summary paragraph of the psychological test report states the issues succinctly:

> Jayne is a child of average intelligence who can function well, given a stable environment which supports her rather fragile defenses. However, *she is easily stimulated to episodes involving loss of reality testing,* primitive oral aggression, *bizarre fantasies, and loss of control* of primitive aggressive impulses. She is also a profoundly depressed child who feels both that she has been quite deprived and quite guilty about ensuing angry feelings. It seems quite likely that in a disruptive environment, further suicidal ideation and attempts will occur. In spite of the extent of the disturbance, Jayne feels the need for and is able to use relationships with others not only to provide nurturance, but to support her defenses and reality testing. The diagnostic impression is of a borderline child.

Douglas was just over age 4 when he was admitted to the children's psychiatric ward. His mother told of a recent history of infantile babbling and of uncontrollable tantrums lasting 2 to 6 hours. An earlier clinic report on this child (age 3) included the notation "psychotic child." On the ward he was initially described as showing "rambling speech, nonresponsiveness to verbal commands, and giving the appearance of being occasionally out of contact with his surroundings." In addition, his disturbance showed itself in the relative *absence* of a number of behaviors that one expects in a normal 4½-year-old—playfulness, some degree of modulated affect expression, cognitive freedom in exploration, and relatedness to others with at least minimal depth. Instead, his preoccupation with making order of his environment seemed to have absorbed all of his available energy.

Douglas's mother, 19 when he was born, was a prostitute, his father a criminal with multiple offenses. His mother reported normal speech at age 2 and then a regression to babbling "for no reason." But following age 2, there were five reported "kidnappings" by his (separated) father who came and took Douglas away, unbeknownst to mother. This is just a sample of his life of instability bordering on chaos.

On the ward, Douglas blossomed in a short few months. He formed an attachment to his therapist, speech returned, the tantrums gradually ceased, he showed positive feelings and playfulness. He soon became the barometer of normality for the ward staff, the measure of what a normal child is like. In spite of a history akin to that of some symbiotic psychotic children (Mahler, 1968), he reversed the regressive process, put back together the pieces of development, and progressed. He was subsequently placed in a residential facility.

The prognosis for these children is far from rosy, partly because after hospitalization they return to the pathogenic home environment or, often, to placements of one sort or another that are pathogenic in their own way. Moreover, it is only the grossest of the pathology that falls away. The history that produced the gross disturbance also produces multiple other disturbances having less of an emergency nature. And it also produces, inevitably, a tendency toward later repetition, toward creating the old situation from inner sources—the situation that, though painful, was nonetheless the form of attachment to the ambivalently cathected love objects.

Incomplete Internalization of Psychosis

This designation could, in a way, have been applied to the previously described material as well, to the children who are reacting to disorganizing environments. But I wish to emphasize here the particular role of the (psychotic) love object, usually the mother, and also problems of incomplete separation and individuation. Children may be *influenced* by a total traumatizing environment, and may show psychoticlike processes that are not yet *stabilized,* as described above. This is different from the child's normal tendency to *internalize* the specific qualities of the love object, which in this case include psychotic features, although this internalization is still *incomplete.*

Akin to this, Anna Freud (1960) once described how the child of a depressed mother could try to follow the mother into her depression, could find the depressed state from her own repertoire of behavior possibilities and cathect it, as a form of attachment to the mother (see also Anthony, 1971).

A while ago, Patti, age 10, arrived on our hospital ward with the report that she had been hearing voices and destroying some of her mother's precious possessions. Patti spoke of this as well. But within a short time she came to be seen by the professional staff as a rather lovely young girl, capable of empathy and insight, and showing no evident pathology. Yet, when her mother visited, she was again severely disturbed for a while thereafter.

After she had been in the hospital for a while, Patti revealed, with terror in her eyes and after getting a pledge of secrecy, that she had not destroyed her mother's possessions; she thought perhaps her brother had; but she had "confessed" to it in fear of her mother and at her mother's insistence. The voices, she reported, sounded to her like her mother's voice calling her (she had only reported them at home); but when she would answer, her mother would say something like: "I'm not calling you, you must be hearing voices; I hear them too." All that we learned in Patti's subsequent treatment and in our contacts with her mother tended to confirm this new story.

Yet, the other had not been just a pose. To say Patti had "lied" earlier misses the point. She had adopted her mother's point of view and presented it (with the accompanying "feel"—affectively and with confusion—of a psychotic child). And whenever her mother visited, Patti again adopted pieces of her mother's character for a while, and showed considerable preoccupation with things that merge into one another (the two halves of her notebook that opened and then folded together, the two overlapping parts—skirt and jacket—of a woman's suit), and with the similarities of and differences between therapist and mother and herself. Human love objects were not automatically experienced as distinct and separate.

Patti's mother, we rapidly came to see, was a grossly paranoid schizophrenic woman, for whom the hospital and one of our staff psychiatrists became the conspiring enemy in her delusional world. She was also a sensitive and intelligent woman who sent a love poem to her doctor, and there is little doubt that Patti's sensitivity reflects some aspect of her maternal care. But in her psychotic periods (of which there had been several, including hospitalization), the mother used Patti as a partner; it was Patti, of all the children, who mattered most to the mother and who was the recipient and object of the psychotic behavior and entanglements. (When Patti was in the hospital, the mother began to use the next younger sibling in the same way—so that we finally had to find a placement for him too.)

For children like Patti, the psychoticlike phenomena seem to be part of the *attachment* to the parent, whether in love, hatred, or both. In this way, their pathology differs from that found in the children who react to gross and widespread pathology with collapse, panic, repetition, or a search for rescue. Patti is enmeshed in and pursuing a specific, partially symbiotic relationship that has grossly pathological features.

To summarize thus far: In both "internal disorganization reactive to external disorganization" and "incomplete internalization of psychosis," a major component of the ongoing pathology results from reactions to the disturbed environment (including the mother), but it is not fully internalized. In the phenomena described under the headings "chronic ego deviance" and "shifting levels of ego organization," the reactive component is much smaller. The pathology has become an integral part of the internal structure, whether as built-in developmental failures (chronic ego deviance) or as defense formations that are grossly maladaptive (shifting levels of ego organization). The next two groups which I shall discuss are characterized by a firmer psychic structure, but also by gross failure or aberration in the development of ego function and/or object relation. They do not show the marked shifts in psychic organization characteristic of the preceding groups, and they rely on more fixed defensive and coping mechanisms.

Ego Limitation

The manual of diagnostic categories for children of the American Psychiatric Association (1968) has a category called "Inadequate Personality." Not a very appealing name, with its judgmental sound, and yet an apt description of certain individuals who, while they may have pockets of peculiarity, show as their most prominent feature a dullness, a meagerness, an inadequacy of their intellect, their judgment, their self-care and planfulness, their sense of self, and more. Such ego limitation is an end result. I shall briefly describe two children who reached that end result by differing pathways. In both, a very early restriction of ego development (in one case due to deprivation, in the other probably due to some combination of intense anxiety and a predisposing minimal cerebral dysfunction) put a stamp of peculiarity on their entire subsequent development. The basic structure achieved early on stunted further growth, so that what would have been the later achievements of the elaboration of thought, the differentiation and modulation of affect, and the enrichment of object relationship did not readily take place. It is the severe stunting of ego development in all areas that makes these children different from those with specific neurotic learning inhibitions or avoidances. The early blockage of ego growth results in the maintenance of a primitive level of functioning.

Russell, an illegitimate, black, ghetto child of a depressed and chronically lifeless mother used to visit the clinic where he, literally, begged, borrowed, and stole to get candy and cookies or money to buy them. Intelligence tests left no doubt that there was no widespread, biologically based intellectual retardation in this boy (whom we knew from age 7 to his teens), but he was (in his words) "in the dumb class" in school, and not learning anything even there. He appeared moronic and lifeless in the way he spoke and thought, and even in his bodily movements. Russell's thought processes were ordinarily not bizarre, though the extent of their stunting was remarkable. He would at times, in a half self-mocking, half self-guiding tone, pronounce stylized verbalisms as he performed some act. Thus, drawing on some of the public safety announcements of his city, he would step into the street at mid-block, saying, "Cross at the green and not in-between," and then come back on the sidewalk. Or, throwing a piece of paper on the street, he would say, "A cleaner New York is up to me," pick up the paper, and throw it in a litter basket.

Our understanding of Russell's history was that the activating role of the mother (Mahler, 1965; Provence and Lipton, 1962) was so grossly lacking that his ego functions did not develop in the vacuum of his home. A lively intelligence, a focused and goal-directed assessment of reality, a planful manipulation of it, and an expressive affective repertoire do not simply unfold in a vacuum; although they are based on biologically given apparatuses, they must be given stimulus and shape by the guiding presence of the mother and are developed as instrumentalities of the relationship to her. Russell seemed to those of us who knew him a true instance of the developmental injuries of "stimulus deprivation," especially lacking the stimulus: mother. He is best viewed as a case of developmental failure rather than in terms of a psychodynamic response to conflict. His character has, of course, a full range of dynamic functions and sources for him, but the initial move into pathology seemed to have been a developmental arrest (as in the "infants in institutions" described by Provence and Lipton, 1962).

William, age 10, on the other hand, the firstborn child of extremely anxious, middle-class, Latin-American parents, presented as a pseudoim-becilic child (Mahler, 1942). Especially when his younger sibling was born, the parents noted a change in his behavior. William, also unquestionably of average to bright-average intelligence, presented himself as a fool, making inane statements and grinning with "dumb pleasure" as he did so. He used neologisms, expressed grossly distorted ideas about the body alongside accurate ones—always untroubled by, indeed broadcasting, his inanity. But for him, the "dumbness" permitted him to remain close to his parents—tormenting them by his illness and yet gratifying himself by continued infantile sexual pleasures (being seen, bathed, dressed) which the parents permitted this "limited" boy.

For whatever reasons (only some of which are known), the signs of William's ego limitation were already apparent quite early, in the preschool years, and by age 10 the loss to the ego of years of deficit in learning could not be reversed by dynamic interpretation alone; he clearly needed major relearning, or rather, first learning as well. In this he differs from a child who has a neurotic inhibition of learning. In such a child the major work of ego development has taken place; the learning inhibition he develops is focused and is based on a specific symbolic meaning. In contrast, William's "choice" of infantile thinking and ego organization as a major adaptive-defensive tool had the effect of distorting the whole of his subsequent development.

Schizoid Personality (*in Childhood*)

This is the category of "isolated personality" in the manual on the classification of childhood disorders by the Group for the Advancement of Psychiatry (1966). Its authors explicitly avoid the term "schizoid" because they feel it is too readily confused with "preschizophrenic." I use it instead (as they use "isolated") in the sense that Schafer (1948) used the term schizoid in adults: characterized by a sharply constricted and underdeveloped affective life, with emotional distance in human relationships, and preoccupation with their own (often rich and at least in part peculiar) fantasy life. The elements of aberration in the thought and fantasy life and of developmental blockage in affective range and expression are what leads me to consider these children among the broad grouping of severely disturbed, yet not clearly psychotic, i.e., "borderline," children.

Brian, age 9, one of several children in a large family, lost his mother 4 years earlier when she died rather suddenly. While the family held together after that, both before *and* after there was little affection and care shown to or by anyone in this family.

Brian looked depressed. His facial muscles were always just about motionless, he spoke in a monotone, and he moved slowly. He made almost no affective and individualized response to people, although he did function in school and was easy to manage. On testing, however, a rich, idiosyncratic, and peculiar fantasy life was evidenced—and this is what most absorbed and occupied him. While he seemed bland and blank from the outside, his thought processes were full, complex, though not lively. Once, at the mention of mother (in a story), he told of a panic—with everyone running so hard that their feet banging split the world apart.

The panic was in the story; *he* remained bland. Fantasy seemed to replace object relationship and was excessively relied upon to retain equilibrium.

Essie, age 7, and a recent immigrant, had not made friends at home or in school. She liked to watch TV alone or just to sit around with her own thoughts. She rarely played with either of her sisters. Seen in consultation, she showed odd ideation around a most unusual imaginary companion (that was more an object than a person) and gave evidence of a prolific imagination which she was driven to express (unable to inhibit) in her sessions with me. The content had to do largely with inanimate, outer-space, destructive images. She revealed it not as a communication, but as a monologue (while drawing). Essie's parents, while concerned about her isolation, were aware of but unconcerned about her unusual and all-absorbing thought content. Indeed, they contributed to it at times in not so subtle ways. When pressed, they said that they felt that she would outgrow it.

Both of these children were preoccupied with peculiar thoughts and were emotionally distant from other persons. Yet other aspects of ego functioning were intact enough to permit passable functioning, for example, in school. They can be distinguished from children previously described by a number of contrasts and comparisons: they carry the pathology within (unlike those responding to external chaos or maternal psychosis); they are more organized than the ego-deviant children; they do not appear retarded (like the ego-limited children); and, while relying heavily on fantasy, they are unlike the children with shifting ego organization in that they do not shift. They simultaneously function in the real world and hold themselves aloof from it emotionally while relating mainly to their odd (but not delusional) thought processes. I am impressed with one critical defining feature: the fantasying works so successfully as a defense (against drive and object relationship) that threat is not experienced in disorganizing ways. These children do not experience panic. Hence they can stabilize a character structure, though at the price of oddness and isolation. In both children, the family style supported isolation and fantasying. Perhaps, therefore, they were not fully alone when they appeared to be isolated, but were somehow still with the family and its way of being.

The G.A.P. report (1966) lists another group to which I wish to refer: the "mistrustful personality"—more usually called "paranoid character"—which is "characterized by a pattern of suspiciousness . . . with intense mistrust of others and marked rigidity of thinking. This latter involves heavy usage of projection" (p. 245). I would include this under the "borderline" category in the belief that it is based on developmental failure of object relations and on failure in the development of a solid boundary and differentiation between self and other. However, the authors of the report suggest (p. 245), and my own experience leads me to concur, that this is rarely seen in a stabilized way in children prior to preadolescence. What *is* seen prior to preadolescence, I believe, are tendencies toward intellectualization, omnipotence, projection, and splitting in some of what I have called chronic ego-deviant children—such that one predicts a movement toward later paranoid character (or paranoid psychosis) in them.

In closing this listing I wish to make explicit what should in any case be clear: that it is neither exhaustive nor mutually exclusive. I have already emphasized the latter. As to the former: it is possible that some syndromes with major organic contributions can profitably be subsumed here, or that subdivisions of what I have called "chronic ego deviance" can successfully be singled out, or that paranoid, impulse-ridden, or sexually deviate borderline syndromes (all considered severe personality disorders in the G.A.P. manual) can be observed in children. If so, they can readily be added here. This listing is intended to expand the individualized diagnostic possibilities (based partly on descriptive and partly on structural-developmental considerations) within the vague land of the "borderline."

I have so far described the "upper" border between this domain and neurosis, and some of the internal borders within it. In now turning to the border between this domain and psychosis, I wish to question whether it is possible to draw a sharp distinction.

ON THE "LOWER" BORDER

In the reading of some of Ekstein's (1966) cases, or in thinking about some of the more severe cases described by Rosenfeld and Sprince (1963)—all discussed as "borderline" in those papers—I have often asked: "Why not consider these children psychotic?"

And when I have spoken of some of the children described here—e.g., some of the chronic ego-deviant or ego-limited children with peculiarities of thinking—I have in turn been asked: "Why not call them psychotic?" And indeed, why not?

Except in the case of some specific entities, such as infantile autism (Kanner, 1942, 1949) and symbiotic psychosis (Mahler, 1952), I believe no sharp distinction, based on any recognizable principle, can be drawn between the borderline children described here and psychotic (or schizophrenic) children. At least I know of no place where such a distinction has been drawn in a conceptually unambiguous way. This problem may be inherent in the phenomena in this realm: absence of structure or else structuralized and adaptive use of quite primitive ego mechanisms. In any event, it seems to me appropriate that clinical wisdom follow what has been viewed as clinical uncertainty until now. That is to say, when a child seems "clearly" psychotic or "clearly" not psychotic (yet severely disturbed) by whatever principles of judgment the individual clinician used, there is no diagnostic problem; but once it is not so clear, it should be recognized that there are no absolute principles, and certainly no widely agreed-upon ones, by which to make a judgment.

This state of affairs can be formalized, and given clinical-theoretical recognition, by stating that there is a continuum from the "borderline" cases discussed here to childhood psychosis. Ekstein and Wallerstein (1954, p. 368), for example, refer to the *slight degree* of control that borderline children have, as a distinguishing mark from psychosis; clearly, then, this is a relative matter. *The more* the thinking peculiarities of the ego-deviant or ego-limited child dominate his thinking, or *the more* the child with shifting ego organization is *"in"* the state of unreality, or *the more* the child with an incompletely internalized psychosis *carries it around* with him, *the more prone we are* to consider this childhood psychosis. And that indeed reflects the state of affairs within the child, who himself is in developmental flux. Consider his developmental position vis-à-vis the flux of reality and fantasy, the normal regressive aspects of his object relations and drives, and the degree to which he is influenced by his surround. There is a continuum between borderline and psychosis colored in part by the ongoing development of the child.

Let me clarify this. Usually, to call a person psychotic we look for some degree of structuralization of the psychosis, some degree of fixity and of impact on many psychic structures, before we can view the pathological phenomena as characteristic of him. But the child is developing and in general shows less characterological fixity because of the flux of development. In addition, the child is in any event more highly responsive to and influenced by his environment than the adult. These two features, characteristic of childhood in general, are also part of what makes it difficult to assess whether a particular child "is" or "is not" psychotic. The problem is *intrinsic* to our diagnostic mode of thinking, and not just peripheral or based on lack of knowledge. Hence the continuum notion (from borderline to psychotic) with no clear demarcations seems to me most appropriate.

I said a moment ago that the borderline syndromes and the psychoses of childhood should be regarded as a continuum "except in the case of some specific entities" of psychosis. Two such entities have been clearly described; a third not at all clearly. The first, "infantile autism," applies to children who, from birth, have been unresponsive to the persons around them. The characteristics have been well described by Kanner in 1942; other work done since then is highly suggestive regarding organic contributions to the syndrome (see the review by Rutter and Bartak, 1971). The second, "symbiotic psychosis" (Mahler, 1952, 1968), applies to children who show more or less adequate early development, with a reversal usually in the second or third year, usually but not always involving a clear precipitating event, often in the nature of a separation, followed by panic in the absence of mother and/or secondary regression to autistic mechanisms (see also Speers and Lansing [1965] for brief descriptions of several cases).

The less clearly defined entity that may stand as an independent form of childhood psychosis, not just as a more severe form along a continuum from borderline, is childhood schizophrenia. The discussion of such cases—under the rubric "is there such a thing as childhood schizophrenia?"—has not proceeded very far. The G.A.P. publication refers to "schizophreniform" psychotic disorder (1966, p. 254) to distinguish it from the adult form of the disease.

Naturally it must be so distinguished. The one thing that is certainly true of childhood schizophrenia is that it occurs in children! It is obviously true of children that much development has not yet taken place. Thus, the reality-fantasy distinction has not been sharply etched. When one asks: "Is this really a hallucination or is it just the fantasying behavior of a child?" the question is meaningless. The particular mental product is the form that hallucination takes in a psychic apparatus that, in any event, readily engages in fantasying behavior. Furthermore, in view of the fact that much development still must take place in the child, the predictive test for whether childhood schizophrenia is "truly" schizophrenia is also meaningless. Will this childhood schizophrenia develop into adult schizophrenia? Naturally the answer can only be "maybe." Similarly, an adult schizophrenic episode can remit, recur, or become chronic. That, quite often, is the best we can say.

For the sake of clarity, I would propose separating out an entity of childhood schizophrenia that is heavily based on *regression* and that culminates in withdrawal and thought disorder (including hallucination or delusions). I say this because earlier I proposed that the borderline syndromes all involve primary developmental failures; and in more severe instances (on a continuum) they would be called childhood psychosis. A child who shows more or less normal development and then undergoes severe disorganization of a regressive sort (in the elementary school age years) may then be considered a case of childhood schizophrenia—the word "schizophrenia" emphasizing the likeness to the adult syndrome, and the word "childhood" emphasizing its differences.

I am not familiar with such cases, *except where there is acute brain disorder or gross trauma that triggers the disorganization.* Perhaps this is just an "ideal type," a theoretical end point that helps us define a variable (in this case the continuum from developmental failure to minimal development followed by regression). For in the childhood period, at least in my experience, we are still close enough to the developmental history of the schizophrenic child to see the failures that have taken place, to see the continuity of the pathology, to see the early signs and signals, so that the idea of normal development (even only "more or less normal") followed by regression carries no real weight. The developmental failures and aberrations are ordinarily all too clear.

Having set apart the clear psychotic entities of childhood, I am proposing that what we call "borderline" shades into what we call psychosis, that there is no sharp distinction, and that each clinician will of necessity label as his leaning dictates. All of the borderline children I have described show developmental failures and aberrations of a sort that, when severe enough, would warrant considering them psychotic. That no sharp line has been drawn, I suggest, reflects the fact that no sharp line exists.

Concluding Remarks

I have been discussing a number of different kinds of severely disturbed children who have been, or can be, considered borderline. As a vehicle for discussion, I have taken the spatial metaphor "borderline" seriously and discussed the borders between this domain and neurosis on the one hand and psychosis on the other, describing internal borders within the domain as well.

I have suggested that what unites these children is the presence of severe developmental failure or aberration in the realm of ego functioning and object relationship. This distinguishes them from the neurotic child characterized by unconscious drive-defense conflict and symptom formation in the setting of more or less normal development. At the lower (more pathological) extreme, I have suggested that in principle there is no real distinction between the borderline child and some forms of psychosis in childhood. The two blend into one another. I have thus tried to treat the general vagueness about the distinction between borderline and psychosis with respect—that is to say, I view it as clinical wisdom, as an indication of the fact (if fact it is) that there *is* no sharp distinction. The exception to this is in the case of certain specifiable entities of childhood psychosis which are discontinuous with the borderline syndromes. These separate entities include infantile autism, symbiotic psychosis, and a form of childhood schizophrenia that is heavily based on regressive processes rather than solely on developmental failures and aberrations.

Most important, however, I have tried to describe a number of different kinds of children who may be considered "borderline." I have spoken of differing "groups of children"—those showing chronic ego deviance, shifting levels of ego organization, internal disorganization reactive to external disorganization, incompletely internalized psychosis, severe ego limitation, and schizoid character. But I have also suggested that it may be better to refer to these groupings as "aspects of the pathological phenomena" instead. By that I mean to say that any one severely disturbed child may show more than one of these features. They hardly constitute a typology, but rather represent forms that severe pathology takes in children.

The principal aim of the paper has been to counter both the vagueness in the way the term "borderline" is used and the search for "the" borderline child—a single syndrome based on a single mechanism or developmental failure. That seems to me too simplistic, and would still leave us with whole groups of very sick children whom we have no adequate way to describe.

BIBLIOGRAPHY

AMERICAN PSYCHIATRIC ASSOCIATION (1968), *Diagnostic and Statistical Manual of Mental Disorders*, 2nd ed. Washington, D.C.: A.P.A. Publications.

ANTHONY, E. J. (1971), *Folie à Deux*. In: *Separation-Individuation*, ed. J. B. McDevitt & C. F. Settlage. New York: International Universities Press, pp. 253–273.

EKSTEIN, R. (1966), *Children of Time and Space, of Action and Impulse*. New York: Appleton-Century-Crofts.

———— & WALLERSTEIN, J. (1954), Observations on the Psychology of Borderline and Psychotic Children. *This Annual*, 9:344–369.

ERIKSON, E. H. (1950), *Childhood and Society*. New York: Norton.

FREUD, A. (1956), The Assessment of Borderline Cases. *The Writings of Anna Freud*, 5:301–314. New York: International Universities Press, 1969.

———— (1960), Four Lectures on the Psychoanalytic Study of the Child, read to the New York Psychoanalytic Society.

———— (1970), The Symptomatology of Childhood. *This Annual*, 25:19–41.

FREUD, S. (1924), The Loss of Reality in Neurosis and Psychosis. *Standard Edition*, 19:183–187. London: Hogarth Press, 1961.

GREENACRE, P. (1958), Toward an Understanding of the Physical Nucleus of Some Defence Reactions. *Int. J. Psycho-Anal.*, 39:69–76.

GROUP FOR THE ADVANCEMENT OF PSYCHIATRY (1966), *Psychopathological Disorders in Childhood*. New York: G.A.P. Publications.

368   *Fred Pine*

HARTMANN, H. (1952), The Mutual Influences in the Development of Ego and Id. *This Annual*, 7:9–30.

KANNER, L. (1942), Autistic Disturbances of Affective Contact. *Nerv. Child*, 2:217–250.

——— (1949), Problems of Nosology and Psychodynamics of Early Infantile Autism. *Amer. J. Orthopsychiat.*, 19:416–426.

MAHLER, M. S. (1942), Pseudoimbecility. *Psychoanal. Quart.*, 11:149–164.

——— (1952), On Child Psychosis and Schizophrenia. *This Annual*, 7:286–305.

——— (1965), On the Significance of the Normal Separation-Individuation Phase. In: *Drives, Affects, Behavior*, Vol. 2., ed. M. Schur. New York: International Universities Press, pp. 161–169.

——— (1968), *On Human Symbiosis and the Vicissitudes of Individuation, Vol. 1: Infantile Psychosis.* New York: International Universities Press.

PINE, F. (1970), On the Structuralization of Drive-Defense Relationships. *Psychoanal. Quart.*, 39:17–37.

——— (1974), Libidinal Object Constancy. *Psychoanal. & Contemp. Sci.*, 3. Riverside, N.J.: Macmillan.

PROVENCE, S. & LIPTON, R. C. (1962). *Infants in Institutions.* New York: International Universities Press.

ROSENFELD, S. K. & SPRINCE, M. P. (1963), An Attempt to Formulate the Meaning of the Concept "Borderline." *This Annual*, 18:603–635.

——— ——— (1965), Some Thoughts on the Technical Handling of Borderline Children. *This Annual*, 20:495–517.

RUTTER, M. & BARTAK, L. (1971), Causes of Infantile Autism. *J. Autism & Childh. Schiz.*, 1:20–32.

SCHAFER, R. (1948), *The Clinical Application of Psychological Tests.* New York: International Universities Press.

SPEERS, R. W. & LANSING, C. (1965), *Group Therapy in Childhood Psychosis.* Chapel Hill: University of North Carolina Press.

WAELDER, R. (1936), The Principle of Multiple Function. *Psychoanal. Quart.*, 5:45–62.

WEIL, A. P. (1953), Certain Severe Disturbances of Ego Development in Childhood. *This Annual*, 8:271–287.

——— (1956), Certain Evidences of Deviational Development in Infancy and Early Childhood. *This Annual*, 11:292–299.

Trauma in the Light of Clinical Experience

MARGARETE RUBEN

IN A SYMPOSIUM ON PSYCHIC TRAUMA (FURST, 1967), RANGELL, Greenacre, Sandler, Solnit, Marianne Kris, Anna Freud, and others attempted to bring together what was known about this phenomenon, to advance new data, and to encourage further investigations. With this challenge in mind, I shall examine the analytic material of a young woman and an adolescent girl in whose lives psychic trauma played a significant part. I shall discuss the influence of severe trauma on the total development of these patients—their psychopathology, their ego development, and their capacity for sublimation and adaptation. This developmental view illuminates the significance of the actual experience and its elaboration in fantasy.

In this paper I use "trauma" in the sense in which Freud (1926) defined it: as an experience of helplessness on the part of the ego in the face of the accumulation of excitation, whether of external or internal origin. In 1956 Ernst Kris distinguished between two kinds of traumatic situations: the single event in which reality suddenly and powerfully affects a person's life (shock trauma) and the effect of long-lasting stress situations causing trauma through cumulative, frustrating tension (strain trauma). Thus it would appear that the concept of strain trauma is helpful in enhancing our understanding of early constrictions in ego development and in elucidating developmental trends that suggest premature character formation. Khan (1963) referred to this process as "cumulative trauma."

The first part of this paper deals with a case of strain trauma

369

experienced by a girl at the age of 4½. The second part is concerned with a shock trauma experienced at age 6 and its developmental consequences. In both cases the traumatic events had been completely forgotten and were remembered only after they had been reconstructed in the analyses. The strain trauma emerged from repression when the patient consciously remembered enormous tensions in her reactions to her younger brother. The shock trauma was reconstructed via dreams and through the transference by the adolescent patient.

A STRAIN TRAUMA

CASE PRESENTATION

A 30-year-old woman, Mrs. Z., who had been given my name by a friend of her mother's called me in obviously serious distress, asking for a consultation. She anxiously pleaded that neither her husband nor her parents and friends must know about her call to me. She revealed in her first interview that she felt overwhelmed by her mounting anxiety about an intense love she felt for her music teacher. She feared that if he continued his flattering approaches, she would succumb and be intimate with him despite her determination always to be faithful to her husband. If this should happen, she would feel she had ruined her life forever.

This sensitive, good-looking woman had married a successful scientist 10 years her senior when she was 21 years old. To her dismay she had become pregnant immediately and had not at all felt ready to bring up children. Her first child was a little girl. Two years later she gave birth to a boy. This age difference of two years was exactly the same as that between the patient and her only brother.

When, after a few sessions, the patient decided to undergo psychoanalysis and revealed her need for treatment to her husband, he agreed only with great reluctance. In his adolescence his mother had committed suicide while she was in psychiatric care.

The analysis soon showed that this intelligent, artistic, and productive woman was devoted to her husband and, to use Winnicott's term, a "good enough mother" to her children. Yet at times she became depressed to the point of having suicidal thoughts. Sexually she had always been completely unresponsive to her husband and incapable of finding pleasure in sexual activities. Her husband, whom I saw once, told me: "If you could see her facial expression during intercourse, you would say that you had never seen a more anxious and sad woman in your life."

The patient's relationship to her parents showed signs of some unconscious ambivalence, though consciously she considered it a relationship of fairly good mutual understanding. The father appeared to be somewhat withdrawn. A biologist by profession, he habitually left his home at 6 A.M. every morning in order "to have time to feed the birds" on his way to work. The mother raised the children strictly, in Victorian fashion, although she had been an actress prior to her marriage.

At the age of 21 the patient and her fiancé eloped to be married. However, she asked her brother to inform the parents of the event, unaware that this information enabled the parents to join the elopers, approve of the marriage, and be part of the celebration.

The patient's relationship to her brother had never been satisfactory and deteriorated further when he became addicted to drugs and was jailed twice. Although he was outstandingly intelligent, he had never succeeded in any professional work. His negligent, unkempt appearance embarrassed my patient to the point that she did not want to be seen with him by her friends. Several attempts at psychiatric treatment had failed.

The patient's analysis gave evidence of her undisturbed development until the age of almost 3. Around this time she began to feel the loss of her position of priority in the family because her brother increasingly became the center of attention. Sharply aware of the differences between the sexes, she attributed her parents' pride in their son to their admiration of his physical masculinity. Her increasing penis envy reinforced her intense jealousy, particularly of her mother's care and preoccupation with the brother. On the other hand, some of her preoedipal drives seem to have been satisfied by the father, who was fascinated with his little daughter's early drawings and paintings. But her intense phallic ambitions prevented her from reacting with any pleasure to her father or her brother. Moreover, she painfully witnessed both parents' continuous admiration of their little boy's precocious intelligence.

One day when the children, still in their prelatency, were left to play without supervision, the little girl's sexual excitement and aggressive impulses drove her to nip her brother's penis. Although there was perforation and some drops of blood, the patient recalled that her father comforted her while her mother attended to her brother. She was not punished; in fact, the incident was never mentioned again.

This traumatic experience of being overwhelmed by her own sexual and aggressive drives, and above all her penis envy, turned out to be the core of disturbance in the further psychosexual development of this patient. The immediate consequence of this event was a regression to preoedipal longings, with the corresponding clinging and demanding attitude toward her mother. Phallic masturbation was given up, and for a short time she was again preoccupied with anal concerns. She withdrew completely from her brother and stated guiltily in analysis: "I will never forgive myself for not being friends with my brother."

She became "painfully shy" in her social contacts and lonely in school, a difficulty that persisted in her analysis. She complained of never having been able to carry on prolonged, close relationships with people, whether in her school years or later on, "though I am able to flirt now," she added. As an example she referred to a man who had flirted with her at a recent dinner party and who had said: "I always get scars from beautiful women."

She reported that she had worked harder than anyone else, both in school and in her art classes. She had felt she "had to," despite her intelligence and giftedness. As she described it, she worked "with the perspiration running down my face." She recalled the moment in grammar school when she made the decision "to become perfect in every way." One day she practiced sitting up perfectly straight in the car with her hands folded, the way her mother liked it. She waited for attention and praise, but none came, she sadly remembered. While her latency ideal to become "perfect" in every way had the character of unconscious atonement, in adolescence she developed narcissistic ambitions by deciding to become somebody special—we can presume: as special as she had experienced her brother to be in early childhood. Yet her desire to become a known painter had not led her beyond achieving a single "one-man show," because as soon as she discovered that her art instructor valued the work of one other student as much as her own, she gave up painting. She became the best player in an exclusive tennis club, but gave up playing altogether when her request to play opposite male players was not granted. One day, during her analysis, she accused herself of being unethical. It turned out that she had not invited her best friends, who had wanted to come, to a party she had given for some well-known celebrities.

The patient's conflict in the relationship to her brother remained her greatest concern in analysis. During one period of her treatment she contacted her brother and enjoyed a few weeks of pleasant meetings with him in the presence of her family. Once she even indulged in a *folie à deux* when she visited him alone and shared one of his marijuana cigarettes. However, a short time later she complained about her parents' softheartedness which made them pay for the brother's rent. Gradually her rejecting attitude toward him returned.

Satisfactory work could be achieved with regard to the patient's masochistic character traits, her infantile narcissism, and her need for a mother. She once told me: "If only you would give me the right advice, I would follow whatever you would recommend." Long periods of work were devoted to her sexual shortcomings based on her penis envy. The patient rationalized that her body must be built differently from that of the average woman. The conflict concerning her brother seemed to remain insoluble in analysis.

However, reality intervened at the time of her son's Bar Mitzvah, when the necessity arose to invite people for the occasion. At this time she returned to analysis (which we had terminated) with the fear that she might again be plagued by terrible guilt feelings if she would not invite her brother. After a renewed working through of her penis envy and her desire to "be the only boy" (in identification with her son) at the Bar Mitzvah, she decided not to include her brother among the guests and afterward she felt pleasure and satisfaction about not having experienced guilt reactions as a result. An important factor in this reaction was that in this situation her mother sided with her. The mother had prepared the brother by explaining to him that his sister did not wish to hurt him by the exclusion, but that their life styles had taken entirely different directions. One can say that once more the patient satisfied her envious desires, but this time on a psychologically permissible level.

DISCUSSION

While Ernst Kris (1956) emphasized that in the reconstructive work during analysis we may not always be able to distinguish between shock and strain trauma, there seems to be sufficient evidence in this case to speak of an accumulation of frustrating tensions that resulted in the violent breakthrough of aggressive drives. While the incident of her nipping her brother's penis can be called the traumatic event, its overwhelming traumatic influence stemmed primarily from the continuing strain and pressure of her guilt feelings.

In "Trauma, Strain, and Development," Sandler stressed the point that the repression of traumatic experiences is due to guilt (a common feature in the history of the Hampstead patients). The motive for the repression stems, not from the traumatic experience proper, but from fear of punishment, which is reflected in internal feelings of guilt, shame, and humiliation (see Furst, 1967).

In my patient it was the absence of punishment that greatly augmented her guilt feelings. Their persistence prevented her from overcoming the trauma and marred her subsequent development. This in turn led to the formation of an excessively severe superego and the retention of masochistic and infantile narcissistic traits. No beneficial change of superego and ego ideal occurred in her further development; on the contrary, the patient's ego continued to undergo painful distortions in order to fulfill the overwhelming demands she made of herself. It is a case of exaggerated adjustment to social demands at the price of incomplete functioning in an anguished life. When she stopped masturbating, her sexual excitement and fantasies could no longer be discharged, but from her life style we can see that her inner need to create scars in men, even if only in symbolic terms, and her need to measure up and compete with men continued in her life until she was analyzed.

But the traumatic event led not only to pathogenesis. This discussion would be incomplete if one were to overlook the patient's remarkable ego strength which allowed her to bear great anxieties and to develop her capacities for adaptation and sublimation. Beginning in latency she pursued her studies in painting; she broadened her intellect in school and college. She lived up to reality demands as a mother and wife and was respected as a civic leader. Last, but not least, her judgment told her to ask for help when she found herself in danger of losing control over her drives.

We have to leave open the question why in her adult life she suddenly felt overwhelmed by outer stimuli. As Anna Freud states: "An individual's adaptation to his environmental circumstances includes, of course, adaptation to the strains and dangers inherent in them. . . . It is unknown to us by what means people succeed under such conditions to raise their sensitivities as a safeguard against breakdown" (see Furst, 1967, p. 238).

A SHOCK TRAUMA

CASE PRESENTATION

Mary was referred to me for treatment when she was 13½ years old. She had previously undergone analysis in Switzerland for 10 months. Her former analyst sent me the following report:

> Mary felt friendless and extremely unhappy in school and had spent much time weeping in the evenings. However, her parents considered her to be the "easy" child of the two girls they had, her sister Lucy being about 3 years Mary's senior. It soon emerged that one precipitating factor in Mary's urgent need for help was her separation from her friend, Amy, whom she had to give up when the family moved to another country. This friendship was idealized and Mary's loss led her to fall back on her sister for friendship, but intense envy and jealousy of Mary made this impossible.
>
> Another basic problem was Mary's inhibition of aggression which affected all her relationships, but especially that with her mother, whom she regarded overtly as perfect until some of the sibling rivalry had been worked through. Mary appears to be highly intelligent and very sensitive. She has a good ego and an overstrict superego, both libidinal and aggressive drives are inhib-

ited so that she loses all pleasure in life, particularly through being
so painfully shy. She seems to be aware of this herself and her wish
to be cured is strong.

When Mary, a well-built and pretty girl, started to see me, she
corroborated her continuous feelings of sadness and her dislike of
her mother, whom she bitterly accused of preferring her sister.
Adding to her feelings of general unhappiness, she had imposed
upon herself the life of a hermit. She had no friends and never
invited or visited classmates. Very reluctantly she put up with her
parents' friends and their children when they came to the house.
The only relationship she pursued was that with her sister, although
she hated her for being her mother's favorite. While she enjoyed
sharing childhood memories with Lucy, she also liked the feeling of
looking down on her because of her inferior intelligence.

Her mother stated that it was "easy to have Mary around." She
was a quiet onlooker at home, always polite, but never actively
participating in family conversations and pursuits. She never
displayed aggression or hostility. When she was reprimanded for
not doing some chores, she never said: "I don't want to do it."
Rather she said: "I'll do it later" and she always did.

Mary's joyless life was intensified by eating fads. She would not
join the family for breakfast, but only gulped down her orange
juice. She ardently watched her diet so as not to put on weight. She
completely avoided physical contact with her parents, never kissing
or touching them. When they wished her "sleep well" in the
evening, she would respond jokingly, "I'll try."

In contrast to her complete emotional blocking, Mary showed
ego strength and superior capacity for sublimation. She very much
enjoyed studying, in school as well as at home. She never
complained about too much work. She also showed great skill and
persistence in dressmaking, an interest Mary had developed in
identification with her mother who spent much of her leisuretime
on this hobby.

Mary's mother was a warm, articulate, and rather dominating
woman, highly respected in the field of labor relations. She was
aware of her daughter's great intelligence and "individuality," as
she put it. At the same time she minimized Mary's pseudoadapta-

tion to life. She jokingly called her husband "a strange man," who was not as successful in his professional and social relationships as she was, but he had a better relationship with Mary. Both parents had been analyzed.

From the beginning of the analysis Mary was a difficult patient. She would jump onto the couch, unload her dislike of me, and idolize her previous analyst. At times her hostility toward me became so overwhelming that her whole body would stiffen in catatoniclike postures on the couch. At other times she would berate me for "not paying any attention to me despite all the material I am offering you"—material, in fact, which was unusable for interpretation. Referring to statements made in earlier sessions, or in analytic discussions at home, she would develop highly sophisticated psychoanalytic theories, including the value of masturbation, and would formulate them in ways an adult could have been proud of.

When she began to understand her reproaches as a craving for total attention, she told me in most apologetic terms of her mother's mistakes in the early upbringing of her sister. The mother had criticized herself for neglecting her older daughter Lucy as an infant. After her own analysis she was determined not to repeat the mistakes with Mary. Therefore she engaged baby-sitters for the two girls when she had to work at her writing at home. The arrangement allowed her to be near the children and to observe them from her room, and they, in turn, were able to see her. This had created a continuously frustrating atmosphere for the lively girls, because the baby-sitters kept them at a distance from their mother. Mary said that she had hated these baby-sitters, who also put the children to bed when the parents went out in the evening.

One of Mary's most painful memories of this time was of a threat by one sitter "to throw her out of the window" unless she would pray to God. Actually, the children were brought up without religious beliefs, but the incident led to phobic symptoms during Mary's early latency. Mary avoided going to places where she would have to face a statue of Christ on the Cross. In addition to such inner conflicts Mary had to adjust to numerous new and strange environments, since the family moved back and forth between several different countries. (Before she started treatment with me, the patient had already moved six times.)

The few pleasurable memories Mary reported from her prelatency period were of playing fantasy games with her sister in which the most prominent figure was a "bad witch." Other moments of happiness had occurred when the mother showed interest in Mary's early reading ability, her intelligence, and avid search for knowledge.

In treatment Mary gradually recognized that these early years had lacked the security, warmth, and closeness to her mother which she had needed. She also began to understand her far more positive feelings for her father as having grown out of oedipal longings.

After 18 months of analysis Mary's reticence and hostility had lessened to such a degree that her parents believed she was far happier than she had ever been before. Her mother called to say that she had received the first spontaneous kiss from her daughter.

Encouraged by such progress and in view of the fact that Mary would soon have to send off her applications for college, her parents requested a consultation to discuss Mary's potential readiness for leaving home and terminating treatment. It was planned that she should enroll in a good local college, move into a dormitory with other girls, and attempt to live more independently. Although great changes had occurred, Mary was still friendless. I had some trepidations about these plans, but hoped that more social gains could be achieved in the remaining nine months of treatment. This hope was, indeed, fulfilled. Mary's pride in soon reaching the age of 16 and in approaching college life considerably lessened her social inhibitions. She made contacts with youngsters her own age and established a real friendship with a boy who had been introduced to her by her mother. In addition, Mary showed brilliant achievements in her senior year in high school.

At this time a most unexpected shift occurred in the treatment situation. One day Mary refused to continue lying on the couch, insisting on sitting up and facing me in her sessions. My acceptance of this was based upon the assumption that the young adolescent's growing-up process had to be respected and that analytic interference might lead to too much resistance. As a result, Mary's vivid dreams and associations led to the recall of a traumatic experience which had been completely repressed until this time.

Mary's family had always spent three months in the summer vacationing at the grandparents' farm in the country. A Negro couple, with children of their own, did farmwork and helped in the grandparents' house. The husband, though reputedly a drunkard and unreliable character, was considered to be somewhat of an adopted son to Mary's grandfather, who had shown interest in him and attempted to improve the man's lot.

One day after the man had done some repair work in the grandparents' house, he invited Mary to come with him to watch the milking of the cows. Full of confidence she put her little hand into his big one and went with him to the barn. Once there, he threw himself into the hay, held Mary, and forced her to commit fellatio. The man's wife, who obviously had become suspicious, came after them and saved Mary from being further molested. She took the child to her own house, cleaned her mouth and teeth, and gave her honey and other sweets to eat. Afterward, Mary played with the couple's children before she ran home, having been warned "not to tell anything." Mary was 6 years old at the time.

This traumatic event had occurred just prior to the departure of Mary's family for a different country, where they stayed for one year. During this year Mary was taught by a Negro teacher in school and, despite her mother's presence and insistence that she shake hands with the teacher, Mary refused. About a year later, again in another city, Mary pleaded with her mother to dismiss a Negro domestic. Although no one in the family understood why the child disliked the woman so intensely, her mother gave in to Mary's desperate pleading. Following this incident complete repression seemed to have taken place, because Mary showed no further acute problems on a trip to South Africa where, instead, her intellectual curiosity was highly stimulated.

Mary's reactions to the reconstruction of the trauma showed a strange mixture of excitement and sober confirmation, which she summed up by stating: "That sounds reasonable." The trauma had emerged shortly before Mary's vacation which she was to spend at the very place where the event had occurred. There was no time to work through the painful consequences this episode had had on her life. Her subsequent letters showed a relatively stable, though ambivalent transference. The first letter from her vacation arrived right after her departure.

> Dear Mrs. Ruben,
>
>   I am writing to you now so that I can be sure that I will start writing and not keep putting it off, as I have this evening been planning to. I decided that otherwise I might never write (like last summer) and that would be awful. I am pushing myself to do this in somewhat the same way as we talked about my pushing myself to be a sales girl this summer to prove nothing will happen again like the thing in the barn and everything is really all right. Yesterday was quite nice. I didn't feel my hour with you was very successful, but then again it wasn't so bad either. I felt in one way rather that we should have done something very important and have a very good hour as the last one. But I suppose that's actually quite silly, since it was the end and everything. But I would have liked you to say something about the dreams that I told you about, but still I suppose you wouldn't even have been wanting to start anything very new, or even not new, but semi-new. (Maybe I also didn't like being let out early, but actually neither yesterday nor today do I feel very angry with you.)

The second letter arrived two months later.

> Dear Mrs. Ruben,
>
>   I am sorry that I have not written again since June, but I suppose that I am angry that I can't instead see you and also (though quite logically) writing is quite unsatisfactory in all sorts of ways and makes me sad that I can't express what I want to or tell you everything.
>
>   I quit my sales job one week ago as I got very tired from it and could do very little else due to both exhaustion and working hours that were longer than I expected. It was lonely even though it was nice to get out of the house and feel independent, but the money and independence weren't enough to make up for my feeling that I was having no summer holiday at all.
>
>   I feel a bit lonely and sad and find myself much more dependent on my family, but I don't want to be a sales girl again. I am thinking about less exhausting and time-consuming jobs for next summer. I think I shall soon settle down, though, as I have not had

a normal first week of liberation (grandparents were keeping me busy—now they have left). The summer, generally, so far, has been very nice in that I have been quite happy and never depressed to any degree. . . .

Thank you for your note, though I think that I was disappointed with it.

I look forward to seeing you in Sept. (around the 13th) and will hopefully write again before then.

I will go into depth about all this later when I can talk (quickly) and tell you everything.

I had a dream last night in which you were saying that I was still very neurotic because I hadn't written you during the summer. I was frightened and angry and felt that my analysis would never finish and sad that I hadn't written (which was the main reason for your feeling I was so neurotic). So now I write.

Love,
Mary

P.S. Reading the letter over, it all sounds very sad. I am truly happy this summer and having a nice time. Don't take it all too gravely.

Immediately upon Mary's return from her vacation it became obvious that her former stable working alliance was considerably shaken. In spite of her conscious wish to keep the traumatic seduction a secret from her parents, Mary dreamed and associated hardly anything but topics concerned with talking, telling, speaking, responding, until she was ready to accept her unconscious burning desire to let her parents know of the event in the past. But before she finally requested that I should talk about it with her parents, Mary went into a tailspin of denial, projection, and particularly identification with the aggressor. She would say, for example: "I really don't remember anything. It was you who said it," defending herself in this way against her intense feelings of guilt. For 10 years she had guiltily avoided social contacts outside of her home, preventing the danger of sexual excitement and possible punishment.

When her parents showed their understanding for her frightening early experience, Mary, freed from guilt feelings, began to excel at school and was declared an "immediate senior": she received

official recognition of early fulfillment of the academic requirements for college entrance. This achievement had repercussions in
her relationship with her parents and with her analyst. Mary
became independent with a vengeance. She insisted on following
her own choice of a college that was 3,000 miles from home. Her
narcissistic pride would allow her nothing less than an Ivy-League
college. She also initiated a sexual relationship with her boyfriend,
which in some aspects was an aggressive repetition of her traumatic
experience in the past. She stayed away from home weekends in
spite of her parents' protests.

At this time in the treatment she arrived one day in great alarm,
fearing she was pregnant. She refused to discuss the situation with
me and threatened to discontinue treatment if I told her parents.
She wanted to solve the problem on her own by going to the Free
Clinic and being examined. Further discussion revealed that her
sexual relationship with her boyfriend consisted only of mutual
masturbation. She feared that the boy's semen, which had landed
on her legs, might have caused a pregnancy.

After the doctor at the Free Clinic had reassured her that her fear
was groundless, she refused the pills offered to her in case her
relationship should progress to sexual intercourse. In her irrational
state of mind she maintained that her parents would not approve of
it. This incident seemed to betray an acting out of her former
fantasy life around the trauma and threw light on her eating
problems as a fear of oral impregnation. Unfortunately most of her
fantasy material was withheld by her in her analysis. After the
clearing up of her unconscious anxiety and the acceptance of her
wish to remain a virgin, she gratefully volunteered to help in the
Clinic until she left for college and did excellent work in interview-
ing and helping clinic patients who were in need of jobs.

Amidst this onrush of exciting activities Mary also became a
social leader among her classmates. Driven as in euphoria, she
finally broke off her analysis before she left for college.

The parents, overwhelmed by what they called Mary's "independence" and her academic and social successes, became totally
permissive, giving in to all of her wishes and decisions. They met my
doubts in her readiness for college life at a great distance (the first
time away from home) and without therapeutic help with the

verdict: "She is much stronger than you think." (And it turned out that they were right.)

All of Mary's applications to first-rate colleges had been accepted and she had greatly impressed all interviewers. She delighted in flying across the country to acquaint herself with the college of her choice and otherwise preparing for her departure.

It turned out that Mary's self-determination to lead a life on her own was severely threatened when the first four months of college and dormitory life became almost unbearable for her as well as for her parents. She was desperate she might not be able to succeed academically. She telephoned home long distance almost daily, wavering in moods from utter despair to "feeling fine, just fine." Her mother was able to arrange no less than six visits with Mary during this time. Each time she found her daughter in continuous tears, which turned into "merciless arrogance" (the mother's own words) when returning home was offered. Mary engaged a tutor and sought psychiatric help at college. She spent her weekends with her boyfriend, who attended another college and had a job in a nearby town. Their meetings consisted mostly of Mary's crying on his shoulder and being comforted. Above all she worked at her class assignments in the library of his school, in endless fear of not being able to pass her mid-term exams. At Christmas she came home and spent her entire vacation studying.

When she had passed the exams with quite satisfactory grades, the crying spells stopped immediately and Mary was rarely anxious or sad again. She reduced her relationship with her boyfriend to a minimum and began dating other students. Her next vacation at home was free from any studies, her contacts with her former classmates were lively, and at the end of the college year she received, to her own surprise, very good grades, which again heightened her self-esteem to a great degree. She now lives a typical student life and feels no further needs for psychiatric help.

DISCUSSION

In her paper on "The Influence of Infantile Trauma on Genetic Patterns," Greenacre stressed the fact that "there are true accidents of fate in which the child has no part in the provocation [of a traumatic event]. These may have the severest sequelae because 'out of the blue' they may overfulfill the child's most powerful fantasies, thereby arousing feelings both of guilt and of omnipotence. . . . they may seriously distort the actual conditions of the child's life" (see Furst, 1967, p. 134).

Studies of children subjected to traumatic events have shown that the frightening, overstimulating occurrence is not understood objectively, but is interpreted by them in terms of their fantasies and their previous experiences. Apparently, Mary had considered the seduction as something of her own doing. At the time of the trauma she had reached the object-centered, phallic-oedipal phase of development. One may wonder whether her fantasy life at that time had not coincided with the reality of dangerous inner urges of oedipal origin, which had been displaced and externalized. Her guilt feelings became evident when she insisted in treatment that she "had been much younger" at the time of the seduction. (Mary's mother confirmed that Mary had been 6 years old because she remembered without difficulty her child's agitation during that particular summer. She herself had linked it up with "either penis envy or masturbation anxiety" and had tried to be reassuring.)

Mary's silence, her self-imposed isolation at home, her ascetic tendencies indicate her latent guilt feelings, which were strengthened by the expressed threat "not to tell anything." She tried to escape into a narcissistic withdrawal. She decided to renounce her need for love and to become self-sufficient. With this goal she was bound to fail. She found some security in being the overly submissive child and courting her mother's appreciation by her intellectual superiority, but her sadness betrayed her helplessness.

The strength of Mary's defenses to guard herself from inner and outer dangers was matched by her unusual capacity for sublimation. She put the same emotional distance between herself and her family as her mother had done with her sister and her. She identified herself with her hard-working mother by being a presence *without contact* while studying and enjoying her own work thoroughly. Sublimation for her was not only a change in mode of energy away from the instinctual toward the noninstinctual (Freud,

1926), but it provided her ego with a different range of aims and activities. Above all, it saved her from more serious psychopathology.

Gross and Rubin (1972) point out that sublimatory activity plays at times a crucial role in the maintenance of reality. This is illuminated in certain pathological states where the sublimation survives as the only bridge to reality and as the sole representative of the object world. Mary's sublimatory activity following the shock trauma not only served defensive and adaptive purposes; it also aided her identification with the studious and active mother. In this way the child was kept in contact with parts of her object world, despite its deprivations. Sublimatory efforts secured object contact and established narcissistic pride and self-esteem.

Summary

In *Moses and Monotheism* Freud (1939) states:

> The effects of traumas are of two kinds, positive and negative. The former are attempts to bring the trauma into operation once again—that is, to remember the forgotten experience or, better still, to make it real, to experience a repetition of it anew, or, even if it was only an early emotional relationship, to revive it in an analogous relationship with someone else. We summarize these efforts under the name of 'fixations' to the trauma and as a 'compulsion to repeat'. . . .
>
> The negative reactions follow the opposite aim: that nothing of the forgotten traumas shall be remembered and nothing repeated. We can summarize them as 'defensive reactions'. Their principal expressions are what are called 'avoidances', which may be intensified into 'inhibitions' and 'phobias'. . . . Fundamentally they are just as much fixations to the trauma as their opposites, except that they are fixations with a contrary purpose [p. 75f.].

Mrs. Z. developed positive reactions to her trauma by wanting to remember the forgotten experience, to make it real, to experience a repetition of it anew. As a result of her self-inflicted trauma she developed an unusually harsh superego and masochistic character traits. Her guilt feelings became the leitmotiv of her life and stimulated a constant fight against her sexual-aggressive drives, which she could never appease but also never suppress for good. However, she remained capable of object love and adaptation to reality. Her sublimatory faculties not only served her personal needs, but were also directed to humanitarian interests.

Mary's reactions to the shock trauma were the negative ones described by Freud. Her feelings of guilt forced her into a retrogressive level of development in which her hatred of her mother gained the upper hand. She avoided outer danger by staying at home or in school, and she protected herself from further inner sexual stimuli by giving up any physical contact with the family. Her sleeping disturbances betrayed her remaining masturbation conflict, and her depressive moods, her sadness, induced an almost complete withdrawal from outer reality, so that she increasingly led the life of a hermit. Her sublimatory efforts served primarily narcissistic purposes and remained her only foothold in reality.

There is no doubt that her pathology was far more severe than that of Mrs. Z. Without analysis Mary's symptomatology would not have taken a turn for the better and would seriously have jeopardized her future development. The severity and nature of her pathological reaction to the trauma resembled those of the patients Anny Katan describes in her paper "Children Who Were Raped." She writes (1973, p. 221): "The tremendous excitement that was aroused in these patients made all their conflicts extraordinarily intense; hence the abnormal amount and quality of guilt that they were forced to cope with."

BIBLIOGRAPHY

Freud, A. (1965), *Normality and Pathology in Childhood.* New York: International Universities Press.

Freud, S. (1926), Inhibitions, Symptoms and Anxiety. *Standard Edition*, 20:77–175. London: Hogarth Press, 1959.

——— (1939), Moses and Monotheism. *Standard Edition*, 23:3–137. London: Hogarth Press, 1964.

Furst, S. S., ed. (1967), *Psychic Trauma.* New York: Basic Books.

Gross, G. E. & Rubin, I. A. (1972), Sublimation. *This Annual*, 27:334–359.

KATAN, A. (1973), Children Who Were Raped. *This Annual*, 28:208–224.

KHAN, M. M. R. (1963), The Concept of Cumulative Trauma. *This Annual*, 18:286–306.

KRIS, E. (1956), The Recovery of Childhood Memories in Psychoanalysis. *This Annual*, 11:54–88.

A Filmed Fairy Tale As a Screen Memory

SANFORD SCHREIBER, M.D.

THIS CLINICAL STUDY FOCUSES ON THE SPECIFIC USE ONE GIRL made of a filmed fairy tale that she saw at the age of 7, several months before she was separated from her mother for a 6-month period. The fairy tale was *The Wizard of Oz*. The fact that my patient, whose case I shall report, saw the movie and did not read the book was most significant in her use of this filmed tale to form a screen memory. The purpose of the screen memory was to help repress this most painful period. In my presentation, I shall focus on those aspects of the analysis which illuminate the formation of the screen memory and not include a more complete discussion of the course of the patient's analysis.

Freud (1913) noted the relationship between fairy tales and screen memories when he wrote, "In a few people a recollection of their favourite fairy tales takes the place of memories of their own childhood; they have made the fairy tales into screen memories" (p. 281). Investigations of the significance of fairy tales for a child's fantasy life (e.g., Buxbaum, 1941; Desmonde, 1951; Ferenczi, 1926; Fraiberg, 1954; Huckel, 1957; Petty, 1953; Rowley, 1951) have all referred to a fairy tale which was either heard or read by a child. In my patient, the visual presentation of the fairy tale was crucial in establishing the screen memory.

Associate Clinical Professor, Yale University School of Medicine; Director of Education and Training, Psychiatry Service, West Haven Veterans Administration Hospital.

I wish to thank Dr. William Pious for his valuable suggestions.

The Literature on Screen Memories

When Freud (1899) first discussed screen memories, he was astonished by the fact that the earliest childhood recollections were concerned with everyday and indifferent events described in great detail, while known significant events, laden with affect, were not recalled. He concluded that these indifferent memories were the result of two opposing forces, the force to remember and a resistance to prevent painful remembering. A compromise is reached in a memory which is substituted for the significant impression and which owes its preservation to an associative relationship with the repressed memory. Since the objectionable elements are eliminated, the resulting memory is often trivial. These screen memories have distinctive features. They are remembered in great detail. Their content is usually indifferent. They are predominantly visual and are remembered in an observing, detached way as if watching oneself perform. This contrast between an acting and a recollecting ego meant that the original impression had been altered. Also, the screening images possessed unusually intense sensory impressions.

Freud (1901) later noted a common quality shared by screen memories and the forgetting of names. Both showed a displacement along superficial associations. He also observed how it was often necessary to know the life history of an individual in order to demonstrate that a childhood memory was a screen memory. Freud (1913) believed that screen memories latently retain all essential childhood experiences. Freud (1910, 1917) provided clinical examples in his analyses of the childhood screen memories of Goethe and Leonardo da Vinci.

Fenichel (1927), elaborating on Freud's papers, believed that screen memories served an economic function. Since repression requires constant energy, screen memories allow repressed material to reach consciousness via displacement. The discharge permitted through this safety valve reduces the work needed for repression. Fenichel spoke of a "hunger for screen experiences" (1927, p. 114), when the ego searches for substitute ideas which are a compromise between the push for recognition of painful percepts and the repressing ego. When substitutive images are found which can be made conscious, relief is obtained and the forgetting of an unpleasant experience is made easier.

Greenacre (1949) significantly contributed to an understanding of the special intensity, brightness, and visual qualities which are so characteristic of screen memories. She hypothesized that the severity of the trauma produces an overflow in the form of a secondary visual excitement. The shock character contributes directly to the bright edge and vividness of the screen memory by means of displacement from the central stress to peripheral innocuous details. The detached quality is attributed to the superego which causes an intense watchful state. Analysis of screen memories is resisted and, where connections are made, it is usually only toward the end of the analysis.

Greenacre (1947) describes the visual experience of a psychic shock, where the overwhelmed child feels bewildered, and can experience sensations of lights, flashes of lightning, bright colors, or an aurora effect. The most common events producing such visual overstimulation in a child are the sight of the adult genitalia of the opposite sex and the witnessing of childbirth. There is a peculiar peripheral luminosity which is characteristic of a screen memory. Affect and color influence each other. While strong emotion can arouse color sensations, the opposite is also true, as in the stimulation of affect from the sudden introduction of color in the Rorschach cards.

A number of other psychoanalysts (e.g., Abraham, 1913; Lathbury, 1957; Simmel, 1925) have described specific screen memories and the conflict-laden earlier memories concealed behind this screen. While Anna Freud (1951) observed that innumerable traumatic memories may be telescoped in a single screen memory, Glover (1956) and Greenacre (1950) have noted that the memories of traumatic events in childhood should be carefully examined for their own screening function. Greenacre observed that prepubertal traumatic events may be induced by a girl to screen the effects of earlier intense preoedipal genital stimulation in which the girl was the passive victim. The affect associated with the more overwhelming earlier seduction is successfully screened by the later prepubertal trauma.

Rose (1960) reports a homicide, where associated screen memories served as an attempt to master, through reenactment, traumatic experiences associated with the primal scene. Reider (1953) has demonstrated that an interpretation which is a reconstruction is followed by screen memories that are derivatives of the unconscious material. The reconstruction is experienced as a command to remember, a reaction first noted by Fenichel (1928). The unconscious memories stimulated by this type of interpretation reach consciousness by associative screening memories.

The repetitive effect of a special screen memory on the writing of Lewis Carroll is described by Greenacre (1955). Of considerable interest is the life of Lyman Frank Baum, who wrote his first successful book, *The Wizard of Oz* (1900), at the age of 44 (see F. Baum and Mac Fall, 1961). An investigation of his life and a reconstruction of the psychic events that influenced his writing this fairy tale will be the subject of a future study.

One reference to the specific use of a fairy tale serving as a screen memory is in a footnote in Freud's paper, "Childhood Memories and Screen Memories" (1901). Unfortunately, no further information is available about the case cited or the name of the speaker. Freud, reacting to a paper given before 1904 at the weekly Vienna Psychoanalytic Society meetings, wrote this poetic analogy, "Dr. B—showed very neatly one Wednesday that fairy tales can be made use of as screen memories in the same kind of way that empty shells are used as a home by the hermit crab. These fairy tales then become favourites, without the reason being known" (p. 49).

Synopsis of The Wizard of Oz

The movie[1] opens with Dorothy and her dog, Toto, returning to their Kansas farmhouse, owned by her uncle and aunt. Dorothy is fearful that a spinster neighbor will have Toto killed for biting her. Her aunt, uncle, and three farmhands ignore Dorothy's fears until the neighbor appears with a court order to take Toto to the Sheriff to be killed. Auntie Em and Uncle Henry reluctantly agree, but Toto jumps out of the neighbor's basket and returns to Dorothy.

---

[1] This is a synopsis of the 1939 MGM movie. The patient saw this movie and did not read or hear the fairy tale.

Dorothy decides to run away and meets Professor Marvel who can see the future in his crystal ball. He convinces Dorothy to return home, but a cyclone suddenly appears. Her aunt, uncle, and farmhands enter their underground storm cellar, but Dorothy returns too late; the cellar door is locked. She then runs into the house and is hit on the head by a loose window, falling on her bed.

Suddenly, the house is lifted into the sky and objects fly by. The neighbor turns into a witch on a broomstick and the house finally falls to the ground. Dorothy opens the door and, at this moment, the film changes from sepia tone to technicolor as the opened door reveals the Land of Oz. All the subsequent scenes in the Land of Oz are in technicolor

The house lands on the Wicked Witch of the East, killing her. Glinda, the good Witch of the North, advises Dorothy to take the dead witch's ruby slippers which will protect her. The Munchkins dwarfs who live in the East of Oz rejoice. Dorothy wishes to return home and is told by Glinda to follow the Yellow Brick Road which will take her to the Emerald City where the Wizard of Oz lives. He may be able to tell her how to return home. The Wicked Witch of the West appears, is menacing, and leaves; but she is able to observe Dorothy's actions by looking into her crystal ball.

Along the Yellow Brick Road, Dorothy meets the Scarecrow who wants brains, the Tin Woodsman who wants a heart, and the Cowardly Lion who wants courage. They join Dorothy in her search for the great Wizard in the hope that they can also be helped. The Scarecrow, Tin Woodsman, and Lion were the farmhands back in Kansas.

The group reaches the Emerald City despite the Witch's attempts to foil them. They are taken to the throne room of the Wizard of Oz where, behind smoke and flames, a huge image of a head appears. They make their requests and the Wizard says they must bring back the broomstick of the Witch of the West, proving their worth before he grants their wishes.

The group has several adventures before finding the Witch, capped by Dorothy throwing a bucket of water at the Witch who begins to melt and finally disappears. They bring the broomstick back to the Wizard. Toto pulls back the curtain revealing an elderly man working the controls and speaking into a microphone.

The group is furious, calling him a humbug and a bad man. The Wizard replies, "I'm a very good man, I'm just a very bad Wizard." But he then gives a diploma to the Scarecrow, a medal to the Cowardly Lion, and a testimonial to the Tin Woodsman, symbolizing the brains, courage, and heart, they wanted. To help her return home, the Wizard offers to take Dorothy with him in a balloon that first brought him to Oz from a Midwestern carnival show. Unfortunately, the balloon begins to rise with only the Wizard inside, for Dorothy was distracted chasing Toto. But Glinda, the good Witch of the North, arrives and tells Dorothy that she always had the power to return to Kansas but that she had to learn first that her heart's desire was only to be found at home. Dorothy is told to tap the heels of her magic slippers together three times and think, "There's no place like home."

Dorothy does this and suddenly awakens in her bed in Kansas, surrounded by Auntie Em, Uncle Henry, the three farmhands, and Professor Marvel. At this moment, the film changes from technicolor back to sepia. Dorothy is told that she had a bad dream. She insists that she was at a real place called Oz where she kept on saying that she wanted to go home. The movie ends with Dorothy saying, "And I'm not going to leave here ever, ever again, because I love you all. And, oh, Auntie Em, there's no place like home!"

Case Presentation

Background Material

I shall focus only on the significant events in the patient's life and on those aspects of her analysis that have a direct bearing on the screen memory. Mrs. R. began psychoanalysis at the age of 30. She had four children, ranging in age from 12 to 3. Separated from her husband for one year, she was legally divorced two months before she began analysis. She was married at 18 because she became pregnant. The following year, her husband left his job and he never worked throughout their marriage. They were supported by his father. In psychotherapy for one year, she was encouraged by her previous therapist to make a decision about her marriage before beginning psychoanalysis and she chose divorce.

Mrs. R. had a Protestant mother and a Jewish father. She had a brother, 3 years older. Her mother had sudden mood changes which the patient later understood to be due to her mother's drinking. Her father regularly appeared nude in front of the family. She recalled peeking into her parents' bedroom and seeing her father hurting her mother in a struggle. She had been involved in sex play with an older male cousin whose penis she had handled, wishing to break it off and have it for her own. She remembered her childhood as having been happy until the age of 5 when she first noticed her parents fighting. Her mother then brought strange men to the apartment, and the girl was left more frequently in the care of the housekeeper.

When the girl was 7, Mrs. R.'s mother suddenly left her husband and children and followed her boyfriend to California where she divorced her husband and married this man. After a separation of six months, Mrs. R. and her brother, accompanied by an elderly unknown woman, left their father and traveled by train across the United States to live with her mother and stepfather. It was their stepfather's third marriage. The girl initially lived with her new stepsiblings, who were 10 to 15 years older. When she was 11, her brother was sent away to school. She was often left alone at night in their big house overlooking the ocean.

The following year, Mrs. R.'s stepfather enlisted in the army during World War II. Her mother, brother, and she then moved to her mother's parents' home in Ohio, where she enjoyed riding horses. They moved back to Boston shortly before her stepfather's return, and her mother began seeing boyfriends again. Her mother and stepfather then returned to California, and the patient, now 13, moved to Rome with her father and new stepmother, where she lived for one year. Returning at 14, she was sent to boarding school for the next three years. She enjoyed drama, singing, and foreign languages, and performed sufficiently well to be accepted by an excellent university.

She met her husband-to-be during her sophomore year at this university. Upset by her own wishes to terminate the relationship she became pregnant by him. Because of her agitation following her pregnancy, she consulted an analyst. She finally decided to marry. Shortly after the marriage, Mrs. R. felt that she had made a serious mistake. Throughout the 12 years of marriage, she turned to her father-in-law for counsel, until she told him of her wish to leave his son. The father-in-law had a heart attack soon thereafter, and she then decided to seek professional help.

ANALYTIC MATERIAL

Early in her analysis, Mrs. R. stated that there was a 6-month period in her life about which she had no memory. This period began when her mother left her in Boston when she was 7 and ended at the moment of reunion with her mother in California 6 months later. One of her expressed goals for analysis was to discover what had happened and how she felt during this time.

Initially, she had only two memories of this 6-month period. On one occasion, she recalled sitting in the living room, seeing an image of her mother sitting in another chair. Another time, she remembered being afraid to sail with her father for fear of drowning. As the analysis progressed, she slowly recalled other incidents from this period. She remembered returning home immediately after school. She would then go to her room and play with dolls. She was very frightened of her father who often returned home after she had gone to bed. She recalled an especially terrifying visual image which occurred while she was lying in bed pretending to be asleep. Father opened the door to her room and she could see his outline in the door, framed by a *peculiarly intense* bright light behind him. At such moments, she was terrified that he would attack her. She visualized this particular image on several occasions during the analysis. For example, once while sleeping in a motel with her daughter, someone tried opening the latched door. The patient screamed with terror before realizing that it was a lost boy. She associated her intense fear to the image of her father at the door of her room.

Mrs. R. saw the film, *The Wizard of Oz*, when she was 7. She did not remember who went with her to see the movie, but recalled enjoying the film. She expressed surprise when her own children were frightened by the movie, for it was the reverse of her own remembered childhood experience. She especially admired the courage of the heroine, Dorothy. She enjoyed the fact that the evil Witch was Dorothy's problem to face and that she was only a spectator. She also recalled feeling disappointed when Dorothy returned home to bleak Kansas. The most significant moment of the film, for her, occurred when Dorothy, transported to Oz, opens the door of her house. At this point the film changed from sepia tone to technicolor. In response to this recollection, she recalled a feeling of happiness and awe which directly reminded her of her reunion with mother in sunny, beautiful California after spending 6 months in a dark, dreary Boston apartment.

Mrs. R. had no memory for the moment when she was separated from her mother. At first, she hypothesized that her mother had not mentioned that she was leaving and had gone away without warning. In the third year of her analysis, she began thinking that her mother had told her, but that she could not remember it now. She recalled an image of an empty corridor outside her apartment leading to the elevator, but there were no people present. This image persisted until separation from her mother was revived in the transference during the termination phase and she finally recalled and reexperienced the moment when her mother had left.

The meaning of Mrs. R.'s frequent associations to the film did not become clear until the final year of her analysis. In reviewing the case material, I was struck by the fact that whenever her associations led to *The Wizard of Oz*, she was experiencing a real or imagined separation from an important person. References to Oz occurred when I had just announced an intended vacation, or had just returned from vacation. When she thought of terminating her analysis, she immediately associated to *The Wizard of Oz*. When she experienced an increase in sexual feelings, she considered eloping with a boyfriend. At these times, fearing my jealous reaction, and concerned that I would leave her because of her sexual desire, she recalled various incidents from *The Wizard of Oz*. Other references to *The Wizard of Oz* occurred when her parents were about to leave her after a visit and return to California, when a close female neighbor was preparing to move away, when her son had not slept at home the night before, and when her father had stopped sending monthly checks. Thus it was clear that associations to *The Wizard of Oz* indicated the experience of a significant personal loss.

On examining the associations during the week following each reference to *The Wizard of Oz*, a pattern began to emerge. She had always stated that the most significant event in the movie was the moment when Dorothy opens the door of her house and sees Oz for the first time, which is also the moment when the movie changes from sepia to technicolor. And she always associated this moment to the actual reunion with her mother in sunny California, after a bleak winter in a dark, gloomy apartment. Thus, it seemed at first that *The Wizard of Oz* symbolized reunion with her mother. But the associations that followed *The Wizard of Oz* in the analysis repetitively recaptured her emotional state, not after the reunion with her mother, but after the abandonment by her mother. The associations recall how she must have experienced this critical period during her mother's absence.

One group of associations consisted of a variety of feared retaliations, especially abandonment, for feeling happy, for feeling sexually aroused by a man, or for experiencing murderous wishes. Another group of associations referred to an angry or fearful relationship with a male authority figure in her present life, after a maternal figure leaves. A third group referred directly to fantasies and feelings experienced during abandonment. These fantasies included the fear of starving, the wish to become pregnant and marry, the wish for perfect parents, and the need to choose one object from two men present (mother left her with Mrs. R.'s father and brother, and mother had a husband and boyfriend).

In addition, the periods of her analysis following thoughts of *The Wizard of Oz* were especially rich in fantasy themes which centered around the attempt to answer two questions. Why did mother leave? How can I be reunited with mother? She felt that only if she could answer these questions could she master the trauma and helplessness of separation from her mother. Associations related to why mother left included these explanations. Mother left because she had died. The girl wanted her mother dead in order to have father for herself. Here, the departure of her mother meant that the patient's murderous wishes were truly destructive. At other times, she felt that her mother left her because of the girl's evil sexual desires and love for a man. This provoked mother's jealousy and punishment of her.

In another group of fantasies she was concerned about how she could be reunited with her mother. The use of magic was one way she fantasied such a reunion. She recalled hoping that her brother, who performed magic tricks, could restore mother; and this reminded her of the magical Wizard's power in Oz. Her disappointment in the Wizard was equated with her disillusionment with her brother's failure to make mother reappear, as well as her disappointment with her analyst for not transforming her.

A third group of fantasies defended against the painful affect of loss through the reversal of roles. Instead of the patient being the lost Dorothy threatened by the evil witch mother, she pictured her mother as lost and herself as the witch. The image of her mother trying to find her was a projection of her own sense of loss and helplessness. In this identification with the aggressor, she felt that she was the wicked Witch. When people important to her withdrew their affection, it made her feel like a witch. When her father stopped sending a monthly check or when the analyst was silent, she associated to the feeling that she was shrinking like the wicked Witch after Dorothy had thrown water on her. She felt she was not loved because she was evil. The associative context before and after references to *The Wizard of Oz* could then be pieced together into a reconstruction of the girl's psychic life during her mother's absence.

Screen Memory Formation in the Analysis

On the first occasion when the analyst raised the subject of termination, Mrs. R. began to cry. She then said,

> I don't like to think about stopping my analysis. I don't know what would replace it. I always have to be replacing things. I have this picture of opening a door and beyond it, it is very bright, nice, but empty. I have the sense of an irreplaceable loss. I don't know what that would be. It is like the loss of one's children. *It reminds me of Oz.* Oz was very beautiful and very bright. I was very impressed when the movie changed from black and white to color. I was never scared of Oz like my children were. It was a secure place, very far away like I felt in California, with plenty of space, where I went wandering around. The place was empty of people. Just a lot of space to walk around and discover new things.

Mrs. R.'s expectation of losing her analyst revives in the transference the affect she experienced when she felt abandoned by her mother. But she is unable to make this most painful connection. At first, she imagines the loss of her children rather than that of her mother. Then she recalls Oz. As soon as she remembers Oz, she is able to maintain her repression for that period when she was separated from her mother. For the thought of Oz enables her to associate directly to California, the place representing reunion with mother. Here, the association to Oz serves as a screen memory by allowing her to reverse the affect of a painful loss to one of discovery. And the visual image chosen with its peculiar quality of intense brightness provides an ideal associative visual link. The memory of being left by her mother is captured in the last visual impression of her mother as she walked out the door of their apartment. Mrs. R. recalled this image only after she had already remembered many of the fantasies, wishes, and fears experienced during separations from her mother. The visual image that she had repressed was the picture of her mother at the door, leaving with a *bright* light behind her—the moment that was associated with her feeling an irreplaceable loss, an emptiness. The image that she chose to substitute was from a movie that she had seen several months before. In *The Wizard of Oz*, the girl is also looking through an open door from inside the house. But now the outside is not empty. On the contrary, the outside is suddenly filled with beautiful color and is a lovely scene. The visual image in the movie has an especially powerful impact because of the sudden and unexpected introduction of color into the movie. The sudden change to technicolor was an interesting film device to dramatize the event.

That color is introduced when a new world is discovered is intriguing. Calef (1954) writes that color in dreams is the last line of defense against the arousal of a particular affect. Color helped this scene to be chosen as a screen memory to substitute for the image of mother's departure. Not only was the content similar—looking out through an open door—but the sudden introduction of color is similar to the shock effect described by Greenacre (1947) when a psychic trauma is experienced as an overwhelming visual sensation of lights, halo, and color. When Mrs. R. was searching for screen experiences to help repress the painful percept, the dramatic, similar visual image of her recent past was most available. Instead of feeling loss, she recalled the discovery of a beautiful scene, where an object was found, not lost.

On the next occasion when the subject of termination was raised, Mrs. R. again immediately recalled Oz:

> I am afraid of making a mistake, afraid of feeling empty once again, like I felt as a child. I guess I'm afraid that I'll feel like I did at 8. That I'll go back to the way I used to be. *But also I'm reminded of Oz.*
>
> When Dorothy returned home to Kansas, I was disappointed. The color changed back again to black and white. If the color had remained, I would not have felt as badly. But she was back in bleak Kansas. She should have stayed in colorful Oz where everything was so interesting.
>
> I had to admire her for wanting to go back home. I also admired her for she was not afraid of the Witch. She went after her and eventually killed her. I was impressed with that.
>
> Oz was also the story of my life because the change from Kansas to Oz was exactly how I felt when I went from Boston to California. When I got off the train, my feeling was as different as Dorothy's coming to Oz for the first time. And there was traveling to it too, with the cyclone reminding me of the train ride. You didn't know what would happen next. Also, the Witch was always there. She would suddenly appear in the background at unexpected times. That's how I felt. That there was always some evil presence lurking in the background.
>
> But I always enjoyed seeing the Witch because Dorothy had to face her, not me. It was a welcome change.
>
> I could never understand why she went back to Kansas. Even though there were evil witches in Oz, there were also good witches.

Recalling the empty feeling after her mother's departure, here revived by the consideration of termination with her analyst, Mrs. R. is again immediately reminded of Oz. But why was my patient disappointed when Dorothy returned to Kansas, for Dorothy was actually most happy to be back? As long as Dorothy was still searching for her lost parents, Mrs. R. could identify with her and hope that Dorothy would find her missing good parents in a manner that would also provide a magical solution for the patient. Dorothy's solution was to come to terms with her own parents who actually did care for her. But Mrs. R.'s experience as she traveled back and forth from California to Ohio and then to Boston and Rome was that she never had both a loving mother and father. While all children at one time wish for the idealized parents of the family romance fantasy, it is easier to come to terms with one's parents, as Dorothy did, when they actually do care. But a child who does not have parents who are lovingly protective must remain dissatisfied with Dorothy's eventual resolution.

Focusing on Dorothy's courage helps the patient to forget her own feeling of helplessness. Dorothy bravely killed the Witch, while Mrs. R. was fearful of being murdered by her mother, in retaliation for her own murderous wishes. This scene evoked Mrs. R.'s admiration, for it enabled her to feel detached, become a spectator, and observe her own fears acted out and mastered by others.

My patient equates the story of her life as represented by Oz with the excitement and happiness resulting from the reunion with her mother. As mentioned earlier, the reverse is true. The story of her life is epitomized by the traumatic loss of her mother and her subsequent lifetime search to be reunited with a good mother.

While Mrs. R. directly associated the cyclone with the train ride to visit her mother, on all other occasions in the analysis, the cyclone represented the forces that cut her off from her mother. The cyclone stood for those feelings of estrangement during her mother's absence when Mrs. R. felt lost in space, bewildered, and alone. Her concerns about exploring space and the fear that she would become lost and confused were exemplified in the analysis by her refusal to leave town while I was away. One of us had to be at home in order for her not to feel lost. She was terrified for the safety of the astronauts who were exploring outer space. The exploration of inner space, as in masturbation, was equally frightening to her.

Her fear of an evil presence lurking in the background characterizes Mrs. R.'s feelings, which were particularly frightening during her mother's absence. It was only during this period that she was terrified to go sailing alone with her father. She was convinced that large waves (mother) would rise over the boat and drown her. The girl actually locked herself in the bathroom to prevent her father from taking her sailing, so frightened was she of her mother's retaliation for her own forbidden incestuous wishes.

The "welcome change" that my patient experienced watching Dorothy confront the Witch illustrates another purpose of the screen memory. Mrs. R. could forget her fears of her own mother and become a spectator rather than remaining a helpless participant. The screen memory also was welcome because Dorothy triumphed over the Witch.

DISCUSSION

SCREEN MEMORY FORMATION IN THE
CONTEXT OF LIBIDINAL DEVELOPMENT

A traumatic event occurred at a particular time in the libidinal development of a 7-year-old girl. Ordinarily, a 7-year-old is considered to be in latency, a period of lessened intensity of the libidinal drives. But because the girl experienced considerable inner turmoil due to her father's exhibitionism, mother's drinking, primal scene exposure, strange men with mother, and sex play with a male cousin, the girl's libidinal development at the time of mother's separation was closer to that of a child still struggling with oedipal concerns.

In addition to the painful loss, other conflictful wishes prompted the development of Mrs. R.'s screen memory. While I have focused on the wish to screen the painful affect resulting from the loss of mother, the fear experienced by the girl who thought she had successfully eliminated her mother and won father for herself was of crucial significance. She was frequently terrified that she would be murdered during her mother's absence. She displaced the subject of her concern from mother to father. For example, she would lock herself in the bathroom rather than sail alone with her father, so convinced was she of drowning. Father was experienced as a dangerous person, which contradicted his benign though seductive availability.

The girl's fear of attack on seeing her father framed in the open door at night is a defense against her own incestuous wishes. The terror is heightened by this particular visual image for it also recalls to the girl the last view of her mother in the doorway, before mother's disappearance. She is thus reminded of her murderous wishes, along with her incestuous wishes. The terror experienced stems from both a defense against incest and a fear of mother's retaliation.

The screen memory formation is the result of both the experience of loss and the forbidden wishes with their attached affects. For screen memories are a condensation of conflicts at many different levels. Greenacre (1949) has noted that one of the motives for forming screen memories is the intensity of the disturbing experience. Where intense aggression is aroused, accompanied by erotization, the resultant overflow of energy causes a secondary visual excitement. This is increased when the ego is weakened or the degree of erotic arousal heightened due to a particular stage of libidinal development. In Mrs. R.'s case, then, the painfully experienced separation from her mother, the intense aggression following her feeling of abandonment, and the erotization due to her incestuous wishes, all contributed to the formation of the specific screen memory.

Kris (1956) has illustrated how single traumatic incidents are woven by events prior and subsequent to them into the life history of an individual. Reconstructions focus on several occurrences which have been highly cathected because they were at significant crossroads in a person's life. "The memories of such events seem then to become nodal points. Hence the defense against the revival of certain memories becomes essential: anticathectic investment is directed against the re-emergence of the derivatives of instinctual forces and the affects attached to the memory image" (p. 77).

For Mrs. R., her mother's leaving was such a nodal point. Before this separation, the girl had often seen her mother with men other than her father. Her parents had fought frequently. Father had also been very seductive, frequently appearing nude before his children. There was an excessive stimulation of the girl's oedipal wishes. Mother's leaving left her unprotected against her own wishes. Moreover, it was experienced by the girl as a fulfillment of her own murderous and sexual impulses which left the child terrified by the fear of castration and murderous retaliation by mother.

Mother's constant preference for men also reinforced the girl's envy of and wish for the penis, for those who had a penis obtained mother's love. The girl hated having to play the cymbals in a school orchestra, preferring the drums which made a loud noise rather than a tinkle. Mrs. R.'s constant wish for a magical transformation from a relationship with a man contained the wish to have a penis, to have a child, and to gain mother's love. Her wish for a child from father was intensified by mother's absence. During this time the girl had a strong interest in her dolls, especially male dolls, which she associated to a fantasy of having her father's child. These wishes and their affects were intensified during mother's absence and the defense against their revival was essential. This was accomplished by the formation of a screen memory.

THE FAIRY TALE IN SCREEN MEMORY FORMATION

There are many reasons for the choice of a particular screen memory. As Fenichel (1927) writes, "The ego searches its store of memories for images to present to consciousness until it finds a suitable one. Even the new perceptions made during the time of the struggle are also scanned by the ego to see whether they are suitable as substitutive images; the ego has a 'free valence' for screen experiences and is economically eased when it finds them" (p. 114).

While I have illustrated the particular significance of the visual presentation and libidinal development, the story of *The Wizard of Oz* touches this patient's inner world in many ways.

The Search for Ideal Parents

The Wizard of Oz represents, in part, a search for one's parents. But the wish is to find the ideal parents of the family romance fantasy, and the search represents a renunciation of the present parents. In the story, Dorothy is raised by her aunt and uncle, and the identity of her true parents is unknown. In the movie, her aunt and uncle do not protect Dorothy's dog but allow it to be taken away. This parental failure is sufficiently great to make Dorothy decide to run away. Dorothy's feeling of being unloved and unprotected is underscored by her remarks on awakening after her return home. Then she declares that she will not leave home again because she loves everyone there and repeats, "There is no place like home," a denial of her wish to find a better home elsewhere. The patient's life consisted of constant shuntings back and forth from one parent to another to school. It was clear that neither parent wanted to keep her. In California, the patient's renunciation of her own parents is illustrated by her expressed wish that her parents would die and she would be adopted by the parents of her girlfriends. Even after reunion with her mother, sunny California only had "plenty of space where I went wandering around. The place was empty of people."

The Wizard As Impostor

Greenacre (1947) describes children exposed to overwhelming visual trauma such as seeing the paternal phallus. Mrs. R.'s father constantly exhibited himself before the girl, who experienced erotic arousal, fascination, and horror seeing his penis. Such children, according to Greenacre, are prone to screen memory formation with peripheral luminosity. They endow others with an overvalued, worshipful love, and keep them inviolate in an overestimation which is also a devaluation. The patient always had one man whom she treated in this way throughout her life. This was transferred to the analyst—"the Wizard of Oz," seemingly all powerful, but in reality a humbug.

Dorothy's and her defective friends' wish for some magical change bestowed upon them by an all-powerful person, to compensate for a feeling of inadequacy, represents a common motivation for entering psychoanalysis. This was especially true for my patient who was content to free-associate, but made no effort to translate her intellectual understanding of her past and present into effective action in her real world. She waited for me to change her by helping her find a loving husband and live happily ever after. She had divorced her husband just prior to beginning psychoanalysis in anticipation of this expectation. To find a loving man also represented her wish to have a child by him, her wish for a penis, and ultimately her wish for a good breast in a final union with a loving mother.

It was only after I acknowledged her lack of progress and therefore my inability to change her that she began looking at the unrealistic way in which she regarded others and thought they viewed her. Confronted with her own unrealistic demands, she began to work on changing herself in relationships with others. Instead of feeling hurt and repetitively disappointed in her expectations, she began to see friends and colleagues at work more realistically, accepting them with their limitations. At the same time, she began to see her mother as less a witch than a frightened, limited, insecure woman. In *The Wizard of Oz*, it is only after the Wizard is revealed as a humbug that Dorothy uses her own resources to accomplish her goals.

The Wish for Stable Companions

The sudden changes from one world to another, causing bewilderment, fear, imagined dangers, and the impressive attempt at mastery made by Dorothy must have been most appealing to Mrs. R., whose life contained repetitive abandonments and consistently shifting objects. Mrs. R. was searching for a stable love object, and constantly attempting to achieve mastery over her fear of aloneness in an uncaring world. Her adoration of a man contained the hope that she would be permanently protected and loved by him. She must have admired Dorothy's fearless persistence and relished Dorothy's faithful companions—the Scarecrow, Tin Woodsman, and Cowardly Lion, who not only remained by Dorothy in times of crisis but demonstrated the qualities of intelligence, loving concern, and courage so lacking in her own parents.

Splitting of the Mother

The splitting of the mother into good and bad objects is a striking characteristic in the movie with its two good witches and two evil witches. Mrs. R. could see people only in terms of good or bad. She recalled being frightened by her mother's dramatic changes in mood. Her mother was good when she was sober and caring and bad when drunk and frightening. She associated to the Jekyll-Hyde splitting that made a profound impression on her while watching this other film. Again the image of the object in an open door reappeared in a scene where Jekyll leaves his girlfriend. The camera focuses on the door which slowly opens, revealing Hyde returning to kill her. This scene reminded Mrs. R. of her father at the door as well as her fear of her mother's return and retaliation for the girl's murderous and incestuous wishes. These wishes promote the splitting into the good and bad mother.

Opening the Door to a New World

The moment when the door opens from Dorothy's world to the land of Oz had a special impact on the patient, who had felt terrified on other occasions when a door had been opened. These include her father opening the door to her room at night, the moment in the Jekyll-Hyde movie when Hyde opens the door to his girlfriend's room, the time when a lost child tried to open her motel door, and the moment when her mother left through the open door. The terror and excitement of opening the door for the patient stem from her primal scene memories of opening the door to her parents' bedroom as a child, and seeing her father hurting her mother in a physical struggle. If the door represents the repression barrier against the emergence of oedipal and preoedipal longings, opening the door to the land of Oz exposes the child to having to deal with his forbidden wishes. One important interest of this tale for children may be in their identification with a child who shares their longings, but who also masters the dangers of the oedipal conflict.

SUMMARY

There is a high degree of overdetermination in the need for and choice of a screen memory. This investigation was initiated in order to understand a woman's repetitive associations to a filmed fairy tale throughout her analysis. It was determined from the associations preceding and following *The Wizard of Oz* that the film served as a screen memory to avoid experiencing the inner conflicts fixated by a traumatic childhood event—separation from the mother.

In addition to the painful experience of loss, the event was traumatic because of its revival of incestuous and aggressive wishes and their accompanying affects. The energy directed against experiencing the painful affects associated with the event led to the formation of a screen memory. This displaced memory had to be associatively similar to the repressed images. The choice of a particular film to serve as a screen memory was especially suitable because the film's content contained unconscious wishes and fantasies which corresponded with this girl's libidinal and aggressive wishes. The use of visual images in the film to screen disturbing memory images is a most interesting determinant in forming this screen memory. Considering that such visual images are becoming increasingly available to children through the greater use of television, I wonder to what extent other children are affected by the innumerable, dramatically presented, visual images that characterize children's television programming. This would be a most worthwhile subject for further psychoanalytic investigation.

BIBLIOGRAPHY

ABRAHAM, K. (1913), A Screen Memory Concerning a Childhood Event of Apparently Aetiological Significance. *Clinical Papers and Essays on Psychoanalysis.* New York: Basic Books, 1955, pp. 36–41.

BAUM, F. & MAC FALL, R. (1961), *To Please a Child.* Chicago: Reilly & Lee.

BAUM, L. F. (1900), *The Wizard of Oz.* Chicago: Reilly & Lee.

BUXBAUM, E. (1941), The Role of Detective Stories in a Child Analysis. *Psychoanal. Quart.*, 10:373–381.

CALEF, V. (1954), Color in Dreams. *J. Amer. Psychoanal. Assn.*, 2:453–461.

DESMONDE, W. (1951), Jack and the Beanstalk. *Amer. Imago*, 8:287–288.

FENICHEL, O. (1927), The Economic Function of Screen Memories. *The Collected Papers of Otto Fenichel*, 1:113–116. New York: Norton, 1953.

——— (1928), The Inner Injunction to "Make a Mental Note." *The Collected Papers of Otto Fenichel*, 1:153–154. New York: Norton, 1953.

FERENCZI, S. (1926), Gulliver Fantasies. *Final Contributions to the Problems and Methods of Psychoanalysis*, 3:41–60. New York: Basic Books, 1955.

FRAIBERG, S. (1954), Tales of the Discovery of the Secret Treasure. *This Annual*, 9:218–241.

FREUD, A. (1951), Observations on Child Development. *This Annual*, 6:18–30.

FREUD, S. (1899), Screen Memories. *Standard Edition*, 3:301–322. London: Hogarth Press, 1962.

——— (1901), Childhood Memories and Screen Memories. *Standard Edition*, 6:43–52. London: Hogarth Press, 1960.

——— (1910), Leonardo da Vinci and a Memory of His Childhood. *Standard Edition*, 11:53–137. London: Hogarth Press, 1957.

——— (1913), The Occurence in Dreams of Material from Fairy Tales *Standard Edition*, 12:279–287. London: Hogarth Press, 1958.

——— (1914), Remembering, Repeating and Working-Through. *Standard Edition*, 12:145–156. London: Hogarth Press, 1958.

FREUD, S. (1917), A Childhood Recollection from *Dichtung und Wahrheit. Standard Edition*, 17:145–156. London: Hogarth Press, 1955.

GLOVER, E. (1956), The Screening Function of Traumatic Memories. *On the Early Development of the Mind.* New York: International Universities Press, pp. 108–111.

GREENACRE, P. (1947), Vision, Headache and the Halo. *Psychoanal. Quart.*, 16:177–194.

——— (1949), A Contribution to the Study of Screen Memories. *This Annual*, 3/4:73–84.

——— (1950), The Prepuberty Trauma in Girls. *Psychoanal. Quart.*, 19:298–317.

——— (1955), "It's My Own Invention." *Psychoanal. Quart.*, 24:200–244.

HUCKEL, H. (1957), One Day I'll Live in the Castle! *Amer. Imago*, 14:303–314.

KRIS, E. (1956), The Recovery of Childhood Memories in Psychoanalysis. *This Annual*, 11:54–88.

LATHBURY, V. (1957), An Interesting Screen Memory. *Bull. Philadelphia Assn. Psychoanal.*, 7:81–84.

PETTY, T. A. (1953), The Tragedy of Humpty-Dumpty. *This Annual*, 8:404–412.

REIDER, N. (1953), Reconstruction and Screen Function. *J. Amer. Psychoanal. Assn.*, 1:389–405.

ROSE, G. J. (1960), Screen Memories in Homicidal Acting Out. *Psychoanal. Quart.*, 29:328–343.

ROWLEY, J. L. (1951), Rumpelstilzkin in the Analytical Situation. *Int. J. Psycho-Anal.*, 32:190–195.

SIMMEL, E. (1925), A Screen Memory *in Statu Nascendi. Int. J. Psycho-Anal.*, 6:454–457.

The Wizard of Oz, Metro-Goldwyn-Mayer, (1939), 90 min. Sound, Technicolor, 16 mm. Motion Picture, Credit: V. Fleming.

APPLICATIONS OF PSYCHOANALYSIS

The Adoption Theme in Edward Albee's *Tiny Alice* and *The American Dream*

JULES GLENN, M.D.

ALTHOUGH ADOPTED CHILDREN EXHIBIT A VARIETY OF PERSONALITY structures, certain conscious and unconscious preoccupations, strivings, and conflicts appear in them with great frequency. This is not surprising, since the fact of adoption calls forth a limited number of parental responses and consequent reactions from the children. Thus, although the approved style of dealing with adoption has changed from time to time, each method necessarily involves complications. I do not wish to imply that all adopted children encounter the same difficulties, or that the difficulties, when they exist, are crippling. Being adopted, however, does influence personality development, and if the child becomes an artist, the resultant fantasies may reveal themselves in his creative products. Moreover, the adopted child's wishes and defenses may serve as the wellspring of his artistic activity.

In this paper I intend to show the role which the adoption theme plays in some works by Edward Albee, who was in fact adopted at the age of two weeks. In *Tiny Alice* (1965), this theme appears in disguised form. The play's main character, Julian, acts as if he were an adopted child caught up in the confusions and cravings typical

Clinical Associate Professor of Psychiatry and member of the faculty of the Divison of Psychoanalytic Education, Downstate Medical Center, State University of New York, Brooklyn, New York.

of many such children. Other features of the play also reflect the adopted child's fantasies. I shall also discuss Albee's *The American Dream*, in which adoption is openly portrayed.

THE PSYCHOLOGY OF ADOPTED CHILDREN

I shall draw on the scant analytic literature and some unpublished reports to pull together the few facts that analysts have established about the psychology of adopted children. While there have been no published analyses of adopted children, a sufficient number have been studied in psychotherapy and by observations of families to allow some generalizations about the characteristics of adopted children (Schechter, 1960, 1967; Peller, 1963; Blum, 1969; Blos, 1963).[1]

Most adopted children, either consciously or unconsciously, know about their adoption. Generally, the new parents tell the child that he is adopted; even if they do not, the child eventually often suspects or overhears the truth. Certainly, the age at which the parent tells the child as well as his method of doing so will influence the child's reaction.

Once the child knows of his adoption, he is faced with the fact that he has two sets of parents. He may well develop mental representations that encompass real and imagined traits of both sets. He may have difficulty differentiating between the "real" and the "false" parents, ascertaining which is which. In trying to clarify these confusions the child may have to sacrifice reality testing, may deny or repress the existence of one set of parents.[2] This may be the case especially if the adoptive parent insists, as he sometimes does,

---

[1] I have confirmed or supplemented the descriptions in the literature with my own experience and that of the members of a study group that meets regularly in Great Neck, New York. Two reports on the analyses of adopted children have been very illuminating as well (Daunton, 1973; Freeman, 1967). The latter's chapter on the "Abandoned Doll" is a report of an analysis conducted by Walter Stewart. Swartz (1973) and Kernberg (1974) also provided unpublished confirmatory data.

[2] Wieder (1974) has made the additional suggestion that the child's being told of his adoption reinforces fears of abandonment that are already present. Defenses against this anxiety include denial and result in a disturbance of the sense of reality.

that he is the biological parent, or if the child is commanded to forget or not to mention his biological origins.

The parent may intentionally or inadvertently tell the child falsehoods about his adoption. He may describe, as has been recommended, how the child was chosen by him. He may say that the original parents are not alive or invent exalted motives for the real mother's surrender of her baby. If, as is often the case, the child is aware of the fabrication, he may himself develop a need to lie, with the concomitant superego defect. Here the child identifies with the lying parent and may take revenge by creating falsehoods in ways that hurt the parent. Or the child may react to parental falsifications with hyperbole, imagining the adults to be totally corrupt.

The child may build fantasies on the fact that adoption involves legal machinery and that money is paid to a lawyer, an agency, or to the mother herself, either for her medical care or in frank payment for the baby. He may feel that an illicit exchange has been carried out behind his back and without his control, knowledge, or approval. Hatred for the deserting parents may be fused with fury at the adoptive parents, who, he imagines, have stolen or bought him in a crass and unfeeling way, who consider him a possession rather than a person. He may fear that, having been deserted once, he may be again. More specifically, he may be returned to his original parents. The adopted child's fantasy that he has actually killed his parents (Rosner, 1974) may stem not only from his hatred, but also from a defensive need to believe that he has actually gotten rid of them, that he has not been the passive abandoned child (Wieder, 1974).

The adopted child often correctly concludes that his situation resulted from his adoptive parents' inability to have children. He then becomes especially preoccupied with the question of how children are born and conceived, with the possible causes of infertility. Illogically, as if he had inherited his adoptive parents' defects, he wonders whether he will be capable of producing a child; he identifies with the sterile parent. The child may attribute the lack of children to parental virginity, impotence, or frigidity.

As is generally true, a family romance fantasy (Freud, 1909) occurs, but it often takes an idiosyncratic form in the adopted child.

In the usual family romance fantasy, the child imagines that he is adopted and that his real parents were truly exalted personages. He was left with a poor family, but one day will rejoin his wealthy or regal biological parents. Such fantasies serve a number of purposes. They console the child for disappointments in his parents; they relieve his guilt by eliminating the incest barrier; they act defensively against the hostility and incestuous feeling to the parents. The form of the adopted child's family romance, however, is colored by what he has surmised or heard about his biological parents. Thus, he frequently pictures his biological family as low people, poor, and even depraved. His father and mother may not have been married, and hence he is illegitimate. Identification with such parental object representations may lead to self-denigration as well as to wishes to create illegitimate children.

I have mentioned that hatred for the parents who have deserted him may be transferred to the adoptive parents. There may be a concomitant idealization of the biological parents with a strong desire to return to them. Being adopted, he may feel weak, deficient, evil, castrated, or lacking in identity. Hearing that his natural parents have died may lead to identification with the deceased and tendencies to self-injury.

When a child's insatiable curiosity is frustrated by parental and societal reluctance to have him know his real father and mother, he may actively search for them when he is older, or he may attach himself to biological parent substitutes as well as surrogates for his adoptive parents. So intense and frequent is the desire of adopted children to find their original parents, to establish their continuity with the past and their present and future identity, that an organization has been formed by adopted people to overthrow the legal barriers to receiving information about their origins.[3]

Knowing that his adoptive parents are not his natural parents may create special sexual problems because the child—and even the parents—may feel that incest is permissible. Temptations may thus be greater, but despite relaxation of restraint, the superego will probably remain intolerant of real or fantasied breaches of the

[3] In Scotland the child at 17 may achieve legal access to his original birth certificate (McWhinnie, 1969).

incest taboo, and the child still feels that he must be punished for his wishes. Indeed he may come to believe that he was adopted as punishment for his incestuous desires.

I wish to emphasize again that what I have described are common confusions and concerns of adopted children, not universal configurations. Nor do the conscious and unconscious solutions of the children to these conundrums necessarily lead to pathology. Indeed, in describing the influence of an adopted child's fantasies on his plays, I am emphasizing one individual's highly adaptive utilization of his concerns.

Whether the conflicts and fantasies I have described develop, and how intense they will be, depends upon a number of factors. These include when, how, and how often the child is told that he is adopted. If the fantasies described can serve a defensive function against other, perhaps more pressing, conflicts, they will become more important. Telling the child early and repeatedly that he has been chosen by his parents, as has been recommended in the past, may lead the child to feel that he is special, an exception, and cause him to develop superego defects. Regardless of how he is told, however, his "sense of identity . . . is insecure at best" (A. Freud, 1972, p. 624).

TINY ALICE

This strange and beautiful play has been denounced as obscure by many critics. The enigma of the drama diminishes when one recognizes the confusions and conflicts of the adopted child which are hidden within it. Although we may elucidate the author's private unconscious symbolism, this is not necessarily the interpretation that Albee intended; he has not disclosed this meaning, contending that it is "quite clear."

The play opens with a scene of vicious confrontation between two former schoolmates, an attorney and a cardinal whom the attorney is visiting. We first encounter the lawyer alone, playfully talking gibberish to his host's caged birds, two cardinals. The ecclesiastic enters, chides his friend, and the two men engage each other in a witty and sarcastic verbal brawl in which despicable traits of each are revealed.

The lawyer has come as an emissary for a Miss Alice, a wealthy woman who wants to donate vast amounts of money, millions of dollars, to the church. The lawyer informs the cardinal that Brother Julian, the private secretary of the cardinal, will be sent for to make arrangements for the delivery of the money.

Brother Julian, a devout lay Catholic brother and apparently an intimate of the cardinal, arrives at Miss Alice's mysterious mansion. A dollhouse, identical with the huge mansion, occupies a prominent place in the library. When a conflagration erupts in the life-sized house, an identical fire burns in the model. When the larger fire is extinguished, the fire in the model disappears. Similarly, lights appear in the smaller house when the larger one is illuminated.

Although the lawyer has requested that Julian be the emissary, the cardinal tells him that he had "chosen" him for this "high honor." Hearing this, the attorney scoffs: "He. Chosen. You." Julian's exact duties are unclear. He is "to take care of odds and ends." Eventually the fact emerges that he is to have an affair with Miss Alice and then to marry her; he is to be sacrificed in order that the church may receive the large grant. But Julian is not aware of the plans; he accepts the strange happenings naïvely and without question.

Julian is courted by the seductive Miss Alice. He reveals to her certain events of the six years of his life that are missing from the dossier that her associates have prepared regarding him. Julian had already revealed to the butler that he had himself placed in a mental home because he could not reconcile himself "to the chasm between the nature of God and the use to which men put . . . God." He contrasts God the creator and the God created by man. As a result of his doubts, his faith "abandoned" him.

While in the hospital, Julian experienced hallucinations and could not differentiate between the real and the imaginary. Hence, he could not be certain whether he had had sexual relations with a patient who fancied herself to be the Virgin Mary. After their possible intercourse the woman "ascended or descended into an ecstasy, the substance of which was that she was with child . . . that she was pregnant with the Son of God." Actually, she suffered from a uterine malignancy and soon died.

In the second act the lawyer and the butler discuss a conspiracy to take Julian from the cardinal in exchange for $100,000,000 a year for 20 years. Julian is to be married to Alice or to Miss Alice, "one through the other." There are indications that the matter is more mysterious still, when occurrences such as identical fires in the mansion and the model adumbrate strange events to come. That both butler and lawyer have been Miss Alice's lovers and that they direct and supervise her activities further confuse the audience and arouse its expectations. The mystery heightens as Miss Alice succeeds in seducing Julian, saying, "You will be hers [Alice's]; you will sacrifice yourself to her."

In the final act we learn that Julian is to marry, be sacrificed to Alice; not Miss Alice, but an unseen being for whom Miss Alice is merely a surrogate. Miss Alice says, "You have married *her* . . . through me . . . you felt her warmth through me, touched her lips through my lips . . . wrapped yourself in her wings . . . your mouth on her hair, the voice in your ear, hers not mine, all hers; her. You are hers." In fact, the lawyer states, "We are surrogates; *our* task is done now."

But Julian must remain with Alice. The cardinal, the lawyer, the butler, and Miss Alice each call on him to "accept," to make "an act of faith." When Julian rebels against this "mockery" of religion and law, the attorney shoots him. All but Julian leave the building.

Julian lies dying, awaiting Alice. Confusing God and Alice, he at last accepts her, as he is engulfed by the shadow of a great presence, and dies in a crucified state.

ADOPTION AND *TINY ALICE*

The analytic literature contains a single paper that deals with this uncanny, moving masterpiece (Markson, 1966); it does not even mention the possibility that Albee's experiences as an adopted child may have influenced his imagery and imagination. Markson finds a plethora of evidence for oedipal inspirations; and of course these are present in *Tiny Alice* as in most or all creative works. He sees the play as "an intense representation of a chaotic passively resolved oedipal conflict" (p. 20). Blum (1969), on the other hand, has traced the adoption motif in Albee's *Who's Afraid of Virginia Woolf?*, but has chosen to omit the fact that Albee is an adopted child.

We see at once that Julian is in a position similar to that of the adopted child. An arrangement has been made for him to be transferred from one family to another, from the family of the Catholic Church and God the Father to the Alice household. This is being done for money, and it is arranged without his knowledge and approval. The latter, of course, is inevitable in most adoptions, since they take place when the children are infants. In the play the transfer, which uses legal machinery, is arranged by the giver and receiver and carries religious sanction. When Julian realizes what is being done, he objects and calls it a mockery; religion and law are being used illicitly. But he is told that he must accept the new situation, the new parent substitute, who is equated with Mother Mary and God the Father. Miss Alice at one point embraces Julian in a Pietà-like posture. In the end Julian calls the engulfing Alice "God."

The imagery of the mysterious transfer from one family to another is foreshadowed and reinforced by repeated references to surrogates and doubles. The play opens with the lawyer talking to *two* cardinals, birds that in turn symbolize their ecclesiastic counterparts. The huge mansion and its model can be understood as symbols for the two mothers, the original one and the substitute that is confused with the biological parent. Early in the play the millionaire's lawyer contends that he "learned never to confuse the representation of a thing with the thing itself" (p. 39). Nevertheless, he and the others are uncertain about the reality of the mansion and the dollhouse. The miniature is said to be a model, but the large one is called a replica. Later Julian learns to his dismay that the visible Miss Alice is not the authentic one. Rather the unseen Alice is the real Alice. As the lawyer, referring to those who have arranged the marriage, says, "We are her surrogates" (p. 156).

The double image appears again in Julian's disillusionment with God. He distinguishes between God the creator and the God that men have created, as the adopted child tries to separate the representations of his biological creators and the parents that men have arranged for him. In the end he fails to separate the true God and Alice.

Julian comes to feel uncomfortable in Alice's mansion. His

former identity is interfered with as he indulges in pleasures and temptations. He feels that he is being tested. Like the adopted child he must be "good" to be accepted, but is uncertain of his allegiances, unclear as to which identifications to adhere to, unable to consolidate the old and the new.

When Julian objects to his new family and wants to return to his established relationship with the cardinal, he is prohibited from doing so. Rather than let him return, his guardians shoot him, as they tell him he must accept and have faith. Certainly, it takes great faith to believe that adoptive parents are true parents and can be trusted. As I have pointed out, the child sometimes sacrifices reality testing as he uses denial to support this belief. Indeed, the uncertainty in separating reality and fantasy is very prominent throughout the play. In addition to the very real element of the audience's confusion, we find that Julian was hospitalized for a psychosis. He had not merely lost his faith; he also lost his capacity for reality testing.

I have noted that the adopted child often ponders over parental inability to have children. He wonders: are they sterile, defective? Do they have intercourse? This preoccupation appears in Julian's relationship with the mental patient who thought she was the Virgin Mary and who bore not a child but a cancer. His uncertainty about their having had sexual relations reflects the adopted child's uncertainties about his parents' sexual activities, internalized and applied to Julian. And the Virgin Mary, like adoptive parents, can have a child without intercourse.

The adopted child may be plagued by lack of clarity as to whether incest is permitted. Who is the forbidden object? Julian showed oedipal desires as he was attracted to a type of mother, the patient who fancied herself Virgin Mary, and later to Miss Alice who posed as Mary. His uncertainty about his sexual activity with the patient is overdetermined: it also suggests the defensive blurring that one may experience in trying to recall prohibited acts or wishes.

Julian's relationship with Miss Alice is interesting for a number of additional reasons. Marriage to her is equated with adoption, i.e., being transferred from one family to another as part of a contract. (As such, it is tolerated incest.) There is a sadomasochistic tinge to their relationship, when she invites him to use his crop on her. Possibly, this feature combines the punishment for incest and the regression from oedipal fantasies.

Julian is timid about marrying Miss Alice, but he is terrified about his union with the real Alice. It is as if the latter were the real mother, the unseen mother, with whom he must not unite, as intercourse with her is truly incestuous. Indeed, he is killed before he can consummate this marriage. Quite possibly there is a negative oedipal, a homosexual, implication here, in that Alice represents the father he wished to fuse with. There are hints in the play that the attachment between the cardinal and the lay brother is more than Platonic.

Folklore holds that incest breeds monsters. This fantasy appears, I believe, in the production of a cancer following intercourse between Julian and the patient who imagined she was Virgin Mary.

We can find other derivatives of the adopted child's picture of his biological parents as well: they were promiscuous and they abandoned him. The behavior of Miss Alice as the mistress of the lawyer and the butler are relevant here. Of course, Miss Alice and the others do desert Julian at the end of the play. Earlier, Julian describes his faith abandoning him. As is often true, the parent surrogates tell Julian that he was chosen. But he is furious, nonetheless, at the abandoners who have lied to him, tricked him, and traded him. His impotent rage is for naught.

Manifestations of primary process thinking, important in any creative work, carry a special significance in *Tiny Alice*. To mention one outstanding example of condensation, the same characters can stand for biological mother and adoptive mother, for God and father. So it is with many adopted children who project the various superimposed representations of their several families onto those about them. The confusion many viewers felt about the play undoubtedly is the result of the intense reality with which symbols are treated.

THE ADOPTION THEME IN OTHER PLAYS BY ALBEE

Tiny Alice is not the only play by Albee in which the latent adoption theme appears. It is perhaps significant that three of Albee's thirteen plays—*Malcolm* (1966), *The Ballad of the Sad Café* (1963), and *Everything in the Garden* (1968)—are adapted from other authors' works, borrowed and reworked—adopted as it were. Albee lends credence to this hypothesis when he equates a play and a child (Flanagan, 1967). Talking of the creative act, he says, "It's a form of pregnancy I suppose, and to carry that idea further, there are very few people who are pregnant who can recall specifically the moment of conception of the child—but they discover that they are pregnant, and it's rather that way with discovering that one is thinking about a play" (p. 344).

Malcolm (1966), based upon Purdy's novel (1959), dramatizes a young man's search for his lost parents. Whereas in *Tiny Alice* Julian dies as he is being enveloped by Alice in a union that has sexual and incestuous connotations, the hero of *Malcolm* dies of excessive sexual intercourse with a young women he finds and loves as he seeks his parents. Here, too, we find the implication that death is a result of, a punishment for, incest with a mother surrogate.

I have already mentioned Blum's (1969) study of *Who's Afraid of Virginia Woolf?*. In contrast to *Tiny Alice*, the protagonists of that drama primarily manifest the traits of adoptive *parents* rather than those of the adopted child. Fantasies about adoption abound in both plays. The four characters of *Virginia Woolf* are potential parents unable to have real children. For the most part the audience identifies with them; the story is told from the point of view of adults who wish to have children but cannot, who thus imagine and invent the offspring they are unable to produce and keep in reality. However, the bitterness of the adopted child reveals itself in the unsympathetic portrayal of the protagonists. At one point, as Blum has noted, Nick, the younger man, changes roles and acquires some of the attributes of the adopted child. He is called a houseboy and a stud; he attains the double "identity of a fantasied adopted son, both sterile and fertile like his father" (p. 895). He also becomes the young adopted child seduced by his mother. By contrast, in *Tiny Alice* the audience identifies primarily with Julian who consistently behaves like an adopted child.

In *The American Dream* (1960), adoption is the *overt* subject matter.

THE AMERICAN DREAM

This early play confirms for us Albee's preoccupation with adoption through the appearance of certain themes that we observe in *Tiny Alice* in a more covert form. The teasing out of the adoption motif, of course, does not exhaust our understanding of the play, but merely elucidates one facet.

The play opens on a bickering family consisting of Mommy, Daddy, and Mommy's old mother, Grandma. Daddy is a wealthy man whom Mommy, originally a poor girl, was fortunate to marry. The materialistic orientation of the family is clear. Inordinately concerned about possessions, the mother talks about her clothing and complains that the landlord, who had been quick to take their rent and security money, is slow to repair the house. Threats to expel Grandma, to send her to a home, complement the picture of the family.

The story hinges on Mommy's and Daddy's invitation to Mrs. Barker to their home to complain about the loss of their adopted child. Mrs. Barker works for the Bye-Bye Adoption Service; when she arrives, Grandma explains the purpose of the visit to her in a somewhat allegoric way, talking of a man and woman like Mommy and Daddy rather than directly stating who is involved:

"The woman, who was very much like Mommy, said that they wanted a bumble of their own; but that the man, who was very much like Daddy, couldn't have a bumble; and that the man who was very much like Daddy, said that yes, they had wanted a bumble of their own, but that the woman, who was very much like Mommy, couldn't have one, and they wanted to buy something like a bumble" (p. 98).

However, the purchased baby was a disappointment. Mutual antagonism characterized the parent-child relationship. When it cried and only had eyes for its father, Mommy gouged out the baby's eyes. Because it masturbated, they cut off its penis and hands. They cut off its tongue when it called Mommy an obscene name. As the child grew older, its most disturbing traits became apparent: ". . . it didn't have a head on its shoulders, it had no guts, it was spineless, its feet were made of clay" (p. 100f.). When the child died the parents were distressed not because they had lost a beloved child, but because the goods they had bought had not been durable. Hence, they telephoned the lady from whom they had purchased the "bumble" and told her to come to their home immediately. They insisted on remuneration for the faulty product.

It is noteworthy that the adopted child is repeatedly referred to as "it"; his gender is never mentioned since he is to his parents a possession to be bought and sold, rather than a human being. His wishes are never considered.

The word "bumble," used to designate the child, is interesting. It is a condensation derived from "bumble," "bundle," and "bungle." "Bundle" is a common term for an infant, derived from the wrapping that the baby is dressed in. The implication is that the baby is a bundle of joy, an ironic comment in this case, in which the child is felt to be merely trouble. "To bungle" means to spoil by clumsy work. This alludes to the adoptive parents' bungling in their attempt to produce a baby. The biological parents, in addition, have bungled by producing a child they did not wish to have and could not care for. "Bungle" also refers to the child who is considered inept and malformed. "Bumble" itself is suggestive of a bumble bee, an insect that frequently stands for a child in dream imagery. Possibly, the word "bum," a loafer, is alluded to as well.

To return to the story of *The American Dream*, the resolution of the difficult and bizarre situation takes place through the appearance of Young Man, who is clearly the twin brother of the adopted child, although this relationship is never explicitly stated. Young Man, who is seeking employment and will do almost anything for money, appears at a crucial moment, apparently by coincidence. Introducing himself, he describes his belief that he is an illegitimate child. "My mother died the night that I was born, and I never knew my father; I doubt my mother did." One of the identical twins, "we felt each other breathe . . . his heartbeat thundered in my temple . . . mine in his . . . our stomachs ached and we cried for feeding at the same time" (p. 114). Albee convinces the audience that the deceased child and Young Man are twins when the latter recalls that he experienced the sensations the dead child did as he was being dismembered. The audience shares the fantasy that twins possess a mystical extrasensory contact.

In the end, through Grandma's manipulations and with Mrs. Barker's collaboration, Young Man, unaware of what is happening, replaces the dead adopted child in the family. Mrs. Barker announces that she will send a bill for her services in arranging the second adoption. Just as Julian is passively bought by Alice in *Tiny Alice*, so the adoptions of *The American Dream* are purchases which are arranged without the child's awareness of the transaction. This was true of the first adoption, as is inevitable, for an infant cannot very well know what is happening. The subterfuge repeats itself, however, when Young Man joins the family. Clearly, adopted children are pictured as possessions which can be bought and disposed of, even castrated if they object to their situation, rather than as persons, as true biological offspring. The grandmother, who is also treated as a thing, can be considered a displaced representation of the adopted child, one who is resourceful and manages to maintain her independence despite family pressures. This is the adopted child's wish come true. Instead of being a defective thing, he wishes to become a whole, independent person.

Parental evasions are prominent both in *Tiny Alice* and in *The American Dream*. In both plays the true situation is often alluded to but never clearly stated. The nature of reality is unclear.

Direct references to the parents' inability to produce a child appear openly in this play, whereas in *Tiny Alice* they are disguised, appear, as I have suggested, in connection with the psychotic woman who imagines herself to be the pregnant Virgin Mary, but who does not actually conceive. In *The American Dream*, Daddy is impotent, both sexually—he no longer "bumps his uglies" (p. 67) on Mommy—and socially, for he lacks masculinity and decisiveness.

The theme of the double, so prominent in *Tiny Alice*, manifests itself in *The American Dream* as well. The two sets of parents are referred to directly in the latter. In addition, the appearance of twins reflects the adopted child's preoccupations with pairs of parents. So does the fact that a grandmother, similar in many ways to her daughter, is present and that Mrs. Barker manifests many of Mommy's traits. We may surmise that the adopted child can picture himself as a double, since he has two sets of parents. The fantasied twinship also serves the defensive role of preserving himself even when he is, or feels he is, mistreated, dismembered, and diminished.

One adopted child's family romance constellation is stated quite clearly in *The American Dream*. Young Man notes the uncertainty of his biological parentage and asserts that his parents were unmarried, did not even know each other well, that his father deserted them and his mother died. Indeed, one of the common fantasies of adopted children, that their original mother is dead, may have a palpable influence on their personality development, leading to self-destructive attempts to reach the lost mother. Perhaps this fantasy throws additional light on Julian's union with his unseen mother surrogate, Alice, as he dies.

DISCUSSION

It is a well-established method to seek to demonstrate how special life circumstances are reflected in the imagery of and the themes chosen by artists. Among the many special circumstances that have been investigated are object loss through the death or illness of a parent or parental desertion (Wolfenstein, 1973; Meyer, 1967; Greenacre, 1955), twinship (Glenn, 1973, 1974a, 1974b), and the birth of siblings in rapid succession (Greenacre, 1955).

Following this tradition, this study has singled out the theme of adoption in the expectation that the application of psychoanalytic knowledge concerning the psychology of adopted children might throw light on what is generally regarded as a puzzling play. While there is no doubt that other factors also shaped *Tiny Alice*, I believe that viewing it in terms of the adopted child's psychological preoccupations provides a key to unlocking the enigma.

In the past, analysts have frequently turned to literature to test the validity and universality of their hypotheses which were derived from observation of patients (Nunberg and Federn, 1962). Others, perplexed by clinical phenomena, have turned to literature in the hope that the poet's intuitive understanding would illuminate their patients' problems (Greenacre, 1971), thus viewing applied analysis as a two-way road. Indeed, Eissler (1968) observes that Freud derived considerable insight from his study of Shakespeare's work.

I have earlier referred to the paucity of analytic papers dealing with the special problems of the adopted child. In line with Greenacre's and Eissler's view of applied analysis, our knowledge might therefore also be enhanced by focusing on how a playwright, who was an adopted child, dealt adaptively with this fact in his artistic products. However, such recourse to literature is no substitute for well-documented reports of individual analyses of adopted children.

An additional aim of this paper, therefore, is to draw attention to an area that seems to have been relatively neglected and to underscore the need for work on this problem.

BIBLIOGRAPHY

ALBEE, E. (1960), The American Dream. In: *Two Plays by Edward Albee*. New York: New American Library.
———— (1962), *Who's Afraid of Virginia Woolf?* New York: Pocket Cardinal.
———— (1963), *The Ballad of the Sad Café*. Boston: Houghton Mifflin.
———— (1965), *Tiny Alice*. New York: Pocket Cardinal.
———— (1966), *Malcolm*. New York: Atheneum.
———— (1968), *Everything in the Garden*. New York: Atheneum.
BLOS, P. (1963), The Concept of Acting Out in Relation to the Adolescent Process. In: *A Developmental Approach to the Problems of Acting Out*, ed. E. Rexford. New York: International Universities Press, 1966, pp. 118–136.
BLUM, H. P. (1969), A Psychoanalytic View of *Who's Afraid of Virginia Woolf? J. Amer. Psychoanal. Assn.*, 17:888–903.
DAUNTON, E. (1973), The Opening Phase of Treatment in an Adopted Child with a Symptom of Encopresis. Presented at the Association for Child Psychoanalysis, Ann Arbor, Michigan.
EISSLER, K. R. (1968), The Relation of Explaining and Understanding in Psychoanalysis. *This Annual*, 23:141–171.
FLANAGAN, W. (1967), Edward Albee. In: *Writers at Work* [*The Paris Review Interviews, Third Series*]. New York: Viking Press, pp. 321–346.
FREEMAN, L., Ed. (1967), *The Mind*. New York: Thomas Y. Crowell.
FREUD, A. (1972), The Child As a Person in His Own Right. *This Annual*, 27:621–625.
FREUD, S. (1909), Family Romances. *Standard Edition*, 9:235–241. London, Hogarth Press, 1959.
GLENN, J. (1973), Further Observations on Plays by Twins. Presented at the Psychoanalytic Association of New York.
———— (1974a), Twins in Disguise: A Psychoanalytic Essay on *Sleuth* and *The Royal Hunt of the Sun. Psychoanal. Quart.*, 43:288–302.

GLENN, J. (1974b), Twins in Disguise: II. Content, Form, and Style in Plays by Anthony and Peter Shaffer. *Int. Rev. Psychoanal.* (in press).

GREENACRE, P. (1955), *Swift and Carroll.* New York: International Universities Press.

———— (1971), Introduction to *Emotional Growth.* New York: International Universities Press.

KERNBERG, P. (1974), Discussion of this paper at the Psychoanalytic Association of New York.

MARKSON, J. W. (1966), Albee's *Tiny Alice. Amer. Imago,* 23:3–21.

McWHINNIE, A. M. (1969), The Adopted Child in Adolescence. In: *Adolescence,* eds. G. Caplan & S. Lebovici. New York: Basic Books, pp. 133–142.

MEYER, B. C. (1967), *Joseph Conrad.* Princeton: Princeton University Press.

NUNBERG, H. & FEDERN, E., Eds. (1962), *Minutes of the Vienna Psychoanalytic Society,* Vol. I. New York: International Universities Press.

PELLER, L. E. (1963), Further Comments on Adoption. *Bull. Phila. Assn. Psychoanal.,* 13:1–14.

PURDY, J. (1959), *Malcolm.* New York: Avon Books.

ROSNER, H. (1974), Discussion of this paper at the Psychoanalytic Association of New York.

SCHECHTER, M. D. (1960), Observations on Adopted Children. *Arch. Gen. Psychiat.,* 3:21–32.

———— (1967), Panel Report: Psychoanalytic Theory As It Relates to Adoption. *J. Amer. Psychoanal. Assn.,* 15:695–708.

SWARTZ, J. (1973), Discussion of this paper at the American Psychoanalytic Association, New York.

WIEDER, H. (1974), Personal communication in discussion at Great Neck Study Group.

WOLFENSTEIN, M. (1973), The Image of the Lost Parent. *This Annual,* 28:433–456.

Jump-Rope Rhymes and the Rhythm of Latency Development in Girls

HERBERT J. GOLDINGS, M.D.

> What are little girls made of? Sugar and spice and
> everything nice—that's what little girls are made of.
> > —Mother Goose, Nursery Rhyme
> Man is only man indeed when he plays.
> > —Schiller

THIS PAPER EXAMINES THE PHENOMENOLOGY OF JUMP-ROPE GAMES (skipping rope) with particular emphasis on the form and content of jump-rope rhymes. The aim of the study is to show how this specific play articulates some of the basic issues of psychological development in girls during the latency period.

The approach of this study is to apply, within a small and manageable compass, a combination of two methods and traditions: the fidelity of the folklorist-compiler, and the experience of the clinical psychoanalyst. Psychoanalysts have long had an interest in observation, experiment, and speculation on the functions of play in childhood. Nor have they been alone in this activity: such diverse colleagues as philosophers, poets, parents, and—most recently—pri-

Assistant Clinical Professor of Psychiatry, Harvard Medical School; Associate Director, Child Psychiatry Services, Massachusetts Mental Health Center; Training and Supervisory Analyst, Boston Psychoanalytic Society and Institute.

Presented at the 20th Annual Meeting of the American Academy of Child Psychiatry, October 1973.

matologists (Suomi and Harlow, 1971) have joined them in studying and theorizing. Hence we encounter a broad, at times intoxicating, spectrum of notions which range from Schiller's poetic conception of the play instinct as a special human gift identified with artistic creativity, to van Lawick-Goodall's (1973) current observation of play as a sign of healthy function in the chimpanzee infant and an activity vulnerable to disruption by loss and mourning. While many such studies have been clinically informative and a valuable stimulus to further theorizing, they frequently suffer from the effort to study the child's play too globally, attempting to encapsulate it within too general a formulation, and over too wide a developmental range, and from a failure to distinguish between "therapeutic play" (play as diagnostic communication and as a therapeutic tool between patient and doctor) and "natural play" (play as a phenomenon of normal development). For the present study, therefore, I have chosen to narrow the field of observation to a single form of play which is (a) a usual, nearly ubiquitous game of healthy children; (b) specifically definable as to its phenomenology; and (c) limited as to the developmental range and the sex of the children who participate in it. Jumping rope is an age-old activity practiced now nearly exclusively by girls during the latency years (ages 6–11). Furthermore, most of the observational data are readily available for confirmation and replication in every schoolyard at recess time for any interested observer.

Review of Selected Literature

Nearly a century ago, and long before Freud's psychoanalytic speculations on the subject, Dame Alice Gomme's (1894–98) monumental compilation of the traditional games of England, Scotland, and Ireland emphasized that children's games served to prepare the child for his adult role and as a model and as practice for the major social and cultural transactions which children would encounter as adults in a "civilized society." Thus, games of war, courtship and marriage, of property, and of authority predominated. She was also aware of the crucial part played by rules, ritual, and magic in children's games, but, lacking the influence of an as yet unborn psychoanalytic perspective, her conclusion from her magnificent and voluminous data was both wistful and Darwin-esque: "It is not, therefore, too much to say that we have in these children's games some of the oldest historical documents belonging to our race, worthy of being placed side by side with the folktale and other monuments of man's progress from savagery to civiliza-tion" (p. 531).

William Newell (1883) was a contemporary of Dame Alice, working in the United States and probably unknown to her. He, too, studied children's games with the method of the disciplined folklorist. He recognized, with precocious clarity, the importance of magic and superstition in the games he observed and collected, but as he also lacked the influence of the later depth psychology he could not make further deductions. In writing, for example, of the "conservatism of children," he said: "The formulas of play are as Scripture of which no jot or tittle is to be repealed. Even the inconsequent rhymes of the nursery must be recited in the form in which they first became familiar; as many a mother has learned" (p. 28).

Later-day child folklorists and compilers, such as the Opies (1959, 1969), began to indicate a greater awareness of the psychological and developmental significance of the data which they accumulated with such scholarly meticulousness:

> These rhymes are more than playthings to children. They seem to be one of their means of communication with each other. Language is still new to them, and they find difficulty in expressing themselves. When on their own they burst into rhyme, of no recognizable relevancy, as a cover in unexpected situations, to pass off an awkward meeting, to fill a silence, to hide a deeply felt emotion, or in a gasp of excitement. And through these quaint ready-made formulas the ridiculousness of life is underlined, the absurdity of the adult world and their teachers proclaimed, danger and death mocked, and the curiosity of language itself is savoured [1959, p. 18].

A number of reviews of both preanalytic and early psychoana-lytic contributions to the theory of play are readily available and need no extensive repetition here (Avedon and Sutton-Smith, 1971; Kéri, 1958; McLellan, 1970; Piers, 1972; Richard, 1960; Sonnen-berg, 1955; Stärcke, 1926).

Freud frequently dealt with the dynamics of play and made numerous references to the play of children in clinical and theoretical papers. In his most systematic statement on the subject (1920), he established the existence of both a "pleasure principle" and a "repetition compulsion aspect" to play. Play in the latter sense represents an attempt to master an unpleasant experience—a point that Waelder (1932) made the central emphasis in his classical treatment of the topic. Repetitive play is a method of "assimilating piecemeal an experience which was too large to be assimilated instantly at one swoop" (p. 218). The symbolism of play and its therapeutic possibilities were recognized and formulated by Melanie Klein (1932) and Anna Freud (1926) and their successors. Subsequently, Bornstein (1945), Winnicott (1968, 1971), Erikson (1972), and others have extended our understanding of play and discussed its specific therapeutic uses. Piaget (1945) and developmental psychologists contributed greatly by their detailed studies of the development and function of play activity. A summary of these views would require us to recognize that play involves (or can involve)—

pleasure (physical, cognitive, and intellectual)
symbolic expression
mastery of trauma (cathartic function)
expansion of ego and adaptive functions
exercise of developmentally appropriate defense mechanisms
rehearsal and preparation for adultlike situations.

A particular game or form of play frequently articulates a combination of these functions at any one time. Consider, for example, the turning of a passive experience (in which the child was helpless) into an active experience (in which the child is master—or aggressor). This is a common and important type of mastery of trauma (cathartic function) in play. The symbolic function of play allows this dynamic to be expressed repetitively and in a multiplicity of play vernaculars and play forms; and the expansion of ego and adaptive functions can themselves be augmented by the increased emotional energies which become available as a result of the catharsis.

One must agree heartily with Margaret Lowenfeld's (1935) early observation: "There is at present no theory of play activity which can be applied to all forms taken by the play of children" (p. 36). In addition, it now seems of highly dubious value to attempt to seek one.

Two recent analytic contributions are especially relevant to the perspective of the present study: Lili Peller's (1954) classical paper "attempting to synchronize the psychoanalytic theory of play with current psychoanalytic insight" has established the value of considering play in the context of the interrelationship between libidinal phases and ego development. With this perspective the roots of some of the differences in the play of oedipal, preoedipal, and postoedipal years become much more comprehensible.

Elizabeth Kaplan's (1965) important study emphasizes the continuity in psychomotor activities during childhood. Thus the latency-age child's rhythmical play activities are seen in a spectrum from the rhythmic head-banging and crib-rocking activities of the infant to the simple strong beat of rock and roll of adolescence. She stresses that (1) progressive rhythmic activities are important in the psychological development during latency; (2) the rhymes accompanying the rhythmic activities may permit the child to dip into the primary process without danger of ego disruption; and (3) it is in the stabilization of a transitional period that such rhythmic activities have special importance in the maturing libido-economic balance.

THE JUMP-ROPE GAME

Elizabeth Kaplan (1965) gives a picture of childhood in motion nearly as vivid and compelling as Peter Breugel's famous painting *Kinderspiele* (Children's Games). She states (p. 220):

When I think of elementary school children, I see them rushing and tumbling at recess, balancing on railings, climbing, sliding, swinging with zest, chanting their rhymes, sucking lollipops, comic books in their hands, tearing around chasing one another. I hear the sound of roller skates on the pavement, hopscotch chalked on the sidewalk, girls skipping rope to chants such as

> Teddy bear, Teddy bear,
> Turn around.
> Teddy bear, Teddy bear,
> Touch the ground.

Let us consider another specific activity: a group of girls perhaps age 6 to 8 bouncing a ball:

> A my name is Alice,
> My husband's name is Al,
> We come from Alabama,
> And we sell apples.
>
> B my name is Barbara,
> My husband's name is Bill,
> We come from Boston,
> And we sell bananas. . . .

In both rhymes, the rhythm, repetition, sequence, and alliteration are enjoyable in their own right and afford a pleasure that is neither dissimilar nor totally removed from rhythmic activities of the infant and preschool child. The rhythmic activities in latency, however, are based upon a more refined use of motor skills, occur in a peer situation, and exercise a child's vastly increased mastery of words, symbols, the alphabet, and learning. If one watches the jump-rope game more closely and listens with greater care, the teddy bear rhyme goes on:

> Teddy bear, teddy bear show your shoe,
> Teddy bear, teddy bear that will do,
> Teddy bear, teddy bear go upstairs,
> Teddy bear, teddy bear say your prayers,
> Teddy bear, teddy bear switch off the light,
> Teddy bear, teddy bear say good night.

The cadence, tempo, and general excitement increase, limited only by the skill of the jumper. One becomes aware of being an observer of a highly sensual experience: disguised, limited, ritualized, carried out in a setting of a group of peers of a single sex, the individual participants highly and intensely involved but utterly unconscious of the developmental roots of the pleasures which they are experiencing.

The techniques and varieties of the jump steps transmitted from child to child in a great oral tradition are themselves highly ritualized and range in difficulty from the simple run and jump over a rope held by two comrades to intricate and difficult figures, e.g., where two ropes are swung simultaneously at right angles while the jumper maneuvers a third rope managing all three loops at once. Between these two extremes are infinite variations in which the skill of the jumper and the excitement of the onlookers intensify as the rope is raised higher and higher or swung faster and faster. In one variation called "snake" the rope is wiggled as the jumpers go over it. The terminology varies from one locale to another for the same or very similar standardized figures. Thus, we find "double Dutch" both in London and in the United States; and "double Irish" is also widespread. There is, in fact, an entire lexicon to be mastered by the latency-age girl. Numerous mimes accompany particular phrases: "say your prayers," "in comes the doctor," "turn your back on the dirty old king"—all of these to be mastered with the exactness, precision, and familiarity of the multiplication table.

Group approval and personal pain are readily observable in this drama. There is approbation and jealous affection for the most skilled jumper. There is no more forlorn a figure than the child who has been relegated to the position of "permanent double-ender"— condemned ever to swing the rope and never to jump it. These observations should come as no surprise when we realize that the rope along with the stick and the ball are the oldest and most widespread of the symbolic paraphernalia of play used in ritual games, dances, fertility rites, initiations and mating ceremonies, harvest rituals, and rain rites. Brown (1955) advises us that "in Europe skip rope was traditionally played on Good Friday and was associated with fertility. In the spring and autumn festivals of ancient China, Korea, and Japan skip rope . . . was among many other ritual contests which formed the major part of fertility rites, as a way of choosing a marriage partner and as rain rites" (p. 4).

We have, then, in the jump-rope game a highly organized and intricate play activity suited to the needs and capacities of the latency girl. The specific and intricate figures and the conduct of the game suggest some of its appeal, but an examination of the rhymes themselves tells us even more about "what little girls are made of."

The Jump-Rope Rhymes

We shall now consider the content and the meanings of content in several jump-rope rhymes. In some rhymes[1] the appeal and pleasure are in the mouthing and hearing of the words (or sometimes the syllables) in their rhythmic context, while the content, from a dynamic point of view, is "meaningless."

> Icka-bicka soda cracker
> Icka-bicka boo
> Icka-bicka soda cracker
> Out goes you.

One is tempted to consider the teddy bear rhyme in this category; but it has another aspect as well—the retelling of a vital, fundamental, and universal achievement of the child in his prelatency years. The child has learned to go to bed, to relinquish the waking ego state for the sleeping state, aided by an ordered ritual so characteristic of the 3- or 4-year-old.

The unwelcome sibling is a frequent topic in jump-rope rhymes: invariably the reference is to a younger sibling and almost always a boy who is, at best, abused and, at worst, exterminated.

> I had a little Brother
> His name was Tiny Tim
> I put him in the washtub
> To teach him how to swim.
> He drank up all the water
> Ate up all the soap,
> He died last night
> With a bubble in his throat.

The manipulation of parental authority is sometimes the weapon employed against the sibling:

---

[1] These rhymes are gathered mainly from children's play, but come also from child patients, colleagues, and from some published compilations (Abrahams, 1969; Ainsworth, 1961; Britt and Balcom, 1941; Brown, 1955; Buckley, 1966; Butler, 1973; Butler and Haley, 1965; Douglas, 1916; Hawthorne, 1966; Herron and Sutton-Smith, 1971; McGee, 1968; Seeger, n.d.; Turner, 1972).

I told ma
Ma told pa
Johnny got a lickin',
Ha, ha, ha.
How many lickin's did Johnny get?
One-two-three-four [etc., until the jumper stops].

In one common rhyme, encountered in several versions, consternation, ambivalence, and a hostile solution find expression:

Fudge, fudge call the judge
Mamma's got a newborn baby.
Ain't no girl; ain't no boy,
Just a plain old baby.
Wrap it up in toilet paper
Put it in the elevator.
First floor—miss
Second floor—miss
Third floor—miss
Fourth floor—KICK IT OUT THE DOOR.

This is a particularly interesting rhyme to study in detail. The introductory expletive is a well-known substitute for two Anglo-Saxon "4-letter-words"—the one anal, the other polymorphously sexual, but both vehicles of hostile exasperation. The notion that mother (?) should be punished is further alluded to in the appeal to the "Judge," while the object of aggressive disdain would appear to be the newborn *ipso facto* and regardless of its sex. Its expulsion is by an anal route, indicating a confusion of anality and the female genitals, which we see illustrated many times over in other contexts.

Sometimes the outcome is less than lethal, but the theme of seeing the baby bathed and wishing it to drown is barely concealed:

Virginia had a baby
She called it baby Jim
She put it in the washtub
To teach it how to swim.
It floated up the river
It floated down the lake
And now Virginia's baby
Has the bellyache.

Some of the hostility to the baby brother in particular is believed to be based in the girl's morose envy of the boy's genital equipment. Perhaps this is the implication of the following rhyme which has a wide appeal; for in many cultures the penis is often referred to as a "little animal" of one sort or another:

> I had a little monkey
> I sent him to the country
> I fed him on gingerbread
> He jumped out the winder
> And broke his little finger
> And now my monkey's dead.

Whatever its origin, the hatred of boys finds consistent and varied expression in a large range of jump-rope rhymes:

> Standing on the corner
> Chewing bubblegum
> Along came a boy
> And asked for some.
> No you little boy
> No you dirty bum
> You can't have any
> Of my bubblegum.

Over and over boys should be rejected because of *their* disgusting anality, whereas girls receive familiar apotheosis from their mothers because of the girls' pleasing, largely oral qualities.

> My mother and your mother
> Live across the way
> Sixteen-seventeen East Broadway
> Every night they have a fight
> And this is what they say.
> Boys are rotten
> Made of dirty cotton.
> Girls are dandy,
> Made of sugar candy.
> Acka-backa soda cracker

> Acka-backa boo
> Acka-backa soda cracker
> Out goes you.

In late latency, however, the picture changes slightly and 10- to 11-year-old girls skip rope to these rhymes:

> Johnny gave me apples
> Johnny gave me pears
> Johnny gave me fifty cents
> And kissed me on the stairs.
> I'd rather wash the dishes
> I'd rather scrub the floor
> I'd rather kiss the dirty boy
> Behind the kitchen door.

Here again the anal note is still audible, though the theme is a more heterosexual one. And still further movement into the dynamics of preadolescence is heralded thus:

> Blue bells, cockleshells
> Evy ivy over.
> I like coffee, I like tea;
> I like the boys and the boys like me.
> Tell your mother to hold her tongue
> She had a fellow when she was young.
> Tell your father to do the same;
> He had a girl and changed her name.

With so much anality, hostility, and envy, can the superego be far away? Besides the "Judge" in the rhyme cited above, other representations of the latency superego make an inevitable appearance:

> Policeman, policeman
> Do your duty
> Here comes Kathy
> The American beauty.
> She can wiggle, she can waggle
> She can do the splits;
> She can pull her dress up

Right up to her hips.
First comes love then comes marriage
Then comes Kathy with the baby carriage
How many babies will Kathy get?
One-two-three-four, etc.

Doing the "splits"—exhibiting the anogenital region—is a surprisingly frequent content of much of the jump-rope rhymes, as it is indeed of several of the steps and figures of the game itself.

Salome was a dancer
She danced the hootchie-kootchie
She shook her shimmy shoulder
And showed a bit too much
"Stop!" said King Herod
"You can't do that here."
Salome said "Baloney!"
And kicked the chandelier.

Although King Herod cuts a feeble figure as an emissary of the superego, the following rhyme is more explicit about the range of instinctual dangers against which control must be sought.

There came two Spaniards just from Spain
Talking about your daughter Jane
My daughter Jane is yet too young
To be controlled by anyone.
Be she young or be she old
For all the money she must be sold
Then don't let her gallop
Don't let her trot
Don't let her play in the mustard pot.

On the one hand there is the threat that the girl, when of age, will be given over to some man's purpose or pleasure for money (again, the anality), and the very sensual excitement of motion (gallop, trot) is a hazard—and defense—against the greater danger of anal pleasures or perhaps anogenital ones. For in our lower vernacular the "mustard pot" is used to refer to the anorectal region, just as the "honeypot" connotes the vulvovaginal area.

Our knowledge of the interrelated dynamics of aggression, guilt, and the primitive superego helps us appreciate the strength of the latency child's curiosity and anxieties about death. This subject, too, receives much attention in the jump-rope rhymes:

> Grannie, Grannie, I am ill
> Call for the doctor get me a pill.
> Grannie, Grannie, will I die?
> Yes, my dear and so shall I
> How many carriages will it take?
> One-two-three-four [until the jumper stops].

Even more lightly, the theme of death may be related to success and failure in the game itself:

> Little Miss Pink
> Dressed in blue
> Died last night
> At quarter past two.
> Before she died
> She told me this:
> "When I jump rope,
> I always miss!"
> Did she go up or down?
> Up, down, up, down, up, down, etc.

Yet another expression of oral danger and of undoing death is illustrated in the following:

> Sally ate a pickle
> Sally ate some pie
> Sally ate some sauerkraut
> And thought she would die.
> Whoopsie went the pickle
> Whoopsie went the pie
> Whoopsie went the sauerkraut
> And Sally didn't die.

Pickles, bananas, pins, and submarines share common contexts in the jump-rope rhymes which treat of sexual issues with frankly aggressive overtones.

Last night, the night before,
A lemon and a pickle came a-knockin' at my door.
When I went down to let them in
They hit me on the head with a rollin' pin
This is what they said to me:
Lady, lady turn around
Lady, lady touch the ground
Lady, lady show your shoe
Lady, lady how old are you?
One-two-three-four-etc.

Similarly, the theme of anogenital exposure and penetration is depicted in a number of variations of the Charlie Chaplin theme:

Charlie Chaplin went to France
To teach the girlies how to dance
"Heel toe around we go
Heel toe around we go"
Salute to the captain
Bow to the queen
Touch the bottom
Of a submarine
[or, And turn your back,
On the submarine].

Or, even more simply:

Charlie Chaplin
Sat on a pin
How many inches did it go in?
One-two-three-four-etc.

Each of these rhymes contain the elements of yet a third in the same genre:

Benjamin Franklin went to France
To teach the ladies how to dance
Heel and toe and around you go
Salute to the captain, bow to the queen
And turn your back on the dirty old king.

The message is anal penetration as a sequel to dancing and sexualized play. This is a continuation into latency of some of the earlier sexual conflicts, confusions, and excitement which the girl encountered initially in the prelatency phases.

A single jump-rope rhyme undergoes elaboration and modification to carry a variety of messages as illustrated by three variations on the "Cinderella" series presented to me in sequence by a 7½-year-old patient. Myra was 5½ years old when she began psychoanalytic treatment because of severe difficulties in going to bed, nightmares, restlessness, fearfulness, and easy tearfulness. One year earlier she had been through a number of frightening hospitalizations for the study of a suspected abnormality of the genitourinary tract. Six months prior to that, when Myra was 4, a 2-year younger brother had an unheralded and life-threatening attack of idiopathic thrombocytopenic purpura; he required a long period of aftercare in which he was treated as a fragile and especially vulnerable child. During the second year of analysis Myra's beginning resolution of her resentful and jealous identification with the fragile brother resulted in a burst of physical activities, latency-type peer relationships and games—including a variety of games with a jump-rope which she occasionally brought to the analytic hours. Transference phenomena and transference reactions at that point in the analysis included both the displacement of oedipal excitement from the father to the analyst and frequent regressive fusions of the figure of the analyst-father with that of the analyst-doctor (urologist) who would cure-excite-expose and possibly harm her genitals. At the beginning of an hour in the 22nd month of analysis, Myra demonstrated a "new" jump-rope rhyme from school.

> Cinderella
> Dressed in yella
> Went upstairs
> To kiss her fella
> How many kisses did she give him?
> One-two-three-four-etc.

Her play and associations then went to kinds of kissing and what kisses from different people would taste like. She became excited

and began to rock her thighs rhythmically, then jumped up to tell
another jump-rope rhyme she just remembered. Jumping with the
rope, she recited:

> Cinderella
> Dressed in yella
> Went upstairs
> To kiss her fella
> By mistake
> She kissed a snake
> How many doctors
> Did it take?
> One-two-three-four-etc.

Myra then took up some clay and made a pair of lips kissing a
snake—"by mistake." I reminded her that it looked like something
else she had made a few days ago—like the model of "doing
bumps" (sexual intercourse). She gruntingly denied this and pushed
the clay into a large ball making a wry face of revulsion (often
associated with her talking of feces and anal matters) and went
back to the jump rope:

> Cinderella
> Dressed in yella
> Went downtown
> To get some mustard.
> By mistake
> Her girdle busted.
> How many people
> Got disgusted?
> One-two-three-four-etc.

This sequence of development in the analytic and jump-rope
material demonstrates the easy movement in Myra from the
oedipal and latency material to the oral, sexual, and death elements
(including the transference danger of erotic interest in and penetration by the doctor), and, finally, to the anogenital excitement
bound by the reaction formation of disgust. The rhymes and the
movement in the hour served to contain both excitement and
anxiety as well as to give pleasure and to exhibit to the analyst. The

rhyme content comes to rest at the anogenital confusion—frequently found in the jump-rope material, but especially relevant for this girl by reason of her medical history of genitourinary tract study. Transference attraction and transference regression permitted the articulation of the material with the other features of the ongoing analytic work.

Finally, there is a group of jump-rope rhymes which deal with "higher" matters. They serve the age-old function of defining the little girl's future life, her lover, her clothes, her home, and her fortune:

> Ice cream, soda, ginger ale, pop.
> Tell me the name of my sweetheart.
> A, B, C, D,
> Does he love me?
> Yes, no, maybe so; yes, no, maybe so.
> What will he be?
> Rich man, poor man, beggar man, thief,
> Doctor, lawyer, Indian chief.
> What will I be married in?
> Silk, satin, calico, rags.
> What will my ring have?
> Diamonds, rubies, emeralds, glass.
> Where will we live?
> Little house, big house, pig pen, barn.
> How many children will I have?
> One-two-three-four-etc.

While this rhyme begins with the oral pleasures of latency (and earlier phases) as a prelude to seeking the *sweet*heart, a nearly identical version of this rhyme begins with a preamble which summarizes succinctly the struggle from which the latency girl is emerging and the universal dynamic antecedent to the girl's later choices.

> I love my Papa, that I do,
> And Mama says she loves him too,
> But Papa says he fears some day
> With some bad man I'll run away

Who will I marry?
[continues as above].

And at the very end, the crucial question is asked again:

Strawberry Shortcake
Cream on Toast
Who's the one *you* love the most?

Summary

A study of the jump-rope game and particularly of jump-rope rhymes illustrates the manner in which a specific type of childhood play articulates basic issues of psychological development in girls during the latency period. In the form of the game, highly sensual motor activity is coupled with ritual, the setting of a group of peers of one sex, and an exercise of recently developed coordinated linguistic and conceptual skills. The content of the rhymes demonstrates the frequent reaching back into prelatency issues by means of chants dealing with sibling rivalry, aggression, jealousy and rage toward boys, and a fear and mastery of death. While some rhymes give "practice" to the girl's fantasy of her future fortune and heterosexuality (as older folklorists would have predicted), there is a striking prominence of themes of anality and anogenital confusion and indications that superego forces are marshaled to defend in particular against the pull of regressive gratifications.

The data of these rhymes tend to confirm some classical impressions regarding the latency period (Bornstein, 1951) and call our attention especially to more recent formulations which recognize that the latency period may be a highly unstable developmental phase for girls in particular (Jacobson, 1964; Kestenberg, 1957). Notwithstanding the lower incidence of clinical psychopathology in girls (as compared to boys in this age range), girls in latency are often in a state of unstable transition, prone to easy regression to pregenital themes and pregenital issues. Other authors have suggested that it is precisely in such transitional periods that rhythmic psychomotor activities have a special stabilizing importance. The jump-rope rhymes are an even more specific articulation of some of the important areas of instability for girls, areas which merit further study in reconsidering the psychology of girlhood during this important developmental phase.

BIBLIOGRAPHY

ABRAHAMS, R. D., ed. (1969), *Jump Rope Rhymes: A Dictionary.* The American Folklore Society Bibliographical and Special Series, Vol. 20. Austin: University of Texas Press.

AINSWORTH, C. (1961), Jump Rope Verses around the United States. *Western Folklore,* 20:179–199.

AVEDON, E. M. & SUTTON-SMITH, B. (1971), *The Study of Games.* New York: Wiley.

BORNSTEIN, B. (1945), Clinical Notes on Child Analysis. *This Annual,* 1:151–166.

———— (1951), On Latency. *This Annual,* 6:279–285.

BRITT, S. H. & BALCOM, M. M. (1941), Jumping-Rope and the Social Psychology of Play. *J. Genet. Psychol.,* 58:289–305.

BROWN, E. (1955), *Skip Rope* (Introduction), Folkways Records Album no. FC7029. New York: Folkways Records and Service Corporation.

BUCKLEY, B. (1966), Jump-Rope Rhymes: Suggestions for Classification and Study. *Keystone Folklore Quart.,* 11:99–111.

BUTLER, F. (1973), The Poetry of Rope-Skipping. *New York Times Magazine,* December 16, pp. 90–95.

———— & HALEY, G. E. (1963), *The Skip Rope Book.* New York: Dial Press.

DOUGLAS, N. (1916), *London Street Games.* London: St. Catherine Press.

ERIKSON, E. H. (1972), Play and Actuality. In: *Play and Development,* ed. M. W. Piers. New York: Norton, pp. 127–168.

FREUD, A. (1926), *The Psychoanalytical Treatment of Children.* New York: International Universities Press, 1946.

FREUD, S. (1920), Beyond the Pleasure Principle. *Standard Edition,* 18:3–66. London: Hogarth Press, 1955.

GOMME, A. B. (1894–98), *The Traditional Games of England, Scotland and Ireland,* Vols. I & II. New York: Dover, 1964.

HAWTHORNE, R. (1966), Classifying Jump-Rope Games. *Keystone Folklore Quart.,* 11:113–126.

HERRON, R. E. & SUTTON-SMITH, B. (1971), *Child's Play.* New York: Wiley.

JACOBSON, E. (1964), *The Self and the Object World.* New York: International Universities Press.

KAPLAN, E. (1965), Reflections regarding Psychomotor Activities during the Latency Period. *This Annual,* 20:220–238.

KÉRI, H. (1958), Ancient Games and Popular Games. *Amer. Imago,* 15:41–87.

KESTENBERG, J. S. (1957), Vicissitudes of Female Sexuality. *J. Amer. Psychoanal. Assn.,* 4:453–476.

KLEIN, M. (1932), *The Psycho-Analysis of Children.* London: Hogarth Press.

LOWENFELD, M. (1935), *Play in Childhood.* New York: Wiley, 1967.

McGee, B. (1968), *Jump-Rope Rhymes*. New York: Viking Press.

McLellan, J. (1970), *The Question of Play*. London: Pergamon Press.

Newell, W. W. (1883), *Games and Songs of American Children*. New York: Dover, 1963.

Opie, I. & Opie, P. (1959), *The Lore and Language of Schoolchildren*. Cambridge: Oxford University Press, 1967.

——— ——— (1969), *Children's Games in Street and Playground*. Cambridge: Oxford University Press.

Peller, L. E. (1954), Libidinal Phases, Ego Development, and Play. *This Annual*, 9:178–198.

Piaget, J. (1945), *Play, Dreams, and Imitation in Childhood*. New York: Norton, 1962.

Piers, M. W., ed. (1972), *Play and Development*. New York: Norton.

Play (1971), *Natural History Magazine*, Special Supplement (December).

Richard, P. H. (1960), The Nature and Function of Formal Children's Games. *Psychoanal. Quart.*, 29:200–208.

Seeger, P. (no date), *Skip Rope Games*, phonograph record no. 7649. Englewood Cliffs, N.J.: Scholastic Records.

Sonnenberg, M. (1955), Girls Jumping Rope. *J. Nat. Psychol. Assn. Psychoanal.*, 3:57–62.

Stärcke, A. (1926), Über Tanzen, Schlagen Küssen, usw. *Imago*, 12:268–272.

Suomi, S. J. & Harlow, H. F. (1971), Monkeys at Play. *Play: Natural History Magazine*, Special Supplement (December), pp. 72–75.

Turner, I. (1972), *Cinderella Dressed in Yella*. New York: Taplinger.

van Lawick-Goodall, J. (1973), The Behavior of Chimpanzees in Their Natural Habitat. *Amer. J. Psychiat.*, 130:1–12.

Waelder, R. (1932), The Psychoanalytic Theory of Play. *Psychoanal. Quart.*, 2:208–224, 1933.

Winnicott, D. (1968), Playing: Its Theoretical Status in the Clinical Situation. *Int. J. Psycho-Anal.*, 49:591–599.

——— (1971), *Playing and Reality*. New York: Basic Books.

Self-Observation, Self-Experimentation, and Creative Vision

OTTO ISAKOWER, M.D.

IN THE COURSE OF STUDYING THE PLACE OF THE ORGANS OF perception in the structure of the ego, I was prompted to acquaint myself somewhat more closely with the history of the physiological investigation of the sense organs. These studies soon concentrated on the eye as one of the foremost tools of recognition in the sciences.

A particular problem attracted my attention: the attitude of the investigator in this field, on the one hand, to observation and, on the other, to experimentation; or even more specifically, to observation of and experimentation with his own person.

Thus I engaged in the study of one particular group of investigators who lived at the end of the 18th and the beginning of the 19th century, the most interesting among them being Johann Wolfgang Goethe, Johann Evangelist Purkinje, and Johannes Müller.

Goethe must be credited with having inaugurated a new departure in the physiological and psychological investigation of the processes of vision. It was his interest in painting that induced Goethe to devote a considerable part of his lifetime to these studies

This paper was read at the New York Psychoanalytic Society on February 27, 1945 and discussed by Ernst Kris, Herman Nunberg, Paul Federn, and Bertram D. Lewin. It is published posthumously. The Editors wish to express their deep appreciation to Dr. Salomea Isakower for making this manuscript available to them.

which were so unrelated to his other activities. From his earliest youth to maturity he tried to achieve technical skill in the pictorial arts, to which, as he confessed, he felt drawn with almost greater impulse and passion than to that which by nature was easiest and most congenial to him. In order to fulfill, through understanding and insight, what Nature had denied him, Goethe sought for technical norms which he could apply in drawing and painting "more than he had ever sought for rules in poetry." His comprehensive work on the *Theory of Color* appeared in 1810.

Here we have a very impressive example of how the urge to comprehend the external world may lead to a preoccupation with the organs designed (or chosen) for its comprehension.

Soon, however, there was someone to tread in Goethe's footsteps: one of the greatest 19th-century personalities in the history of physiology, Johann Evangelist Purkinje, who, from 1819 on, published his highly important contributions to the subjective aspects of vision, the results of his unremitting observations of experiments with his own eyes.

Inspired by Goethe and Purkinje, a third man set to work in this field, and it is his story that I have chosen to present. He was not the most brilliant in the pursuit of the studies in question; yet in other respects he is, I think, the most instructive example. I am speaking of Johannes Müller.

In his case, self-observation and self-experimentation were directly responsible for an almost psychotic breakdown, offering the picture of an acute hypochondriac neurosis and resulting in a far-reaching transformation of his entire personality and career after his recovery. This short, but decisively important episode in his life is the central part of this investigation.

Johannes Müller was born in 1801, in Coblenz on the Rhine, the first of five children of a humble shoemaker. What little is known about his early childhood I shall come back to later. After a brilliant career at school he went to Bonn where he studied medicine, and took his doctor's degree at the age of 21. He became lecturer and later, in 1830, professor at the University of Bonn. In 1833 he was appointed to the chair for anatomy and physiology in Berlin and held the professorship until his death in 1858.

Both as a teacher and as a scientist he worked with unique

success; the circle of disciples he gathered around him has few parallels in the history of science, in respect either to their accomplishments or to the fame which many of them attained.

In order to achieve a deeper understanding of Müller's personality, it is necessary to go back to his childhood and give a few more details of his life history. We do not have any actual material which would give us insight into Müller's early psychological development. We know that he was a quiet boy who had a vivid imagination; he was not gregarious, and kept to himself from an early age. His parents spent all their limited means on his education, urging him to enter the service of the Catholic church; as early as in his eighth year the boy talked of becoming a Catholic priest. There is some important material in an autobiographical report (1826a), which provides evidence for the significant role of early introspection.

> Often, during the years of my childhood, the plasticity of my imagination in the dark and light visual fields intrigued me. One impression I remember most vividly. Through the windows in the living room of my parent's home I could see an old house directly opposite on which the plaster had become blackened in many places; in others, however, it had fallen off in multiform patches so that older and even the oldest layers of color had become visible. When I was not allowed to go out, I spent many hours of the day near the window, occupied with all sorts of things, and looking again and again through the window at the old, dilapidated wall of the neighboring house. Then I would succeed in recognizing in the outlines of the fallen-off and the remaining patches of plaster many a face which, through repeated observation, became quite expressive. For hours, the old house with its walls remained the only specific object in my light visual field, and it kept returning in its uniformity; small wonder that creative imagination finally brought some kind of life into this monotonous landscape. When, however, I tried to draw the attention of the others to the fact that one was forced to see all sorts of faces in the dilapidated plaster, nobody would agree with me; yet I saw them most distinctly. This refusal to appreciate my imagination even made me sullen; my seeing of faces became something mysteriously secret to me [p. 47f.; My tr.].

Müller had published two papers prior to his trip to Berlin, in the spring of 1823. He had worked on the first, *On the Respiration of the Foetus*, at the age of 20, as a student, before he had had time to take even a first glance at the biological sciences.

His methods impress us, even for that time, as incredibly cruel and primitive. He performed 57 vivisections of pregnant animals. The ensuing publication in Latin gives an enthusiastic account of the enlightening results of his investigation—results which he readily disavowed later, in his *Handbook*.

The other publication was a treatise on the Laws and relations of numbers governing the Movements in the various classes of animals, in particular of insects and arthropods. Emil Du Bois-Reymond, his successor and first biographer, said of this paper that Müller might have been prompted to this detailed analysis by the very disgust which the swarming legs of the centipedes aroused in him. For, says Du Bois-Reymond, such was the working of Müller's intellect that this disgust would itself immediately be transformed in his mind into a physiological problem. From early childhood on, Müller had a spider phobia which he never got rid of. Intent on studying precisely the laws of the movements of the spiders, which because of their rapidity the eye could not distinguish, he starved the creatures for weeks until their movements became slow enough for him to follow with his eyes. Less cruel observers of fast movements later invented the stroboscopic apparatus, the kymograph and kinematograph; that is to say, they modified the apparatus of perception rather than the object. On the merits of this paper on the movements of spiders Müller received, after six semesters of study, the degree of doctor of medicine. His treatise is full of phrases gleaned from the mystic-speculative eccentricities of natural philosophy. In his old age Müller is said to have destroyed all the copies of this fantastic production he could lay his hands on.

In 1823 Müller went to Berlin on a scholarship. There he came under the influence of Karl Rudolphi (1771–1832), who held the chair of anatomy and physiology. Rudolphi was highly esteemed and admired by his disciples and friends, both for his scientific zeal and his noble character. He abhorred vivisection, declaring that not even the prospect of worldwide fame could induce him to commit such atrocities. He also worked hard to purge biology of the mysticism which had been introduced by natural philosophy. His scientific approach was that of "pure observation."

Müller was deeply impressed by Rudolphi, both as a scientist and as a person. The two men developed an intense father-son relationship which was bound to promote in Müller a complete identification with Rudolphi, the loving father, especially since Müller had lost his own father the year before.

Having erected this new ego ideal in himself, Müller could no longer in his scientific work maintain the callous, cruel approach to the object of investigation, nor could he continue the mystic-dreamy conversion of real processes into an unreal, pseudorational fabric of speculation. "Pure observation," he was told, had to become his new creed and scientific method.

When, in the fall of 1824, Müller returned home from Berlin, he found the beloved of his youth, Nanny Zeiller, in the society of merry and spirited young men and women. Among them were Jakob Henle, who later became famous, as an anatomist, and his sister. Müller impressed both of them as "awkward and peculiar." He appeared so absorbed in his thoughts that he frequently became taciturn and brooding even in the most animated company.

Shortly after his return from Berlin, Müller was appointed lecturer without salary at the University of Bonn. He tried to practice medicine as a sideline, without much success, however. Later he used to tell that the death of a friend who died under his care from rupture of the intestines had induced him to give up his practice. He needed money; repeatedly and with increasing urgency he wrote to Rudolphi, asking for a position as professor with a regular salary. Nanny, his fiancée of many years, again and again suggested to Müller that he give up his plans for marriage. Nothing can be found out about the real nature of the relationship between the two.

In his public inaugural lecture Müller launched upon a heated condemnation of the "bloody experiment." Addressing himself especially to Magendie in Paris, Müller now proclaimed the principle of pure observation. This public action has a touch of opportunism in it and betrays a side-glance toward the teacher and influential patron in Berlin; but it certainly is more than that. It is the first attempt at a reorientation. However, the inner conflict cannot be resolved by the superficial effort of a "declaration of intention." This was proved by subsequent events. The instinctual source of his energy had not been renounced. Apparently a compromise solution had been looked for and had been found.

He directed his zeal and his curiosity to the study of the organ of vision. He made his own eye the object of investigation and observed the processes in it intensively, relentlessly, and to the point of exhaustion. This cost him a tremendous expenditure of energy, and his persistent ruthlessness finally almost destroyed him.

The results of these efforts are two books which were published in quick succession in the same year. The first and larger one, *On the Comparative Physiology of the Sense of Vision in Man and Animals*, appeared in February 1826. The book contains a wealth of well-observed, important, and often completely new facts about vision in man and animals. It was composed entirely in Goethe's spirit and written very much in Goethe's style. What attracted Müller most in Goethe's observational method in optics was the fact that it started from subjective phenomena.

In his enthusiasm, however, Müller wanted no less than to base the entire physiology of the senses, including even the anatomy of the sensory sphere, upon subjective phenomena, i.e., upon intro-spection, or still more precisely, upon psychology. Thus, for instance, he offers a new but entirely erroneous explanation of the formation of the chiasma opticum—on the basis of subjective observations! This leads him to contradict older authors, such as Newton and Wollaston who with their comparatively much less adequate technical means had developed a correct conception entirely in agreement with the modern one. (That was not the first time he had gone astray in his investigatory zeal.)

At this time Purkinje, who had followed Goethe's lead, had already made a number of remarkable discoveries in the dark field of his own eyes. These discoveries were of lasting value. Müller welcomed the work of Goethe and Purkinje as landmarks of a new epoch in sense physiology. He himself put in the center of the science of the physiology of the senses the specific energies, deriving this doctrine from the fact that one and the same sense organ, however stimulated, will always react in the selfsame manner. Moreover, each sense organ is able to produce its own type of sensation as "fantastic sensory phenomenon" without any external stimulation. By applying this doctrine to physiological investigations, Müller moved right into the core of the deepest psychological problems.

Several months later, in September of the same year 1826, Müller published the little book which deals exclusively with these fantastic visual phenomena. He presented it as a gift to his early friend and fiancée of many years, along with a poem in which he promised her immortality in the union with him. The book, *On the Fantastic Visual Phenomena*, starts with the fantastic imagery that, as a boy, he had seen in the contours on the wall of the house across the street.

Müller now made these fantastic sense perceptions the object of incessant observation in his own eye. He pursued them from their most insignificant beginnings to a level which is accessible only to a few, particularly gifted men; from the delicate luminous dust which so often covers the black velvet of the dark visual field with a golden shimmer, to the perfectly sharp, colored, luminous appearances of peculiarly shaped forms of men and animals which he had never seen, of illuminated rooms in which he had never been. Not the slightest connection can be traced between these phenomena and his experiences during the day.

Müller saw in his dark field of vision such pictures as he had been used to seeing in his earliest childhood. He succeeded in watching them appear, move, change, disappear, and reappear—and not only before falling asleep; he was also able to produce them at any time of the day, when, sitting in a darkened room, he would, with a feeling of relaxation of his entire body and of the muscles of his eyes, ward off all thoughts and all judgments, and become entirely absorbed in the darkness of the visual field. During this state, he was intent on observing only "what was going to appear in the darkness of the eye as a reflex of internal organic conditions in other regions of the body."

He spent many an hour of repose with closed eyes, yet far from sleep, in order to observe these phenomena. If only the place was dark enough, if he himself was quiet enough mentally and free from passion, he could be sure of the apparition, though there was no question of sleep.

Repeatedly he emphasized that the phenomena occurred most readily if he felt entirely well, if there was no special mental or physical stimulation in any part of the organism, and, particularly, if he had abstained from food. Through fasting, he said, he could bring the phenomena to a "marvelous vividness." He was never able to perceive them after he had had wine.

He then explained these phenomena as being identical with those of the dream, well known even to people who show hardly any inclination toward producing them. During the process of falling asleep they are transformed into dream images, which, conversely, frequently remain in the visual field for a short time after awakening.

Müller's intention in his subjective experiments, to observe "what, in the darkness of the eye will appear as the reflection of organic states that obtain in other parts of the body," seems to indicate that he threw the whole amount of movable cathexis from all the other regions into the eye, while the remaining zones of his body were permitted to make themselves felt only feebly and indirectly, and only in the form of entoptic visual sensations. Such an interpretation of his attitude toward the body is corroborated, I think, by the ascetic preparations which Müller made to induce the proper receptive mental state for these observations.

Not many people can induce "subjective phenomena" with the same intensity and ease as Müller could. That is not to say that the majority of people cannot induce such phenomena at all. In some cases, according to our observations, they can do so in precisely the same manner and intensity as described by Müller. The phenomena will appear with ease, clarity, and vividness if, immediately upon waking from sleep, during the night, and in a dark room, the subject will devote his entire attention to them. This would seem to indicate that at such a moment the attunement of the visual sphere is still exactly the same as during sleep, or at least much closer to it than it is during waking hours, provided the waking state is not immediately preceded by sleep.

This, however, leads us to the conclusion that Müller was able to manipulate his *visual sphere alone* to assume the same attunement as obtains in sleep, to a much greater extent and at a greater speed than he could manipulate other ego functions.

From all this it would appear that for the scientific investigation of processes going on in one's self, it is a prerequisite that the subject be able to put himself into a state very much akin to that between sleep and waking, to remain in this state, and to let the apparatuses of his ego become active.

Why should this have to be so? And what indications do we have for its having been so? There seem to be certain attitudes inherent in this in-between state—the first one being a particular form of self-observation.

In a discussion of certain hypnagogic phenomena (1936), I tried to point out how this state between waking and sleep entails of necessity the observation of one part of the ego by another, as conditioned by the phenomena of disintegration of the ego, which is peculiar to the process of falling asleep. But this relation may become manifest only if the process of falling asleep is disturbed or retarded by certain influences (from outside the ego proper), and if this phase is extended and has a chance to establish itself as a state of some duration.

Between the state thus defined and the state of the investigator, there is a wide gap, I admit; a gap that has to be filled or bridged, and with more solid material at that, than is the conviction of the faithful: "For so He Giveth his Beloved in Sleep."

If we look across this gap, we find the investigator: absorbed in systematically induced self-observation, apparently wide awake, yet deeply submerged "in himself." This assertion is based on facts, that is, autobiographical communications whose honesty cannot be doubted; nor can it be doubted that this very state is identical with that of fully developed "research," with all essential criteria: concentration upon a specific object, curiosity, systematic observation, and objectifiable results.

I now turn to a somewhat detailed account of Müller's development prior to the time when we find him engrossed in his subjective studies. I have previously quoted the account he himself gave of seeing variously shaped, meaningful configurations in the broken patches of plaster. Onto this screen, the boy was able, for many

years, to project all his fantasies. The faces and shapes which these
accidentally formed patches assumed for him remained as fixed
images of childhood curiosity. In a sense they even fulfilled the
function of screen memories. They were at the same time an
admissible displacement substitute.

It is important to note that there was no motion in these illusory
configurations. Nor did Müller forget to mention his efforts to
persuade others to share these observations with him, in order to
lend to his configurations a greater degree of external reality. For it
was of the utmost importance to Müller that others should confirm
the reality of what he saw, and recognize these shapes and
configurations as being exactly as he saw them. When the others
refused, or, as he said, "refused to accredit at least my imagination," he became sullen and withdrawn. His "seeing of faces"
became his secret possession, something which he was forced to
consider as abnormal and peculiar to himself. At the same time,
however, it is clear that these images were extremely important to
him, and became the exponents of his most vital interests. "In later
years," he continued, "I no longer could succeed, and although I
could still see those images clearly in my mind, I could no longer
find them in the contours out of which they had originally sprung"
(1826a, p. 48).

Thus, when the ingenious attempt to render these strange forces
harmless by projecting them into the light of day failed, it was
followed, quite consistently, by the inclination of the boy to observe
the processes in his own visual field. After this first rejection by his
environment, he was compelled to withdraw the representatives of
his fantasies into his inner self. Only at night, in the dark, could he
summon them to appear, to delight and terrify him in the form of
hypnagogic hallucinations. But he never succeeded in controlling
them, in summoning them up and dismissing them at will.

He then proceeded to develop an extraordinary control over the
motor apparatus of his own body. It is told of Müller that in his
student days he entertained his colleagues with the most amazing
distortions of his powerful face. He had taught himself, in front of a
mirror, to move each one of his facial muscles voluntarily. He
himself reports, in his *Handbook of Physiology*, that he could even
voluntarily move the muscles of the inner ear, so that people

standing next to him could hear the auditory ossicles crack. With one eye covered, he could also completely control the dilation and contraction of the pupil of the other eye.

Once again, he called upon his environment to witness and substantiate his power. Here we can already see how the purely receptive attitude in observation combines with the motor tendency toward mastery, and turns against the ego. What has been pure self-observation now clearly takes on the character of self-experiment. Müller still requires living witnesses and admirers for his exploits, which he carries out with great narcissistic gratification.

His next attempt was to direct both his destructive tendencies and his visual curiosity (once more combined) toward objects in the external world. This took the form of the unbelievably crude and primitive vivisections which he performed as a student of 19, in order to study the respiration of the foetus. In the publication of this study the names of two witnesses are duly recorded beside each of the 57 vivisections he performed.

Then there was his aversion to spiders, which he attempted to overcome by making the spider a subject of scientific curiosity and investigation. He destroyed the object while he wrested its secret from it—and at the same time exalted his own ego. For with this thesis he achieved the degree of doctor of medicine.

When immediately thereafter he came to Berlin, a happy solution of the conflict (for it was a conflict) offered itself in the person of Rudolphi, who showed him fatherly love and at the same time a new and promising method of scientific investigation: the method of pure observation.

Until then Müller had gloated in the destruction of the object and had feasted his eyes on quivering, bleeding bodies. Rudolphi's strict precept was directed simultaneously against cruel experimentation and philosophical speculation. As a reward for giving these up, Rudolphi offered Müller love and the fulfillment of his most ambitious desires for academic honor and fame.

Müller went so far as to reconstitute, to a large extent, his superego, identifying himself with Rudolphi. But Rudolphi failed to gratify either his desire for love or his ambition immediately and completely. He did not give Müller his daughter: she went to Dr. Purkinje, whom Rudolphi also immediately helped to achieve the dignity and office of full professor at an important Prussian university, while he let Müller return to Bonn, as a lecturer without an income. And as a reward for having given up his uninhibited visual curiosity Rudolphi presented Müller with—a microscope! Müller's frustration and disappointment were bitter.

Back in Bonn, Müller's precarious financial situation and his subordinate academic position made independence impossible. He had to look around for a new father-protector. For Rudolphi he now substituted Goethe. This was all the easier since the principles of scientific investigation which Goethe proclaimed were practically identical with Rudolphi's. In addition, Goethe was already surrounded with an almost godlike halo; and finally, Goethe not only had enthusiastically upheld the cult of visual experience in his poetry, but he had fought for its recognition as a principle of science. It was thus, precisely, that he had paved the way for the scientific triumphs of Müller's brother-competitor, Dr. Purkinje. Moreover, he had given Purkinje in recognition for his achievements both fatherly love and admiration. Above all, Goethe had appeared to Müller, long before Rudolphi, as the Savior in the difficulties of his adolescence.

In Müller's book on the *Fantastic Visual Phenomena*, there is one paragraph which follows immediately the detailed description of his own subjective images in the dark visual field. In this paragraph he quotes a passage from Goethe's novel *Elective Affinities* (1809), which describes the hypnagogic hallucinations of the girl Ottilie. In that pleasant state between waking and sleeping, Ottilie would see the figure of Edward, clad in shining armor, the man whom she loved secretly and hopelessly. The whole description of the girl's hallucinatory experience is really striking in its resemblance to Müller's description of his own subjective phenomena, and Müller confesses with enthusiasm that here for the first time he had found these phenomena outside his own private experience. I have carefully established the biographical detail that Müller became acquainted with Goethe's novel when he was about 15 years old.

The interpretation presents itself that Müller identified himself with the girl Ottilie, idolizing the man Edward-Goethe as a hero and as a redeemer from secret anguish and helplessness. This occurred long before he embarked upon scientific investigations of any kind; at that time his investigations and troubles had been rather of a generally human, intimate nature. Goethe, in the paragraph on Ottilie, became for him the liberator from the harassing feeling of being afflicted with a secret peculiarity. Through the book, as it were, Goethe had conveyed to him the message that these were experiences common to all human beings, about which one could speak and even write. For that Müller was grateful and for that he worshipped and loved Goethe.

Subsequently Müller learned that Goethe had raised these same subjective experiences to objects of scientific research. He then endowed the old ideal with new glory and devoted himself enthusiastically to the study of subjective optic phenomena. He not only identified himself with Goethe, but introjected Goethe's and Purkinje's penetrating visual power. He proceeded to look with the eyes of these two men.

But now the unexpected, the horrible, occurred. Goethe brusquely rejected the first gift which Müller placed at his feet. This happened in the following manner:

Just as soon as the first copies of the *Comparative Physiology of Vision* had come off the press, Müller rushed a copy of this first major work of his to Goethe. With the book, which was written entirely in Goethe's spirit, even in Goethe's style, he sent a letter, dated February 5, 1826. Thus, for the first time, he approached the man to whom he felt particularly indebted for his intellectual development and who was to him, as to so many others, an exalted father figure (I tried to make clear the specific sense in which this was true for Müller). This letter reflects the attitude of an entirely trusting disciple presenting his success to the master—doubtless with considerable filial pride—and at the same time demanding with unmistakable urgency some echo, some response, some reward. This letter was written on February 5. Goethe did not reply until March 29.

From Goethe's diary it may be seen that during these intervening weeks he had composed various drafts of a reply—quite an unusual procedure for Goethe. In the answering letter he finally sent to Müller, Goethe established an insurmountable distance between them with a few stilted and exaggeratedly formal sentences. He stressed emphatically that there could be no question of a common road of which Müller had been so proud; rather, he pointed out the difference in their respective methods and aims, adding that he had completely discarded his interest in the sciences since he was thoroughly occupied with the final edition of his collected works. Concluding, he forced from his pen a "faithful handshake," at the same time indicating unequivocally that this was his "good-bye."

This becomes a certainty when we compare this letter with the one Goethe wrote on the very same day to Purkinje to thank him for his second communication: "Whatever I experienced and discerned in the course of persistent studies in the realm of seeing, looking, observing, remembering and imagining is in complete agreement with your presentation, and through it has been raised to the level of consciousness."

The next event we know of Müller's private life occurred at the beginning of the following year. In 1827 his fiancée Nanny Zeiller wrote him that she did not want to curtail his full freedom to work. Whatever happened thereafter—the wedding was set for the 21st of April. Two weeks before this date Müller fell ill, but the wedding nevertheless took place. Immediately afterward, he suffered a complete breakdown. He became highly irritable and incapable of any strenuous intellectual work, or even of any physical movement. He believed that his legs were completely paralyzed, that he was suffering from a spinal disease, that he was doomed. When writing he felt spasmodic jerks in his fingers and in his hand.

In the meanwhile the rumor of Müller's illness had spread to Berlin where it was believed that he was really suffering from raving madness. The physician in charge had difficulties in convincing the minister of education that it was nothing but a case of not very serious hypochondriasis; he obtained a leave of absence for Müller and a grant for a vacation trip, and by October Müller was fairly well on his way to recovery.

Emil Du Bois-Reymond, Müller's successor and his first and most understanding biographer, has the following to say about his illness: "Apparently, what deranged him, above all, were those subjective observations with which even Rudolphi disliked to see him occupied, this eavesdropping of his sense organs on themselves, their duplication, as it were: it is also known that as a consequence of similar experiments Plateau completely lost his sight and Fechner almost did so. To Purkinje alone was it granted to brave with impunity what was almost a law of nature; as Goethe says of him [Purkinje]: to look into himself without undermining himself." Thus Goethe and Du Bois-Reymond both show deep understanding of the dangers inherent in the investigatory attitude toward one's own person.

It is striking that the eyes apparently did not participate in the symptomatology of the acute crisis of Müller's illness. What specifically is the psychic process which underlies this clinical peculiarity?

Müller, the patient, did not complain about his eyes. He did not allow them to make any demands upon his narcissistic concerns. He condemned them to silence—he refused them his recognition. Turning away from them, he allowed all the other parts of his body to complain loudly and overbearingly, and to receive his entire sensitive compassion.

The eye, this priceless instrument and representative of the world, became useless and an object of hatred. For it represented at the same time the two men—Purkinje and Goethe—who had thrown him into the abyss. They were his enemies. Just as eagerly as he had previously identified himself with them he now must throw them out. If he had to work further with his eyes, he would have to destroy himself.

At the same time, however, this permitted the revival of Rudolphi's strongly ethical precept: not to submit to that visual curiosity which was so inextricably bound up with destruction. It is conceivable that if Rudolphi, the former father ideal, so long overshadowed by the radiant figure of Goethe, had not come into the foreground once more, Müller might have succumbed to his destructive lust for revenge and actually destroyed Goethe—that is, destroyed his own eyes physically.

When as a young man Johannes Müller came to Berlin to study under Rudolphi, he devoted himself at the suggestion and under the guidance of his teacher to specific physiological problems. These investigations were interrupted and left unfinished by his departure from Berlin and his subsequent preoccupation with subjective optical studies; among other things, he had been working at that time on experiments with Bell's law on the motor and sensory roots of the spinal nerves. Much later, long after his recovery, he resumed these investigations and brought them to a successful conclusion by experiments on frogs.

Certain symptoms of his illness, for instance, his hypochondriacal fear of suffering from a spinal disease, or the idea that his legs were paralyzed, apparently reflect these neglected studies—and in more ways than one: first, they represent a reproach from Rudolphi for not having carried through these investigations; secondly, they imply an identification with the animal experimented upon; and then, again, Rudolphi himself may have been meant as the object against which these destructive tendencies were directed.

The imago of Rudolphi was unequivocally placed in the foreground of the conflict, with the entire process of the illness and recovery centering around it; while Goethe—and the eyes—had been pushed out of the center of the struggle. The demands of ethics and of scientific methodology, both personified by Rudolphi, prevailed. It even seems probable that the process of restitution of the ego had already been foreshadowed and initiated when, in the form of hypochondriacal self-observation, the patient had turned to physiological investigation of his own body. One more detail may be mentioned here: at the very onset of his illness, Müller suddenly announced—for the first time in his academic life—a course of lectures on physiognomy. He quickly canceled it, however, and never lectured on this subject. He must have sensed that in carrying out this seemingly academic project, he might have embarked upon a narcissistic-magic display of his muscular virtuosity.

The crisis occurred when, in the course of this self-observation, the sense organ was threatened with being flooded by narcissistic libido. The visual sphere had replaced the object; more than that, it had replaced the entire object world with all its parts, the environment as well as the body, inasmuch as the body is experienced as an object.

Just as the onset of the crisis was characterized by the fact that Müller abruptly stopped his dangerous activity, so were the end of the crisis and his new scientific career characterized by a turning toward the outside world as its exclusive object. A strong, and heavily fortified defense against any form of introspection was established. One example will illustrate the intense and unconditional character of this defense. When, in 1851, his disciple Helmholtz invented the ophthalmoscope, Müller stubbornly refused to familiarize himself with this instrument, or even to examine it more closely.

Thus he emphatically turned away from studying the processes going on inside himself. Soon he altogether withdrew his active investigating interest from human anatomy, embryology, and paleozoology. In the morphological sciences the visionary power of his eyes achieved triumphant successes; it was as if he were able to penetrate opaque matter with his eye, to see forms and their evolution which no one had seen before him.

How it came about that his visual faculties not only emerged unimpaired from this crisis, but even developed an extraordinary degree of penetration, remains intriguing enough as a problem. But instead of attempting to pursue it here, in the stringent theoretical manner that it would require, I shall review in detail the most outstanding chapter of his late scientific career, one that marks the zenith of his achievement, in more than one respect. It is his discovery of the larvae and the metamorphosis of the echinoderms, which he created out of nothing, as it were. This enterprise covers a period of five years, from his 44th to his 49th year.

In the fall of 1845 he was engaged in marine research on the coast of Helgoland. While examining seawater microscopically, he came upon a number of most peculiar forms which puzzled him greatly. He checked in his mind all known divisions of the animal kingdom—these shapes would fit none. The strangest of these forms Müller called, since everything must at least have a name, *Pluteus paradoxus,* because it looked like an easel with a garment thrown over it. But he had no idea about its origin, its place, or its significance. In the following year he found the solution: the pluteus was the larva of a starfish. This was the first step toward discovering the secret of the origin of the great class of echinodermata.

Having ascertained the general principle of the metamorphosis of an echinoderm, Müller succeeded, on his microscopical fishing excursions, in discovering other larvae, and following them up through their metamorphosis into unmistakable echinoderms. There was one form which still bore some resemblance to the pluteus. But instead of an easel, it looked to him more like the case of a grandfather clock on four legs, with the rudiment of a mouth swinging from the back like a pendulum. On one of the sidewalls of the case, where ordinarily there would be no clockface, there grew a thing looking just like a dial; namely, the radial echinoderm. It finally became a sea urchin.

Müller illustrated the metamorphosis of both larvae described so far as follows: "The larvae are related to the fully developed echinoderms as is the painter's easel"—and here he uses the same simile in a functional sense—"to the picture or the embroidery frame to the embroidery." The only part of the larva to be fully taken over by the new creature is the stomach. The mouth is formed anew; the star, at first quite small, keeps growing, the larva decreases steadily, and finally vanishes completely.

In the next year, in the sound of Helsingør, he observed a new larva which he named the "rococo-larva of Helsingør" for its coquettishly curved strings of cilia. When he detected the anlage of the final star figure at the top region of this larva, above the arms, he recorded it with these words: "just as one would visualize the celestial globe on the shoulders of King Atlas, who knows all the secrets of the stars."

The history of the discovery and investigation of the larvae of the echinoderms and their metamorphosis passes before our eyes as a kind of triumphal procession in celebration of the creative power of the organ of vision. Müller had already believed himself close to such a victory 20 years earlier, when, in his entoptic observations, he had tried, with a terrific expenditure of energy, to force his visual functions to maximum productivity. At that time he had failed.

But if one compares these early efforts to experience and grasp the object with his experiencing and grasping of the object toward the close of his life, one can guess at the tremendous change which must have taken place, and the painful development which lies between these two events.

Most significant, however, is the intrinsic correspondence between the two. Is it not fundamentally a repetition of the same process—now, in the oceanic adventure, and then on the bare stage which he populated with his phantoms, in the dark visual field, and still earlier, on the bare crumbling wall opposite his window? Then, as later, he saw himself faced with the same task! Through the visual organ of recognition (under the guidance of the reality principle) first to give meaning to the contours and that which they enclosed, and later to assign these phenomena to their rightful places.

Earlier the problem was to recognize these objects as *unreal* (fantastic), despite their most hallucinatory vividness and reality; later it was to recognize these "unreal" fantastic configurations, which presented themselves as something so uncommon, so foreign, so unrelated to any known or recognized form of organic, living matter, as real forms of life, and to coordinate them into a larger pattern.

The things which he saw then were similar to those which he had seen earlier, that is, they were fantastic in appearance and entrancing in the richness of their color, their incredible strangeness, and the incomprehensibility of their forms. For hours he peered into the microscope, as he had formerly stared day after day at his wall, and night after night into the dark field of his vision. It was as if the old spell would draw him again with sweet, demonic power—he had almost to submit to the compulsion.

But one thing *had* changed! In his searches, he now handled the new objects in precisely that manner which he had since learned to apply to the recalcitrant objects of investigation; the manner in which, still earlier, he had treated living creatures with a violent hand. He forced the delicate, fragile, and elusive forms to remain immobile under his gaze, for as long as he willed it—and then to turn and twist at his command. (How wonderfully had he succeeded in thus disciplining the earlier phantoms!) For this purpose he created *ad hoc* a technique for directing these perishable forms, and devised the most delicate instruments to control them. He manipulated them with the most refined, and at the same time with the most carefully adjusted movements of his skillful hands, and with the speed and keenness of his analytic, dissecting eye.

This was no longer the highly passive self-abandonment to phenomena which crowded in on one—for which one had opened one's eyes wide to let them in. Now it was the purposeful, controlled activity of overpowering the object, or, more exactly, the optimum combination of the two.

Müller the scientist, at the height of his fame, and almost past the zenith of his powers, found himself once again, through the extraordinary character of his findings, under the old breathtaking tension and suspense. He felt compelled to place all the reserves of his visual power at the service of this unexpected adventure. Completely infatuated, he was prepared to give up everything for the possession of these new, enchanting objects.

Was there not the risk that the guards who had been on duty for 20 years would be called off? Then the banished phantoms, forced so long to lurk in the depths, could seize the opportunity to break in again on the now cultivated and pacified territory—all the more since they so resembled these forms approaching from outside as almost to be taken for them. They came threateningly close.

But once again there was an unexpected turn. The master felt their presence, trapped the evil spirits before they could conquer the visual battlefield, and forced them to serve him—the only rational treatment for powerful, but recalcitrant elements. He disenchanted them, devaluated them, and forced them to relinquish their forms to him. The old images, now empty lifeless shells, were just good enough to serve as an iconography for the description of the new fantastic creatures. He dragged *them* out of the realm of "historic truth" into which they sought to lure him back. He forced *them,* with powerful exorcism, to help him pronounce something about the reality of the external world, the reality of the here and now.

Müller described these newly discovered phenomena not as organisms are usually described, but by borrowing the names of inanimate objects, for the most part odd household articles stored in the attic. There is only one stirring poetic image, the one of "King Atlas," who knows "the secrets of the stars." The configurations are composed of heterogeneous elements, put together apparently without making sense, in the manner of the wildest surrealist compositions—and thus, once again, with a touch of the uncanny, the dreamlike, the fantastic. The language makes use of symbolism as the dream does, and thus leads back once more into childhood. Similar also to the mechanism of the screen memory, the inanimate objects represent the corresponding earlier scenes. One is reminded of Freud's remarks on the dream of the Wolf-Man (1918): "rigid" instead of "in violent motion."

We seem to have here one of those rare and direct glimpses into the dynamic structure of sublimated activity *in statu nascendi*.

Again and again with fanatical obsession, Müller returned to the sea, until he had solved every single problem of the morphology and development of these forms, of their relation to one another, and until he had assigned them a place in the world of all living forms. He created the system of echinoderms as a separate class of animals.

The completion of this task obviously exhausted his entire strength, for he never even began another large scientific project. In fact, when toward the end a problem arose in the study of the echinoderms themselves and he could not find a satisfactory answer quickly enough, he became restless and depressed. More or less accidentally he had come upon a specimen of an echinoderm, a sea gherkin, with a number of small, fully developed snails inside it. Had the echinoderm in a moment of caprice decided to procreate snails? Could one no longer depend even on the most fundamental laws of nature? The answer—that this was a case of parasitism— never even occurred to him. Once again the old conflict of 20 years ago seemed to rear its head. Rudolphi had been a pioneer in parasitic research, and all subsequent research in this field had been based on his work. But Rudolphi, curiously enough, was convinced that the parasites or their eggs are produced by pathological processes inside their host, whereas otherwise he emphatically denied the possibility of spontaneous generation. The controversial figure of Rudolphi blurred the resolving power of Müller's vision. The snail which Müller found still bears the name: *Entoconcha mirabilis Mülleri.*

After this he rapidly sank into a state of alternating agitated and dull depression, accompanied by renewed hypochondriacal complaints. Physically this was most certainly precipitated by cerebral arteriosclerotic changes which progressed rather rapidly.

One morning in April 1858, not quite 57 years old, he was found dead in bed. A rumor, that in despair he had committed suicide, was never contradicted.

A few years earlier, however, he had had the great triumph of his life. At the height of this triumph, an impressively concise and dramatic phrase escaped the long since sobered Müller; the simile of "King Atlas, who knows all the secrets of the stars." Full of implications and associations, it is an elliptic reference to a verse in Homer's *Odyssey*, in which Atlas is described as the "wizard who knows the depths of the whole sea, and keeps the tall pillars which hold heaven and earth asunder."

BIBLIOGRAPHY

Du Bois-Reymond, E. (1859), *Gedächtnisrede auf Johannes Müller.* [Reprinted from *Abh. k. Akad. Wiss.*] Berlin: Dümmler Verlag.

Freud, S. (1918), From the History of an Infantile Neurosis. *Standard Edition,* 17:3–123. London: Hogarth Press. 1955.

Goethe, J. W. (1809), *Elective Affinities,* tr. R. J. Hollingdale. Harmondsworth: Penguin, 1971.

——— (1810), *The Theory of Color,* tr. Charles Lock Eastlake. London: Cass, 1967.

Isakower, O. (1936), A Contribution to the Pathopsychology of Phenomena Associated with Falling Asleep. *Int. J. Psycho-Anal.,* 19:331–345, 1938.

Müller, J. (1823a), *De respiratione foetus commentatio physiologica.* Leipzig: Cnobloch.

——— (1823b), *Dissertatio inaug. physiolog. systema commentarios de phoronomia animalium.* Bonn: Marcus.

——— (1826a), *Über die phantastischen Gesichtserscheinungen.* Leipzig: Johann Ambrosius Barth, 1927.

——— (1826b), *Zur vergleichenden Physiologie des Gesichtssinnes des Menschen und der Thiere: Nebst einem Versuch über die Bewegungen der Augen und über den menschlichen Blick.* Leipzig: Cnobloch.

——— (1834), *Handbuch der Physiologie des Menschen.* Coblenz: Hölscher.

The Development of the Influencing Apparatus

A Study of Freud's Article "A Case of Paranoia Running Counter to the Psycho-Analytic Theory of the Disease"

MAURITS KATAN, M.D.

THE TITLE OF FREUD'S PAPER REFERS TO THE THEORY WHICH HE developed in his article on Schreber's psychosis (1911). The persecutor, of the same sex as the patient, was or is the person who basically is loved homosexually by the patient. This thesis seems to be contradicted, however, because the female patient described in 1915 appears to be persecuted by a young man. Even today this problem has not lost any of its intriguing qualities and therefore awakens our full interest. Let me add that the importance of Freud's contribution is greatly enhanced by Edward Bibring's remark (1929) that in this article Freud also touches upon another new subject, namely, the persecution by means of an apparatus (Katan, 1946; Eissler, 1971, p. 272). Over the years this subject has attracted considerable attention as a result of Tausk's paper on the influencing machine (1919). Bibring's remark makes it clear that Freud (1915a) was ahead of Tausk in investigating this subject.

Freud did not seem to be aware, in his analysis of the case, that

Dr. Katan is Professor Emeritus, Case Western Reserve University, Cleveland.

he was also covering the phenomenon of the influencing machine. It remained for Bibring to reveal this aspect of Freud's article. It must have escaped Tausk's attention as well, for he never mentions it in his long study (1919).

In order to make full use of Freud's beautiful description of the case, I shall quote from the text:

> Some years ago a well-known lawyer consulted me about a case which had raised some doubts in his mind. A young woman had asked him to protect her from the molestations of a man who had drawn her into a love-affair. She declared that this man had abused her confidence by getting unseen witnesses to photograph them while they were making love, and that by exhibiting these pictures it was now in his power to bring disgrace on her and force her to resign the post she occupied. Her legal adviser was experienced enough to recognize the pathological stamp of this accusation; he remarked, however, that as what appears to be incredible often actually happens, he would appreciate the opinion of a psychiatrist in the matter. He promised to call on me again, accompanied by the plaintiff. . . .
>
> Shortly afterwards I met the patient in person. She was thirty years old, a most attractive and handsome girl, who looked much younger than her age and was of a distinctly feminine type. She obviously resented the interference of a doctor and took no trouble to hide her distrust. It was clear that only the influence of her legal adviser, who was present, induced her to tell me the story which follows and which set me a problem that will be mentioned later. Neither in her manner nor by any kind of expression of emotion did she betray the slightest shame or shyness, such as one would have expected her to feel in the presence of a stranger. She was completely under the spell of the apprehension brought on by her experience.
>
> For many years she had been on the staff of a big business concern, in which she held a responsible post. Her work had given her satisfaction and had been appreciated by her superiors. She had never sought any love-affairs with men, but had lived quietly with her old mother, of whom she was the sole support. She had no brothers or sisters; her father had died many years before. Recently an employee in her office, a highly cultivated and attractive man, had paid her attentions and she in turn had been drawn towards him. For external reasons, marriage was out of the question, but the

man would not hear of giving up their relationship on that account. He had pleaded that it was senseless to sacrifice to social convention all that they both longed for and had an indisputable right to enjoy, something that could enrich their life as nothing else could. As he had promised not to expose her to any risk, she had at last consented to visit him in his bachelor rooms in the daytime. There they kissed and embraced; they lay side by side; he admired her partly revealed beauty. In the midst of this idyllic scene [*Schäferstunde*] she was suddenly frightened by a noise, occurring just once, a kind of beating or ticking. It came from the direction of the writing-desk, which was standing across the window; the space between desk and window was partly taken up by a heavy curtain. She had at once asked her friend what this noise meant, and was told, so she said, that it probably came from the small clock on the writing-desk. I shall venture, however, to make a comment presently on this part of her narrative.

As she was leaving the house she had met two men on the staircase, who whispered something to each other when they saw her. One of the strangers was carrying something which was wrapped up and looked like a small box. She was much exercised over this meeting, and on her way home she had already put together the following notions: the box might easily have been a camera, and the man a photographer who had been hidden behind the curtain while she was in the room; the click had been the noise of the shutter; the photograph had been taken as soon as he saw her in a particularly compromising position which he wished to record. From that moment nothing could abate her suspicion of her lover. She pursued him with reproaches and pestered him for explanations and reassurances, not only when they met but also by letter. But it was in vain that he tried to convince her that his feelings were sincere and that her suspicions were entirely without foundation. At last she called on the lawyer, told him of her experience and handed over the letters which the suspect had written to her about the incident. Later I had an opportunity of seeing some of these letters. They made a very favorable impression on me, and consisted mainly in expressions of regret that such a beautiful and tender relationship should have been destroyed by this 'unfortunate morbid idea'. . . .

[The patient's story contradicted Freud's theory.] My own

observations and analyses and those of my friends[1] had so far confirmed the relation between paranoia and homosexuality without any difficulty. But the present case emphatically contradicted it. The girl seemed to be defending herself against love for a man by directly transforming the lover into a persecutor: there was no sign of the influence of a woman, no trace of a struggle against a homosexual attachment [p. 263ff.].

Freud hoped that if the patient would consent to see him a second time, he would be able to obtain more information regarding this theoretical problem.

Thanks to the lawyer's influence I secured this promise from the reluctant patient; and he helped me in another way by saying that at our second meeting his presence would be unnecessary.

The patient's second story did not invalidate the previous one. However, it provided sufficient supplementary information so that all doubts and difficulties were removed. Above all, she had visited the young man in his rooms not once, but twice. It was on the second occasion that the noise had occurred which aroused her suspicion; in the first report, she had suppressed the first visit, omitting it because it no longer seemed important to her. Nothing noteworthy had happened during this first visit, but something did happen on the day after it. Her department in the business was under the direction of an elderly lady whom she described as follows: 'She has white hair like my mother.' This elderly superior had a great liking for her and treated her with affection, though sometimes she teased her; the girl regarded herself as her particular favourite. On the day after her first visit to the young man's rooms he appeared in the office to discuss some business matter with this elderly lady. While they were talking in low voices, a feeling of certainty suddenly developed in the patient that he was telling her about their adventure of the previous day—indeed, that the two of them had for some time been having a love-affair, which she had hitherto overlooked. The white-haired motherly old lady now knew everything, and her speech and conduct in the course of the day confirmed the patient's suspicion. At the first opportunity she took her lover to task about his betrayal. He naturally protested

---

[1] In his study on Schreber (1911), Freud states that these friends were Jung and Ferenczi (p. 59).

vigorously against what he called a senseless accusation. For the time being, in fact, he succeeded in freeing her from her delusion, and she regained enough confidence to repeat her visit to his rooms a short time—I believe it was a few weeks—afterwards. The rest we know already from her first narrative [p. 266f.; I have changed a few words of the translation because I think the substituted words come closer to expressing Freud's meaning.]

First, let us try to find Freud's main line of thought underlying his explanation of the case.

In the first place, this new information removes any doubts as to the pathological nature of her suspicion. It is easy to see that the white-haired elderly superior was a substitute for her mother, that in spite of his youth her lover had been put in the place of her father, and that it was the strength of her mother-complex which had driven the patient to suspect a love-relationship between these ill-matched partners, however unlikely such a relation might be. Moreover, this disposes of the apparent contradiction to the expectation, based on psycho-analytic theory, that the development of a delusion of persecution will turn out to be determined by an over-powerful homosexual attachment. The *original* persecutor— the agency whose influence the patient wishes to escape—is here again not a man but a woman. The superior knew about the girl's love affairs, disapproved of them, and showed her disapproval by mysterious hints. The patient's attachment to her own sex opposed her attempts to adopt a person of the other sex as a love-object. Her love for her mother had become the spokesman of all those tendencies which, playing the part of a 'conscience,' seek to arrest a girl's first step along the new road to normal sexual satisfaction—in many respects a dangerous one; and indeed it succeeded in disturbing her relation with men [p. 267].

Thus Freud traces back the origin of the patient's conflict to her infantile relationship with her parents. He concluded that the patient had a strong homosexual attachment to her mother. This attachment was displaced onto the elderly lady, the patient's superior. The young woman tried to conquer her homosexual attachment by entering into a love affair with a young man. It is clear that Freud conceived of the basic conflict as one between a homosexual and a heterosexual instinctual drive. The ego used the heterosexual drive as a defense against the homosexual one. On the basis of this concept of the conflict, Freud was able to state that in the present situation, too, the original persecutor was not a man but a woman.

Freud must have found this conclusion very satisfying. The contradiction which originally existed between the clinical manifestations and the theory was now eradicated. This contradiction was the key word in the title of the article. Therefore, Freud had achieved the main goal of his article, a goal which he had set forth in the title. Of course, he also had to include the vicissitudes of the basic conflict.

Before reviewing these vicissitudes, let me return first to the patient's delusion of persecution. Compared with Schreber's delusions of persecution, this patient's delusions are quite different. According to Freud, strong feelings of guilt form an essential part of this type of delusion. For certainly in the more normal part of her mind, this patient must have thought that if the elderly lady knew what the patient had done, the older woman would have disapproved of her. Even for this normal reason the patient must have felt very guilty. Yet these normal feelings of guilt were immediately accompanied by far stronger guilt feelings of a psychotic origin. In her delusion, the patient imagined that her lover told the lady everything about her love affair. In connection with this information, the patient developed delusions of reference in which the lady showed her disapproval. This delusional disapproval was already the projection of the patient's guilt. However, she was not at all aware of this. She perceived the situation quite differently because, to her, it was the lady's disapproval that caused her guilt. I shall come back to the origin of her guilt feelings later. Indeed, her persecutory ideas were quite different from the usual delusions of persecution. However, this entire group of delusions, individually different as they may be, share the common factor of originating from warding off intolerable homosexual strivings.

Freud's conclusion that the antagonism between the patient's heterosexual and homosexual instinctual drives is at the center of her conflict directs the course of the remainder of his paper. He states that the conflict "is dealt with in the form of one neurosis or another, according to the subject's available disposition" (p. 267f.; the word "available" is missing in the English text). Freud points out that the neurotic reaction is determined by the infantile and not by the present-day relationship to her mother. He makes a similar remark about the way the patient tries to rid herself of the homosexual component: "her disposition, which need not be discussed here, enabled this to occur in the form of a paranoic delusion" (p. 268).

By not discussing the patient's disposition, Freud avoids any attempt to differentiate between a neurotic and a psychotic reaction. Not until several years later did he make a start by differentiating between normal, neurotic, and psychotic jealousy (1922). In an article about paranoia (Katan, 1969a), I have tried to expand this idea of Freud's. At the time when Freud was writing about this particular patient, he was still at the very beginning of his attempt to develop metapsychological insights. At that time it would have been impossible for him to explain how the same conflict could occur under normal, neurotic, prepsychotic, and psychotic conditions.

A remark similar to those quoted appears in 1911: "An intense resistance to this phantasy arose on the part of Schreber's personality, and the ensuing defensive struggle, which might perhaps just as well have assumed some other shape, took on, for reasons unknown to us, that of a delusion of persecution" (p. 47).

As early as in his correspondence with Fliess, Freud had commented as follows about paranoia: "There could be no doubt whatever about the defence; but it might just as well have produced a hysterical symptom or an obsession" (1950, p. 111). Thus, over a long span of time, Freud was puzzled why what seemed to be the same type of conflict could be mastered on some occasions only by a psychotic reaction, whereas on other occasions hysterical or obsessional defense mechanisms sufficed.

Freud next tried to determine how the basic conflict about the homosexual urge could be transformed so extensively that in the second eruption of delusions the woman no longer plays a role. He concluded that a displacement had taken place from the woman (the mother figure) to the man (the father figure). Freud explicitly defended his conviction that in this phase[2] (i.e., the phase of the formation of the second delusion) the man would never have become the persecutor if the displacement had not occurred via the mother and as a result of his relation to the mother, who in the preceding delusions had been endowed with the main role.

In another place Freud tried to explain how it happened that the elderly lady no longer appeared in the second delusion. During the second meeting which the patient granted her lover, she radically did away with the beloved mother figure. She had taken over the mother role through a "narcissistic identification" with the elderly lady. The patient's ego had withdrawn all the libido from the mother object, and this withdrawn libido was used to establish this primitive mother identification. We observe that Freud followed the example he had set in his study of Schreber. Reality was abandoned because the ego had withdrawn the libidinal charges away from the object, and through the resulting increase of narcissistic libido the delusion of grandeur was formed. This mechanism Freud considered the psychotic equivalent of the mechanism of repression. I have strong objections to this concept. Why would this mechanism lead, in Schreber, to a delusion of grandeur, whereas in the case under consideration this type of delusion is absent?

In "Mourning and Melancholia" Freud discussed this narcissistic identification more extensively. I regard Freud's viewpoint as a preliminary attempt to clarify the primary identification. Freud's final metapsychological concept of the primary identification was developed much later (1921, 1923) and differed considerably from this concept of the "narcissistic identification." I do not think that

---

[2] In my opinion, the translator, by writing "this [first] phase" (p. 268), has made a definite mistake. He thought, incorrectly, that Freud was speaking here of the *first* phase, whereas actually Freud had in mind the *second* phase. The translator's mistake can be easily explained. In the first group of delusions the persecutor was a man, and this man even caused the elderly lady to participate in the persecution. Freud thought that this first group of delusions was the psychotic elaboration of the patient's attempt, through a heterosexual affair, to defend herself against her homosexual attachment to the older woman. However, in the delusions which were formed a few weeks later, Freud thought that the man had inherited the role of the female persecutor. In the formation of the first delusions, the man did not play this role.

Freud's concept of this form of identification can be used to explain melancholic delusions.

We are now ready to study Freud's explanation of the patient's complaint about the ticking of a clock which disturbed her during her second *tête-à-tête* with her lover. Freud connects this type of disturbing noise during a love scene with primal scene observations. Practically always, listening to the noise the parents make causes anxiety in the child, for he is afraid of betraying his "spying presence" by making a noise himself.

As one might expect Freud to do, he suddenly opens a new vista upon the symptomatology of the case by conceiving of the noise as a hallucination. The woman's situation justified the sensation of a throbbing or "knocking" in the clitoris. "And it was this that she subsequently projected as a perception of an external object" (1915a, p. 270). Freud bases his interpretation on the dream of a hysterical patient; in the dream, there was a knock which woke her up. Nobody had knocked at the door, but during the preceding nights painful "sensations of pollutions" had awakened her. To prevent this from happening again, the dream was formed at the precise moment when she felt the first signs of her genital excitement. "There had been a 'knock' in her clitoris" (1915a, p. 270). Freud assumes that the same process of projection was responsible for the sound his paranoic patient heard.

During her fleeting acquaintance with Freud, the patient showed every sign of feeling herself unkindly coerced. Therefore Freud doubted whether she gave him a truthful account of all that had taken place during both amorous meetings.

> But an isolated contraction of the clitoris would be in keeping with her statement that no contact of the genitals had taken place. In her subsequent rejection of the man, lack of satisfaction undoubtedly played a part as well as 'conscience' [p. 271].

Thus Freud's remark reveals that the patient quite pertinently had told him she did not have sexual intercourse with her lover.

Freud's remark needs further discussion for still another reason. I conceive of this remark as meaning that because sexual intercourse, which could have been satisfying to the patient, did not take place, only an isolated clitoral contraction could develop. As a result, the patient remained unsatisfied. This lack of satisfaction, in addition to her conscientious objections, caused the patient *in her delusion* to reject the man. In my opinion, Freud overlooked the fact that he himself had explained that her hallucination warded off the development of a clitoral orgasm. Therefore it is not correct to say that "an isolated contraction would be in keeping with her statement that no contact of the genitals had taken place." Furthermore, Freud did not consider the possibility that the patient was far removed from having any desire to engage in intercourse, an attitude which would prevent vaginal satisfaction. (I shall return to this point. If I am correct, then Freud's conclusion is erroneous.)

Freud's brilliant interpretation that the patient hallucinated hearing a noise similar to the ticking of a clock at the moment when she could have become conscious of a clitoral excitement throws new light on this fascinating case. Edward Bibring (1929) has fully acknowledged the significance of Freud's achievement:

> One could also assume for Freud's case that the delusion about the box, respectively the camera, represents an initial or rudimentary phase of an influencing apparatus. The tracing back of the ticking noise of this apparatus to the beating of the clitoris shows that Freud has here a genital projection in mind. The influencing apparatus represents the libidinally cathected organ that causes hypochondriacal sensations and is operated by the love object or his representative [p. 60; my translation].[3]

In view of later interpretations, it is worth while to quote Bibring's opinion that in this process the projected organ has merged with the persecutor.

I want to emphasize that although the instrument, in a projected

---

[3] Peculiarly, Bibring's remark has an unexpected value for the resolution of a current controversy created by Roazen (1969), who claims that Freud was jealous of Tausk's achievements, especially Tausk's ideas about the "influencing machine." Bibring's remark shows that Freud not only had preceded Tausk but also far outdid Tausk in developing insight into this puzzling psychotic symptom. Eissler (1971), in his thoroughgoing criticism, has covered practically every aspect of Roazen's slipshod contentions. Niederland (1971) has also protested the absurdity of Roazen's conjectures.

form, symbolized the patient's clitoris, this is certainly not the most important aspect of Freud's interpretation. Its real significance lies in the fact that the hallucination of the sound made by the instrument serves as a defense. The hallucination prevents the outbreak of genital (clitoral) sensations. This aspect overshadows by far the symbolic meaning of the instrument. However, although Freud explained very clearly the defensive role of the hallucination, he did not offer any metapsychological insight into its structure.

In the interest of a good understanding of the case, I want to make a brief evaluation of Freud's explanation. The outcome of his analysis of Schreber's psychosis, especially the homosexual origin of the delusion of persecution, directed him in his scientific approach to the present case. In 1915 Freud was fully engaged in developing the preliminaries of a metapsychology. Thus he could not yet have found the necessary support from metapsychological concepts for the understanding of the psychotic process. It is still noteworthy that more and more he began to make use of the concept of defense. This particular patient was clinging desperately to reality; moreover, her psychotic symptoms still bore a semblance of some reality orientation. For instance, taking the lawyer as an example, we see that the patient had influenced him to the extent that he thought her complaints might have reality value.

In spite of my objections, I want to express my conviction that Freud's explanation shows fully the touch of his genius. The patient's complicated psychotic development inspired Freud with ideas, still in a rudimentary form, which later became the center of his article "Female Sexuality" (1931). Let me elucidate this theme. The psychotic patient's basic conflict, as Freud saw it, was caused by a fixation of what we would now call the patient's preoedipal relationship with her mother. This fixation prevented her positive oedipus complex from coming to full bloom. As a result, her attempts to ward off her homosexual attachment by entering into a heterosexual relationship with a father figure ended in failure. This failure led to the outbreak of her psychosis.

To this idea Freud added that the role of the persecutor was displaced from the mother representative to the father figure. In 1931 Freud further clarified female development by stressing that in the woman's relationship with the father, elements appear which have their origin in the preceding relationship with the mother. Therefore I consider Freud's trend of thought in his report of a case of paranoia a forerunner of the ideas he developed in "Female Sexuality."

I have made the foregoing remarks for still another reason: to show that Freud, in his explanation of the patient's psychosis, leaned heavily upon normal and neurotic mechanisms. Beautiful as his ideas may be, however, I do not think they are applicable to a psychotic development, as I hope to show further along in this paper.

I want to add an impression. It would seem as if Freud expresses a certain doubt in his explanation. For instance, in the midst of his explanation, he remarks: "It still seems strange that a woman should protect herself against loving a man by means of a paranoic delusion" (p. 268). Here he breaks off to examine the meaning of the sound she heard. Then, after finishing this examination, he repeats:

> Let us consider again the outstanding fact that the patient protected herself against her love for a man by means of a paranoic delusion. The key to the understanding of this is to be found in the history of the development of the delusion. As we might have expected, the latter was at first aimed against the woman. But now, *on this paranoic basis, the advance from a female to a male object was accomplished.* Such an advance is unusual in paranoia; as a rule we find that the victim of persecution remains fixated to the same persons, and therefore to the same sex to which his love-objects belonged before the paranoic transformation took place [p. 271].

Is it not as if Freud, despite his strenuous scientific efforts, is unable to shake off his doubts about his own method?

I have already mentioned that around the year 1915 the circumstances were not favorable for an explanation of a psychotic process. An independent research on the case should be based upon Freud's discovery of the patient's homosexual attachment to the elderly lady and the interpretation of the patient's complaint about the ticking of the clock. *Without this last interpretation, a deeper understanding of the case would still be impossible.* In addition to these two factors, there is a third factor which encourages the reader to reexamine the patient's psychosis.

Freud felt compelled at the beginning of his article (in the second paragraph, to be exact) to make the following comment:

(Before I continue the account, I must confess that I have altered the *milieu* of the case in order to preserve the incognito of the people concerned, but that I have altered nothing else. I consider it a wrong practice, however excellent the motive may be, to alter any detail in the presentation of a case. One can never tell what aspect of a case may be picked out by a reader of independent judgment, and one runs the risk of leading him astray.)

The parentheses enclosing this comment are missing in the original text. Neither are they included in Glover's translation as it appeared in 1933 (*Collected Papers*, Vol. II, p. 150). These parentheses, apparently thought necessary by Strachey, interrupt the close relationship that exists between this comment and Freud's ideas about the case. I have expressed my conviction that Freud was unable to silence a certain doubt about the validity of his explanation. His comment points markedly to his awareness that another viewpoint is possible. In the interest of science, Freud generously puts the material at the disposal of anyone who wants to form an independent opinion. The translator, by placing the comment between parentheses, has acted exactly contrary to Freud's intention as it is contained in his remark.

More than 40 years ago I saw a number of schizophrenics who were delusionally influenced by an apparatus. My memories are now too vague to be of any help. Yet none of these patients, I believe, showed such a complete picture of the development of the instrument as Freud's patient. At least—which perhaps comes closer to the truth—I failed to detect it. Freud's portrayal of the case is of unequaled beauty; his sensitive mind has recorded everything that can be of help to an understanding.

These various considerations all stimulate me to assume the role of "reader of independent judgment" who will "pick out" a different aspect of the case than Freud has done.

A New Approach to Freud's Case

Faced with the choice of what aspect of the case to select, I shall

settle on the suddenness with which the psychosis manifested itself.
Nobody could have foreseen that a love relationship desired by both
partners would have brought such an immediate disastrous result.
It has been my experience that if one is able to study accurately
such overhurried developments, one finds that practically always
there were preceding signs indicating that a psychotic process was
in the making. Are such warning signs detectable in the outwardly
uneventful life of this patient? If so, then in our search for warning
signs we may expect help from the manner in which the patient
told Freud of her experience. In her first interview with him she did
not mention that she had visited her lover twice. She omitted
mention of the first meeting with her lover because nothing out of
the ordinary occurred at that time. Thanks to Freud, we know that
such omissions hide the key to a better understanding. Accordingly
our attention is directed toward the patient's first set of delusions in
which she accused her lover of having betrayed her. These are very
complicated delusions. At first sight, we do not know how the
various parts fit together to form one cohesive idea. Notwithstanding the irrationality of psychotic thinking, it does not make good
sense that the man told the elderly lady with whom he had already
engaged in a sexual relationship that he had started a love affair
with the patient as well. The older woman, as far as he was
concerned, did not seem to mind his escapade at all. However, in
sharp contrast to her attitude toward the young man, she disapproved of the patient's behavior. The only conclusion I can arrive
at is that the man had lured the patient into this affair in order to
show her in a bad light to the elderly lady. It takes some time to
arrive at an understanding of the motivation behind his conduct.
Apparently the young man thought—of course only according to
the patient's delusional thinking—that the patient was trying to
interfere in his relationship with the elderly lady. Her bizarre
thinking now begins to make sense; though it is madness, yet there
is method in it. Clearly, she must have thought the man was
excessively jealous of her and feared her as a competitor for the love
of the elderly lady. In order to remove the young girl from
competition, he persuaded her to have an affair with him. As a
result of his informing his elderly friend of this affair, the latter
withdrew her love for the young girl. We can understand the

patient's anger with her lover, but why did the elderly lady's disapproval arouse so much guilt in her?

For the time being, it appears that we have derived from this group of delusions the maximum benefit available. Let us see whether our investigation of the observation which triggered the appearance of this complicated delusion will help us along further.

The young man came to the office in order to tell the elderly lady something about the business. To an outsider, the conversation between these two persons contained nothing unusual. Given the professional relationship among the three individuals, it can be safely assumed that the patient must have witnessed such a conversation a great many times in the past. Indeed, this assumption is corroborated by the patient herself. She suddenly experienced a feeling of certainty that not only did the young man tell all about this sexual adventure to the elderly lady but also he and this woman had had a sexual relationship for a long time, although the patient had not been aware of it before. Thus she confirmed that for a long time she had seen her lover and the elderly lady conversing together, but had not attached any special *conscious* thought to these previous observations. Light now begins to fall upon the mysterious origin of the patient's psychosis. The delusion in which the patient corroborates my assumption also reveals that from the very start, when she began perceiving these two persons together, her observations had already aroused in her those elements which on the last occasion triggered the sudden outbreak of her psychosis. From the very beginning, these observations had aroused *unconscious feelings and thoughts,* which in the long run weakened her personality structure. Let me be careful not to make an overstatement. I do not mean that these observations were the cause of her psychosis. I simply want to stress that her special reaction to these observations indicated that a psychosis was in the process of development. As far as the available information is concerned, her prepsychotic phase dates from the time she first perceived the young man and the elderly lady together. Thus my previously mentioned experience is confirmed that prior to the sudden outbreak of her psychotic symptoms, for a period of a certain duration, the patient had started to deviate from normality.

What were these unconscious feelings and thoughts which, in the long run, would destroy her reality testing? As suggested by Freud, the white-haired elderly lady was a mother substitute. As a result of this woman's dealing with her in either a tender or a friendly teasing way, the patient had become strongly attached to her homosexually; she considered herself to be the woman's special darling. From the time when she first saw this elderly superior talking with the engaging young man, she must have felt afraid that the older woman would prefer this man to herself. Her fear indicates that she intensely wished to be a man. Only if she were a man could she feel sure that her elderly superior would not withdraw her love for her. In short, the patient must have felt very jealous of the young man! However, according to her own admission, until the moment when her first delusions erupted she had never formed any suspicious thought about the possible nature of the relationship between the young man and the older woman. Accordingly I conclude that her ego had warded off these feelings of the loss of love and jealousy as well as their associated thoughts; her ego had successfully excluded these affects and thoughts from becoming conscious.

The patient's appearance and behavior betrayed nothing of what went on in her unconscious. According to Freud, this 30-year-old girl did not show her age; she possessed an unusual charm and beauty and made a genuinely feminine impression. The jealousy certainly did not show up in her behavior, for she responded favorably when the young man began to court her. Outsiders might have thought that finally Prince Charming had arrived—the one who would awaken the Sleeping Beauty from her dreams. However, the events that followed have a very different lesson to teach.

We were led to believe from the text that the patient yielded to the young man's beseechings for her love. What little of her unconscious motivations we have so far discovered is in sharp contrast to the impression created by the text. As soon as her jealousy was aroused, she tried to drive a wedge between the elderly lady and the young man. She could not compete with the young man for the love of the older woman, so she tried to make him love her! If she succeeded, it would mean that she had lured him away from the older woman. Her charm and beauty did not seem to meet much resistance; immediately the young man began to court her.

The sequence of events, as I have deduced it, is exactly the opposite of the sequence as suggested by the text.

In retrospect, the observation that she looked much younger than her age might have aroused the suspicion that she was extremely narcissistic.[4] This narcissism, in addition to the fact that she was her mother's sole support, might have been the main reason why she had avoided contact with young men. Otherwise her appearance would most certainly have drawn out frequent attempts on the part of young men to come in closer contact with her.

Because of circumstances that are not mentioned, marriage between the two was not possible. This factor could not have exerted an inhibiting influence upon her attitude, for it permitted her to continue to live with her mother and to hold her business position. Therefore neither her relationship with her mother nor her relationship with her elderly superior was threatened by the impossibility of marriage.

A very significant problem is posed by the question: how should we conceive metapsychologically of the girl's efforts to lure the man to her? Freud's opinion regarding this point is, of course, most valuable. He never considered that the patient might be jealous, but instead he conceived of her love for the young man as a defense against her homosexual attachment to the older woman. I am not ready to join Freud in this conclusion. In the first place, the girl did not fall in love with the young man, but she tried to make him fall in love with her. This attempt was an ego defense, because it aimed at preventing the formation of her jealousy, but it was not a defense against homosexuality. For by succeeding in making the young man fall in love with her, she achieved her goal of removing him from competition with her for the love of the older woman. Using the term coined by Ernst Kris, I would call the patient's attempt to win the man's love a heterosexual instinctual drive "in the service of" her homosexual attachment. Her success in winning the young

---

[4] There is a group of people, men and women alike, whose egos seem to be narcissistically fixated at the phase of young adulthood. They may be homosexuals, but frequently they are not. Their experiences, sexual and otherwise, are shallow and do not leave a deep impression. Their faces reveal this fact; they appear younger than they really are.

man over means basically that her homosexuality was victorious. It is obvious that her preoccupation with the young man formed an excellent screen behind which her love for the older woman could remain hidden.

For a woman to try to lure a man away from another woman whom she unconsciously loves is perhaps not a rare occurrence at all. If her effort is successful, ordinarily she will suffer only difficulties of a neurotic nature; her ties with reality will remain fully intact. In this respect Freud's patient was completely different. First of all, the young man was not a real competitor for the love of the elderly lady. The patient only imagined it. Second, this patient's attempt to win the man over to her ended in a psychotic development. Therefore I conceive of her attempt as a prepsychotic defense, which metapsychologically differs markedly from the attempt of a woman who superficially behaves in a similar manner but stays within the boundaries of normality. In the patient's prepsychotic state, homosexuality is not warded off because of guilt, but, as I previously tried to explain, because the homosexuality poses a threat to the maintenance of reality testing. The patient's attempt was a last defense, for it was followed by the sudden outbreak of her psychosis.

Comparing the analytic results of her presychotic defense and the results of the first set of delusions, I am struck by the similarity between the motivations for her prepsychotic conduct and those for her delusional accusations. In these delusions she accused her lover of having maintained for a long time a sexual relationship with the elderly lady and in this way having betrayed the patient. Through his betrayal, her lover successfully removed the patient as his competitor. *Accordingly, in her delusional accusations she ascribed certain motivations to her lover, which were the projections of her own prepsychotic intentions.* For she had loved the elderly lady for a long time and was striving to remove her lover from competing with herself. Finally we have achieved a beginning insight into the secret code of the relationship between her prepsychotic and her delusional defensive system.

Our next step is to become much better informed about the events which caused the transition from her prepsychotic reactions to her psychotic development. I have selected the suddenness with which the psychosis manifested itself as the starting point for my examination of this case. I deduced that it was the patient, and not the young man, who was the dominant force working to promote a love affair. Her penis envy made her extremely jealous of the young man, but her ego succeeded in keeping these feelings unconscious. Becoming conscious of this form of jealousy would be synonymous with becoming fully aware of her homosexual wishes. In the prepsychotic state, this form of jealousy differs from the neurotic form. In this state, the patient no longer merely wished to be a man. Her homosexual desires could be fulfilled only by becoming a man. These desires were irreconcilable with the fact that she was a woman, and therefore they constituted a threat to her ties with reality. According to the patient's prepsychotic thinking, she had to be a man in order to be assured of the elderly lady's love. It becomes clear that her defense against her jealous feelings toward the young man hid her homosexual feelings and thus gave support to the maintenance of her reality testing. However, it was a very precarious support, for, as we have just discovered, in order to keep her jealousy of the young man unconscious, she had to win his love. He would then no longer constitute an obstacle to her love for the elderly woman. This means that her homosexual desires would be satisfied. In this event the warded-off would be victorious, a result which would deal a deadly blow to her attempt to maintain reality testing.

These theoretical considerations give rise to the question whether the first amorous meeting between these two lovers resulted in satisfying the warded-off, and whether this result in turn was responsible for the precipitous course taken by the psychotic development after this first meeting.

This question forces us to return to the clinical facts. It puts the first meeting between patient and lover in the limelight. However, we are confronted with a practically insurmountable obstacle, for, according to the girl's story, nothing unusual took place. Thus the patient's resistance brings any attempt at inquiry to a halt. It should be stressed that during the first meeting she remained free of any psychotic symptoms. These erupted the next day. Fortunately, we are a little better informed about the second amorous meeting, through Freud's interpretation of the sound the girl insisted she had heard. The formation of an auditory hallucination prevented the development of a clitoral excitement. Therefore, during the second amorous meeting, in contrast to the first, she developed a psychotic symptom. Accordingly, in the first meeting, the patient was in a completely different frame of mind than in the second meeting, and I do not think the psychotic symptom, the hallucination, permits me to draw any conclusion about what might have happened during the first meeting. Again, our way toward the acquisition of further information is blocked.

We do not have to become discouraged, however, for not every source of information is yet exhausted. At their second meeting, the two lovers lay side by side; he admired her partly revealed beauty. Of course, there is nothing abnormal about the exhibitionism she displayed in this way. It was at this second meeting that she hallucinated hearing a ticking sound. On her way home, she connected this ticking sound with the sound of a camera shutter. She then accused her lover of having hidden a man behind a curtain so that he could take a picture of the love scene at the moment when she was in the most compromising situation. This was the moment of the ticking sound when she was on the verge of having a clitoral orgasm. She prevented the occurrence of an orgasm by having a hallucination. Her description seems to reveal the pathological nature of her exhibitionism. However, she did not speak of her *exhibitionism; rather, she emphasized that her lover was a voyeur* by having this particular picture taken. By showing this camera picture, he would have it in his power to bring shame on her and force her to resign her business position.

I have already stressed that projection was the central feature of her delusional defense. Affects and thoughts which she warded off in herself were ascribed, through projection, to her lover. Thus I conclude that similarly her lover's voyeurism, as it is contained in her accusation, was the projection of her own strong tendencies to observe her partner. By accusing her lover of wanting to make public that she was on the verge of an orgasm, she was conveying, although in a distorted way, something comparable that she had observed in him. *She must have observed that he was having an orgasm!*

I want to repeat that this happened during the second meeting. We know that she responded to her lover's orgasm by becoming excited herself. An important detail of information is that her vagina did not partake in her excitement. Her excitement revolved around the clitoris, and through her hallucination she prevented the development of a clitoral orgasm.

We have now considerably increased our knowledge of what took place during the lovers' second meeting. However, our goal was to gather new information about the first meeting. Are we now justified in applying our newly acquired insight to attain this goal? As far as the man is concerned, we are permitted to do so. He was so eager to establish a sexual relationship with the girl that, as a matter of course, he would have had an orgasm the first time as well. The man, however, is not the center of our investigation; he can be of help only if through our study of him we are better able to understand the girl's behavior. How did she react to her lover's orgasm on that first occasion?

Let us again picture the state she was in. On her first visit to the young man's apartment she was not yet psychotic. Driven by her jealousy of him, she tried to win him over to her, to pry him loose from his supposed attachment to the elderly lady whom she wanted to love her instead of loving him. I have called this a heterosexual defense in the service of a homosexual drive. At this point we are ready to ask: what, for her, was the most convincing sign that her reaction was successful? One cannot escape the answer: the moment when she observed her lover's orgasm signified that she had triumphed. He belonged to her and not to the other woman. This victory meant that simultaneously her homosexual goal had been achieved! *The road toward loving the woman was no longer blocked by the man. She had removed him from competition with her for the love of the woman; she was no longer threatened by her feelings of jealousy, for they were dissolved!*

It is evident that such a victory could not leave her without an adequate emotional reaction. With what affect did she appropriately respond? Keeping in mind that her jealousy was aroused by her thought that a man was better equipped than she was to win the older woman's love, and therefore in her prepsychotic state she needed to become a man, we may conclude that at the moment of victory she must have felt herself the equal of this man. In other words, she identified with the man in his orgastic state. *Accordingly, she experienced a clitoral orgasm, in strength comparable to that of the man.*

It remains obscure which actions were engaged in by each of the participants in order to achieve this result. The satisfaction of the patient's need to see the process of her lover's genital orgasm enabled her to identify with him. Her voyeuristic tendencies would have been thwarted to a great extent, I think, if she had engaged in intercourse. Thus we may safely assume that intercourse was excluded.

In my explanation I have not been specific enough about how her need to be a man was fulfilled. To say that she identified with the man does not explain how she could become a man. It must have been a very primitive form of identification experienced during the orgastic ecstasy which enabled her to feel herself a man. One immediately thinks of a primary identification, and is then reminded of Freud's definition: "Identification is known to psychoanalysis as the earliest expression of an emotional tie with another person" (1921, p. 105). A few years later Freud provided a somewhat clearer picture of the primary identification: "At the very beginning, in the individual's primitive oral phase, object-cathexis and identification are no doubt indistinguishable from each other" (1923, p. 29). This primary identification is the sign of an object relation. It does not, however, mean that object and subject merge, with the subject becoming the object. It becomes clear that a more primitive reaction is necessary than the one contained in Freud's beautiful formulation if the patient is to feel herself a man. It must be a state in which neither subject and object, nor inner and outer world, are any longer differentiated from each other. In her orgastic ecstasy the patient must have regressed to this earliest mental level in order to satisfy her need to be a man.

In a previous article (Katan, 1954) I have tried to explain why orgasm during the final stage of prepsychotic development is detrimental to the patient's reality testing. Let me try to apply this rule to the psychotic development of Freud's patient. In order to keep the intricate meaning of the patient's reaction in focus, I repeat its peculiar features. Her attempt to win the young man's love warded off her jealousy of him. This jealousy was caused by her need to be a man herself. Thus her attempt to win the young man's love enabled her to keep her need to be a man in check. This defense was able to function as long as circumstances did not cause her to have an orgasm during which she felt herself to be a man. Once her orgastic experience had passed, she found herself confronted with the prospect that reality would force upon her the realization that she had not become a man. The recognition of this failure is synonymous with having to accept castration. When this point is reached, the patient will surrender reality testing. Most patients during the prepsychotic phase suffer from an inordinate amount of anxiety, which is caused by the threat of castration. By establishing a contact with the young man, Freud's patient warded off the various feelings akin to anxiety.

The patient's loss of reality testing did not follow immediately her orgastic experience, as sometimes happens with other patients. The day after the amorous meeting, the outbreak of her delusional symptoms occurred. Her observation of her lover talking to the elderly lady about business affairs triggered the outbreak of her psychosis. A sudden feeling of certainty guided her in extracting from this innocent observation her various accusations. Thus the question is appropriate: what caused this sudden feeling of certainty?

Until that moment the patient had retained her reality testing. She must therefore have been fully conscious that in the near future she would again observe her lover and the elderly lady having a discussion about business affairs. I deduce that if this observation engendered surprise, the origin of this surprise must have resided within herself and not in the actions of the other two persons.

My attention is now tuned in on the patient again. Previously I deduced that she must have felt a sense of victory when she observed that her lover had an orgasm. She had separated him from the other woman, and through this feat her feelings of jealousy were temporarily dissolved. As a consequence, she was able to release her own orgastic feelings.

One might expect that the patient's sexual satisfaction would be useful to her ego as a strong defense against eventual future disappointments. Indeed, this is true under normal and neurotic conditions. However, these conditions no longer existed, and therefore the sudden outbreak of her psychosis does not corroborate this expectation. The content of her delusion shows that she thought her lover regarded her as a threat to his relationship with the older woman. Driven by his jealousy of the patient, he succeeded in separating her from the older woman. In my opinion, this delusion revels that when the patient observed her lover and the elderly lady talking together, the patient had an inkling of a sudden rising feeling of jealousy of her lover. How was this possible?

Apparently the sexual meeting was followed by *a period of unconscious "meditation"*; her ego did not want to acknowledge the existence of the jealousy. As an aftermath of the amorous meeting, the victorious feat lost its luster. The identification with the man had not provided her with a penis. In retrospect, her clitoral orgasm was followed by feelings of inferiority; her orgasm could not be considered the equal of his orgasm. Her jealousy then returned and she felt guilty for having given in to her orgasm, which in the long run proved to be of no value at all. For in order to achieve this clitoral orgasm, *she had been unfaithful to the elderly lady whom she loved. It had all been in vain, and this negative result gave rise to guilt.* Again I want to stress that she still maintained reality testing and that these mental processes remained unconscious, but they were ready to rear their heads as soon as circumstances were favorable. This opportunity arrived when the patient saw the older woman and the young man talking together. These various processes were then at the threshold of becoming conscious. If this had happened, her ego would have become convinced of the unconscious motivations underlying her behavior.

However, we know that nothing of this kind happened. At the moment when she saw her lover and the elderly lady together, suddenly a *certainty* developed in her that he was telling the lady about the sexual adventure—"indeed, that the two of them had for some time been having a love affair, which she had hitherto overlooked." What was the origin of this sudden feeling of certainty (a question I have asked before)?

In view of the patient's projections, the thought arises that she had wanted to speak herself to the lady about her love affair. For at that particular moment, when the motive for her behavior was on the threshold of becoming conscious, there must have been in the foreground especially a feeling of certainty that she did not love the young man; on the contrary, for some time already she had loved only her motherly friend, whose darling she had been. For this reason she wanted to confess her sexual adventure—how wrong this had been and how her unfaithfulness to the older woman had filled her with guilt. To my amazement, I discover that at the very last moment before the outbreak of her psychosis a current of realistic thinking was still trying to keep her on the right track. Yet the weak link in this current was the fact that she needed to be a man in order to win the elderly lady. Therefore the feeling of certainty that she was discovering the truth about herself never got a chance to materialize in that form, for at that particular moment her ego abandoned reality testing, and psychotic thinking took over. *The examiner catches the ego in a state of transition from prepsychotic to psychotic state.* The feeling of certainty became part of her psychotic thinking and then lent impetus to her delusional accusations. *She* did not talk about herself to the lady; *he* did! The contents of her delusional accusations were projections of those thoughts which a split second before had still been part of what I have called a current of realistic thinking.

At that particular moment of transition her ego became powerless to maintain the secondary process thinking which was necessary for normal reality testing. Out of impotence, the ego had to rely upon the primary process in order to cope with the danger that had not ceased to exist. I can only emphasize that that part of her total personality which was involved in the conflict had finally regressed to the undifferentiated state (Hartmann, 1939).[5]

I return to the patient's first visit to Freud. She omitted telling anything about her first amorous meeting and the delusions which occurred the next day. She had omitted this episode because it no longer seemed important to her. During her first meeting with her lover nothing conspicuous had happened.

Apparently the patient meant that no psychotic symptom developed during the first meeting, in contrast to the second meeting, when she had a hallucination. I gain the distinct impression that the patient was unwilling to part with any

[5] In the past I have discussed this regressive process in a series of papers (1940, 1950, 1954, 1969a, 1972), but the examination of the regressive process in this particular patient can be done better in combination with a discussion of Freud's paper "The Unconscious" (1915b).

information about either her own or her lover's orgasm. Indeed, in a lovers' meeting such feelings are "usual" and are considered too intimate to be mentioned. Also, the delusions that followed the next day had less influence on her attitude than those which erupted a few weeks later.

The patient's resistance against revealing anything about her first sexual experience can be better understood after we take note of the psychotic defenses that she developed subsequently.

Next, a period of approximately two weeks ensued when her delusional accusations were countered by her lover with a strong protest against what he called a senseless accusation. For the time being he succeeded in freeing the patient from her delusion and she "regained enough confidence to repeat her visit to his rooms a short time—I believe it was a few weeks—afterwards." This period forms a sort of interlude between her two eruptions of psychotic symptoms and is of the greatest interest to us because of the improvement of her reality testing. What changes took place in her defensive system during this interlude, changes which made this improvement possible?

In this connection I am curious why the patient felt sufficiently confident to repeat her visit, in view of the disastrous result of her first visit. The fact that she prevented the development of a clitoral orgasm proves that on her second visit she had a completely different attitude than on her first visit. To clarify the difference: the first time, the patient yielded to a sexual satisfaction; the second time, she did not. Thus, apparently her confidence in repeating her visit was based upon the hope that during this second meeting she could muster sufficient resistance not to become sexually excited. Her hope was in vain, however, for she again became excited and was forced to resort to the psychotic defense of a hallucination. Question follows question: upon what did she base her hope?

In order to solve this problem, I shall return to "the period of unconscious meditation" which followed her clitoral orgasm. In this orgasm, by merging with her lover, she felt that she had become a man herself. When her excitement had passed, reality forced her to acknowledge that she had not changed at all. She found herself again prey to unconscious feelings of jealousy toward her lover. Next, I want to emphasize that in the aftermath the memory of her clitoral orgasm became disturbing. Just as her lover's orgasm was proof that she had won him over to her, so her own orgasm was a sign that she had been unfaithful to the woman she loved, a recognition leading to considerable guilt. Not becoming a man was synonymous with acknowledging her castration, which caused her ego to abandon reality testing.

After a few weeks, having recovered somewhat, she paid a second visit to her lover. She had now changed her strategy. Her full cooperation for the purpose of causing her lover to have an orgasm was still aimed at prying him loose from his supposed attachment to the elderly lady. Simultaneously, by not becoming sexually excited herself, she hoped to avoid the disastrous results of their first amorous meeting. Remaining frigid would mean that she had not surrendered herself to her lover. Thus she would not be unfaithful to the lady, and no guilt feelings would ensue.

Obviously, her recovery during this interlude does not deserve that name. Her new strategy had the earmarks of the same irrationality as her previous prepsychotic reaction. Indeed, in her so-called recovery she had returned to a prepsychotic reaction, although it differed from the first one. Both prepsychotic reactions were full of contradictions. To sum up these reactions: in order to win the elderly lady, the patient had to become a man. To achieve this end, she had to be unfaithful to the lady. However, faithfulness to the lady excluded the possibility of becoming a man. I have digressed here in order to show how desperate the patient's situation must have become that she found it necessary to resort to such irrational defenses!

During the second meeting, when her lover's excitement very obviously was mounting to an orgasm, the patient again became sexually excited herself. She had planned to remain frigid, but her excitement took her off guard; she was not prepared to meet it with an adequate defense. At the first sign of the pulsating sensation in her clitoris, her ego immediately surrendered its reality testing. In the content of the hallucination the pulsating sensation was represented by the sound of ticking or knocking. The hallucination was not merely a displacement of the clitoral sensation; it interfered completely with the development of her clitoral excitement. The occurrence of the hallucination brought the interlude to an end.

The sight of what started to happen to her lover's genitals, notwithstanding her intentions to the contrary, threatened to arouse in her a clitoral orgasm. It seems to me that only at the very last moment did her auditory hallucination interfere with the process of her mounting sexual excitement. Therefore I assume that the ego used this defense only as a last resort in an attempt to prevent a repetition of a clitoral orgasm. Taking into account that the danger, for the patient, started with the stimulation of her voyeuristic tendencies, I am able to formulate my opinion more precisely. The hallucination could only prevent her clitoral orgasm but had no influence upon her aroused voyeuristic drives. The latter, so to say, were rampant and could cause the patient any moment to become sexually excited again. For instance, these drives could lead to fantasies about what she had observed in her lover, fantasies which very probably would be discharged in masturbatory activities. These considerations convince me that the hallucination as a defense had its shortcomings. It covered only a part and not the total danger situation.

Accordingly, the hallucination did not provide sufficient reassurance. At this point the question arises: did she try to find additional defenses which would afford better protection than the hallucination alone was able to do? Only the clinical facts will supply the answer.

Thus I must find out what was the first clinical fact after the patient experienced her hallucination. On her first visit to Freud, the patient informed him that she had immediately asked her lover what the cause of the sound was and had been told it was probably the little clock on the desk. Freud, however, did not believe she had asked this question on that occasion. The sound, according to him, became significant to her only after she met the men on the stairs. Although Freud's opinion makes excellent sense, I am more inclined to think the patient was right. The hallucination had not afforded her sufficient reassurance. She needed to get a better grip upon her excited state and therefore either had really asked or had thought of asking her lover for an explanation of the sound. It is apparent that she did not receive any satisfactory reassurance; as a result, she set out to find an explanation on her own. My curiosity is aroused: what information did she want to wrest from her lover?

The patient succeeded surprisingly soon in finding an explanation. As she left her lover's room, she met on the stairs two men who, upon seeing her, whispered something to each other. Then she shifted her gaze to the little covered box that one of them was carrying. On her way home, her mind was busy toying with this incident. Very soon the little box became a camera; the ticking sound, the click of the shutter; one of the men, a photographer hired by her lover. And within a very short time her accusation had taken on what was for her an acceptable shape: her lover possessed pictures of her in a particularly compromising situation. Now it was in his power to bring shame upon her and to force her to resign her business position.

The question is whether the patient, after leaving the apartment, used the first available observations to distill from them a suitable explanation, or whether she was guided by an idea which, after she made some adjustments, would be confirmed by her chance observations. Related to this question is my previous conclusion that her hallucination did not cover the total danger situation. Therefore it was necessary to complete the defense, of which the hallucination formed only a beginning, in order to cope with the danger situation as a whole. Indeed, the possibility that a picture showing her in a most compromising position could be used against her was sufficient to destroy any future incentive to become excited! Accordingly, did she have this picture in mind when she made these chance observations?

I want to stress that we have here another opportunity to observe the patient in a state of transition. Her prepsychotic ego was struggling with the temptation to yield to a clitoral orgasm. Too weak to exert control over this temptation, the ego was forced to fall back upon a psychotic defense. When the patient visited her lover for the first time, this defense had not yet become necessary. After the influence of her clitoral orgasm had died down, she was forced to acknowledge that she had not become a man. For this reason, on her second visit she did not want to get sexually excited again. As I see it, a picture of her in this most compromising situation would prove that she was not a man. She was simply a woman, lacking a penis. Is it not too much of an imputation that she had in mind a *printed* picture of herself in that situation? At that moment she was still prepsychotic, and this formed a valid reason for assuming that she was still thinking more realistically. My conclusion is ready: to both partners the other's genitals were visible and therefore bare. When she was at the point of becoming conscious of the spectacle which she herself was offering her partner, it was apparently too late for her to establish a psychotic defense which would undo the stimulating influence of her voyeuristic tendencies. Thus her ego had to switch to the auditory hallucination which could only prevent her mounting sexual excitement from culminating in a clitoral orgasm. The hallucination did not give her sufficient reassurance, and in her upset condition she asked her lover what might have caused the sound. In that way she did not hint at the real cause of her anxiety. Under these circumstances it was impossible for her lover to give her any reassuring answer.

Upon leaving her lover's apartment and while still on the stairs (around the year 1910 in Vienna elevators were a rarity) she met two men. It was her thought that, upon seeing her, they began whispering together. When previously she had seen her lover talking with the elderly lady, she had felt certain he was revealing their secret to her. Thus I assume that according to the patient, the two men must have been informed of her sexual affair. For the time being, we do not know how this might have been possible.

Next, the patient shifted her gaze to the little covered box that one of the men was carrying. On her way home, her mind was busy with this inconsequential incident instead of, as one might expect, with her love affair. There was a very good reason, however, for her preoccupation. The little covered box symbolized what she had seen uncovered—her lover's genitals. In the first amorous meeting, the sight of his orgasm had led to her own clitoral orgasm, and then she had merged with his masculinity. In the second meeting, almost the same thing had occurred. Accordingly, the little box symbolized her lover's penis as well as the one which she believed she possessed during her orgasm. Thus far the displacement from her lover to one of the men on the stairs, and the displacement from the role of the genitals to the little box, must have encouraged the patient to continue her trend of thought. If she could only make a connection between the box and the clicking sound, the box could exert a disturbing influence upon the origin of her sexual excitement. To this self-imposed task she responded beautifully. The box became a camera; the ticking sound, the click of the shutter; and the man, a photographer who, at the instigation of her lover, took a picture of her in a most revealing pose. Thus she had finally been able to bring the disturbing picture of herself exposed to her lover into the general psychotic defense which was to prevent her from becoming sexually excited. This shameful picture of herself had the purpose of keeping her voyeuristic tendencies in check. The goal of these tendencies was represented by the box. This displacement to the box took on the form of a projection as far as she was concerned, but this projection was missing in the connection between the box and her lover. In the final picture of the delusion, the clicking sound became an attribute of the box; this box, by representing the merger of her masculinity with her lover's masculinity, then became a better means of defense than the auditory hallucination had been originally.

I want to discuss a number of aspects of the role of the camera in order to shed more light on the development of the influencing apparatus and its function. Bibring's conclusion is of inestimable value: the camera is such an apparatus! Bibring believed that the patient's projected organ had merged with the persecutor. I have just concluded that the patient's projected organ is the penis which she believed she possessed during her orgastic ecstasy. However, it has also become clear that the camera represents a totally different meaning as well, namely, her lover's penis. Thus two different meanings are condensed in the influencing apparatus. In that way the camera symbolizes her merger with her lover's masculinity at the moment of the orgastic union. Her orgasm became the straw that broke the camel's back, and it was this experience that brought about the removal of the last defense against the outbreak of her psychosis.

The lover persuaded her to visit him a second time. At this second meeting she focused on not getting excited again. Although the temptation to experience again the merger with her lover's masculinity was great, she succeeded at the very last moment in preventing this from happening. What she abolished inwardly became through projection part of her external world—a camera. Thus she psychotically endowed the camera with the role of serving as an intermediary between herself and her lover. In her delusion, she could not become identical with this man, but by creating an intermediary she at least maintained a tie with his masculinity! *Therefore I regard the camera as a transitional object.*

By using the camera as a transitional object, she could participate delusionally in the possession of her lover's penis, but she could not derive pleasure from it. The camera became the backbone of her psychotic defense against ever becoming sexually excited again by her lover.[6]

My last remark leads me to another point. According to Bibring, "the camera represents an initial or rudimentary phase of an influencing machine." It is possible that Bibring thought this because the camera was used only once. I do not agree with Bibring's opinion and I think the camera is really a fully developed influencing apparatus. Through the creation of this apparatus, the auditory hallucination became the click of the camera shutter. Instead of being only a final intervention in an excitement that was aiming toward a climax, the changed meaning of the auditory hallucination served to prevent the development of any sexual excitement at all. The picture of the patient took care of that. Thus, in the final issue, the importance of the camera was passed on to its product, the picture! It is easy to see that she no longer was persecuted by the camera. It was the existence of the picture which became the center of her persecutory ideas. She could not desist from showering her lover with verbal and written delusional accusations, delusions which were beyond correction. I conceive of her behavior as a defense. She was in continual danger of reliving in her fantasies the sexual episode with her lover, and her delusional accusations had the aim of preventing the recurrence of her sexual excitement.

---

[6] During the war I discovered that a blanket in a story by Schnitzler represented the last object to whom the hero was attached, as well as the hero himself, when he was dying. I based this interpretation on my study of schizophrenics. I thought that such a phenomenon could occur only in schizophrenics, but I could not find a single example. Later Winnicott (1953) revealed that the transitional object is a part of normal development. Only recently I discovered that the influencing apparatus is such a transitional object.

A brief remark concerning the patient's ideas of reference is necessary. Take, for instance, the delusions which had the task of propping up the limited defensive power of the hallucination. Immediately following the hallucination, her goal led her to form a psychotic defense which would cover the total danger situation. She did not form a new hallucination, but instead made use of reality observations which on the spur of the moment had to be adapted to her goal.

My preceding considerations give me reason to stress that the formation of the influencing apparatus was necessary for the execution of this plan. Both the hallucination and the subsequent delusions have in common the function of preventing a danger. This conclusion is at odds with a long-standing conviction of mine. It was my thought that a hallucination prevents the occurrence of a danger, whereas a delusion is formed after the damage has already been done. The delusion results from an attempt at restitution. I can now no longer defend the validity of that distinction. This is one of the reasons why I no longer believe that a delusion results from an attempt at restitution.

Another comment concerns the functioning of the primary process. We have had some opportunities to observe the transition from prepsychotic to psychotic thinking. Displacements, condensations, and the primary form of projection become noticeable. I speak of primary projection, for what originally was part of the patient's mind now reappears as if it belongs to the outer world. Thus primary process thinking steps into the foreground. In this special case the psychotic ego used the primary process to endow the camera with the role of serving as an intermediary between the patient and her lover.

It is now time to turn to the problem that inspired Freud to write about this patient. It is the unusual phenomenon of the female patient being persecuted by a man. The patient began by attempting to lure the young man away from the elderly lady whom she unconsciously loved. The courtship led to the patient's clitoral orgasm, which then became the immediate cause of the outbreak of her psychosis. In the aftermath of her sexual adventure, she conceived of her orgasm as a proof of having been unfaithful to the lady. She incorporated the ensuing guilt feelings into her ideas

506 Maurits Katan

of reference, reading in the lady's conduct signs of disapproval of herself. Thus, in the first set of delusions her relationship to the lady still played a prominent role.

Yet, at the second amorous meeting, by preventing a clitoral orgasm from occurring, the patient did not consider that she had been unfaithful and no guilt feelings appeared. It may seem as if the elderly lady had now totally disappeared from the scene. However, in comparing this second set of delusions with the first set, it strikes me that both follow the same pattern. In the first set, her lover had informed the elderly lady verbally of his love affair with the patient. Next she became aware of the lady's disapproval, etc. In the second set, her lover, by displaying the picture of her, could bring shame on her and cause her to lose her business position, a consequence which would be synonymous with losing contact with the older woman. Here the picture is the piece of evidence substantiating the patient's amorous adventure.

I would say that the older woman had not disappeared entirely: the focus of attention had been displaced away from this woman onto the man. In trying to formulate the displacement of the patient's attention more accurately, we may describe the outcome by saying that she had shifted her emphasis away from the love object (the elderly lady) onto the penis of the man.

Freud thought that through a displacement the man had acquired the significant role of the mother figure. If I were to apply Freud's thinking to the development of this case, all I could say would be that her lover represented the phallic mother. The *available* material does not support such an application.

Basing my conclusions upon this available material, I feel permitted to say that when the patient reached adulthood, the process set in which many years later led to her psychotic breakdown. It impresses me that she was never able to use the capabilities with which nature endowed her. Her attractiveness to a young man, contrary to what one might expect, manifested the quickly approaching psychosis.

Can the origin of her illness be traced back to childhood? Freud indicated that the contents of her delusions bore the imprint of primal scene observations. It is easy to assume that she reacted to these observations with masturbatory fantasies in which her desires for masculinity were predominant. But even if these conjectures are correct, does it prove that she was different from any other girl who had the same fantasies but did not become psychotic?

Greenacre (1973) has recently described convincingly the influence of the primal scene on the development and functioning of the sense of reality. However, she does not mention the case of anyone who later became psychotic.

I have not changed my long-standing conviction that psychogenetic, constitutional, and organic factors all contribute to the development of a psychosis. Furthermore, when the mind, because of an organic factor, is forced to function differently, the symptoms will remain psychologically explainable.

It may well be that after a person passes through adolescence, either very soon or even a long time afterward his personality will show itself to be insufficiently anchored in reality, by virtue of the fact that an organic factor has come to the fore which causes a part of the personality to regress to the undifferentiated state. At that point of regression the ego has only the primary process at its disposal to cope with the conflicts which it was unable to master on a higher level.

The discovery that a hallucination may cover only a part of the danger situation came as a complete surprise to me. As a result, the patient in a great hurry formed delusional ideas of reference in order to prop up her too weak defensive system.

Although repetitions will be unavoidable, there is a certain advantage in gathering the impressions which this patient evoked in other people. The elderly superior displayed a motherly love for her and accepted her as a favorite child.

Next, the lawyer. The patient leaned upon him for protection. Since her own father was dead, she wanted the lawyer, as a father figure, to force her lover to behave himself. The young man should stop accosting her! Apparently she had so charmed the lawyer that it was extremely difficult for him to see the pathological nature of her accusations.

The patient was afraid of Freud. He had interviewed her years before he wrote about her. This case became of special interest to him after he was convinced that the persecutor was always of the same sex as the patient. Although we cannot be certain of the exact

year when Freud saw the patient, it must have been at a time when
his fame was already rising. Undoubtedly the patient would have
heard of his new discoveries. She must have been very suspicious
that he would find out what she wanted to hide most, namely, what
had occurred on her first visit to her lover. Originally she had
completely omitted telling that part of the story. Freud was struck
by the fact that, notwithstanding her psychotic complaints, she
made a genuinely feminine impression. Moreover, in the first
interview with Freud she did not betray any shameful inhibition, as
might have been expected, corresponding to her resistance against
Freud.

Her lover's attitude is most interesting. Truly he cared a great
deal for her, and I assume that he was without any psychiatric
knowledge. How did he feel when, after their first love affair, she
attacked him with her delusions? He called her behavior a senseless
accusation. Nevertheless, it did not stop him from continuing to
court her, and he asked her for another meeting. Even after their
second amorous meeting, when her accusations took on larger
dimensions and she besieged him verbally as well as with correspondence, his letters to her expressed mainly his regret that "such
a beautiful and tender mutual understanding" was being destroyed
through "this unfortunate morbid idea."

As I see it, the young man's love for her and his lack of
psychiatric knowledge cannot wholly explain his attitude. In my
opinion, he seemed to be suffering from confusion; he was unable to
understand how a woman who had shared his wishes for an
intimate relationship, something they "had an indisputable right to
enjoy," could suddenly exhibit such contrasting behavior. During
their meeting together she had partially undressed and, according
to my conclusion, not only had been cooperative in satisfying him
but had not remained emotionally cold herself. Intercourse did not
take place, but her emotional reaction must have aroused in him
the hope that another time she would relinquish her resistance to
this act. Indeed, he had become so much involved that he could not
read the ominous meaning in her first accusations. Otherwise he
would have broken off relations then and there.

During the patient's initial interview with Freud, she omitted
telling him about her first visit to the young man's rooms.

Everything that had followed that visit made its remembrance extremely painful to her. Is it not as if the girl and her lover unwittingly corroborated the constructions which are so difficult to come by?

Perhaps some people will ask why I have omitted all mention of Tausk's paper on the influencing machine. This article is so interwoven with Tausk's other publications that one can do it justice only by discussing his works in their totality. Let a single remark suffice: Tausk's patient did not provide any information from which a deeper analytic insight could be obtained.

My study of Freud's case of paranoia will be followed by a discussion of his article "The Unconscious." The intricate problems about the role of the primary process in psychoses can be better and more definitely dealt with there than it has been possible to do in my present article.

BIBLIOGRAPHY

BIBRING, E. (1929), Ein Fall von Organprojektion. *Int. Z. Psychoanal.*, 15:44–66.

EISSLER, K. R. (1971), *Talent and Genius.* New York: Quadrangle Books.

FREUD, S. (1911), Psycho-Analytic Notes on an Autobiographical Account of a Case of Paranoia (Dementia Paranoides). *Standard Edition*, 12:3–82. London: Hogarth Press, 1958.

———— (1915a), A Case of Paranoia Running Counter to the Psycho-Analytic Theory of the Disease. *Standard Edition*, 14:261–272. London: Hogarth Press, 1957. CP 1924, 2:150–161.

———— (1915b), The Unconscious. *Standard Edition*, 14:159–215. London: Hogarth Press, 1957.

———— (1917), Mourning and Melancholia. *Standard Edition*, 14:237–260. London: Hogarth Press, 1957.

———— (1921), Group Psychology and the Analysis of the Ego. *Standard Edition*, 18:67–143. London: Hogarth Press, 1955.

———— (1922), Some Neurotic Mechanisms in Jealousy, Paranoia and Homosexuality. *Standard Edition*, 18:221–232. London: Hogarth Press, 1955.

———— (1923), The Ego and the Id. *Standard Edition*, 19:3–66. London: Hogarth Press, 1961.

———— (1931), Female Sexuality. *Standard Edition*, 21:223–243. London: Hogarth Press, 1961.

———— (1950), *The Origins of Psychoanalysis: Letters to Wilhelm Fliess, Drafts and Notes 1887–1902*. New York: Basic Books, 1954.

GREENACRE, P. (1973), The Primal Scene and the Sense of Reality. *Psychoanal. Quart.*, 42:10–41.

HARTMANN, H. (1939), *Ego Psychology and the Problem of Adaptation.* New York: International Universities Press, 1958.

KANZER, M. (1972), Victor Tausk: The Creativity and Suicide of a Psychoanalyst. *Psychoanal. Quart.*, 41:556–584.

KATAN, M. (1940), Die Rolle des Wortes in der Schizophrenie und Manie. *Int. Z. Psychoanal.*, 25:138–432.

―――― (1946), De Grondbeginselen van de Waanvorming. Doctor of Medicine thesis, University of Leiden.

―――― (1950), Schreber's Hallucinations about the 'Little Men.' *Int. J. Psycho-Anal.*, 31:32–35.

―――― (1954), The Importance of the Non-Psychotic Part of the Personality in Schizophrenia. *Int. J. Psycho-Anal.*, 35:119–128.

――――(1969a), A Psychoanalytic Approach to the Diagnosis of Paranoia. *This Annual*, 24:328–357.

―――― (1969b), Schnitzler's *Das Schicksal des Freiherrn von Leisenbohg. J. Amer. Psychoanal. Assn.*, 17:904–926.

―――― (1972), The Role of the Word in Mania. *Bull. Philadelphia Assn. Psychoanal.*, 22:4–41.

NIEDERLAND, W. (1971), On the Pitfalls of Biographical Writing [Review of Paul Roazen (1969)]. *J. Hist. Behav. Sci.*, 7:100–105.

ROAZEN, P. (1969), *Brother Animal: The Story of Freud and Tausk.* New York: Alfred A. Knopf.

TAUSK, V. (1919), On the Origin of the "Influencing Machine." In: *The Psychoanalytic Reader*, ed. R. Fliess. New York: International Universities Press, 1948, pp. 52–85.

WINNICOTT, D. W. (1953), Transitional Objects and Transitional Phenomena. *Int. J. Psycho-Anal.*, 34:89–97.

Little Black Sambo

MARJORIE McDONALD, M.D.

LITTLE BLACK SAMBO, LONG A FAVORITE CHILDREN'S TALE, IS regarded today as a prime example of racism in children's literature. Goodman, in her study of race awareness in 4-year-old children (1952), is openly critical of *Little Black Sambo* and she cites two instances of the antipathy of American Negroes for the story. She quotes a Negro mother, talking about her child, as saying:

> "Now I just see that he doesn't have books like *Little Black Sambo*. . . . We're not 'black'—we're *brown*. I detest that book and I detest the word. Jimmy was called 'black' once. . . . So was Susan, 'black nigger' to be exact—and right here in the Project where there are nothing but colored children!" [p. 184].

At 4 years of age a Negro boy had already acquired a distaste for Black Sambo. Goodman writes about him:

> Paul's race awareness is of a medium order, but his feelings are strong. He is not clear about kinds of people, though he has a notion that there is a "black" kind, and another kind which he only occasionally labels "white." He sometimes calls the black kind "black Sambo." Paul probably sees himself as being actually very dark, and he clearly prefers not to do so. He always finds white figures prettier and nicer and he rejects "black" [p. 190].

In a recent book, *Black Child, White Child* (1971), Porter says, "Overt stereotypes of blacks, such as in *Little Black Sambo*, now appear more rarely in children's books than they did in the past" (p. 17). Later on in her book she goes further and labels Sambo "blatantly stereotypic" (p. 202).

Dr. McDonald is a psychoanalyst in Cleveland, Ohio.

In "The All-White World of Children's Books" (1965) Larrick singles out *Little Black Sambo* for special mention as "objectionable" in its portrayal of Negroes. It was given this rating by four Negro children's librarians in New York, Chicago, and Baltimore. But not everyone shares this prevailing rejection of Sambo. Larrick quotes Albert R. Levinthal, president of Golden Press, who says, "Almost every time we reissue *Little Black Sambo*, we receive mail deploring it. When it is not available . . . we have had letters asking why we do not keep this classic in print!"

Little Black Sambo has indeed been regarded by authorities in children's literature as a classic, and an outstanding one at that:

> One of the very few modern fanciful tales which might easily be mistaken for a folktale (except for the anachronism of the umbrella!). It has already given unusual delight to two or three generations of small children and is the despair of writers who attempt to imitate it [Moore, 1934, p. 367].

> A masterpiece had appeared and the color line was abolished. [Americans] took [Sambo] to their hearts and into their homes by the hundreds of thousands. Other publishers pirated the book. Unauthorized stories of Little Black Sambo written by other writers . . . began to appear [Stokes, 1936, p. 374].

> It was published about 1900, caused no particular stir . . . at the time Stokes published it in the United States . . . But American children took it to their hearts with a fervor and unanimity that have necessitated reprint after reprint ever since its first appearance in the United States.

> *This story, which might almost have come out of some folklore collection, has about it an effortless perfection which baffles analysis. Its extreme simplicity is deceiving. Just try to duplicate it!* [Arbuthnot, 1964, p. 336; my italics].

Arbuthnot struggles to resolve the paradox that a superb classic must today be rejected for its presumed racism.

> In this age of color and race consciousness some people wish that Mrs. Bannerman had not woven the word *black* into her repetitive cadence of colors. Indeed its use, together with the stylized pictures, has brought about the exclusion of the book from most reading lists. If *black* applied to people is a cause of grief to some of our children, then the book should be omitted from school lists. But Sambo is happy and completely triumphant, the envy of all young hero

worshippers—he outwits the tigers over and over. He has the right
kind of parents, just the kind every child would like to have. And in
the history of children's literature *Little Black Sambo* remains an
important innovation. It has theme, plot, and felicitous style. The
text of the story and the pictures are perfectly synchronized. It
remains a model for the picture-story type of literary composition
[p. 336].

In the few years since Arbuthnot phrased this dilemma, the word
"black" has undergone a startling transformation into a preferred—
even a proud—term. But *Little Black Sambo* seems to be as rejected as
ever.

So a story of only a thousand words has succeeded in generating
some startling contradictions. *Little Black Sambo* is called "blatantly
stereotypic," but its publishers believed it had abolished the color
line. Its reissue is deplored, but its disappearance from print is
protested. It is banned from children's reading lists, but it is a classic
"modern fairy tale" (Arbuthnot, p. 326) worthy of preservation. It
could have come out of folklore, but in fact it is a late 19th-century
tale of known authorship. It is especially beloved by Americans, but
its author happens to have been a Scotchwoman living in India. It
is written with "extreme simplicity," but "just try to duplicate it."
And a final paradox can be contributed by psychoanalysis, for this
story of "effortless perfection which baffles analysis" is in fact rather
easily psychoanalyzed.

At first glance the story of *Little Black Sambo* appears to have
almost none of the usual overt implications of racism, although the
characters are of course black. The language is not in dialect, and
Sambo and his parents are not caricatured according to any
American Negro slave stereotype. It is true that the author, who is
also the original illustrator, has drawn Sambo's mother as fat so
that it is possible to mistake her for a Southern black mammy. But
her correct name is Black Mumbo. Furthermore, Sambo has both a
father and a mother. Black Jumbo, like Black Mumbo, is a fine
parent—"just the kind every child would like to have"—and hardly
fits the stereotype of the weak or missing or unknown American
Negro father.

A contrasting children's classic is "Epaminondas," whose hero is
also a little black boy (Wadsworth, 1927). This lesser known tale is

overtly racist. It begins, "Epaminondas was a little darkey boy who lived with his Mammy." Mammy speaks in dialect and her favorite refrain to her son is, "You ain't got the sense you was born with!" There is no mention of a father in the story, and Epaminondas is a hapless go-between in the feminine world of his Mammy and his Auntie.

Since *Little Black Sambo* is so much more widely known than "Epaminondas" it may seem natural that *Sambo* has become the prototype of a racist children's story. But the paradox remains that *Sambo*, unlike "Epaminondas," does not appear to be overtly racist. For that matter if white people in America had such an overwhelming need for a racist tale, why didn't they take "Epaminondas" to their hearts rather than *Sambo*, which, after all, is not even an American story? An analysis of the two stories suggests an answer. The power of *Little Black Sambo* lies in its roots in the unconscious regions of deeply repressed childhood fantasies and conflicts. The weakness of "Epaminondas" lies in the limitation of its message largely to the realm of consciousness. *Little Black Sambo* presents an appeal to unconscious wellsprings of prejudice while safeguarding against their eruption into consciousness. (At least until recently this was so.) "Epaminondas" presents only a conscious, undisguised expression of prejudice and consequently may be too openly offensive ever to have gained the universal popularity of *Sambo*.

The Author of Sambo

The author of *Little Black Sambo* was Mrs. Helen Bannerman, a Scotchwoman married to an army doctor stationed in India. What meager information there is available about her has been recorded by two representatives of her American publisher, who visited her for "a good Scotch tea" at her home in Edinburgh in the mid-30s. She was then a widow, living with one of the daughters for whom she had written *Sambo*. The first visitor went with a special request (Stokes, 1936) to be discussed later, and the second for the express purpose of obtaining biographical material which so many *Sambo* readers had requested (Fish, 1937). Mrs. Bannerman is described as "a small, quiet, gray-haired Scotchwoman, with a kind face and what might be called a dignified twinkle in her eyes." Fish goes on:

Then Mrs. Bannerman told me about her life, with characteristic modesty, as though she thought it couldn't be of the least interest to anyone. She was born in Edinburgh, daughter of an army chaplain who had been stationed in various far-flung corners of the Empire. His large family went with him, and when his daughter Helen was two years old they were sent to Madeira, where they remained for ten years. Then she had several years at home and in Germany, at school, and later she married an army doctor. The thirty years of her married life were spent in India, and it was in 1889, when she was returning to India after leaving her two little girls at home in Scotland for their health and education, that she wrote *The Story of Little Black Sambo*. But it was to send home to amuse them, and partly to comfort *herself* on the long railway journey that took her away from them that she wrote the story. . . . Mrs. Bannerman loved India and must have been a true help to her husband in his important work of stamping out plague in Madras and Bombay, but she spoke sadly, as mothers in the Indian service do, of the intermittent years of separation from her children. Her daughter told me how she and her brothers and sister had loved the illustrated letters their mother wrote them through those years. She still cherishes them, as children all over the world cherish those two little books about Sambo [p. 356f.].

Thus the author herself explains that *Sambo* was written as a creative effort to master a most painful separation. Judging from the story she wrote for them, I would assume that the children must have been very young and the pain of parting very acute. Although the separation was rationalized as necessary for the children's development, one of the mother's preoccupations on her lonely journey homeward probably concerned the adequacy of her preparation of her two small daughters for their venture alone into the world.

An Analysis of *Little Black Sambo*

The story of Sambo begins with just such a situation. Sambo is outfitted in "a beautiful red coat and a pair of beautiful little blue trousers" made specially for him by his mother. And he wears purple shoes with crimson soles and crimson linings and carries a beautiful green umbrella, both purchased specially for him by his father. Thus bedecked Sambo goes out for a walk all by himself into the jungle.

From a psychoanalytic point of view the clothing made by the mother could represent the child's transitional objects which enable him to endure the developmental separation from her. And the father's gifts of royally colored shoes and an umbrella symbolize the phallic strength which the father passes on to his son. In the original illustrations by the author the father is himself shown with an umbrella.[1] Just why the author has chosen a phallic little boy as her hero rather than a heroine or even two heroines, in this story for her two daughters, is a matter for speculation. Perhaps unconsciously she regarded a boy as better equipped to face the world on his own. Possibly she also was responding to her little girls' phallic wishes.

The parents in this story, it will be recalled, are "the right kind of parents, just the kind every child would like to have." And what every child would like to have as he ventures forth alone into the jungle of life is magic protection. That Black Mumbo and Black Jumbo are the wished-for magic protectors is symbolized not only in their gifts to Sambo but in their very names, Mumbo and Jumbo. Webster's dictionary defines "Mumbo Jumbo" as follows:

1. among certain African tribes of Western Sudan, a medicine man who is supposed to protect his people from evil and terrorize the women into subjection.
2. an idol or fetish.
3. any object of fear or dread.

In the jungle Sambo's adventures begin:

---

[1] In her appraisal of *Sambo* Moore said that the story could be a folktale, "except for the anachronism of the umbrella!" The *Columbia Encyclopedia* (third edition) says of the umbrella: "used as a protection against the sun in China, Egypt, and elsewhere in remote antiquity. *It was often an emblem of rank* [my italics]. During the Middle Ages the umbrella became almost extinct in Europe; its usefulness was not rediscovered until the late 16th century, when it was introduced as the *parapluie* (against the rain). Its use did not become general until the late 18th century, when it is said to have been introduced in England by Jonas Hanway; umbrellas were first manufactured on the continent after 1787." In the story of *Sambo* the umbrella serves an important function as an unconscious "emblem of rank." It is an especially apt phallic symbol because of its erectile and protective properties. For Sambo it also symbolizes control and strength.

And by and by he met a Tiger. And the Tiger said to him, "Little Black Sambo, I'm going to eat you up!"

And Little Black Sambo said, "Oh, please, Mr. Tiger, please don't eat me up, and I'll give you my beautiful little red coat."

So the Tiger said, "Very well, I won't eat you up this time, but you must give me your beautiful little red coat."

So the Tiger got poor Little Black Sambo's beautiful little red coat, and went away saying, "Now I'm the grandest Tiger in the Jungle."

And Little Black Sambo went on, and by and by he met another Tiger. . . .

And so the plot unfolds, as Sambo "outwits the Tigers over and over" to escape being eaten up. The second tiger takes his beautiful little blue trousers. The third tiger has too many feet to wear Sambo's purple and crimson shoes, but Sambo persuades him to take the shoes and wear them on his two ears. When the last tiger cannot carry Sambo's umbrella because he needs his paws for walking, Sambo convinces him, "You could tie a knot in your tail and carry it that way." The tiger does just that and like his three predecessors goes away proclaiming himself "the grandest Tiger in all the jungle." The author's illustration of this last tiger with Sambo's umbrella knotted in its tail and proudly opened over its head leaves little doubt about the umbrella's phallic symbolism.

At this point the "effortless perfection" and "extreme simplicity" of the narrative make it not only undesirable but quite impossible to condense its climax. The passage has to be quoted verbatim:

And poor Little Black Sambo went away crying, because the cruel Tigers had taken all his fine clothes.

Presently he heard a horrible noise that sounded like "Gr-r-r-r-rrrrrrr," and it got louder and louder. "Oh! dear!" said Little Black Sambo, "there are all the Tigers coming back to eat me up! What shall I do?" So he ran quickly to a palm tree, and peeped round it to see what the matter was.

And there he saw all the Tigers fighting, and disputing which of them was the grandest. And at last they all got so angry that they jumped up and took off all the fine clothes, and began to tear each other with their claws, and bite each other with their great big white teeth.

And they came, rolling and tumbling right to the foot of the very tree where Little Black Sambo was hiding, but he jumped quickly in behind the umbrella. And the Tigers all caught hold of each others' tails, as they wrangled and scrambled, and so they found themselves in a ring round the tree.

Then, when the Tigers were very wee and very far away, Little Black Sambo jumped up, and called out, "Oh, Tigers! why have you taken off all your clothes? Don't you want them any more?" But the Tigers only answered, "Gr-r-rrrr!"

Then Little Black Sambo said, "If you want them, say so, or I'll take them away." But the Tigers would not let go of each other's tails, and so they could only say "Gr-r-r-r-rrrrrrr!"

So Little Black Sambo put on all his fine clothes again and walked off.

And the Tigers were very, very angry, but still they would not let go of each others' tails. And they were so angry, that they ran faster and faster, till they were whirling round so fast that you couldn't see their legs at all.

And they still ran faster and faster and faster, till they all just melted away, and there was nothing left but a great big pool of melted butter (or "ghi," as it is called in India) round the foot of the tree.

Disguised in this jungle drama of *Little Black Sambo* is the story of a small child's reactions to seeing the primal scene. Sambo, helplessly looking on at the fighting tigers, is the little child transfixed as he watches his parents in intercourse. No longer is he the manly little adventurer, the master of his own fate who can even outwit tigers. The final surrender of his umbrella—the symbol of his masculinity—marked the destruction of that illusion, and without his protective umbrella Sambo gets wet—for it is just then in the story that Sambo starts to cry.

In his regressed and frightened state, without his clothes or umbrella, Sambo hears a horrible "Gr-r-rrr" and fears the tigers are coming back to eat him up. But this clever little fellow does not even run away to save himself. Instead he hides behind a palm tree and "peeps" out to watch the tigers fighting over who is the grandest. This interpretation of the fight as a narcissistic struggle for power is the most likely explanation the little boy can think of for a fight. It also reveals that the child feels *himself* to be the instigator of the disturbance. After all, is it not Sambo's finery that causes the tigers to quarrel over who is the grandest?

The primal scene continues as the tigers take off their clothes and claw and bite each other. Then they come rolling and tumbling right to the foot of Sambo's tree. That is to say, the little onlooker feels himself being engulfed in the excitement. But Sambo is ignored as the tigers catch hold of each other's tails in their mouths, wrangle and scramble, and form a ring around the tree. This is a child's conception of intercourse, in which both parents, with their tiger tails, are portrayed as phallic and intercourse is performed using the mouth.

Next the reader is informed that the tigers appear "wee and far away," although strangely enough they are not in fact moving into the distance. It must really be the little child who feels "wee and far away," lonely and excluded from this strange fight that is going on between his parents. It is just at this moment of feeling deserted that Sambo jumps out of his hiding place and calls out to the tigers to ask why they have taken off their clothes (no—not *his* clothes!) and whether they don't want them any more. He must be the frightened child who feels his parents may not want *him* any more. The tigers hear Sambo call to them, but they will not let go of each other's tails so they respond to him with a "Gr-r-r-rrr." The angry parents growl at the child who is interrupting their lovemaking, but their growls must further convince the child that the parents are in a fight and that he has something to do with it because they are angry at *him*.

The tigers continue running round and round the tree, trying to eat each other up—"whirling around so fast that you couldn't have seen their legs at all." At the climax they all melt away "and there was nothing left but a great big pool of melted butter around the foot of the tree." But just as it was Sambo, not the tigers, who was "wee and far away," so it must be Sambo who has made the big pool of melted butter, for in his excitement Sambo must have lost control and urinated. He has lost his umbrella, the powerful phallus which would give him control and protect him from the rain of his urination. The author's illustrations intuitively expose this conflict by drawing the umbrella in a fully open position. In the scene where Sambo watches the fighting tigers he is hiding behind the open umbrella holding it with the handle extended in front of him, symbolizing his erection. Less perceptive illustrators have closed the umbrella, but one (Wadsworth, p. 90) has gone so far as to remove the author's symbolic drawing of the erection as an umbrella. As he "peeps" Sambo is shown grasping his genitals with his left hand!

After the primal scene has ended the parents in their undisguised form suddenly reappear in the story. The sexual excitement of the wild animals is over and once again they are human and civilized—"the right kind of parents, just the kind every child would like to have." To interpret Arbuthnot's remark, every child wants to deny his parents' sexuality.

Black Jumbo, on his way home from work, just happens to pass by with a big brass pot in which he collects the "lovely melted butter" to take home to Black Mumbo. Black Mumbo makes pancakes with flour, eggs, and sugar, and fries them in the melted tiger butter, which makes the pancakes "just as yellow and brown as little tigers." Black Mumbo ate 27 pancakes, Black Jumbo ate 55, "but Little Black Sambo ate a hundred and sixty-nine, because he was so hungry."

It hardly comes as a surprise to find that the aftermath of the primal scene is little tigers—babies. And these babies have been conceived, according to a child's theory of creation, by the father's urinating into the mother. The melted butter is symbolically put into the big brass pot. In a restatement, the butter is combined with eggs—in the pancakes—and the result is yellow and brown little tigers.

The eating of the pancakes, like the tigers' threats to eat Black Sambo, further symbolize oral conception. Probably the brown color in the yellow and brown little tigers symbolizes the completion of the child's gastrointestinal theory of creation. The orally conceived baby is delivered anally, like brown feces. That Little Black Sambo is the hungriest and eats the most pancakes is simply a child's longing to be able to make a baby himself. With the abundant gratification of this wish 169 times over, the story comes to an end. At least it ends for about 40 years, until its sequel appears in 1936.

The small detail of why there are four, not two, tigers requires clarification. The changed number of course protects the disguised identity of the two parents. In addition, this multiplier of two seems to balance another numerical disguise which relies upon a divisor of two. The author's two little girls become the solitary Sambo of the story. The detail that Black Mumbo is illustrated as fat can now be interpreted as representing her pregnancy.

As Arbuthnot implies, the "repetitive cadence of colors" in the story is very important. The colors are vivid and cheerful, reflecting the good spirits of the story and contrasting with the black skin color of the characters. Whatever the racial implications (to be discussed later), the bright colors seem to achieve a reversal of affect which successfully defends against the intrusion of the author's underlying black mood of loneliness and sadness into the story.

THE AUTHOR AS A CREATIVE WRITER

Surely this psychoanalytic revelation of the concealed primal scene story can only enhance the reader's respect for *Little Black Sambo*. In the "extreme simplicity" and "effortless perfection" with which the story reaches to the depths of the human personality it well deserves its rating as a classic that could be mistaken for folklore. Moreover, it merits a further investigation—beyond the content of the story to the author who created it. How was Helen Bannerman able to write this story?

It is known that she produced *Sambo* following a painful separation from her two small daughters and also from Scotland, her native country and her home for the first two years of her life. When she wrote it she was traveling, something she had often done as a child, so that the traveling itself must easily have called up early separations. Furthermore, her loneliness must have been intensified by the fact that she was traveling alone; presumably her husband was in India awaiting her return.

The author's concern about having prepared her children for their new life without their parents underlies the opening of the Sambo story. But quickly the primal scene takes over. Is it not reasonable to suppose that in this primal scene the author, like any mother who has just sent a child off to school, is expressing a wish to replace her lost children with a new baby? The natural wish of the grown woman to return to her husband and to become pregnant then finds unconscious reinforcement in repressed primal scene memories from early childhood. No longer is it just the author's children, but now it must become the author herself who is the left-out and frightened little onlooker at the vividly portrayed primal scene. And it is her own childhood sexuality which then gives the compelling foundation to her story. The story reveals the typical coexisting wishes of a little girl to be a boy, but also to be able to have a baby herself. In the "*lovely* melted butter" there is the wishful denial of the loss of control and shame in the wetting that follows the masturbatory excitement of the primal scene. But in the loss of the umbrella and the ensuing wetting there is the crying little girl's recognition of her genitals as castrated. The masturbatory guilt at this castration, however, is not clearly identifiable in the story, and this omission will require an explanation later.

The question can be raised whether the *Sambo* story draws upon an actual witnessing of parental intercourse or only a childhood fantasy about it. The vivid technicolor portrayal and the quality of Sambo's ego state—he is an intense, frozen, peeping onlooker—leave little doubt, for me at least, that the author is indeed drawing upon her own childhood visual experience and not merely a fantasy. It is not possible to reconstruct more specifically the connections in the author's early childhood between primal scene exposure and separations. Both situations have in common the arousal of lonely, left-out, and lost feelings. *Perhaps* they might have occurred together, during the disorganization of family life that comes with moving. *Perhaps* a primal scene exposure could have happened at 2 years of age during the departure from Scotland—her birthplace and her homeland—but this is mere speculation.

However, I believe it is a reliable conclusion that it was the indispensable contribution from her own unconscious that enabled the author to write *Little Black Sambo*. It is a universal story of childhood sexuality, presented in palatable disguise. It holds an appeal not just for the author's children but for children everywhere, and especially *white* children in the United States.

Helen Bannerman's creation of *Little Black Sambo* is a thorough verification of a formula composed by Freud in "Creative Writers and Day-Dreaming" (1907):

> A strong experience in the present awakens in the creative writer a memory of an earlier experience (usually belonging to his child-

hood) from which there now proceeds a wish which finds its fulfilment in the creative work. The work itself exhibits elements of the recent provoking occasion as well as of the old memory [p. 151].

In the same paper Freud goes on to say, "How the writer accomplishes [his creative writing] is his innermost secret" (p. 153). In the 67 years which have elapsed since Freud's paper was published no analyst has yet succeeded in explaining *how* creativity happens. For all that this psychoanalytic study of *Little Black Sambo* has revealed, it has failed to penetrate the "innermost secret" of its author's creativity.

THE SEQUEL TO SAMBO

In 1936, some 40 years following the original *Sambo* story, Mrs. Bannerman wrote its only sequel. Both the circumstances of her doing so and the sequel's content beautifully confirm that *Little Black Sambo* is a primal scene story, written under the influence of a separation.

The American publisher of *Sambo*, Frederick A. Stokes Company, had tried for many years to persuade the author to write more *Sambo* stories, but always she had refused. A speculation is that circumstances surrounding the requests had always failed to call forth the unconscious reinforcement she sensed to be so necessary to her creativity. Without this pressure from within she could not duplicate her own "effortless perfection." Rather than compromise her standards for *Sambo* she wrote nothing, and no promise of financial reward could change her mind. Not until the visit of her publisher, Horace W. Stokes, in 1936, was she able to write more about Sambo. Stokes describes this eventful visit:

Mrs. Bannerman wrote other books . . . successfully published . . . but the child of her heart and of her public was *Little Black Sambo*. She refused to write more about him.

The writer of this article has, like Mrs. Bannerman, two little girls. Time and time again he was begged to get Mrs. Bannerman to write another Sambo story. Letters were written to her but remained unanswered. Finally, in March of the present year, he begged for an interview from London.

"I'll be glad to see you," replied Mrs. Bannerman, "but I cannot write another story of Little Black Sambo. You must remember that nearly forty years have passed. Little Black Sambo is a middle-aged gentleman now!"

Mrs. Bannerman is a sweet-faced, elderly Scotchwoman, but she has a firm chin.

"I won't—I can't—I tell you it's impossible. I couldn't possibly write anything more," she reiterated.

"My own little girls have been giving me no peace. They even have a dog named Little Black Sambo. They *must* have the new book!" said the publisher.

He left apparently defeated, but three weeks later in his room in London he was startled and delighted by the manuscript of *Sambo and the Twins* by Helen Bannerman. The illustrations, forty of them, by Mrs. Bannerman herself, came promptly.

"You must remember," she wrote to the publisher, "that this is your own children's book. If it had not been for them I should never have written it at all" [p. 373f.].

Stokes gives the distinct impression in this article that his daughters were separated from him—at home in the States. So, after 40 years, the separation of two little girls from a parent reawakened the author's own separation from her children which had led her to write the original story of Sambo. Now, at last, she was able to write the sequel.

Amazingly, the sequel, *Sambo and the Twins*, resumes exactly where the original had left off, as though there had been a lapse of only 9 months since the primal scene and not 40 years. The story begins:

Once upon a time Little Black Sambo was very busy. He was building a house for himself, and his father Black Jumbo had given him a big hammer and a lot of long nails. So he was nailing two bits of wood together when he heard someone calling, "Little Black Sambo! Little Black Sambo!" He looked up and saw Black Mumbo standing at the door.

"Yes, Mother," he shouted. "What is it?" "Come here and you'll see," said Black Mumbo. So Little Black Sambo ran to the house, and there he saw two darling little black babies lying in a big basket.

"Oh!" said he, "are they for me?"

"Yes," said Black Mumbo, "they are yours for always and always."

"How lovely!" said Little Black Sambo. "I shall call them Little Black Woof and Little Black Moof."

The story goes on to tell how Sambo raises and takes care of "his" children—obviously his siblings. It is practically predictable that the main event concerns a frightful separation. Two wicked monkeys kidnap Little Black Woof and Little Black Moof. The babies cry. Little Black Sambo cries. "And poor Black Mumbo sat down and threw her apron over her head, and cried and cried and cried, for she thought she would never see Little Black Woof and Little Black Moof again." (Forty years later, the publisher's separation from his two daughters—Little Black Woof and Little Black Moof—brings back the author's intense despair at leaving her own children, and perhaps at being left herself as a child.) Finally, a kind eagle rescues the children and the story ends with the reunited family sitting down to a feast—"an ENORMOUS DISH OF PANCAKES."

Six of Mrs. Bannerman's stories have been collected in a volume, *The Jumbo Sambo*. Five stories, including the two Sambo stories, are about jungle adventures and black children. The last story in the collection, "Little Kettle-Head" seems quite out of place. It is about a little white girl living in India, who was "very fond of poking fires." She ignores repeated scoldings and one day, in a ghastly accident, she gets her head burned off. She manages to conceal the loss by substituting a kettle for her head, until that very night, which happens to be Christmas Eve, Santa brings her a pretty new doll's head with long golden hair. Here at last is the missing childhood story of masturbatory castration and guilt and punishment that come with poking exciting forbidden fires. Significantly, the author, the daughter of a Scottish clergyman, assigns these dire consequences of masturbation to a little *white* girl.

EPAMINONDAS

In contrast to *Sambo*, the story of Epaminondas contains little of psychoanalytic interest. It is an American version of an English folktale, "Lazy Jack," a "noodle story" concerned with foolish people. Lazy Jack manages in the end to get himself a wife. In the

American story the hero's foolishness earns him only condemnation —"you ain't got the sense you was born with"—and a spanking from his mother.

In ancient history Epaminondas was a brilliant Greek general who lost his life in battle. His namesake, the "little darkey boy," is a foolish child who can't do anything right. He naïvely misunderstands and misapplies all of his mother's good advice, with the result that he destroys everything he carries home to her from his Auntie's house. He crumbles a cake, melts butter, drowns a puppy, and drags a loaf of bread home on a leash through the dirt. Finally, his exasperated Mammy makes the trip to Auntie's herself. Before she leaves she bakes ten big blackberry pies and sets them on the porch to cool, cautioning Epaminondas, "Mind about stepping in those pies." So Epaminondas dutifully does just that. "And when his Mammy came home and found how Epaminondas had minded about stepping in the pies—well, you can just guess what happened to Epaminondas then!" And so the story ends in this minor key.

Easily recognizable behind the façade of stupidity in Epaminondas is the passively resistant, stubborn, angry, anally fixated little boy. There are no hints as to the unconscious roots of these character traits, and the reader can hardly avoid recognizing the unfortunate Negro stereotype.

Sambo and Racism

The impassioned rejection of *Little Black Sambo* by American Negroes, and more recently by sympathetic whites as well, cannot possibly be denied. Regretfully it has to be accepted that somewhere in this children's classic there must lie some justification for its "racist" reputation. As already mentioned, there is little overt racism in the story. But even when it is subjected to a psychoanalytic interpretation, there still appears to be no obvious evidence of racism. All that psychoanalysis reveals is a fascinating glimpse of childhood sexuality. *Sambo* is just a story of growing up, of separation, of a primal scene and conception, and of childhood excitement and castration anxiety. It is a story of childhood sexuality in disguise. *But it is just this unconscious childhood sexuality that underlies* Sambo's *racism!*

The book is the story of a little *black* boy's sexuality. That the author has "woven the word *black* into her repetitive cadence of colors" is not mere chance. The black skin color is an essential element in the story and the cadence of brightly colored clothing helps to underscore that the story is about *color*. The "racial" message of *Sambo* is that forbidden sexuality belongs to little *black* boys and their families.

The white reader uses this story to deny his own childhood sexuality. *Sambo* reassures him that the sexual thoughts and feelings of childhood belong just to primitive black people from the jungle, not to civilized white Americans. However, underneath the skin black people are no different from white, and they too would like to deny childhood sexuality. The story of *Sambo* is for blacks a blatant contradiction of that denial because it assigns the forbidden sexuality specifically to people with their own black skin color. Thus the black reader's rejection of *Sambo* resembles the impassioned rejection which greeted Freud's discovery of infantile sexuality.[2]

Now the difficult question must be raised whether the author of *Little Black Sambo* was racially prejudiced. It has to be acknowledged that *unconsciously* this white woman, in racially segregated India, projected childhood sexuality onto a black figure. Furthermore, her story of "Little Kettle-Head," who suffers a castration for poking at forbidden fires, affirms that sexuality is taboo for a little *white* girl. (Probably it is more taboo for girls than for boys, too.) But is this evidence of prejudice?

Would it not be more reasonable to judge Mrs. Bannerman on the basis of her conscious thought and deed rather than her unconscious primary process displacement of sexuality onto skin color? The little evidence available suggests that she led a highly worthwhile life which was directly beneficial to India's dark-skinned poor people. It might even be that the creative discharge of her unconscious childhood conflicts in *Little Black Sambo* liberated her from their detrimental influence upon her conscious life, thus preventing the formation of a prejudice.

In the unlikely event that Mrs. Bannerman lived long enough to see the tragic fate of *Sambo*, by now a quite elderly gentleman, it

---

[2] *Little Black Sambo* is not the only evidence of a displacement of the problems of childhood sexuality onto skin color. I have studied this subject at length (McDonald, 1970).

must have caused her great agony. Like peace-loving Alfred Nobel, appalled at the destructive power of the dynamite he had discovered, Helen Bannerman would, I believe, be appalled at the destructive turn taken by the elemental forces in her story.

To achieve an understanding of a creative author is an enriching experience for a psychoanalyst. But in the case of *Little Black Sambo* the achievement is tempered by the frustration that enlightenment brings no solution. Indeed, it is not possible to improve on Arbuthnot's reluctant recommendation: "If 'black' applied to people is a cause of grief to some of our children, then the book should be omitted from school lists." It remains for future generations to abolish the color line and restore *Sambo* to its rightful position as a classic "modern fairy tale."

BIBLIOGRAPHY

ARBUTHNOT, M. H. (1964), *Children and Books.* Glenview, Ill.: Scott Foresman.

BANNERMAN, H. (1900), *Little Black Sambo.* Philadelphia: Frederick A. Stokes.

———— (1942), *The Jumbo Sambo.* Philadelphia: Frederick A. Stokes.

FISH, H. D. (1937), Book Visits in England and Scotland. *Horn Book Magazine,* 13:355–358.

FREUD, S. (1907), Creative Writers and Day-Dreaming. *Standard Edition,* 9:141–153. London: Hogarth Press, 1959.

GOODMAN, M. E. (1952), *Race Awareness in Young Children.* New York: Collier Books, rev. ed., 1964.

LARRICK, N. (1965), The All-White World of Children's Books. *Saturday Review,* September 11, pp. 63–65, 84–85.

McDONALD, M. (1970), *Not By the Color of Their Skin.* New York: International Universities Press.

MOORE, A. E. (1934), *Literature Old and New for Children.* Cambridge, Mass.: Houghton Mifflin, Riverside Press.

PORTER, J. D. R. (1971), *Black Child, White Child.* Cambridge, Mass.: Harvard University Press.

STOKES, H. W. (1936), Sambo and the Twins. *Horn Book Magazine,* 12:373–374.

WADSWORTH, W. C. (1927), *The Real Story Book.* New York: Rand McNally.

Index

DATE DUE